Inside Book Publishing

Praise for previous editions

'The definitive text for all who need to learn about the publishing industry'
Publishing Training Centre

'An excellent book ... I recommend this book to everyone'
Gillian Clarke, *Editing Matters*, Society for Editors and Proofreaders

'A crucial title if you are looking to enter the industry'
Suzanne Collier, bookcareers.com

'Well worth reading as an overview of the global industry and publishing process'
Thomas Woll, *Publishing Research Quarterly*

'Fabulous to have as a shelf reference whatever your department'
Rachel Maund, Marketability

'No writer equipped with this book need ever feel like an ignorant outsider again'
Chris Holifield, WritersServices

Now in its fifth edition, *Inside Book Publishing* remains the classic introduction to the book publishing industry, being both a manual for the profession for over two decades and the bestselling textbook for students of publishing.

This new edition has been fully updated to respond to the rapid changes in the market and technology. Now more global in its references and scope, the book explores the tensions and trends affecting the industry, including the growth of ebooks, self-publishing and online retailing, and new business models and workflows. The book provides excellent overviews of the main aspects of the publishing process, including commissioning, product development, design and production, marketing, sales and distribution.

The book remains essential reading for publishing students, those seeking a career in publishing, recent entrants to the industry and authors seeking an insider's view. The accompanying website (www.insidebookpublishing.com) supports the book by providing up-to-date and relevant content.

Giles Clark has recently retired from The Open University, where he was the Copublishing Adviser, Learning and Teaching Solutions.

Angus Phillips is Director of the Oxford International Centre for Publishing Studies at Oxford Brookes University, UK.

Inside Book Publishing

Giles Clark and Angus Phillips

Fifth edition

Routledge
Taylor & Francis Group

LONDON AND NEW YORK

First published 1988 by Blueprint

Second edition published 1994

Third edition published 2001

Fourth edition published 2008
by Routledge

This edition published 2014
by Routledge
2 Park Square, Milton Park, Abingdon, Oxon OX14 4RN

and by Routledge
711 Third Avenue, New York, NY 10017

Routledge is an imprint of the Taylor & Francis Group, an informa business

© 1988, 1994, 2001 Giles Clark
© 2008, 2014 Giles Clark and Angus Phillips

British Library Cataloguing in Publication Data
A catalogue record for this book is available from the British Library

Library of Congress Cataloging in Publication Data
Clark, Giles N. (Giles Noel)
   Inside book publishing / Giles Clark and Angus Phillips. -- Fifth edition.
   pages cm
   Includes bibliographical references and index.
   1. Publishers and publishing. 2. Publishers and publishing--Vocational guidance.
   3. Publishers and publishing--Great Britain. I. Phillips, Angus II. Title.
   Z278.C557 2014
   070.5--dc23
   2013047921

ISBN: 978-0-415-53716-2 (hbk)
ISBN: 978-0-415-53717-9 (pbk)
ISBN: 978-1-315-77776-4 (ebk)

Typeset in Scala
by Saxon Graphics Ltd, Derby
Printed by Ashford Colour Press Ltd, Gosport, Hants

Contents

Expert, focus and skills boxes

Tables

Illustration credits

The publisher would like to thank the following companies and individuals for permissions to reproduce the following illustrations:

page 12, IPA; page 17, John Taylor; page 39, Random House Group; page 47, Quercus; page 49, Faber & Faber; page 55 (left and right), Random House Group; page 61, Pearson UK; page 70, Palgrave Macmillan; page 90, Bloomsbury Publishing; page 91, Illetisim; page 113, Faber & Faber; page 124, HarperCollins; page 128, John Taylor; page 133, John Taylor; page 147, John Taylor; pages 155–7, Routledge; page 183, Routledge; page 185, Publishing Training Centre; page 194, Pearson UK; page 201, Antony Rowe; pages 216 and 217, Clays; page 229, Bradt; page 238, Profile Books; page 239 (top), Kate Wheeler; page 239 (bottom), Finn Beales; page 240, HarperCollins; page 247, John Taylor; page 283 (left and right), Angus Phillips; page 289 (top), Angus Phillips; page 289 (bottom), Mladinska Knjiga; page 295, John Taylor; page 298, Jaffé and Neale; page 301, John Taylor; page 303, Waterstones; page 305, John Taylor; page 310, Scholastic; pages 316, 328 and 329, John Taylor.

Preface to the fifth edition

The previous edition of this book was published in 2008, at a time when many publishers were facing a perfect storm. The start of a prolonged recession in Western markets coincided with unprecedented technological disruption and innovation which challenged their businesses. The large technology companies saw opportunities in the area of books, and the newly arrived Kindle reading device, first launched in the US in 2007, was to drive the purchase of ebooks by the public and create a new distribution channel for self-published authors. The uncertain economic climate helped to accelerate change across many dimensions as publishing houses searched for efficiencies. By the time of the writing of this edition, the industry has proved to be both resilient and adaptive, and most publishers continue to operate successfully and profitably. New start-ups arise constantly and the possibilities of digital make this the most exciting time to be in publishing for centuries.

In this fifth edition, we cover the characteristics, dynamics and core functions of the business, including: diversity by sector; the growth in globalization; the strategic concentration in ownership and the dynamism of smaller firms; the move from the sale of products to the provision of services; and how publishers operate within the digital world. Publishers are navigating the transition from print to digital publishing. We show the new ways in which they produce, market, sell and distribute books in print and digital formats to benefit readers, authors and shareholders. Some of their business models are fading and there is much experimentation in this area. We equip students and recent entrants to publishing with the knowledge and understanding to navigate the industry. The book also gives an insight into the industry for authors working with publishers, as well as authors who self-publish.

A good publisher guides, supports and invests in authors. Christoph Chesher (Group Sales Director of Taylor & Francis Group, which includes Routledge) suggested to the authors that the new edition should be more international in scope. Thus this book now takes a broader view and is bigger. Niall Kennedy, our development editor, likewise read drafts and provided helpful comments. He kindly supplied the costing information on this book reproduced here in the case study. We thank them greatly.

The book continues to be supported by a certificated course from the Publishing Training Centre. Called Train for Book Publishing, the course is largely completed online. It summarizes key learning points from the book and reinforces the learning through a series of self-test exercises, before requiring delegates to submit an essay or project on a book-related topic for final assessment and grading. For further information please visit the website: www.train4publishing.co.uk or call the Publishing Training Centre on 020 8874 2718.

January 2014

ACKNOWLEDGEMENTS

We are indebted to cartoonist John Taylor for his wit; to the copy-editor Ruth Bourne and the production editor Anna Callander; to Niall Kennedy, Aileen Storry, Susan Dixon, Sarah Hartley, Christoph Chesher and other colleagues at Routledge for producing, marketing and selling this book.

A number of friends and colleagues have given their help with the new edition. The following read chapters in draft and offered many useful comments on the text: David Attwooll, Emma Bourne, Adrian Bullock, Suzanne Collier, Clare Fletcher, Sheila Lambie, Sylvia May, Sue Miller, Lynette Owen, Beverley Tarquini, and Anthony Watkinson. The illustrations are credited separately but in all cases there was a cheerful and prompt response to the authors' requests. A variety of people helped the search, including Clare Christian, Charlotte Clay, Martin Collyer, Kath Donovan, David Fickling, John Gerrard, Jonathan Glasspool, Donald Greig, Jon Howells, Sally Hughes, Ruth Killick, Kate McFarlan, Sylvia May, Stephen Mesquita, Patrick Neale, Richard Ogle, Bahar Siber, Beverley Tarquini, and Henry Volans.

All the contributors of the boxed panels deserve our gratitude for their readiness to have their arms twisted to write for the book.

Angus would like to thank Ann, Matthew, Charlotte and Jamie for their patience and support during the writing of the book; distractions were offered by our two cats, Ginger and Whiskers.

Giles would like to thank Julia, the sausage dog and two black and white moggies for their humour and perseverance during the writing.

Preface to the first, second, third and fourth editions

The history of this book's publication reflects the dramatic changes in publishing over the decades. Since its conception in the 1980s, the copyright of *Inside Book Publishing* has passed through six changes of outright publishing ownership, has appeared under five publishing imprints and been worked on by seven editors. This story is not unique in publishing today.

In the 1980s, the Society of Young Publishers (SYP) asked Giles Clark to write a book for the benefit of its members, to give an overview of publishing and the careers available. His employer, The Open University, supporting the project, gave him special leave to undertake the primary research: over 150 publishing managers were interviewed. The first contract was with Allen & Unwin, a long-established, family-owned publisher of medium size and diversity most noted for its general list, including the classic works by J. R. R. Tolkien – *The Lord of the Rings* and associated titles. This publisher also had a respected school textbook list, and higher education and professional titles in the earth sciences and the social sciences. By the time Giles had pulled together his research, Allen & Unwin had been taken over by another privately owned company and became Unwin Hyman. The first editor Adam Sisman left the restructured company (later going on to write a well-received biography of A. J. P. Taylor), and the new editor cancelled the contract and paid compensation. Unwin Hyman was then bought by HarperCollins, the international book publishing imprint of Rupert Murdoch's News Corporation. The Tolkien classics joined the ranks of other famous dead and living authors of HarperCollins and were to become in the next century reissued bestsellers tied in to the international film series, but at the time of purchase the staff were surplus as were the more specialist titles. A few of the Unwin Hyman managers formed University College London Press, which was later acquired by Taylor & Francis, and the social science titles were acquired from HarperCollins by Routledge, the respected academic imprint of the International Thomson Organization.

Giles was thankfully saved from the wilderness of being unpublished by Gordon Graham, then President of the Publishers Association and Chief Executive of Butterworths (legal and technical publishers) and subsequently the founder of the renowned publishing journal *Logos*, who introduced him to Dag Smith of the Book House Training Centre (renamed the Publishing Training Centre), who in turn contacted Blueprint Publishing – a new small publisher spearheaded and owned by Charlotte Berrill. She successfully focused on books on publishing and printing. Giles's work was adapted to the brief they drew up. The first edition of *Inside Book Publishing* (1988) was energetically published and sold by Blueprint.

Blueprint Publishing was later acquired by Chapman & Hall, the scientific and professional book imprint of Thomson. In 1993, Vivien James (the publisher in charge of the Blueprint list) needed a thoroughly revised second edition, which duly appeared in the autumn of 1994. German translation rights were sold to Hardt Wörner, which published their edition in 1996. During the summer of 1995, International Thomson conducted a reorganization which included combining the business and management lists of Routledge and Chapman & Hall into a new company, the International Thomson Business Press, and the transference of Blueprint to the media studies list of Routledge under the editorship of Rebecca Barden. By the autumn of 1995 the first printing of the second edition of *Inside Book Publishing* had fortuitously sold out, enabling the reprint to appear under the Routledge imprint. A management buy-out of Routledge occurred in 1996, supported by the venture capitalist Cinven. In 1998, the UK journal and book publisher, Taylor & Francis bought Routledge. The third edition appeared in 2001, reprinted three times and was translated into Vietnamese. In May 2004, Taylor & Francis and Informa merged under the public listing of Informa to provide specialist information to the global academic and scientific, professional and commercial communities via publishing, events and performance improvement.

The publication of the fourth edition in 2008 marked a step change in the book's development with the aid of a new co-author Angus Phillips and a redesign. Why? When first published in 1988, the book was never conceived as a textbook but over the years it had become an 'accidental textbook'. It was widely adopted by lecturers as a key set text on the growing number of respected courses on publishing, and student purchasing kept it alive. Textbook publishing is long term. Publishers need to issue new editions of successful books to keep them current, to fend off competition and to overcome the attrition in sales from the used book market. They also face the possibility that the original author may not have the time to undertake yet another new edition alone, or more problematically, be able to consider their work afresh. Katrina Chandler, the development editor at Routledge, found for Giles Clark a new co-author, Angus Phillips, who brought significant new ideas for additional content, structural reorganization, publishing knowledge, and teaching and illustrative approaches. Her successor, Aileen Storry, saw the book through to publication. The redesign of the book in a larger textbook format to match market needs and the finding of a new co-author of complementary strengths to work alongside the original author in a highly productive way, are good examples of a publisher adding value, a theme which runs throughout this book. Angus created the accompanying website www.insidebookpublishing.com which stimulated internet interest. (By a happy coincidence he also succeeded Gordon Graham as editor of *Logos*.) An ebook edition was published after the publication of the printed edition, but its sales were modest initially. The book was translated into Romanian, and the rise in importance of Asian publishing was further reflected by translations into Korean and Chinese.

Special thanks are therefore due on the first edition to all Giles's friends in the SYP, to The Open University, Gordon Graham, Dag Smith and Charlotte Berrill; on the second edition to Vivien James; on the third edition to Rebecca Barden; on the fourth edition to Katrina Chandler and Aileen Storry. Furthermore we are indebted to the many dozens of people who have helped with *Inside Book Publishing* over the years.

THE AUTHORS

Giles Clark, with a family background in publishing, and educated at University College London, worked at The Open University UK, where he was the Copublishing Adviser. He organized copublication arrangements between the University and a wide range of publishers from small to large, across most academic disciplines. The partnerships forged with commercial publishers extend the university's readership internationally, reduce its costs and give it entrepreneurial income. He now chairs the Graham Greene Birthplace Trust in Berkhamsted, serves on other charities and works on business ventures.

Angus Phillips is Director of the Oxford International Centre for Publishing Studies at Oxford Brookes University. He has degrees from Oxford and Warwick Universities, and many years' experience in the publishing industry including running a trade and reference list at Oxford University Press. He has acted as consultant to a variety of publishing companies, and trained publishing professionals from the UK and overseas in editorial, marketing and management. He is the author of *Turning the Page: The evolution of the book* (Routledge, 2014), and the editor, with Bill Cope, of *The Future of the Book in the Digital Age* (2006) and *The Future of the Academic Journal* (second edition, 2014). He is also the editor of the premier publishing journal *Logos*.

CHAPTER 1

Introduction – publishing trends and digital transformations

WHAT PUBLISHERS DO

Book publishing serves the million-copy fiction writer and the specialist author with sales of under 300 copies. Books can be published profitably for tiny markets which though limited in scale are many in number. As a long-established industry, publishing developed over time a worldwide distribution system through which its output of physical books could be traded in a regulated and controlled way. This ecosystem now coexists with digital distribution through which content can be sold and distributed right around the world on to mobile devices such as smartphones and tablets. Whilst this offers an exciting opportunity, at the same time publishers have to compete vigorously against other forms of entertainment, learning processes and information sources.

The primary definition of 'to publish' given in the *Oxford English Dictionary* is 'to make public'. In a world where anybody can post content on their blog or Facebook page, is this enough of a definition? Michael Bhaskar suggests the following thought experiment: 'you write a novel, and leave it on a park bench. Is this a published novel? Let's say you print 1,000 copies, leaving them on 1,000 park benches. How about now?' (page 18). Professional publishers go much further and undertake a range of activities. Publishers are not printers or mere 'middle men' interjecting themselves between authors and readers while creaming off the profits. They both add value to authors' works and protect the value of their copyrights. If they are doing their job well, they will develop an author's career and make a market for their works. Publishers commission authors (often before manuscripts are written), confer the authority of their brand on authors' works, project manage the publishing process, finance the production and marketing and sell the works in multiple forms and ways wherever possible. The publisher, aiming to generate a profit for its owners and a surplus to finance further activity:

- researches the markets in which it specializes,
- builds contacts, audiences and brands,
- seeks authors (in competition with other publishers) and is sought by them,
- matches marketable ideas to saleable authors,

- assesses the quality of the author's work (sometimes externally refereed), costs of production and marketing, and the sales prospects,
- decides whether to risk its investment funds in projects to appear under its own brand or sub-brands, and sometimes pays risk capital to authors in the form of an advance against future royalties,
- negotiates and manages contracts with licensed suppliers (including authors, agents, other publishers and media); purchased suppliers (for example production specialists); resellers (often retailers); and end-users (for example institutions),
- edits and designs the work to meet market needs,
- produces a source file of the work to enable it to be sold in multiple formats,
- specifies, buys and oversees the activities of suppliers which help produce the work, print and distribute it,
- exploits new technology to reduce costs and stock levels, adopts new systems, products and allied services, and collects and analyses data to facilitate sales and marketing techniques and publishing effectiveness,
- builds a worldwide sales network,
- markets and sells the work to intermediary resellers (retailers, wholesalers, and overseas firms) – the channels through which the works are mainly sold,
- markets the works to their intended audiences and users, and as appropriate, builds community sites to generate sales, and offline and online services,
- licenses the works to third parties, for example publishers in other countries,
- operates an e-commerce platform, sometimes with additional services, to promote and sell directly to end-users,
- holds bulk stock of titles, where necessary, to satisfy demand,
- fulfils orders, distributes the works in many forms and collects the money, paying royalties or sums to licensed suppliers (authors) on sales made, and
- protects the work and brand against illegal activity.

Additional income benefiting the publisher and author may be made from various licensing arrangements that enable other organizations at home and abroad to exploit the work in different ways, in different media and languages.

The problem with this list of activities is that they all involve costs to the publisher. Unless the publisher can add sufficient value to the author's work over and above the costs to make a profit from revenue received, the publisher will go out of business. Publishers' business models (the ways in which they make money) and the ways in which publishers add value to authors and shareholders are explored in Chapters 4 and 5.

Whilst the specialist staff of large publishers carry out all the above activities, some work (such as the detailed editing of books) is often contracted out to freelancers or possibly to other firms. Smaller publishers may not have the resources to employ their own sales staff or to distribute the books themselves so they may use larger publishers, or specialist firms. Apart from the decision to publish a book and raising the finance, all the other work can be outsourced, either to freelancers or to separate companies. Publishers of all sizes have increasingly outsourced work in order to reduce their staff overhead costs, a process that began in the editorial and production departments. But there are potential drawbacks: the publisher may have less control over the way the books are produced, leading to a diminution of quality; lose the marketing emphasis projected by its own employees committed solely to its books; run the risk of outsourcing core competences including skills; and contribute to the profit margins of sub-contractors.

In the above list, the word 'work' is used rather than 'book' for the following reasons. First, the so-called 'book publishing industry' encompasses significant non-book publishing operations, such as the publication of scholarly journals and database reference works. Moreover, the definition of what constitutes a 'book' is becoming increasingly elusive. In the physical world, children's publishers stretched the definition through their publication of 'novelty books' for babies and toddlers and upwards. In the digital world, content may be published as apps, enhanced ebooks, or on websites. However, for the majority of book publishers the sale of printed books still constitutes by far their largest source of sales and revenue.

Second, publishers have traditionally defined themselves through the printed book: an icon conveying authority, prestige and great cultural significance over the ages. Publishers are shifting from selling physical products to licensing digital content, for example in the form of ebooks. This is a fundamental change affecting workflows and the whole mindset of the organization. Another way of defining publishers is to say that they are traders of intellectual property (IP). The author creates the IP, and under copyright owns it, and is able to give it away for free or to sell it, usually via a publisher by means of an exclusive publishing licence – a publishing contract. The contract between the author and publisher not only conveys the right to the publisher to sell the work as a book, in whole or in part, but also other rights which enable the publisher to exploit and sell the work in many different ways. In the transition from printed books to digital publishing, the ways in which authors' works can be sold are multiplying. The 'book' as a printed container of content represents a too restrictive view. In the 1980s, some publishers started describing books as products and were slated by authors and critics. Today some say that they are publishers of content and receive similar criticism.

Stephen King says that 'books are life itself' (*Vanity Fair*, 14 April 2014)

Demand and supply-side publishing

The above list of publisher activities is based on two main assumptions. First, the publisher at its own risk and expense undertakes the production, marketing and the selling of the work. Second, the publisher attempts to earn its revenue from the demand-side, the market, with a view to making a profit. The assumption underlying most publishing is that publishing is a service to both authors and readers.

There is an alternative: supply-side publishing. The authors or their sponsors pay for the cost of publishing at their risk and expense, and the resulting product may be given away for free or charged for, but usually at a low price. The receipt of revenue from market demand may be of little or of no consequence. During the twentieth century, the Soviet Union adopted this method of financing publishing and extended the model by controlling politically the means of production (including authorship) and distribution. In the West, supply-side financed publishing has been present as well. For instance, in some countries, ministries of education pay publishers to produce textbooks for schools: the publishers earn their profit from the service provided. Universities subsidize the publication of scholarly works through their own presses. In this century, some supply-side publishing models have been growing enabled by digital technologies. In the USA and subsequently elsewhere, there has been an enormous growth in authors (especially of genre fiction) self-publishing books at their own risk and expense, and paying the author services companies for distribution and often for production and marketing. Philanthropists and universities finance the production of Open Educational Resources (OER) available for free. In learned journal publishing, some researchers, consumer groups and politicians advocate free public access to online journal articles. Under the gold open access model the research funders pay the publishers for the cost of publication. When publishers or service companies charge for their work, they primarily provide a service for their customers (authors or sponsors), rather than readers. The creation of content abundance usually underpins the business model of supply-side firms.

MARKET SECTORS AND PUBLISHER SIZE

The publishing industry divides into various market sectors within which the publishers specialize. The trade or consumer publishers (sometimes called 'general' publishers) produce books for the public. They have historically been called 'trade' publishers because their business was and still is mainly conducted through the book trade.

Non-consumer publishing embraces other significant sectors based around readers' places of study and work. The educational publishers produce textbooks and other instructional resources, which may be described as tools for asynchronous learning, for schools and higher education. However, educational publishing is usually more narrowly defined as serving primary and secondary schools. They are sometimes referred to as 'curriculum publishers'. Educational publishing is mainly non-international and defined by countries or sub-national regions. In North America, school publishing is referred to as El-Hi (Elementary-High School) or K-12, an abbreviation of kindergarten (4–6-year-olds) to 12th grade (18–19-year-olds). Trade education publishing describes learning materials used at home reflecting the convergence of home and school learning. English language teaching for all age-groups, both American and British English, is a significant international market and is called ELT publishing.

The publishers serving higher educational and professional markets are differentiated into overlapping sectors. Academic publishers concentrate on the humanities and social sciences (HSS); and STM publishers focus on science, technical and medical areas. Sometimes engineering is added (STEM), or scholarly (STMS), to embrace other academic disciplines. All these publishers produce a wide range of products, such as textbooks for students, high-level books and reference works for researchers and practitioners, and learned journals. In the USA, the textbook business is so large it warrants its own name and the companies are referred to as college textbook publishers. The professional publishing sector for practitioners' research, reference and training overlaps with academic and STM publishing, and additionally includes law, accountancy and business information. Sometimes it may overlap with 'trade', such as through the publication of books on management and business (professional/trade).

Subsequent chapters in this book expand on this topic. The key points here are that publishing is a very diverse industry, that there are significant differences between the sectors (and within them the numerous subsectors), and that the business models operated by publishers differ markedly. The London Stock Exchange usually lists publishers under media. Overall, publishing is one of the most important creative industries, and it has a prominent place in the UK economy:

> Book, journal and electronic publishing contribute over £5 billion to the domestic economy every year ... The value of UK book exports is higher than the export turnover of any other creative industry; in fact, the UK exports more than any other publishing industry in the world.
> (allpartypublishinggroup.org.uk, accessed 20 September 2013)

There is a controversial view that there is no such thing as the 'publishing industry': publishing activity should be seen as a subset of much larger groupings. Trade publishing is part of the leisure/entertainment industry; educational/college publishing part of the education industry; and STM publishing part of the research/professional information industry. To paraphrase an old industry saw: 'the only thing that the 7,000 publishers exhibiting at the annual Frankfurt Book Fair have in common is that they attend the Frankfurt Book Fair'. Moreover, many kinds of organizations, such as corporates, not-for-profit enterprises, universities and societies publish books and employ staff who undertake the publishing work described in this book. Their activities may not appear in publishing statistics – not least because they publish and sell directly to their communities.

The global publishers

Table 1.1 (page 8) reveals the international nature of the publishing business and how its ownership is dominated by European and US corporations and those from Japan. While the news media and publishing blogs give much coverage to the consumer book publishers, the industry's giants are Pearson (UK), Reed Elsevier (UK/NL), Thomson Reuters (US) and Walters Kluwer (NL), all of which are non-consumer publishers. Reed Elsevier is the world's leading STM publisher, while Thomson Reuters and Wolters Kluwer concentrate more on professional markets. These three companies derive much of their revenue from publishing high-priced products on a subscription business model to a relatively small number of organizations.

The world's largest publisher, primarily in education (including ELT) and higher education, is Pearson. In 2012 it had global revenues of £6bn, employed more than 40,000 people and operated in 70 countries; digital revenues accounted for over a third of the company's turnover. Although it was previously referred to as variously an unfocused conglomerate, a major book publisher, or as a media company, it now calls itself the world's leading learning company. Whilst Pearson is listed as a public company in the UK, over half its revenue derives from the North American education market (K-12 and college texts), and just under a quarter from Europe. International sales outside the US are growing, and like many other publishers, it has made large investments in fast-growing markets in China, India, Africa and Latin America. Pearson has invested heavily in technology and acquired companies to aid student learning outcomes and assessment, teacher support and a range of services to help education organizations (K-12 and higher education) run their operations more efficiently.

Global ranking of publishers

Rüdiger Wischenbart, Journalist and consultant

In 2012, the 50 largest publishing groups worldwide had combined revenues of €54,800 million (up from 48,935 million in 2008), of which the 10 largest groups controlled over half (or 55 per cent, down from 57 per cent five years earlier). A number of new companies have entered the global rankings, notably publishers from emerging markets such as Brazil, Russia or China, with educational publishing being the focus of much of that growth. In the decade between 2001 and 2010, a process of consolidation and restructuring, coinciding with the move from print to digital, had already reframed the segment of Science, Technical, and Medical (STM) publishing.

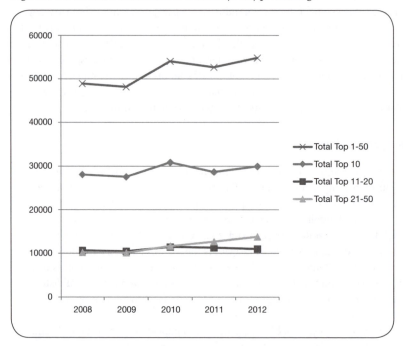

The STM segment now accounts for 41 per cent of reported revenues, while educational publishing represents around a third, or 34 per cent, and trade (or consumer) is down to 25 per cent. The gap between the share of educational and trade publishing is opening ever wider, highlighting that 'educational' is currently perhaps the most competitive sector of the industry.

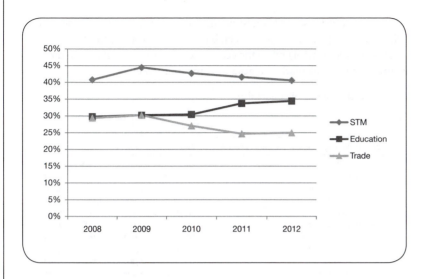

At a first glance, the top segment of the global publishing industry seems to reflect a surprising stability and continuity, since the top four companies have remained in the same order for the past three years. Indeed the top ten list has not opened up to a new entrant despite the impact of the world economic crisis, and regardless of digital change and globalization. But taking such continuity as proof of stability would utterly misread the tidal shifts which are taking place. In fact the whole ecosystem of books and reading, and with this, the industry catering to it, is being re-invented. What used to be a sector governed by a few large conglomerates based in Western Europe, New York and Japan, now sees the publishing groups of China, Russia and Brazil becoming relevant on the global stage. They are not just heavyweights in their respective domestic markets, but also are ready either to partner internationally or, in the case of China, to reach out and become international players in their own right.

A closer examination of the ranking reveals that three out of the top ten focus on STM and professional publishing (Reed Elsevier, Wolters Kluwer and Thomson Reuters). One group has a similar focus on educational (McGraw-Hill), while both the number one, Pearson, and number ten, Holtzbrinck, report revenues from educational that exceed those from trade. After a period of stability in trade publishing, 2012 and 2013 saw a major round of consolidation, including the merger between two of the leading trade houses, Penguin (Pearson) and Random House (Bertelsmann). But among local and regional publishing groups, some new perspectives and aspirations cannot be overlooked. In Scandinavia in 2011, Swedish Bonnier and Finnish Sonoma swapped their respective trade and educational divisions. In 2012, when Italian RCS put its French division, Groupe Flammarion, up for sale, Madrigall, the holding company of Gallimard, considered this as the opportunity to double its size and become the clear number three in France (Hachette Livre is number one). The country's second largest publishing group, Editis, had already been taken over by Spanish Grupo Planeta, but their prospects for further expansion were severely hit by the economic crisis that brought down the entire Spanish book market in 2012 by some 10 per cent.

Table 1.1 Global ranking of 25 publishers

Rank	Rank			Revenues €m	Revenues €m	Revenues €m
2012	2011	*Publishing Company (Group or Division)*	*Country*	2012	2011	2010
1	1	Pearson	UK	6,913	6,470	6,102
2	2	Reed Elsevier	UK/NL/US	4,479	4,395	5,387
3	3	ThomsonReuters	US	4,080	4,181	4,248
4	4	Wolters Kluwer	NL	3,603	3,354	3,556
5	8	Random House	Germany	2,142	1,749	2,897
6	5	Hachette Livre	France	2,077	2,038	2,165
7	7	McGraw-Hill Education	US	1,627	1,466	1,443
8	6	Grupo Planeta	Spain	1,675	1,772	1,829
9	10	Scholastic	US	n/a	1,334	1,389
10	9	Holtzbrinck	Germany	1,608	1,501	1,423
11	11	Cengage	US	1,510	1,443	1,514
12	12	Wiley	US	1,351	1,341	1,282
13	13	De Agostini Editore	Italy	n/a	1,344	1,389
14	14	Shueisha	Japan	1,108	1,320	1,204
15	15	Kodansha	Japan	1,035	1,195	1,129
16	19	Springer Science and Business Media	Germany	976	875	866
17	18	Houghton Mifflin Harcourt	US	974	996	1,260
18	16	Shogakukan	Japan	949	1,112	1,086
19	20	HarperCollins	US	901	846	956
20	21	Informa	UK	850	826	783
21	23	Oxford University Press	UK	849	773	710
22	NEW	China Publishing Group Corporate	China	835		
23	NEW	Phoenix Publishing and Media Company	China	814		
24	26	Kadokawa Publishing	Japan	756	696	599
25	24	Grupo Santillana	Spain	734	720	642

Source: The statistics are taken with permission from the *Global Ranking of the Publishing Industry 2013* by *Livres Hebdo*; copublished in the United Kingdom by *The Bookseller*; research by Rüdiger Wischenbart.

Looking further down the table at other major K-12 and college textbook publishers, there is McGraw-Hill Education (spun off from its parent McGraw-Hill), Cengage Learning (also includes reference) and Houghton Mifflin Harcourt (includes trade). The latter two are owned by private equity and such investors have played an important part in the reconfiguration of publishers and their assets. Wiley (US) is a significant college textbook publisher but is mainly a STMS and professional publisher. It has been divesting its pure trade publishing interests – for example in travel publishing – in order to acquire databases and educational technology companies.

Reed Elsevier dominates in the field of STM, publishing learned journals, reference works and databases, and to a lesser extent books. Much of the content is searchable and accessible via the online platform ScienceDirect. From a user's standpoint – a researcher or student – demarcations between previous format containers (journals, reference works, books) have broken down. The other main

STM and professional publishers are Springer Science (owned by private equity) and Informa (the holding company of Taylor & Francis, which includes the HSS publisher Routledge, the publisher of this book). Reed Elsevier and Informa both operate significant professional events businesses. The STM and professional publishers supply digital content, plus tools and services to improve their clients' workflow.

Just outside the top twenty largest publishers is Oxford University Press (UK), which is a department of the University of Oxford. Tracing its origins to 1478, today OUP is by far the world's largest university press. Its international publishing spans education (including ELT), STMS, reference and some trade (children's and adult) publishing. It acts as a local publisher in many countries and publishes in 40 languages. Other university presses such as Cambridge University Press and many American presses publish beyond their core scholarly publishing remit and may publish in educational, STM and trade publishing markets.

Consumer book publishers

The ownership of international consumer book publishing is dominated by continental European publishers, mainly French, German and Spanish, and by a few US corporations. Some of the US media companies divested their book publishing operations to concentrate on television and movies decades ago. Today, two major publishers dominate: Random House, owned by the German media company Bertelsmann (privately held by the Mohn family and trusts); and Hachette Livre, owned by the French media company Lagardère. The operations of these media companies span books, magazines, newspapers, TV and radio. The consumer book publishers derive most of their revenue from the copy sale business model, selling books at low prices to very large numbers of people.

In 2013, Penguin (owned by Pearson) was merged with Random House (owned by Bertelsmann) to create the world's largest consumer book publisher. The combined group has around a 30 per cent market share in the USA and UK, and is the publisher of many bestselling authors and titles. Bertelsmann's book publishing imprints as a whole derive revenue mainly from the English, German, and Spanish languages (plus Portuguese in Brazil). Under the Random House brand, there are 200 independent publishing imprints in 15 countries. These include publishing houses such as Doubleday and Alfred A. Knopf (USA); Jonathan Cape and Bodley Head (UK); Plaza & Janés (Spain); Sudamericana (Argentina); and Goldmann (Germany).

Hatchette operates in 40 countries and is the leading publisher in French language markets. Its imprints, outside France, include Grand Central Publishing and Little, Brown (USA); Hodder Headline and Orion (UK); Anaya, Salvat, and Bruño (Spain); Aique (Argentina); and Patria (Mexico). Just under a fifth of Hachette's revenue comes from education publishing. The other major English language trade publishers appear well down the global list and, like Penguin Random House, are headquartered in New York: HarperCollins, owned by News Corporation, and Simon & Schuster owned by CBS.

Grupo Planeta (Spain) is the world's leading Spanish language book publisher, operating in Spain, Portugal, France, and Latin America with more than 100 imprints. (The USA has many Spanish speakers but most read their books in English.) It also owns the second largest French publisher Editis and is associated with newspaper, magazine, TV and radio interests. It purchased Spain's main book club from Bertelsmann, which used to own the major book clubs in the UK and elsewhere. Similar to Hachette it publishes part-works sold from news-stands and on subscription. Part-work publishing is still popular in southern Europe and Latin America. The Italian publisher De Agostini also publishes part-works, trade and educational books; Mondadori is the largest trade and education book publisher in Italy with a market share above 20 per cent.

Holtzbrinck (Germany), founded by Georg von Holtzbrinck, is family owned and active in over 80 countries. It publishes across the sectors of consumer, education, STM and professional – and newspapers. Outside Germany, its well-known English language imprints include the trade publishers Farrar, Straus and Giroux in the USA and Macmillan in the UK, the academic publisher Palgrave, and the science brands *Nature* and *Scientific American*. Scholastic (US) is similar in size to Holtzbrinck. It is the world's largest publisher and distributor of children's/young adult (YA) books, including via its book clubs and book fairs based in schools. Outside the US, it has major operations in the UK, Asia and Australia. It has applied new technology to media products, platforms and services for entertainment and education. Bonnier (Sweden) and Egmont (Denmark) are leading Scandinavian media companies spanning trade books, magazines and new media products. Both are especially strong in children's publishing and related products and services.

Small and medium publishers

While the trend is towards larger publishers, there will always be room for innovative, imaginative and entrepreneurial small publishers that are more agile compared to larger competitors either overburdened with bureaucracy and complexity, or slow to respond to fast-changing markets and technological development. The larger the giant publishers become, the more niches they leave open for smaller publishers to exploit. Small publishers must work hard at choosing and marketing their titles carefully, and at developing authors and books that endure on the backlist. Small publishers run the risk of losing their successful authors to larger publishers. Publishers of all sizes typically earn much of their revenue from established titles – their backlist. They can offer a more personal service to authors, who can receive less special attention from the larger publishers. All publishers give most attention to their important new books (frontlist titles), especially in respect of marketing and sales effort.

A sign of a vigorous industry is the frequent start-up of new firms – compared with many industries, publishing needs only a little equipment and a relatively small amount of investment capital. The entry costs have become lower with the rise of digital publishing and printing. However, new publishers usually take at least four years from scratch to turn a profit. Some companies spring from management buy-outs of lists or imprints surplus to a large firm; some start-ups are created by employees leaving large companies. No professional qualifications are needed to be a publisher – publishing is commonly called a trade rather than a profession, and entry is unrestricted. Across all sectors, there are number of serial publishing entrepreneurs: individuals who create new publishers and sell out or move on repeatedly. A good example in the UK is Anthony Cheetham, who founded Century (1981), Orion (1992), Quercus (2004), and House of Zeus (2012). Some of the small and medium-sized publishers grow at a much faster rate than larger companies. In comparison to the large corporate publishers, the smaller publishers are often far more open to discussing their innovations and sharing experiences.

The medium-sized publishers are arguably in a more difficult position because they have neither the scale and financial benefits of major publishers nor necessarily the agility and focus of smaller publishers. They are prime targets for takeovers by larger publishers provided they have valuable backlists which fit the objectives of the larger organization, and increasingly, if they possess digital publishing assets. These will include content and IP, and digital capital such as brand recognition and an established community of authors and readers. One of the fascinating aspects of publishing is that publishers do not need to be the size of Pearson, Elsevier, or Random House to be successful in the home market, to reach world export markets and to apply innovatory technology to expand sales and services.

MAJOR BUSINESS TRENDS

There are a number of trends which affect the business of publishing around the world.

Tectonic shifts in the world economy

US and European publishers of all sizes are looking beyond their traditional and mature (slow-growing) markets of North America and of Europe – Western economies may also be heavily indebted – to the faster growing economies of the East and of the South. The faster growing countries often have rising populations, are investing heavily in education and research, and have expanding middle classes – people who are interested in self-improvement and business books, international fiction and non-fiction, and children's books. In respect of geographical organization, Anglo/American publishers usually divide the world into vertical hemispheres: the Americas; Europe, Middle East and Africa (EMEA); and Asia. Meanwhile, Asian and Latin American publishers are growing and are looking to expand exports to the North and the West.

Globalization of publishing

The publishing industry used to be rather narrowly defined by geography and limited by language, by nation states and empires. From the nineteenth century, the British publishers published in English and exported books to a worldwide empire and to America, the French publishers to their colonies in Africa and elsewhere, and the Spanish to Latin America. The very large German publishing industry exported to neighbouring countries where German was spoken. Meanwhile US publishers benefited from a home market that became the world's

Global publishing markets

Rüdiger Wischenbart, Journalist and consultant

E★PERT

Global publishing is not a level playing field. The six largest publishing markets alone, by value at retail (or consumer) prices, account for over 60 per cent of the global industry. Taken as a whole, the European Union would, technically, own the largest share in the international book market, but given it is fragmented by different languages as well as by largely diverse local traditions for both books and culture in general – with different tax regimes and reading habits – it can hardly be dealt with as one integral market for the trade in books.

The global map of publishing markets represents domestic publishing markets by market value at consumer prices

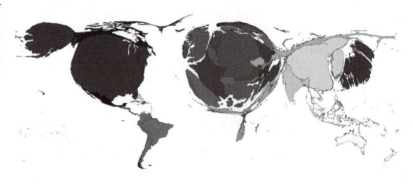

A world map of the publishing industry illustrates how book publishing mirrors much larger economic and social characteristics across the continents. The recent rise of China, today arguably home of the second largest book market worldwide after the United States, reflects the prominent role of books in all emerging economies – as a key media in the modern knowledge society. But also Brazil, South Korea, India, Turkey and Russia are to be found among the 20 largest publishing nations, along with much smaller, yet much wealthier countries such as Italy, the Netherlands, Poland, Belgium, Switzerland or Norway. With a total market value of €95.6 billion, we must assume that the 20 largest publishing markets account for just under 84 per cent of global spending on books, estimated at a total value of €114 bn.

Among all the various publishing, media and entertainment industries worldwide – which also include TV (subscriptions and advertisement), newspapers, magazines, movies and entertainment, video games and music, with a combined value of around $1,000 billion – books represent some 15 per cent, topped only by TV and newspapers, and outsizing both film and music.

Most markets in Western Europe and North America are highly mature or even showing a steady, albeit mostly modest, decline in recent years. The economic crisis of 2008 took a significant toll on those countries hit the hardest, such as Spain or Italy. In this context, ebooks are one of the few sectors of growth, for example in trade publishing in the USA, and even compensating in the UK for the decline in print sales.

Assessing the scope of local book publishing is a difficult exercise for many other parts of the world, especially in the Arab world and in Sub-Saharan Africa, as most books in these regions are not produced domestically, but imported from notably the United Kingdom, followed by the United States and, in West Africa and in the Maghreb, from France. Also hardly any reliable data are available with regard to the modest domestic production in those markets.

Table 1.2 Global ranking of publishing markets

Country	Year	Publishers' total net revenue (€m)	Total market value at consumer prices (€m)	New titles & new editions per 1 m inhabitants	2012 GDP per capita PPP* in USD (Worldbank)	Population
World			114,000		12,189	7,046,368,813
USA	2012	20,750	29,643	1,080	49,965	313,914,040
China	2012		14,200	306	9,233	1,350,695,000
Germany	2012	5,407	9,520	1,115	40,901	81,889,839
Japan	2012		7,878	617	35,178	127,561,489
France	2012	2,771	4,534	1,321	36,104	65,696,689
UK	2012	3,736	3,975	2,459	36,901	63,227,526
Italy	2012		3,072	1,049	33,111	60,917,978
Spain	2011	1,820	2,890	1,692	32,682	46,217,961
Brazil	2012	1,884	2,810	339	11,909	198,656,019
Korea, Rep.	2012		2,734	1,257	30,801	50,004,000
India	2010	1,675	2,500		3,876	1,236,686,732
Canada	2010	1,535	2,342		42,533	34,880,491
Turkey	2012	1,096	1,682	564	18,348	73,997,128
Australia	2011		1,520	877	44,598	22,683,600
Russian Federation	2012		1,494		23,501	143,533,000
Netherlands	2012		1,363	1,412	43,198	16,767,705
Poland	2012	654	1,053	775	22,162	38,542,737
Belgium	2011	519	850		39,788	11,142,157
Switzerland	2011		806		53,367	7,997,152
Norway	2012		743	1,486	65,640	5,018,869
Top 20 Publishing Markets			95,609			
Other Markets			18,391			

*purchasing power parity

richest and largest. Post war the USA dominated popular culture, science and technology, grew exports and became a major source of college textbooks that were sold to overseas markets or adapted. The UK, USA, France and Spain are still the main exporters. UK publishers owned by US and continental European publishers are sometimes used to expand the parent's international English language reach, helping to make the UK one of the world centres of international publishing expertise.

While national and regional markets are still defined by language (less so in science and technology where English is the world's language), the international publishers increasingly operate in many countries. They publish original books in the local language and may export a selection in one or more of the main transnational languages of English, Spanish and French; and they translate or adapt selected imported books, which they have originated and published elsewhere. Smaller publishers that do not own their own overseas companies are able to export by selling their books through networks of other companies and have them translated by other publishers. In addition ebooks can now reach all parts of the world. There is a significant market opportunity for publishers with the growth of the English language and reading in English in many countries.

The globalization of the supply side of publishing means that books may be printed in China or Hong Kong, or printed for sale in local markets using digital printing. The outsourcing of editorial, design and typesetting, for example in journal publishing, may lead to publishers merely retaining a project management function at their headquarters.

Strategic concentration

Major publishers have progressively sold off publishing operations that do not fit with the main sectors in which they operate. The aim has been to be a major player in some sectors and markets, and to exit the other areas. From the 1980s, Anglo/American managements especially concentrated on sectors. Most of the owners of the trade publishers sold off their educational, academic, STM and professional publishing interests. The STM and professional publishers continue to sell off remnants of their trade book publishing operations which they see as lower margin and higher risk businesses, or educational publishing units requiring significant scale and technological investment, or if in professional publishing, print publishing units which are not amenable to the development of digital services.

There may be a counter trend developing. Some consumer book publishers and media corporations are investing in education; or they are diversifying into other sectors. For example, the consumer book publisher Bloomsbury re-invested profits from the Harry Potter books in a series of acquisitions of academic and professional publishers.

Consolidation through merger and acquisition

The major publishers have raised their market share in their chosen sectors through organic growth and by acquiring or merging with similar publishing companies, or those serving adjacent markets or new geographies. They may also acquire technology companies or start-ups which are disruptive of their business models. For example in 2008, Springer bought the publisher BioMed Central which at that time was pioneering open access. They like to search for companies which add value (including those providing related services), can be easily absorbed, and do not create or introduce undue risk. They try to avoid companies that are over-priced, passing peak value, or which are not conducive to digital publishing and exploitation. In each Western market sector, three to four major publishers have come to dominate and together may account for more than half of a market sector's revenue, with the leader accounting for around one quarter or more.

Collaboration

In a fast-changing business environment, impacted by technology, there is a greater need for publishers to collaborate with other firms, even if they are competitors. Experimentation in new areas forges partnerships and, for example, a publisher collaborates with software developers or film or games companies to produce new products. The importance of scale in the aggregation of content encourages publishers to form alliances with other publishers to strengthen their marketing and sales in existing or new markets, or those overseas. The cost of developing new technologies and software prompts publishers and partners to share costs, for example, in the development of platforms. Common goals to improve the user experience (UX), such as enabling an ebook to be portable across platforms and readable on different devices, or a researcher to link to citations in an article, drive publishers to support the development of universal standards. The third party infringers of IP, unauthorized copying and changes in copyright law in respect of digital content, necessitate the sharing of information among publishers to reduce such risks and their support of organizations that defend IP rights globally.

THE DIGITIZATION OF PUBLISHING

Digitization is the mega trend of the age and affects every aspect of the publishing process from authors to readers. Digital publishing is far more than just publishing ebooks. The transition from print to digital publishing might suggest that printed book publishing will end but that is not expected in the foreseeable future as purchasers still appreciate the appearance, collectability, gift value, usability and permanence of the physical object.

The use by publishers of digital processes stretches back decades. During the 1970s and the 1980s, typesetters applied computers and software (the forerunner of today's text mark-up languages) to the composition of books and lowered the cost to publishers. From the mid-1980s, desktop publishing and the development of word-processing programs aided authors, typesetters and publishers alike. Such technologies facilitated the origination of printed books. At this point the publishers had little use for the typeset files of their books because there was no market for selling books electronically. Indeed even into the new century the major consumer publishers did not hold digital files of their books.

The professional reference and STM publishers realized early on the threats and potential opportunities of digital publishing. For example, Reed Elsevier purchased the legal database LexisNexis in 1994 (which had offered full text searching of US legal cases from 1980) and Wolters Kluwer the medical information database Ovid in 1998 (which had developed the first online interface in 1984). From around the mid-1990s onwards, the STM publishers applied digital methods to the peer review process and to the production of journal articles, and made their printed journal content available online to researchers, via libraries, in PDF format. From around 2006, the main consumer book publishers began to digitize their new books and selected backlist books.

Reading devices, ecosystems and walled gardens

In the late 1990s, dedicated ebook reading devices came to the market though ebook sales were limited to enthusiasts. However, the launch of Amazon's Kindle in the USA in 2007, and subsequently in the UK and elsewhere in 2010 had a dramatic impact on the public's purchase of ebooks. The upward demand curve resembled a hockey stick as ebook sales started from a low point and accelerated upwards on a steep incline. The largest US bookstore chain, Barnes & Noble (at the time largely unknown outside America), launched its dedicated reading device, the Nook in 2009. Amazon had already become the leading online retailer of printed books through a focus on excellent customer service and a long-term strategy to gain market share. It had developed a very large database of loyal customers: avid readers who were quick adopters of ebooks, especially non-illustrated narrative titles that were amenable to reading on the black-and-white dedicated reading devices of the period. Amazon is credited with creating the first ecosystem that encouraged people to buy publishers' ebooks easily and legally. The founder of Amazon, Jeff Bezos, says 'Amazon isn't happening to the book business. The future is happening to the book business' (Stone, page 11).

Apple launched the iPad in the USA in 2010 along with its iBookstore for purchasing ebooks. This led to an explosive growth in the purchase by consumers of tablet computers with the connectivity to consume all kinds of media. The increased availability of the new reading devices, linked to compelling websites for ease of purchase, drove ebook demand. The sharp rise in the use of mobile phones or smartphones on which people read books continues worldwide, and larger phones or *phablets* are popular in markets such as China.

Lying behind the impact of the reading devices on ebook uptake are the very different business models of the technology firms. Amazon is primarily a retailer of products and services, intent on increasing the value of the user's shopping basket. It develops software and sells hardware at cost. Apple, by contrast, is primarily a hardware firm, that requires content to help sell its high margin products. Other companies, such as Sony and Kobo, developed reading devices with ebook stores. The business models of Google and Facebook are based primarily on attracting advertising revenue deriving from the search technologies of the former and the social network of the latter. It is in Google's interests for content to be kept outside paywalls and to be freely searchable.

During this brief period of technological change, the importance of an entire proprietary ecosystem with a social component has emerged. In this respect, Amazon and Apple stand out. Both have developed *walled gardens* of content and services. Their customers benefit from the ease of remaining within their favoured system but the proprietary software locks them (and the publishers) into the system in various ways. The printed book, in contrast, has a universally available and non-proprietary operating system.

When there are a few buyers, such as Amazon and Apple on the demand side, facing a large number of sellers (the publishers on the supply side), the market demonstrates imperfect competition. Unless the publishers agree to the terms set by the buyers, they face the threat that the retailer will take down the 'buy button' against their books or remove the books from automated recommendation systems. On the other hand, the major publishers that issue the majority of bestsellers can exert counter pressure by refusing to supply 'must have' titles to the main retailers. In previous eras, the publishers have faced similar concentration and buying power from bricks-and-mortar retailers.

Character of ebook sales

The growth in sales of consumer ebooks occurred first in North America, followed by the UK and Australia. The sales of genre fiction led the way whilst the ebook sales of highly illustrated titles, children's books and textbooks were sluggish. The most popular books in the early phase of the ebook format were those with strong narrative content, and little or no illustration. They might be read in bed or while travelling, and their sales were not so dependent on the quality of the packaging and presentation. The US ebook market is the most advanced and provides insights around the effects on authorship, publishing and bookselling. However, the uptake of ebooks in consumer markets worldwide is occurring at different speeds and caution is required around the extrapolation of US trends.

Disruption

The invention of the web and more recently the trend to mobile are often described as 'disruptive technologies', a term devised by Clayton Christensen who subsequently preferred 'disruptive innovations'. Such innovations do not just

disrupt the business models of technology firms but those engaged in the publishing business, along with many others. Christensen also developed the theory of 'disruptive competitors' – those firms which start by selling inferior goods at low margins in areas ignored by incumbents operating on high margins, but which move up the value chain to eventually challenge and possibly replace the incumbents.

The main disruptors in the world of publishing are the big tech companies – Amazon, Apple and Google. Amazon is arguably more of a disrupter than Apple and Google because for many publishers it controls the main retail channel (pbook and ebook) to readers. Amazon started in 1995 as a mail-order discount bookseller, a direct to consumer (D2C) business. At that time, mail-order bookselling was generally seen as a low margin if not loss-making area of business and was ignored by large incumbents. Through the application of innovatory technology and its diversification into other products beyond books, Amazon overtook Barnes & Noble, expanded internationally and rose to threaten in size the world's largest retailer Walmart. It provided a self-publishing service to authors most of whom would not receive a contract from a traditional publisher; and installed digital printing technology to manufacture books. It moved up the value chain in many areas such as becoming a consumer book publisher in its own right; though in the latter endeavour, competing booksellers boycotted its books thereby hindering sales of its titles.

During the last decades of the twentieth century and into the first decade of the twenty-first, most physical retailers (including the bookselling chains in the USA and UK) spent their resources investing in new and ever larger stores with more staff, in expensive real-estate locations with high foot-traffic. However large their stores were, the shelf-space to display titles was limited. Amazon in contrast did not invest in high cost real-estate but in technology. It had no limits on the number of titles it could display on its website. Provided it could sign up the supplying publishers, the inventory of titles on its website was limitless. Amazon when negotiating with publishers argued that it should receive a high discount from them because of its wide title offer and far lower return rate of unsold books compared to that of the physical book stores. Although it built its own warehouses to store books, Amazon also fulfilled orders by using the main US book wholesalers (Baker & Taylor and Ingram) to deliver books to readers in Amazon boxes. Another key advantage, lost on other retailers of the time, is that retailing is not just about enticing and retaining customers, but also about collecting data on those customers in order to sell them more products and services. Books and other media are described as passion products. Once the customer is acquired online they are likely to be retained.

The online retailers offered convenience, speed of delivery, discounted prices and greater title availability. Internet selling aided the smaller specialist publishers since physical booksellers did not stock their titles. It gave them greater reach into export markets. The overall book market widened and deepened. During the long recession in Western markets, the online booksellers increased their market share against the physical stores. There are several reasons for the decline in physical bookselling but among the chief ones are the switch by consumers to online ordering of printed books; the ease of using smartphones in store to check comparative prices (a behaviour called showrooming); and the rapid growth in the purchase of ebooks, especially in some fiction genres. The decline of book display also occurred in other stores which had previously stocked books as a sideline. The US international companies, such as Amazon and Apple, threaten the once dominant national bookselling chains around the world; but in those same local markets they in turn face new competition. For example, Deutsche Telekom, in partnership with major German publishers and booksellers, launched the Tolino brand of e-reader in 2013.

The decline of retail bookshelf space in the USA, Australia and to a lesser extent the UK, and the rise of online retailers, arguably presents the greatest challenges to the consumer book publishers. The business model of such publishers has traditionally relied on their ability to sell and distribute large quantities of printed books into physical retailers. The retail exposure drives sales of printed books and of ebooks, fosters the discovery of books come across by chance, encourages impulse purchases, aids the launch of new writers and provides a venue for Christmas gift buying. As the physical consumer book retail market is being disrupted and reduced, the business model of consumer book publishers is being disrupted and potentially weakened. The key challenge is to aid discoverability in a world where the high street store is disappearing.

Since publishers have traditionally marketed and sold books through bookstores, they had no direct contact with readers. They are largely business to business (B2B) firms. In other words the publishers, particularly the trade book publishers, long ago surrendered their customer relationship to intermediary firms, the channels through which they sold their books. The retailers do not provide publishers with information on the customers to whom they sell. Publishers now recognize that it is of increasing importance to focus on end-users (rather than retailers) and to establish two-way relationships with them. Readers, however, are still likely to purchase books from retailers.

The educational, STM and professional publishers have supplied for decades their products directly to end-user organizations, cutting out suppliers, and increasingly do so via their own platforms, though various kinds of intermediaries still exist.

Disintermediation

The internet lowers transaction costs in the supply chain, for instance the cost a publisher incurs when handling orders from booksellers, which were once hand-written and which are now processed electronically with fewer people. Moreover, the internet offers the potential for removing, or 'disintermediating', entire businesses in the supply chain from author to reader. Many specialist intermediaries punctuate the linear supply chain. All of them, such as authors' agents, publishers, printers, wholesalers and booksellers, add costs and profit to their activities. The internet and other digital technologies revolutionize the ways in which books are produced and sold. Books can be published faster and cheaper.

All parts of the traditional supply chain are under pressure: each is prone to disintermediation. There are many examples. Authors self-publish stories and cut out agents and publishers. Librarians act as university publishers. Agents offer publishing services to authors and cut out publishers. Printers may supply customers direct; wholesalers may act as printers. Publishers cut out wholesalers and retailers. And online retailers act as publishers, printers, aggregators and libraries thereby attempting to disintermediate everyone in order to create a total vertical business from author to reader. It is conceivable that synthetic authors might replace authors. An intelligent computer program might be devised that uses semantic textual analysis of competing and similar works and real-time analytics of current trends, information, interests and cultures to write books.

The publishing value chain is in a state of flux. At the turn of the last century, publishers feared the end of the book and of their continued existence. Since then fears have receded and publishing as a whole has expanded and adapted.

Scarcity and abundance

Before the digital age, books were scarce and costly to reproduce. There was a scarcity of publishers that had the resources to produce, print and distribute them. The publishers were gatekeepers that made books available to readers. The booksellers were gatekeepers of the retail channel to market; guarding the shelf space on which books were displayed and sold to readers. Libraries were gatekeepers through their selection of titles, had limits of funding and of shelf space to store books for reference and lending. Scarcity helped the publishers to control pricing.

The coming of the web broke down over time the barriers to the scarcity of content and information, and abundance emerged. The connectivity afforded by the internet has given rise to a range of free-to-end-user business models that are used by businesses and organizations outside the publishing industry. Free sources of information, such as Wikipedia, eroded the sales of printed reference titles; and sites with user-generated content, such as TripAdvisor, challenged the publishers of printed travel guides. Classic books that were out of copyright (in the public domain) were digitized and made freely available. Piracy of in-copyright titles is a growing problem though far less prevalent than in the film and music industries. Freemium selling, whereby readers can sample the content before purchase, is a variant of the user-free model. Amazon's Look Inside the book and Google Books have opened up the contents of books to readers which helps publishers sell to global audiences.

There has also been a philosophical shift around how content is created and appraised. Rather than rely on a few gatekeepers to assess the value of content, why not put it up for everyone to see, review, and offer their reaction? This shift is reflected in the huge growth in user-generated content and extends to the peer review of papers in some academic journals post publication.

However, scarcity is still present and comes in different guises, especially in respect of the resources needed to publish. Readers and institutional buyers have limits on their purchasing power. There are also and importantly individual limits on the amount of time available to read, be it a novel or a scientific paper, versus competing media and activities: time is a scarce commodity. Good authors who people want to read are scarce, whether their writings are paid for by readers or available for free. From a publisher's standpoint, it costs money to find, select and buy such authors. It takes resources to develop the author's work for market needs, and to produce the book in whatever formats the content is published. The marginal cost of a digital file may be close to zero, yet there is still a cost to the publisher to create a book and then distribute it through channels to market that are controlled and charged for by others. The sales and marketing costs to capture readers' attention, to help them discover books, do not disappear in the transition from print to digital publishing.

In a world of abundance, the publishers offer a vital service in selecting authors and developing their content to meet readers' needs. They manage the authors' brands and focus readers on the books they have selected. That service is worth paying for when time is scarce. To attempt another definition: the publishing process may be described as managing the scarcity of good authors and content to drive profitability.

Vertical communities and connectivity

Publishers have always published books for people sharing common interests, termed vertical communities. The non-consumer publishers have the advantage over the consumer publishers in that the places and objectives of work or study define communities of interest and are identifiable. In the pre-digital age, the consumer publishers had to rely on booksellers and mail-order book club operators to reach readers. The readers of books were difficult to identify and reach, and had no direct contact with the publishers. Readers spread through the general population too had great difficulty in connecting and sharing views with others. The internet and the development of social media tools have fostered the development of vertical communities, and the connectivity between readers, authors and publishers. Mike Shatzkin argues: 'The shift from horizontal to vertical is inexorable, unstoppable. People need to understand what this means and, as uncomfortable as it is for many leaders of today's trade, they need to start adjusting their business to meet that shift' (Shatzkin, 19 March 2009).

Aggregation and curation

The 'aggregation' of content is the assembly of different objects from different sources to form a whole. In the publishing world, the largest aggregators are the online booksellers, wholesalers and library suppliers, and technology companies such as Google. The larger the amount of content they gather, the greater the benefit they offer to their customers, the greater amount of customer data they collect, and the greater their commercial prospects. Amazon is the premier aggregator in the world of books and dominates the consumer market in many parts of the world. Publishers too benefit from the aggregation of content, for example in the area of journals and databases – one important reason behind their merger and acquisition activity.

The term 'curation' (borrowed from the museum world) is the appraisal and selection of books. Mike Shatzkin writes about the connection between curation and aggregation: 'the concept [of curation] in the digital content world means the selection and presentation of these disparate items to help a browser or consumer navigate and select from them. Aggregation without curation is, normally, not very helpful. Curation creates the brand' (Shatzkin, 21 September 2009).

A number of players in the value chain carry out curating activities. Authors' agents act as gatekeepers and curators of the authors they represent. They curate the projects of their authors for submission to selected editors at publishing houses. Authors too may be described as curating publishers in that they appraise and select the publishers to whom they submit their ideas and projects. They want publication in an aggregation of similar books, such as an imprint, or, if a research scientist, in the most prestigious journal in their field – journals are curated, peer-reviewed and branded aggregations. In turn the editors curate authors and projects through their decision to publish a very small number from a large number of projects submitted. Agents and publishers sort the wheat from the chaff. The publishers curate projects and then publish, whereas the practice on the internet is to publish first and curate afterwards.

The aggregation of published book titles forms the publisher's imprint (a list of books within a publisher's overall publishing programme). Publishers give great attention to building trusted brands in the minds of consumers, both of authors and imprints. The curation of projects to fit the objectives and personality of the imprint creates the brand. The publishers sell the aggregates of their brands to the booksellers or institutions. Additional curation within the publisher's programme occurs at the sub-imprint level. The marketing staff select titles for promotion to different audiences and media. Sales staff select titles which are most attractive to the book buyers of intermediary firms, or sell bundles of journal titles or collections of ebooks to university libraries. The staff selling translation rights to foreign language publishers match selected titles to selected editors of the publishers overseas.

The booksellers are of course both aggregators and curators. Physical stores curate titles by displaying them on shelves devoted to subject categories or by placing bestsellers in the window or on tables at the front of the shop. The online booksellers use the metadata (data about data, for example book title, author, cover, description) supplied by the publishers to place books in subject classifications or to populate the algorithms which create recommendations for consumers.

Finally readers are curating content on the web, and a good example is Maria Popova with her blog Brain Pickings – 'a human-powered discovery engine for interestingness, a subjective lens on what matters in the world and why, bringing you things you didn't know you were interested in – until you are' (brainpickings. org, accessed 21 September 2013).

Granularity and personalization

The container of the printed edition of the book or journal fixes its content and presentation. The economics of print production necessitate boundaries on length: short books or very long books are problematic and uneconomic to publish. Digital publishing reduces or removes such boundaries. Additionally, it gives the opportunity for users to download a chapter or article – the container is chunked at the granular level. The publisher is able to offer users the ability to personalize content for themselves or, if a teacher, to customize resources for students. The scope to chunk and re-purpose content varies across publishing sectors and product types. The long-form book, as such fiction or narrative non-fiction, is not susceptible to disaggregation in the same way as the music album. At the level of content aggregation, publishers are able to offer digital subject collections of books to academic libraries that would have been hitherto uneconomic to do in print, or bundle a novelist's titles for sale.

There are broader issues connected with the granularization of content – how easily can the rights be licensed in a piece of IP (say an image or extended piece of text), when the value of the transaction may be quite low? The system of digital object identifier (DOI) – common in journal publishing – has not yet reached the rest of publishing. As Richard Hooper comments, 'Even in the publishing industry I am not sure you have cracked the system for identifying, uniquely, a chart or a paragraph within an article or a book – i.e. a subset of an ISBN' (Hooper, page 37).

Digital printing

Digital printing is a transformative technology that developed at the turn of the century and which was pioneered by Lightning Source, owned by the US wholesaler Ingram. Books have traditionally been printed on offset litho presses, which require print runs of at least 1,000 copies. A publisher, in advance of publication of a new book, estimates the quantity that could be sold in, say, one year, and places the order with the printer. The printed copies are stored in the publisher's warehouse and dispatched over time to fulfil customers' orders. The publisher ties up its cash in the stock, which may not sell or be damaged, and pays for storage. Digital printing, by contrast, enables the production of just one copy and that copy can be printed after the customer order has been received: pure print on demand (POD). Digital printing also enables economic short print runs of say 10–500 copies. Formerly, backlist titles selling only small quantities went out of print and became unavailable because the publisher could not afford to reprint them using litho presses. Digital technology reduces the publisher's costs and risks, and allows books to remain in print and available for sale. For publishers of specialist books in particular, it offers the prospect of 'zero-inventory' (the publisher has no stock or warehouse). As digital printing improves in cost-effectiveness and quality in comparison with litho and storage costs, the trend is from long litho print runs to short digital runs and POD. The quality and economies of digital colour printing are also improving.

ADAPTATION AND INNOVATION

Every aspect of the publishing process is changing. Publishers are finding authors in new ways. They are developing streamlined digital workflows that enable the work to be published in print, ebook and web formats. Content management systems are used to hold the publisher's IP in codified and retrievable form. The abundance of content on the internet makes it progressively difficult to capture readers' attention. The publisher's signal has to rise above the noise. People discover or come across books in many ways, and their behaviour is constantly changing. The influence of book reviews in the traditional media has been in decline. Retail shelf space devoted to books, so important for discovering consumer books and new writers through browsing, is in decline. Word-of-mouth recommendations among readers remain as important as ever.

Digital marketing offers to the publisher new routes to interact with consumers and to make books visible within search and communities. Publishers are seeing the importance of book recommendation sites, social media and bloggers; and building their own community sites to facilitate a dialogue with readers. Authors too are adapting by building an online profile through their own website, blog and Twitter.

In the pre-digital era, publishers held data on their content in separate parts of the business – often on paper. Examples were contracts, book production specifications, bibliographic data, and customer sales information. It is now essential to impose consistency on the data and its structure, to ensure speed of retrieval and to connect content to the relevant data. Metadata helps computers and readers to discover books and content in the online environment. As Richard Hooper says, 'The digital world drives data and is driven by data in a way that the analogue world is not. Sloppy data can just about get by in the analogue world but not in the digital world' (Hooper, page 36). Data analytics informs publishing decisions: real-time sales and social media information help the analysis of the effectiveness of marketing; data about readers guides the creation of new content and the way publishers interact with users across the whole value chain.

The velocity of change affects every aspect of the publishing process. Former methods of working become uneconomic, ineffectual or redundant. Flexibility is key, as highlighted by Tim Hely Hutchinson of Hachette UK: 'We used to have to print 10,000s, but I can get an economical print run now with 1,500 copies, so we can keep the stock low, and wait to see which formats the books are selling in' (*The Bookseller*, 21 June 2013). Enduring business models that were once profitable begin to fade. Constant experimentation forms an important part of navigating successfully the transition from print to digital publishing. Business models may vary from giving content away free to encouraging subscriptions, to pricing ebooks cheaply to gain market share, to bundling content together into a service.

The move from simply the creation and sale of products to the provision of services and solutions is apparent across all publishing sectors. Many of the services related to content are designed to make it more useful, personal and valuable to users. Services supplied to authors help them publish and build their brand. Services supplied to teachers help their professional development and teaching through using the publisher's content. Online assessment services provided to students aid their learning outcomes. Tools supplied to researchers and professionals improve the speed of searching for relevant content, and aid their productivity and competitiveness. In some areas, the addition of services to the core business of publishing content is a way of occupying more of the value chain to gain new sources of revenue. All such services are examples of investment in developing the value of online vertical communities.

A criticism of publishers is that since they have traded through booksellers and in the academic context negotiate with librarians, they have little knowledge of, or direct connection with, readers. In turn a criticism of college textbook publishers is that they have focused mainly on the teachers, who adopt the textbooks which students buy, more than on the students' learning. Most ebooks are replicas of printed books and do not yet take account of digital opportunities to aid users. User-centred design is still in its infancy.

In response to the transition, publishers' resources and infrastructure devoted to declining or uncertain revenue sources, such as printed books, are reduced or outsourced. Reductions occur in the staff categories primarily engaged in the manufacturing, selling and distribution of printed books, along with warehouse space. Conversely, increases occur in the staff categories engaged in digital production, marketing and selling, along with investment in technology, digital distribution and services. Moreover, the former distinctive activities of editorial, production, marketing and sales are overlapping, and merging into new job roles. Disruption and opportunity occur not only in the external environment but on a constant basis within the organization. It is essential for publishers to alter their mind-set to focus more clearly on the end-user and how they would like to interact with the product or service, whether they are reading for pleasure, teaching a class, or consulting must-have information. One of the key success factors for all organizations is to be able to manage change successfully.

Sources

Michael Bhaskar, *The Content Machine: Towards a theory of publishing from the printing press to the digital network*, Anthem Press, 2013.

Clayton M. Christensen, *The Innovator's Dilemma: When new technologies cause great firms to fail*, Harvard Business School Press, 1997.

Richard Hooper, 'Copyright Licensing: Fit for purpose for the digital age', *Logos*, 24:2 (2013), pages 33–40.

Angus Phillips, *Turning the Page: The evolution of the book*, Routledge, 2014.

Mike Shatzkin, *The Shatzkin Files*, Kobo Editions, 2011. This collects together a number of pieces from Mike Shatzkin's blog.

Brad Stone, *The Everything Store: Jeff Bezos and the age of Amazon*, Little, Brown, 2013.

Web resources

Kent Anderson, '73 Things Publishers Do', 22 October 2013, available from http://scholarlykitchen.sspnet.org/2013/10/22/updated-73-things-publishers-do-2013-edition/

www.bbc.co.uk BBC R4 programme, *The Bottom Line: Books*, Saturday 9 February 2013.

www.digitalbookworld.com Digital Book World (USA).

www.futurebook.net Blog from *The Bookseller* (UK).

www.idealog.com Blog from Mike Shatzkin (USA).

www.scholarlykitchen.sspnet.org Blog established in 2008 by the Society for Scholarly Publishing.

CHAPTER 2

The development of modern trade publishing

The aim of this chapter is to provide an overview of the development of modern trade publishing in the UK. Broad themes include the vertical integration of the hardback and paperback publishing houses, an increase in scale through merger and acquisition, the democratization of authorship, and the growth of digital sales, in particular of ebooks. Running alongside is the change in culture from a product-led to a market-led business.

STABILITY AND EXPANSION

In the 1950s book publishing was broadly based with around 50 medium-sized UK firms each employing around 50 staff and issuing several hundred titles per year, usually in hardback. The publishers were privately owned, usually by family members who held a majority share. They concentrated on fiction and non-fiction – termed 'general' or 'trade' or, more recently, 'consumer books' – although they also developed educational and academic lists subservient to the general book side.

The judge in the *Lady Chatterley's Lover* trial asked the jury: 'Is it a book you would wish your wife or servants to read?'

The 1960s brought great optimism as in other cultural industries such as music and fashion. Rayner Unwin of George Allen & Unwin talks of the 'informal, almost casual, publishing that was still possible during the sixties' (Unwin, page 238). For example, work on the travel writer Eric Newby's book, *Grain Race* (1968), took place in Unwin's flat in the evenings. Censorship was dealt a blow with the publication of the unexpurgated version of D. H. Lawrence's *Lady Chatterley's Lover* on 10 November 1960 – a victory for Penguin, which had won the right to publish the previously banned novel against a charge that it was obscene. The first print run of 200,000 sold out on the first day and within a year Penguin had sold 2 million copies. 'The trial was a turning-point, and after it was over previously forbidden works like *The Ginger Man* and *The Kama Sutra* were finally published in this country' (Lewis, page 333).

Throughout the 1960s and 1970s (apart from in the recession of the early to mid-1970s), much of the publishers' fast-growing prosperity was based on readers' affluence and increasing public expenditure (Table 2.1, page 27). Sales of hardback adult and children's books were underpinned by generous government funding of schools and libraries. Mass-market paperback publishing grew substantially and was carried out by separate firms. In the main they acquired reprint paperback rights from the houses that originated titles in hardback. Literary agents, who increasingly began to represent the interests of fiction and non-fiction authors, were resented by some traditional publishers, who saw them as unwarranted intruders into the publisher–author relationship. New publishers arose producing highly-illustrated non-fiction books in full colour at low and affordable prices – viewed by traditionalists as 'down-market'. Paul Hamlyn (1926–2001), the greatest exponent of affordable illustrated books, made a series of fortunes from illustrated book publishing. In turn he sold his Paul Hamlyn imprint to the magazine company IPC, founded Octopus by buying back the Paul Hamlyn imprint for a nominal sum, plus liabilities, and then sold his imprints to Reed Consumer Books for an enormous sum. In his lifetime, he founded the Paul Hamlyn Foundation to give greater access to the arts.

Table 2.1 Number of titles published in the UK from 1950 to 1980 (*source*: Norrie, page 220)

Year	Number of titles and new editions
1950	17,072
1960	23,783
1970	33,489
1980	48,158

The publication of *The Reader's Digest Great World Atlas* (1961), which had double-page spreads displaying superb full-colour graphics, and extended captions not unlike those found in magazines, and the *Treasures of Tutankhamun*, tied in to the British Museum exhibition (1972), were inspirational to some embryonic book packagers. They went on to produce highly illustrated full-colour information books which they presold to publishers around the world to be marketed and distributed under the publishers' imprints. In the late 1970s, the highly illustrated publishers brought colour books into the supermarkets by producing own brand books for them at very low prices.

By the end of the 1970s the era of the 'gentleman publisher' was fast disappearing. The phrase had been used to describe grand publishers of literary fiction, typically derided as gentlemen who ran their companies by the seat of their pants, who adopted a paternalist management style, or who according to some literary agents exhibited ungentlemanly behaviour in their contractual arrangements with authors. Some of the foremost publishers, who had personally built great publishing companies, had reached the end of their careers. Some of their descendants, given senior management positions, were either incompetent or ill prepared for the changes to come.

The stable and expansionary publishing world of the 1960s and 1970s was rudely shattered by the recession of 1980 which forced publishers to cut their lists and overheads – making redundant both older staff and the weaker staff sucked in during the era of fast growth. From then on progressive cuts in public expenditure throughout the English-speaking world would be the order of the day. Reductions in public funding adversely affected the publishing and availability of some kinds of books including hardback fiction destined for public libraries and children's books supported by school libraries. Further factors of the 1980s and early 1990s were high book-price inflation (there was a steep rise in the cost of paper) and the appreciation of sterling against the currencies of countries to which UK publishers traditionally exported. This led to a continued decline in export sales to the benefit of US publishers. General books from America, particularly mass-market paperbacks, were more competitively priced in mainland Europe and Australia.

MERGERS AND ACQUISITIONS

The rise of European publishers through their purchase of US publishing began in the 1970s. The UK banking, investment and publishing group Pearson, owner of the *Financial Times*, bought the UK publisher Penguin in 1970, and the New York based Viking Press in 1975. The German media group Bertelsmann broke out of Europe through the purchase of the US publishers Bantam Books in 1980, Doubleday in 1986, and Random House in 1998. By 2013 Penguin had merged with Random House to create the world's largest consumer book publisher (Penguin Random House) with its headquarters in New York.

> Founded in 1929, Faber & Faber remains an independent publishing house. William Golding's *Lord of the Flies* was published by Faber in 1954

In the UK, the 1980s were an important period of mergers and acquisitions that restructured the publishing industry and saw, like in the USA, its ownership largely transferred overseas. In the next century three large international publishing groups (Bertelsmann, Hatchette and HarperCollins) came to control a large part of the UK home market; long-established, medium-sized British owned firms were to become a rarity – today Faber & Faber is one of the few left. The deregulation of financial markets led to the increased availability of equity and debt financing allowing the large players to take over medium-sized publishers, and small publishers to expand or start in business. Book publishing was attractive to investors who could see that the industry had consistently, that is until 1987, returned pre-tax profits and return on capital above the average level of all industries. News International, having acquired the US publisher Harper & Row, took control of the UK publisher Collins in 1988 and created HarperCollins. Random House, at the time in American ownership, bought Cape, Chatto, Virago and Bodley Head in 1987, Century Hutchinson in 1989, and subsequently Secker & Warburg and Heinemann before it itself was purchased by Bertelsmann in 1998. Around that time the German Holtzbrinck media company acquired Macmillan. In 2004–6, Hachette (owned by the French media corporation Lagardère) purchased the UK trade publishers of Hodder Headline, Orion and John Murray; and the US trade publishers owned by Time Warner which included Little Brown and Company and the paperback publisher Grand Central Publishing.

The turn of the new century was marked by an increase in the gathering strategy of European-based publishers to acquire US publishers and the willingness of some of the giant US media corporations to sell off their book publishing interests. From the latter's perspective, book publishing represented a small fraction of their stock market capitalization and was seen as a mature and niche business in comparison to their faster growing and central media interests (television and the internet). By contrast, the smaller European-based media corporations, focused to a greater extent on book publishing, seized the opportunity. Their purchase of US publishers gave them access to the world's largest and richest nation and the ability to grow quickly their dominant market share of English language book publishing worldwide. The steady earnings growth derived from book publishing in US and UK markets is more attractive to mainland European publishers, some with a strong history of family ownership; in France and Germany companies have historically been less exposed to the vagaries of the stock market and activist shareholders.

VERTICAL INTEGRATION

The restructuring of UK book publishing in the 1980s affected all types of publishing but its effects were most dramatic in consumer publishing, the fault lines having appeared in the 1970s. Ownership was traditionally divided between many hardback publishers and around a dozen separate mass-market paperback houses. In 1969 the top paperback houses were Penguin (selling 27 m copies), Fontana (13 m), Corgi (13 m) and Panther (9 m).

The publishing strategy was to establish a book in hardback at a high price and subsequently to reissue it, around a year later, in a paperback format at a lower price to a wider audience. Hardback fiction and non-fiction were published in half-yearly seasons (the spring/summer, and autumn/winter) headed by major 'lead titles' and sold to booksellers, libraries and book clubs. Mass-market paperbacks were fast-moving books published in monthly batches, with each month headed by lead fiction and non-fiction titles, with various genre category titles forming the remainder. Paperbacks were published in A format – 'pocket' or 'rack-sized' books. They were often straight reductions of the original hardbacks – pages of the hardback edition were, in a pre-digital age, photographically reduced to the size of the paperback edition. Printed in large quantities on cheap paper, they reached a wider retail market beyond bookshops and were sold in a way more similar to that of magazines, mainly through merchandising wholesalers which stacked the racks in outlets at monthly intervals.

The respective character of hardback and paperback publishers was very different. The hardback publishers inhabited their fine but slowly decaying Georgian houses in Bloomsbury, around Bedford Square, and in other high-class central London locations. The palatial former reception rooms, with Adam fireplaces, hung with chandeliers, were impressive settings for the managing director or the editorial director. When Tom Maschler decided to pursue a career in publishing in the 1950s, he went to see André Deutsch (1917–2000), who was to publish in hardback some of the most important names in post-war fiction, including John Updike, V. S. Naipaul, Philip Roth and Norman Mailer. When Deutsch told him that he had no openings, Maschler responded that the salary was not important. 'At that he asked when I could start. We settled for the following Monday' (page 39).

The editors were very much in control and women were in the majority in the publishing workforce. Diana Athill, who also worked with André Deutsch, writes in her memoir *Stet*: 'All publishing was run by many badly-paid women and a few much better-paid men: an imbalance that women were, of course, aware of, but

Stet (2000) by
Diana Athill is
a memoir of
her fifty years in
publishing

which they seemed to take for granted' (page 56). The production staff, who hired the printers to produce the books, and the marketing and sales staff were crammed in smaller offices in the basement and the attics. The mass-market paperback reprinters occupied office blocks in cheaper London locations. Theirs was a sales driven operation.

The hardback publishers played their traditional role of nurturing new writing talent and working closely with authors on manuscripts. Their backlists were complete with great and loyal authors, and some enduring money-spinning books. Their formidable reputation ensured that new books were reviewed (literary editors ignored paperbacks), that the public librarians would automatically order sufficient quantities, and that the compliant independent booksellers would display and stock their titles. The advent of book clubs supplied another outlet. The booksellers complained that the book clubs were undermining their business by offering their members new hardbacks at discounted prices by mail order. The publishers were pleasantly surprised by the paradoxical increased sales through bookshops stemming from a book club's large-scale consumer advertising campaigns. However, by the early to mid-1980s, hardback publishers found themselves making hardly any profit from selling copies themselves (the copy sales business model). They derived their profit and laid off risks by making rights and co-edition sales to others: to paperback publishers, book clubs, US publishers and foreign language publishers (the licensing business model). While the hardback publishers employed highly talented editors, they also had editors who favoured their pet projects and authors who produced books which few wanted to buy.

The false dichotomy between hardback and paperback publishing could not survive. The book market was rapidly changing, readers' expectations were altering, competition between publishers to secure bestselling authors was intensifying and literary agents were far more adept in extracting maximum advance payments for their authors from publishers. Bookshops had steadily increased the display space for paperbacks, and publishers such as Penguin had provided free paperback shelving for bookshops.

The hardback publishers were used to acquiring the exclusive right to publish an author's work for the full term of copyright in hardback and paperback, even though they had no mass-market paperback publishing capability; and similarly to acquiring US rights which they in turn licensed to US publishers. The hardback publisher would sublicense to a UK paperback publisher – for a fixed period (on average eight years) – the right to publish the paperback on which it would pay the hardback publisher a royalty of 7.5 per cent on the published price, rising to 10 per cent or more after specified large quantities had been sold. The hardback publisher would share the royalties received with the author. The paperback publisher would want to acquire its main titles two years ahead of paperback publication. The originating publisher would secure at that time a large advance payment from the paperback publisher, similarly shared with the author.

Paperback publishers facing escalating advances increased their output of original titles, sometimes licensing rights to hardback publishers. Since authors derived most of their income from paperback sales (and sometimes US sales), it made sense for agents to cut out the hardback publisher's share of such sales. Agents looking to maximize income would license the book separately to an independent hardback publisher, a paperback publisher, and a US publisher, thereby obtaining advances from each party and full royalty rates for their authors (less the agent's commission). The general publishers which owned both hardback and paperback firms (vertical integration) paid authors full royalty rates on each edition and were therefore better positioned to capture the leading authors. Paperback and hardback publishers without a hardback or paperback arm became increasingly desperate – sometimes they entered into alliances in order to bid for the big books jointly.

Another strand leading to the amalgamation of consumer book publishing, again reaching back to the late 1970s, was the weakening polarization between the traditional formats. The mass-market paperback houses, facing increasing competition in the industry and higher title output, recorded lower unit sales per title. Paperback prices rose and the ownership of paperback houses became more concentrated. Furthermore readers' expectations created a new market for certain books and authors to be published in the larger B format – quality or trade paperback. Peter Mayer, Chief Executive of Penguin from 1978 to 1996, had launched this concept when he was at Avon Books in New York in the 1970s. Literary fiction and a range of non-fiction could be published at higher prices in B format; and Mayer applied this idea to more commercial fiction, such as M. M. Kaye's *The Far Pavilions*, which was to sell 400,000 copies within six months of its publication in paperback in 1979. Such books could be reprints from hardbacks, reissues or originals. Both mass-market paperback and hardback houses started up trade paperback imprints and some hardback houses ventured into the A format field, usually with disastrous consequences. Over time, the use of the trade paperback (and larger formats) to publish original fiction and non-fiction has grown apace.

The second wave of the feminist movement in the 1960s and the subsequent rise of women's studies courses in the 1970s and 1980s not only created a new market for books but also inspired the foundation of women-run, women-centred publishing houses whose range and diversity reflect the multiplicity of female experience and writing. Virago was founded in 1973 by Carmen Callil, and later (in 1995) sold to Little, Brown. Its series of Virago Modern Classics, launched in 1978 with *Frost in May* (1933) by Antonia White, was instrumental in the rediscovery of a forgotten female tradition. Persephone Books, established in 1999, reprints neglected fiction and non-fiction by mid-twentieth century (mostly women) writers.

Intellectual property rights

The main financial assets of a publishing company are its intellectual property rights (IPR). These are enshrined in the contracts it holds with authors (negotiated directly or via their agents) and with companies to which it has sold rights, such as English language and foreign language publishers. The original IPR derives from the author – the publisher then adds value. Ultimately the value of the IPR depends on consumers buying the product.

By the end of the 1980s and early 1990s, most of the formerly independent hardback houses were part of the major publishing corporations, which had the capability of publishing and acquiring rights in all formats: mass-market paperback, trade paperback and hardback. Their imprints were gathered together in modern London offices. The new owners combed through the old contracts entered into by their hardback houses with the paperback publishers in order to uncover the titles which had, from other takeovers, fallen into the hands of rival paperback imprints and to determine the termination dates of the licences. In due course they would claw back the paperback rights to those books for their own paperback imprints, much to the consternation of the bereft paperback houses, and some authors and agents. Most of Graham Greene's novels were published from the 1920s by the hardback publisher Heinemann and from the 1960s by The Bodley Head, and sublicensed in paperback to Penguin. Then Random House, having subsequently purchased the hardback publishers, reverted the paperback rights from Penguin and reissued his major works under the Vintage Classics imprint.

The pressure to control rights internationally prompted US general publishers to acquire UK imprints, and vice versa, and both UK and US publishers were attractive to the mainland European publishers, especially to the German media corporation Bertelsmann, and to the French group Lagardère. Once the major consumer book publishers had sister imprints on both sides of the Atlantic, the obvious move in the light of growing international sales of ebooks was to acquire world English rights in the works of bestselling authors. However this is still constrained by the US and UK literary agents, who continue to license UK and US editions to imprints in competing ownership.

A change in culture

The hardback general book publishers, which had developed valuable IPR over decades, held an increasing rarity value and at the peak of the merger boom commanded high prices. As for the staff of the newly taken-over general publishers, the outlook for many was bleak. If not made immediately redundant, they found themselves entering the world of corporate publishing. The editors especially had worked in a small company culture, where they had enjoyed considerable autonomy over the kinds of books they wanted to publish. They carried with them a set of values quite often at odds with those of their new employers, which emphasized sales and profit and sometimes demanded clean and tidy desks, clear of manuscripts and books, in an open plan environment. Some editors blamed the accountants for preventing them from doing the books they wanted to publish. It was not the accountants per se: the whole culture had changed. The nature of consumer book publishing had changed from being product-led to being market-driven. As Alan Bartram noted at the end of the twentieth century,

> the practice of financing a potential poor-seller by profits from successful books, as a publisher such as Victor Gollancz would do because he, personally, believed it deserved publishing even if it cost him money, or as university presses considered it their duty to do – behaviour once considered normal practice – has almost disappeared. (Bartram, page 9)

Editorial individuality is still present in the large corporations. Some major publishing groups have attempted to regain some of the advantages of the smaller publisher by retaining or creating individual imprints. It is vital for innovation that they can lead the market by introducing new authors, publishing books in different formats, and marketing and selling them in different ways. Furthermore, while major publishers attract talented staff from smaller publishers, senior staff of major publishers also leave to start up new companies or to reinvigorate smaller publishers. In a world of brand authors, changing business models, and digital experimentation, publishers are hiring new kinds of staff, sometimes from other media industries. They want publishers who are entrepreneurial, can manage talent, and develop properties into brands suitable for licensing or direct investment across games, film and other media. Francesca Dow, of Penguin Children's, talks of thinking beyond the book: 'Part of our strategy is to develop brands in ways so that we are moving away from being a publisher to an owner and investor in new content ... As a very strategic move, we acquired media rights in *The Snowman* – that is part of our strategy to grow in a new way beyond books' (*The Bookseller*, 11 October 2013).

THE RESHAPING OF RETAIL

While trade or consumer publishing was being restructured, the increased availability of finance in the 1980s also aided the transformation and concentration of UK bookselling. Traditionally, UK bookselling had meant the major chain WHSmith (which had its roots in station bookstalls and high street stationery outlets), small independently owned chains, and a large number of independent or small bookshops. But in the 1980s and 1990s, large bookselling chains, principally Waterstone's and Dillons in the UK (Barnes & Noble, Borders and Waldenbooks in the USA), brought a new kind of bookselling – large, well-stocked bookshops, stocking up to 50,000 titles in the UK, three to four times the size of many independents. Amazon began its operations in the USA in 1995 and in the UK in 1998. The US bookstore chains started to discount bestselling hardbacks, as did the UK chains from the late 1990s, thereby reducing sales of mass-market paperbacks. As John Thompson writes:

> The financial formula that had underpinned the industry in the 1950s and 1960s was being turned on its head: increasingly it was the frontlist hardcover, not the backlist paperback, that was the engine of growth for the industry. By the early 2000s, paperback sales, especially in the mass-market format, had begun to fall off, undercut by the decline in the price differential between hardcover and paperback editions and the widespread availability of attractively produced, heavily discounted hardcovers. (page 378)

The independents lost market share. The new chains expanded aggressively and argued that they needed higher discounts from publishers and extended credit periods (the time to settle invoices). In the USA, the Robinson-Patman Act (1936) has prevented producers (for example publishers) favouring particular customers since they have to offer the same wholesale terms to everybody in order to protect small merchants.

The first Waterstone's was opened in 1982 by Tim Waterstone in Old Brompton Road, London

The first book sold by Amazon, on 3 April 1995, was *Fluid Concepts and Creative Analogies* by Douglas Hofstadter

The consumer book publishers benefited from the well-stocked and branded bookshops displaying their books, and agreed to better discounts, easier credit and the continued right to return unsold books. The power relationship between publishers and booksellers, for so long weighted in the publisher's favour, began to tip towards the major retailers, as is common in most consumer goods industries. Furthermore by the mid-1990s, the major supermarkets were devoting more space to bestselling books and were intent on driving down book prices to the consumer, and their costs of supply. The growth of the supermarkets in general forced the closure of small shops, including in the UK the confectioners, tobacconists and newsagents (CTNs), outlets for mass market paperbacks. The paperback wholesale distributors, which had supplied the CTNs and supermarkets before the latter switched to direct supply, went bust. The decades either side of the new century marked the high point of the physical retailing of books. The bookselling chains (to a varying extent) and the supermarkets operated centralized buying of books which were scaled out to their branches. The book buyers of such 'national accounts' – numbering several dozen of people in the UK – largely determined which books were displayed and bought by the public. Publishers reduced the number of their sales representatives who visited booksellers. Subsequently the growth in online retailing of print and latterly of ebooks reinforced the dominance of Amazon compared to physical book stores.

Another factor impinging on the publishers' margins, pushing up the average discount on sales made to UK customers, was the rise of the trade wholesalers supplying the declining and fragmented independent bookshop sector. From the early 1980s to the early 1990s, the proportion of a publisher's sales passing through the wholesalers grew from around 10 per cent to over 20 per cent, at the expense of direct supply to bookshops. While the chains won discounts from the publishers of well above 40 per cent off the published price, the small independents were stuck with the traditional discounts of 33 to 35 per cent. The trade book wholesalers argued they needed at least a 15 per cent margin between the price they bought the books from the publisher and the price they sold them to a retailer, thus they pressed for a 50 per cent discount or more from the publisher. WHSmith and the bookseller chains, meanwhile, ratcheted up the publishers' discounts still further. Overall, from the mid-1980s to the late 1990s, the average trade discount given by the consumer publishers to their UK customers increased by 10 to 15 per cent.

The major publishers also locked themselves into a battle of paying rocketing levels of advances for lead titles in order to keep their share of the limited number of such titles available. Consumer expenditure on books peaked in 1993, and by the time many of those books with high advances were published, the consumer book market was in decline. The return of unsold books from booksellers, a long-time feature of consumer book publishing (especially of paperbacks, usually pulped), surpassed more than 25 per cent of the publishers' sales as booksellers destocked hardbacks and paperbacks. On some lead titles, the actual sales fell far short of the expected number on which the author's advance against royalties had been calculated – the advance was thus unearned. A publisher which may have budgeted an author's royalty rate of between 15 to 20 per cent of the publisher's revenue, may have paid an advance (in effect a non-returnable fee) which equated to an effective royalty rate of 30 per cent of sales income, or more in disastrous

cases. The consumer book publishers emerged from the recession of the early
1990s leaner and fitter but with low levels of profitability.

In the immediate aftermath of the collapse of the Net Book Agreement (NBA)
in 1995, under which publishers set minimum prices for books, consumer
spending on books bottomed out in the spring of 1996, and then staged a steady
recovery to a new peak in 1998 – a vintage year for bestselling titles. Heavy
discounting by retailers of the new, most popular hardback titles became the
norm. Publishers increased their recommended retail prices above the general
rate of inflation to accommodate the higher discounts given to both retailers and
the public.

Fixed book prices

Various forms of fixed pricing exist in some mainland European countries,
including France and Germany. Governments there are supportive of their
cultural heritage expressed through their indigenous publishing industries
and are also keen to see the continued existence of physical bookshops. Fixed
prices are regarded as helpful to smaller and independent bookshops, as well
as to all bricks-and-mortar stores, which face competition from the lower
prices of internet retailers. At the beginning of 2012 a law came into force in
France allowing publishers also to fix the prices of ebooks.

There are differing levels of tax applied to books around Europe and
efforts continue to harmonize rates between countries and formats. Under EU
law ebooks are not eligible for a lower rate of tax and the standard rate must
be applied, but there is an exception for printed books. This was reflected in
the UK in 2013, where the full rate of VAT was applied to ebooks, but print
books were totally exempt; and in Germany, where the rate of VAT applied to
ebooks was 19 per cent, and to print books 7 per cent. By basing its European
headquarters in Luxembourg, Amazon was able to take advantage of the
country's low (and controversial) rate of VAT on ebooks (3 per cent).

There are no fixed prices for books in the UK following the collapse in
September 1995 of the Net Book Agreement (NBA) – or resale price
maintenance (RPM). The purpose of the NBA was to create a well-ordered
book market in which a large number of dedicated booksellers could afford to
stock a wide range of new and backlist titles, and to offer free customer
services, sure in the knowledge that they could not be undercut by predatory
retailers taking the cream of the narrow range of current bestsellers and
fast-selling backlist titles.

For most of the twentieth century publishers set the retail prices of books
(the 'net price'). Retailers were not allowed to sell net books to the public
below the stated prices, prohibiting the price incentives commonly used for
other kinds of products. In that virtually all the main consumer book
publishers were members of their trade organization, the Publishers
Association (PA), and were voluntary signatories of the NBA, the PA was
highly successful in enforcing the NBA amongst retailers, and defending it

FOCUS

against critics. The PA regulated the operation of the market in other ways, such as negotiating the rules governing the operation of book clubs, which were allowed to offer books at discounted prices to their members by mail order. Also libraries, under a special licence, were allowed to purchase books at 10 per cent off the net price.

Prior to the demise of the NBA, consumer spending on books continued to fall, and pro and anti arguments concerning RPM raged amongst publishers and booksellers. By the 1990s opponents of the scheme argued that price was an important lever for generating sales. Some retailers, such as the bookselling chain Dillons and the supermarket chain Asda (owned by WalMart), presented themselves in the press as championing the consumer's right to low book prices, by selling books at deeply discounted prices from publishers which had abandoned the NBA – these retailers and publishers such as Hodder Headline and Reed Consumer Books appeared to be gaining a competitive advantage. The pro-NBA publishers and booksellers faced expensive and uncertain legal proceedings to defend the NBA in the courts, threatened by the government's Office of Fair Trading and the European Commission. Then in September 1995, the announcement of a cut price promotion by major trade publishers Random House and HarperCollins with WHSmith triggered the collapse. With no consensus among publishers and booksellers, the NBA passed into UK trade history and was formally ended in 1997.

Publishing after the NBA

The low company valuations of the consumer book publishers in the 1990s were in marked contrast to the boom of the 1980s. While most of the owners persevered, Reed decided to sell its consumer imprints in order to concentrate on STM and professional publishing, recording a massive write-off in the process. Nevertheless, newer independent UK publishers, such as Bloomsbury, Fourth Estate, Orion and Piatkus grew strongly. Another source of new publishers were the book packagers, usually concentrating on illustrated non-fiction and reference, many of which decided to publish their books in English under their own imprints in the UK, and sometimes the US, rather than license them to publishers.

By the end of the century, the main consumer publishers had mostly recovered their levels of profitability, and the retailer WHSmith paid what was considered by some competitors to be a high price for the UK publisher Hodder Headline. The commercial logic of a retailer owning a publisher was to come under question (the publisher was sold on in 2004 to Hachette), although in 2011 Amazon began its own trade publishing operation.

It took many years for the full effects of the removal of resale price maintenance to work through the supply chain. Early gainers were the bookselling chains, which grew at the expense of the independents and expanded their number of branches. The chains came to compete on price and adopted the 'three for two' promotional offers at the front of their attractive and well-stocked stores. Losers in the post-NBA world were the businesses which benefited from pricing regulation: the bargain bookshops (a large number had to close); the book clubs (which were to lose sales to the online retailers); and independent booksellers (who could not compete on price). Subsequently the chains came under pressure themselves from the price cuts and expanding ranges of the supermarkets (led by Tesco), and from the ultimate range discount bookseller, Amazon. Supermarket and internet sales have increased in market share in relation to the faltering bookseller chains carrying excess stock and expensive retail space. The pressure on margins throughout the supply chain also forced the consolidation and diversification of the major book wholesalers and library suppliers.

Today readers are able to purchase heavily promoted bestsellers at large discounts off the publishers' recommended published prices from a wide range of retailers, which compete for consumers' attention primarily on price. Consumers have enjoyed a period of book price deflation. As the UK economy enjoyed continued growth from 1992 into the new century, publishers experienced a period of increasing book sales, albeit made at yet higher discounts to wholesalers and retailers.

Legacy practices of the NBA era endure in the world of print. Consumer publishers still display the price on the book's cover, and author royalties are usually based on the recommended price, albeit with let-outs for sales at high discounts. The arrival of ebooks has brought a new dynamic with the ability to change prices at will, both by publishers and retailers, whereas previously printed stock had to be restickered in the warehouse. With Amazon leading the development of the ebook market, publishers have struggled to maintain prices at the levels they consider reasonable whilst attempting to create alternative models for the business relationship with intermediaries.

Wholesale and agency models

Consumer publishers use the *wholesale* pricing method when they trade through all kinds of intermediaries, such as retailers, to reach consumers. It lies at the heart of their transactional or 'copy sale' business model. (The use of the word 'wholesale' in this context is different from 'wholesaler' – an intermediary between a publisher and a retailer.) Under the wholesale pricing method, the retailer buys the book from the publisher at a set price and is free to sell it to a consumer at any price. The set price to the retailer is arrived at by deducting the percentage discount off the recommended retail price which is set by the publisher. The percentage discount (referred to as the 'trade discount') in the UK is the outcome of the negotiation between the publisher and the retailer. The more powerful the buying power of the retailer in terms of the quantity of books ordered or its market share in relation to other retailers, the higher the discount it can extract from the publisher. Thus, for example, if the trade publisher grants a big retailer a 50 per cent discount and sets the recommended published price of the book at £12, the retailer buys it from the publisher at £6, and is free to sell it to the consumer at any price and determine its own margin. The retailer might sell it to a consumer at £12, or discount it to £6, or even below its cost price in order to gain market share, termed predatory pricing. The high trade discounts won by the dominant physical retailers and Amazon were transferred to embryonic ebook sales and became established.

The alternative *agency* model for ebooks came to a controversial fore with Apple's launch of the iPad and its iBookstore in 2010. Famously Steve Jobs, CEO of Apple, had claimed previously 'the fact is that people don't read anymore' (*New York Times*, 15 January 2008). While Apple had become the dominant music retailer and sold other media excluding books, its innovatory and high-priced tablet needed ebooks to compete against Amazon's popular and established low-priced Kindle, and others such as the Nook and Sony Reader. At the time, Amazon enjoyed almost complete domination of ebook sales in the USA with a market share of 90 per cent. To the chagrin of the big trade publishers, their hardcover bestsellers, typically priced at say $25.00, were sold by Amazon as ebooks to consumers at the heavily discounted price of $9.99. Since Amazon probably bought the books from the publishers at around $13–15, it sold ebooks at a loss (a negative margin) to maintain its dominant market share. The publishers feared that it would only be a matter of time before Amazon pressured them further on terms and prices and would control every part of the industry.

Apple in contrast offered the major trade publishers the agency model under which the publisher sets the price of the ebook to the consumer and appoints the retailer which acts as its agent to sell the ebook to the reader. The agent takes a sales commission on the sale, in this case 30 per cent. The publisher has a contractual relationship with, and hence direct liability to the reader, including VAT or other sales tax compliance. Apple supplied the publishers with maximum retail price grids for publishers to set the ebook prices of their titles. New releases of ebooks were typically set between $13 to $15, from which Apple deducted its 30 per cent commission. On such indicative figures, the publishers and their authors received less money per copy sold through the iBookstore than through Amazon, but it was argued that short-term pain would lead to long-term gain.

The major publishers in the USA, which published most of the biggest authors and titles, were at the time called the 'Big Six': Hachette, HarperCollins, Macmillan, Penguin, Random House and Simon & Schuster. With the exception of Random House (the largest), the other five accepted the agency model. The agency contract with Apple included an unusual 'most favoured nation' (MFN) clause which allowed Apple to sell ebooks at least as cheaply as others. It was argued that it was used by the publishers to compel other online retailers, including Amazon, to switch to the agency model on similar terms to those agreed with Apple. The retailers were told that they might not receive ebooks unless they adopted the agency model. Random House by delaying its own decision to transfer to agency pricing gained a competitive advantage and escaped being targeted by the regulators (the US Department of Justice and the European Commission). Consumer groups were angered by the imposed higher prices of ebooks that were close to paperback prices. The regulators launched investigations in 2011 as to whether there was collusion between Apple and the five publishers to conspire to fix the prices of ebooks thereby limiting price competition on a global scale, which might violate regulations that prohibit cartels and restrictive business practices. By the end of 2012, the regulators concluded their investigations and began to sue Apple and some of the publishers. Apple and the publishers agreed to terminate their particular agency contracts. The legal cases were settled with the publishers and compensation paid. Some publishers then produced modified agency contracts or reverted to the wholesale model.

A CHANGE IN PUBLISHING STRATEGY

From the late 1990s, the major publishers were to reverse their former 'scatter-gun' strategy of publishing as many titles as possible in the hope that one or two would be hits. Facing increasing polarization in the market between the bestselling titles and the also-rans (the 'winner takes all' maxim common in the creative industries), they cut their new title output progressively to concentrate on books and authors considered marketable, especially those that would fit the retailers' promotional plans. As the UK trade magazine, *The Bookseller* noted (18 December 2009), the greatest effect of the demise of the NBA 'was discount driven frontlist growth'. The big four publishing groups (Hachette UK, Random House, Penguin and HarperCollins), which had the power to acquire bestselling authors, to negotiate with national booksellers and pay for book promotions, pulled ahead of the other publishers and by 2006 had taken 50 per cent of the UK consumer book market.

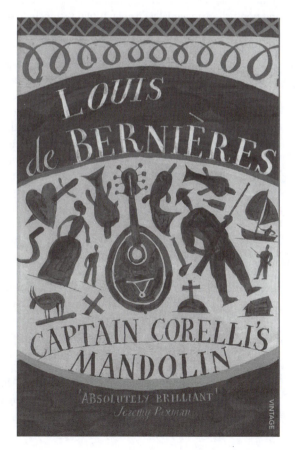

Few book covers have the iconic status of album covers. One example, however, is the 1995 design for *Captain Corelli's Mandolin* by Louis de Bernières

The so-called 'midlist' authors were casualties, not that publishers admit publicly to having a midlist. Writers whose works had been well received within the writing community, who were previously supported by publishers over a number of books – awaiting their sales breakthrough – could be seen as on their way out much earlier and were rejected after only their first few books. Some moved to smaller and welcoming publishers while others were dropped by their agents too.

The major publishers' other strategies (apart from reducing the advances and royalty income of less-favoured authors), included giving greater emphasis to brand authors and series. They also entered into 'licensed' partnerships with television and film companies to merchandise their intellectual properties, and marketing and sales partnerships with smaller publishers sometimes through equity stakes.

Trends in fiction and non-fiction – a US perspective

Edward Nawotka, Founder and Editor-in-Chief of Publishing Perspectives

E★PERT

The US market is geographically, demographically, economically and culturally vast, and accordingly the subjects covered by general trade fiction and non-fiction are equally diverse. When you include self-published titles, there are easily more than a million books published in the United States a year. It is an astonishing figure.

The past few years have seen the internet and self-publishing cater to ever more niche interests, particularly in genres like romance, paranormal and crime. Name your fetish and it will be catered to online. Trends in popular fiction come and go quickly: one year chaste Amish romance novels are all the rage, while the next, uber-explicit erotic fairy tales top the bestseller lists. Always though, you have the stalwarts: thrillers and detective novels in which the lone-wolf hero decides to take matters into their own hands. Likewise, in literary fiction, it is often the same: an individual battling an unacknowledged threat, acting counter to the prevailing trends in society.

Why? Americans are, generally speaking, raised to resent or rebel against authority. It was the founding principle of the country. Characters at the heart of bestselling American fiction tend to reflect this attitude. This applies to non-fiction as well as fiction. A prevailing trend in non-fiction works is to take an idea and flip it to reveal heretofore unknown 'truths'. The 'counterintuitive revelation' is often at the heart of much general non-fiction – from sociological essayists like Malcolm Gladwell to humourists like David Sedaris to conservative political pundits and talking-heads, who reliably clog up the bestseller lists. In the US, political pundits are to bestseller lists as celebrity tell-alls are to the bestseller lists in the UK and Europe.

Americans are weaned on the idea of 'individualism' and, accordingly, the literature they produce is largely character-driven. This is why American historians tend to shy away from writing long, sweeping general histories that summarize the 'world in a book' and tend to focus on a series of events through the prism of an individual, rather than a family, group or a larger movement. Likewise, characters in American books tend to be victims of other individuals and not society-at-large. Ironically, despite this individualism, Americans do follow the herd when it comes to bestseller lists and you can expect two or three 'must read' titles to dominate each season.

Finally, it is a common refrain to say that Americans are not interested in 'foreign books'. And this is, for the vast general populace of readers, entirely true. Why? Because America largely contains a significant percentage of people who, though they may have been born abroad, now consider themselves as Americans. Look at the number of assimilation narratives produced in the US: hundreds of books a year tell the story of several generations of an immigrant family where the parents adhere to the values of the 'old country' and the children live by the rules of their new home. These books might be set in New York, Milwaukee, Dallas or San Francisco and feature families from India or China, Russia or Brazil. But the one thing they have in common is that they are all American books. Unlike in the UK or Europe, if you are born abroad and want to become an American – all you have to do is call yourself one. Accordingly, the USA (mistakenly) believes it has little to learn from the world, since it already contains the world within its borders.

Some firms want to fulfil the traditional role of publishing fine literary works, but only a few authors and books become part of the perennial backlist alongside Austen, Dickens and Orwell. Publishers are opportunistic – they must respond fast if they want to capture a well-known author or celebrity, or take advantage of current fashions, media events or topical issues on which to hang a book's promotion. Books are firmly positioned in genres and categories (see Table 2.2, page 42), whether crime, fantasy or horror in fiction, or home and garden, history, or popular science in non-fiction. This is reflected in the cover design and associated marketing. As Claire Squires remarks about literary publishing:

> By the turn of the twentieth and twenty-first centuries, the necessity of finding arrangements for the 100,000+ books produced yearly by the UK industry is readily apparent. The prolific and diverse nature of the marketplace demands it; the sheer number of individual product lines calls out for some sort of taxonomy. (page 71)

A new category may be initiated by smaller companies before being adopted by mainstream publishers. If the market then diminishes, the category is often left to specialist publishers to pursue. Some publishers make a category their own. Harlequin Mills & Boon (later bought by HarperCollins) had over 70 per cent of the romantic fiction market in the UK in the early part of the twenty-first century, and 3 million women regularly read one of their books. 'Mills & Boon' even entered the Oxford English Dictionary, with the definition 'romantic story book'.

The success of the erotic trilogy *Fifty Shades of Grey* then encouraged other publishers to boost their profile in this market category.

Table 2.2 Top five book genres for fiction and non-fiction (*source*: 2009 data from Book Facts Online)

	Fiction	Non-fiction
1	General popular	Biography
2	Crime/mystery	Cookery/food/drink
3	Adventure/thriller	History
4	General literary	Maps/atlases
5	Fantasy	Travel guides

Table 2.3 Top five book genres for men and women (*source*: 2009 data from Book Facts Online)

	Genres bought for Men	Genres bought for Women
1	Biography	General popular
2	Adventure/thriller	Biography
3	History	Crime/mystery
4	Crime/mystery	Adventure/thriller
5	Maps/atlases	Cookery/food/drink

The public libraries aid, but to a heavily diminished extent, the hardback publishing of fiction and non-fiction. Between 2002 and 2012, four authors recorded borrowings of over 10 m in the UK: James Patterson, Jacqueline Wilson, Danielle Steel, and Josephine Cox. The most borrowed adult fiction book of the decade was *The Da Vinci Code* by Dan Brown, and the most borrowed children's fiction title was *The Story of Tracy Beaker* by Jacqueline Wilson.

THE RISE OF DIGITAL PUBLISHING

There has been a series of overlapping developments which have impacted trade publishing in the most recent period. All are part of the rise of digital in the area of consumer publishing, with growing sales of ebooks and constant experimentation around digital products by both authors and publishers. The following are key developments:

- arrival of the large technology players,
- the rise of self-publishing,
- growth of ebooks,
- digital product development,
- the rise of social networks and communities.

Arrival of large technology players

The landscape of publishing has changed significantly with the entrants of major players including Amazon, Apple, Google and Sony. This kickstarted and then accelerated the move towards ebooks with devices, from the Kindle to the iPad, facilitating a high-quality user experience, and digital content being made widely available. Amazon's strategy of aggressive pricing has opened up the market for ebooks, and publishers have encouraged the other players in the market in the hopes of easing the internet retailer's domination. Publishers have had to learn to work with the technology companies, encountering differences in culture and mind-set.

Google began scanning books in December 2004, firstly at major university libraries in the USA and in Oxford (the Bodleian Library), at the New York Public Library, and subsequently at other libraries. By 2013, it was thought that 30 million titles had been scanned. Google not only scanned in titles that were out of copyright, in the public domain, but also books which were in copyright. Google did not ask, in advance, the rights owners of the latter for permission to copy or offer them compensation, and thus invited controversy and legal cases from authors and publishers. There were other concerns, such as from the library community, that Google might be privatizing access to the world's knowledge. While Google's original concept became legally mired, the outcome today is that readers can search, through Google Books, works in the public domain and view them in full, and copyright books can be viewed in selected amounts with the agreement of the publishers. Ebooks are also sold through Google Play.

There were further significant consequences arising from Google's initiative. The publishers realized that unless they gave the search engine companies, such as Google and Microsoft, access to their content for indexing they and their authors would face potential invisibility on the internet. From around 1996, they were stimulated into digitizing their books before ebook sales took off, rather than relying on a third party to supply them with digital files of their own books. The initial dominance and searchability of digitized English language books prompted similar initiatives from publishers and governments of other languages, which sometimes collaborated with Google.

The rise of self-publishing

Authors have always published themselves, without publishers, but with some difficulty and expense. In the pre-digital world, the so-called vanity publishers, or presses, manipulated authors' often life-long desire to be published by charging them large sums for printing (but rarely marketing) their books in considerable quantity, typically delivered to their homes, where the stock remained. Authors were stigmatized for their vanity – being unable to attract a real publisher to invest in their work – and duped by rogue 'publishers'.

However, from the turn of the century, the availability of print on demand (POD) technology enabled new companies, such as Lulu Enterprises, to offer production and distribution platforms for authors to self-publish their own books at much lower cost than hitherto. Amazon purchased BookSurge (a POD operation) in 2005, and offered authors through CreateSpace a similar service. Author Solutions was founded in 2007 and SmashWords (an ebook distribution company) in 2008. These four author services companies (sometimes referred to as 'subsidy publishers') came to dominate the US self-publishing market. In the USA, Bowker research (prnewswire.com, accessed 24 October 2012) revealed that by 2011 'the number of self-published books produced annually in the USA has nearly tripled, growing 287 per cent since 2006, and now tallies more than 235,000 print and "e" titles'.

Their supply-side business model is the opposite to the curatorial/risk-investment model of the trade publishers. It is founded on creating content abundance, charging authors a small percentage on sales made through their own platform or through other sales channels, and through offering authors charged-for services, such as copy-editing, design and marketing. Critics called it the monetization of the slush pile. The authors receive a high percentage of sales income on each copy sold compared to receiving a low percentage, expressed as a royalty on each copy sold, from an investing trade publisher. Customers are given cloud-based production services, an application of technology which is in advance of the publishers' offline production systems. While physical booksellers do not stock self-published authors, the advent of ebooks gives authors direct access to the reading public. Some kinds of authors are no longer dependent on securing the services of a literary agent and a contract from a publisher to reach readers: authorship is democratized. They are also free to experiment with new business models (looking for a profit share rather than taking a royalty) or new forms of writing including digital story-telling, perhaps in collaboration with other authors.

Most major online retailers offer authors self-publishing services but their sales are restricted to the retailer's channel. The major trade publishers too offer self-publishing imprints, sometimes in partnership with the author services companies. In 2012, Pearson acquired Author Solutions and its technology, by which time it had aided 160,000 authors to bring to market 200,000 titles. Online writing websites, such as Wattpad, emerged for writers to reach and communicate freely with readers. Community sites offer authors the facility to publish fan fiction (their take on a TV series or a novel) or original web fiction, sometimes in serial form. Authors can use such sites to build a fan base or trial out stories. The hugely successful *Fifty Shades of Grey* by E. L. James first appeared as a piece of Twilight fan fiction.

The *Fifty Shades of Grey* trilogy had sold over 100m copies worldwide by 2014

The self-published authors and the author services companies disintermediated literary agents, publishers and physical bookstores from the supply chain. They grew their market share against the trade publishers mostly in terms of title output more than in sales revenue. The companies offered their services to other organizations (for example universities and corporates), and interestingly to literary agents and publishers, both of which wanted to extend their own operations into this fast-growing business of charging authors. The authors labelled themselves as independent publishers; not to be confused with the many thousands of independent publishers which select authors and invest in publishing their works in the usual way.

A small number of *indie* authors (as they became to be known), especially prolific writers of genre fiction (for example crime, science fiction and fantasy, romance), topped the US ebook bestselling fiction charts. They gained triumphant media coverage, fuelling the prospect that authors could potentially make far more money through self-publishing, rather than through an investing publisher, and have total control over the way their books were published. Other indie authors, termed *hybrid* authors, both self-publish some titles and publish other titles through the mainstream publishers. Commentators disparagingly referred to the incumbent trade houses as 'legacy publishers': conjuring an image of corporations locked in their New York glass towers, trapped in analogue mind-sets, and clinging to past systems and behaviours through which they had once controlled authors and markets. However, over time the traditional publishers consolidated their position in the fiction ebook bestseller lists and earned profitable revenues from their higher ebook prices and strength in the international and print book markets.

The entrepreneurial indies primarily compete for readers against the publishers by using very low pricing strategies, even giving their ebooks away for free (the *freemium* business model with a view to charging subsequently). Some established authors took the view that the indies were devaluing writing, that it was being commoditized (producing titles that were easily substitutable and hence worthless), not dissimilar to the comments made earlier in the age of pulp fiction.

The author services companies also impact on the ways publishers inform authors about sales and pay them. The trade publishers send authors, at say six monthly intervals, their royalty statement showing aggregate sales of printed books and give themselves a three-month credit period to pay up. Authors wanting to know their sales have to contact their publisher's editor or agent. In contrast, the author services companies, such as Amazon, see authors as customers and provide them with current sales information and pay them monthly. Authors can check their sales in real time and see how their pricing and promotional activity is influencing sales. In response, some trade publishers, such as Hachette, Simon & Schuster and Random House, provide authors with a dashboard to provide current sales information and marketing advice, and others are starting to pay monthly on their new digital only imprints.

The aim of many new indie authors, however, remains to achieve a contract from a publisher. The self-publishing websites and forums form talent pools for publishers and agents to spot new writing talent. Furthermore, the communities which develop around their writing provide a ready-made audience for the publisher to build greater sales success.

A striking example of author self-publishing occurred in 2012, when J. K. Rowling launched her revolutionary Pottermore site to sell ebooks of the Harry Potter series in many languages and to serve the fan base (the print editions were originally published by Bloomsbury in the UK and Scholastic in the USA, with Rowling retaining the digital rights). By leveraging the strength of the super brand, the online retailers agreed to act merely as shop windows. Readers visiting Amazon, for instance, were directed to Pottermore which owned the customer relationship and fan base, and the ebook could still appear on the Kindle. The retailer receives an introduction or affiliate fee. Pottermore thereby controlled the ebook prices across all channels and Potter readers had the freedom to download the ebook into many different kinds of devices of their choice. The Harry Potter brand is a prominent example of transmedia publishing: a multi-platform property spanning books, films, games, the web and communities.

Growth of ebooks

Most ebooks are little more than replicas of the print edition – so-called *vanilla* ebooks. Printed books are reproduced from a high resolution fixed page PDF file. The first generation of ebooks were simply low resolution PDF files of the print files in order to facilitate downloading over the limited bandwidth networks of the period. They were exact page replicas, usually read on desktop computers with large screens. Reading PDF files on small screens of the emerging dedicated reading devices was problematic and so new file formats were designed to enable text to be reflowed on smaller screen sizes. Readers could also customize the font and type size. Publishers were faced, and still are, with a multiplicity of file formats, some of which are proprietary, such as from Amazon and Apple, thereby hindering interoperability across ecosystems and increasing publishing costs. The ePub file format, supported by publishers, is designed as a universal standard.

The sale of ebooks rose steeply after the introduction of Amazon's Kindle in the USA in 2007; and in 2010 in the UK, along with devices and online bookstores from other international retailers such as Apple, Kobo, and Sony. Barnes & Noble launched its Nook reading devices in 2009 and began to sell them in the UK in 2012. The UK initially lagged behind the USA by one to two years in the availability of devices and consequent ebook sales.

At the outset, some publishers took the view that ebook publication would cannibalize print sales and should occur sometime after the first publication in print. But the traditional pattern of hardback to paperback was disrupted by the arrival of ebooks, and the new convention was that the ebook should be published simultaneously with the first print edition to maximize marketing exposure. Sometimes there was *digital first* publication, and later on *digital-only* imprints in areas such as science fiction and romance. Consumers expected ebooks to be priced very much lower than print editions, while the publishers wanted to hold up prices as long as possible. The biggest early shifts in the purchase of ebooks occurred in the area of fiction, and genre fiction in particular. In 2012, publishers were reporting ebook sales of up to 50 per cent of total sales on some individual new fiction titles, and the UK print market for crime alone fell by 25 per cent. Some publishers believe that readers who would before have bought the paperback edition, published up to 12 months after the hardback edition, now buy the ebook edition instead. The migration from print to ebook formats of highly illustrated books, despite the rise in the purchase of tablet computers, has been slow.

Publishers' revenue from ebook sales is derived mainly from the copy sales business model, enacted through licences with resellers. The use of subscription business models by the non-consumer publishers is long established and more prevalent. However, third party subscription sites for consumer ebooks that mimic the business models of Spotify for music or Netflix for movies are developing worldwide. It is argued that book consumption is closer to that of movies than to music tracks because a consumer takes a long time to read each book, and the number they can consume each month is limited by time scarcity, though a small percentage of so-called 'power readers' may consume more than 10 titles per month.

The Spanish company 24Symbols offers readers using smartphones and tablets access to titles held in the cloud using a freemium-based model (with advertising) or its monthly subscription service. Other companies experimenting with subscription services for trade books include Amazon, Oyster and Scribd. Publishers license curated aggregations of titles, such as backlist or genres, to the subscription companies, with the aim of generating new revenue streams

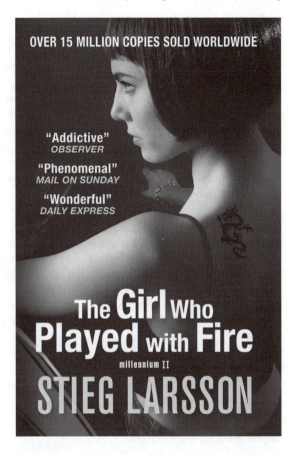

In 2011 Stieg Larsson became the first author to sell 1 m ebooks on Amazon

without disrupting their normal sales revenues. Payments to publishers may be triggered by the usage of their titles. Some of the trade publishers, from Bertelsmann to niche publishers, are experimenting with their own subscription services. Customers who pay a monthly subscription are given access to a collection of titles, usually designed for vertical communities in particular genres. In emerging markets, where piracy may be high, subscription services offering streamed content may be preferable to the pay and download business model.

Table 2.4 Sales from digital – 2011 and 2012 (*source*: Association of American Publishers, Publishers Association)

	USA Proportion of publisher net revenues	UK Proportion of publisher net revenues
2011	17 %	8 %
2012	23 %	12 %
Sales of consumer ebooks	$1.5 bn	£216 m

Public libraries

The lending of ebooks through public libraries is a difficult issue. Librarians want to extend their ebook lending services and retain their purpose of providing products and services free to end-users. But publishers fear that unrestricted lending would undermine book sales and thus publishers' and authors' revenue, and that of physical bookstores. UK public libraries tend to lose a demographic of borrowers from the late teens through to the child-rearing age. Supporters point to the physical importance of the library for book discovery and for stimulating books sales. Public libraries are an important place to introduce children to books and reading. Nevertheless, UK public library closures accelerated during government spending cuts from 2012 onwards; and their expenditure on books had fallen previously, in 1995 it was 17 per cent of total expenditure, by 2008 it was just 12 per cent.

The large US and UK publishers were resistant to ebook lending, and began trials limited to selected backlist titles. However, from around 2012, some of the main publishers allowed the lending of new books. Ebook lending mimics the restrictions of physical book lending, for example, the authentication of the borrower, limits on the number of simultaneous borrowers, loan expiry periods, and 'degradation' through usage of per copy purchased. The purchase price of a book to the library may be higher to reflect multiple usages. The ebook lending distributor, OverDrive (USA), became an important intermediary between the publishers and the public libraries and school libraries, in the USA and internationally. Major wholesalers, such as Baker & Taylor (USA) and Gardners (UK) also entered the library supply aggregation market.

Digital product development

The development by Apple of its app store in 2008 and the launch of the iPad in 2010 opened up an opportunity for publishers to produce, often in collaboration with app developers, titles which contained rich media (audio and video) along with interactive features, similar to those developed by Dorling Kindersley in CD-Rom form over a decade earlier. Publishers' apps were initially limited to Apple's iOS operating system (a 'closed' system) though later some were available on Google's Android system. The development of apps proved very costly, initially with six figure investments. Touch Press, in partnership with publishers such as Faber & Faber, produced some notable titles for adults – Steve Jobs used the *Solar System* app in his launch of the iPad 2 in 2011. However, Apple's app store is populated with large numbers of free apps, marketing apps, apps sold on a freemium model, and paid-for apps available at very low prices. It is not a conducive place for publishers to charge higher prices for quality products. The content of Apple's store was not open to the search engines and with the discovery of apps difficult, most publishers scaled back or abandoned the production of content app titles for adults, but continued modest developments of story book apps for children and young adults, incorporating gaming techniques. Publishers increasingly use web-based apps for content delivery and marketing purposes across many devices.

💬 PERSPECTIVES

▶ I. THE BURIAL OF THE DEAD

Seamus Heaney is one of Ireland's best-loved poets. Considered by many to be the most important Irish poet since Yeats, he was awarded the Nobel Prize in Literature in 1995. He has published more than fifty works of poetry and fiction and is a leading expert in Anglo-Saxon literature. He lives in Dublin.

Seamus Heaney

Encountering Eliot's poetry for the first time

The process of reading Eliot   ✓

Reading the end of 'The Fire Sermon'

Reading 'Death by Water'

Paul Keegan

Eliot and illness

Eliot's collaboration with Ezra Pound and Vivienne Eliot

Eliot's legacy

🏠

I.   The Burial of the Dead

April is the cruellest month, breeding
Lilacs out of the dead land, mixing
Memory and desire, stirring
Dull roots with spring rain.
Winter kept us warm, covering
Earth in forgetful snow, feeding
A little life with dried tubers.
Summer surprised us, coming over the Starnbergersee
With a shower of rain; we stopped in the colonnade,
And went on in sunlight, into the Hofgarten, 10
And drank coffee, and talked for an hour.
Bin gar keine Russin, stamm' aus Litauen, echt deutsch.
And when we were children, staying at the arch-duke's,
My cousin's, he took me out on a sled,
And I was frightened. He said, Marie,
Marie, hold on tight. And down we went.
In the mountains, there you feel free.
I read, much of the night, and go south in the winter.

Enhanced ebooks are similar to apps in that they include rich media and interactive features but can be traded through all book channels to market. The HTML format, which renders an ebook through a web browser, and the ePub3 standard format (itself based on HTML) are designed to enable such features. The enhanced ebook equivalents of highly illustrated books, where text, illustrations and captions are closely related on fixed layouts, are at the experimental stage and have yet to be proven commercially viable. The iBooks author tool is also being used for such developments.

A screenshot from *The Waste Land* app from Faber and Touch Press (released in 2011; Seamus Heaney died in 2013)

The transition to digital in trade publishing is expected to encounter further disruption and innovation. Digital publishing breaks the economic constraints of the printed book container, enables faster publication, and updates. In the print only era, short stories (typically up to say 20,000 words) were published only in collections or anthologies, and their sales were modest. Novels often had to be at least 40,000 words, and novellas fell somewhere in between. Newspaper and magazine articles were limited in length by their publishers.

Amazon at the start of 2011 launched its Kindle Singles programme and kickstarted a new channel for short-form digital fiction and non-fiction, published at low prices, up to $2.99 or £2.50, to drive impulse purchase. Short-form digital publishers and publishing programmes arose; and magazine and newspaper organizations conceived the publication as ebooks of long-form journalism. Digital shorts are roughly in the range of 5,000 to 30,000 words, or more narrowly 10,000 to 15,000 words. Digital publication reduces the publishing cost

FOCUS

The rise and fall of multimedia publishing

In consumer publishing, the first wave of new media excitement – the publishing of multimedia titles on CD-ROM – occurred in the early to mid-1990s. At that time there were large numbers of US imports. Analysts pointed to the rapid rise in the number of computers with CD-ROM drives being purchased by UK households. This would lead, it was argued, to an exponential rise in the consumer purchase of suitable content. Some of the major trade publishers, such as HarperCollins, Penguin and Reed, and the illustrated book reference publisher Dorling Kindersley, established new media divisions. The world's main encyclopedia publishers converted their works on to CD-ROM; Microsoft created the encyclopedia Encarta (which eventually closed in 2009), localized around the world; multimedia start-ups appeared; and major entertainment companies such as Disney exploited their character properties on the new medium. But by 1996, most of the UK trade book publishers, with the exception of Dorling Kindersley, withdrew from the marketplace bearing large losses. No mass market appeared for these products and the publishers could not cover their high development costs. The booksellers did not stock the titles sufficiently and the publishers were left to compete in the computer stores, an alien and difficult setting for their business. By the late 1990s, the remainder dealers had extensive stocks of lifestyle titles from around the world to sell off for a few pounds per title. The publishing of multimedia titles on disk then continued mainly in the educational (home and school), cartographic and text-based professional reference fields.

The failure of multimedia publishing reinforced many publishers' sceptical view of new media publishing and negatively coloured the response of senior managers to the news of ebook growth in the USA in the late 1990s. If the business model for multimedia publishing on disk was loss-making, they argued, what hope would there be for publishing on the internet, a generally free medium devaluing the price of information, with few viable business models for selling content? This view was confirmed by the internet dotcom bubble of the late 1990s, which saw investment pouring into many start-up companies that later became worthless. Yet publishers took little or no action to future-proof their business for the digital age. Comforted by the oft-quoted mantra 'content is king', few foresaw that in the next century big money would be made from consumers searching for content on the internet, especially by Google, a company that would turn its attention to book content.

by removing the cost of printing which amounts to say 10 to 15 per cent of the cost of publishing the book. Furthermore, it is not constrained by the six to nine month marketing and sales lead times of the print supply chain. Writers may self-publish their short fiction or via their publishers. Short fiction and serial release may be used to promote a future novel through generating pre-orders; or help readers discover and sample established or new writers. Some news and magazine publishers entered into partnerships with the book publishers to create lists for long-form journalism on topical issues.

At the other extreme, the sheer length of major references works and the necessity to update them led in 2012 to *Encyclopaedia Britannica* announcing that it would no longer publish its print editions; Oxford University Press had made a similar decision for the *Oxford English Dictionary* (*OED*). The online *OED* is sold under licence to libraries on a subscription business model, and licensed to corporations to bundle with their hardware and services. In 2013, the Reader's Digest book company in the UK was closed marking the end of its publication of highly illustrated reference printed books that had inspired a previous generation of publishers, such as at Mitchell Beazley, Octopus and Dorling Kindersley.

Some of the consumer publishers' output crosses over to education markets: school and higher. For example, Bloomsbury and Faber & Faber aggregated their drama lists and in 2013 opened a content platform, Drama Online, for higher education markets. The inclusion of learning tools and stills, for instance, from the Victoria and Albert Museum, mimics Bloomsbury's Berg Fashion Library published online earlier.

The transition from print to digital publishing was acutely felt by the publishers of travel guides. The travel guide publishers migrated their content to the internet, especially helpful to travellers searching on mobile devices. BBC Worldwide bought the guidebook publisher Lonely Planet from the founders in 2007 and got full control in 2011; it sold it at a loss in 2013, despite having grown a significant digital publishing and community operation. In 2012, Wiley divested the US travel guide publisher Frommer's to Google, which previously had purchased Zagat, the mainly consumer-rated restaurant and hotel guides. Nine months later Google sold the Frommer's brand back to its founder, Arthur Frommer, who recommenced the book publishing. Google, however, retained the social media data of the brand's serious followers, and integrated travel content into Google+ Local and other Google services. It was speculated that Google had bought Frommer's primarily for the metadata it offered on places around the world.

The rise of social networks and communities

The enormous growth of social networks such as Facebook and Twitter, and of sharing sites such as Pinterest, creates new opportunities for publishers and authors to hold conversations with readers and potential readers. Since the retailers do not provide publishers with information on customers, it is imperative for publishers to form direct relationships with readers and customers, not least in order to understand how they are engaging with the publisher's products. While the conventional review media are still important for publicizing books, all-important word-of-mouth recommendations are increasingly fostered through the use of social platforms and communities.

The rise of subject interest, or vertical, communities, favours niche publishers that develop in-depth specialist sites for enthusiasts and which provide associated services to authors as part of their brand innovation. Publisher-led communities in genre categories help fans discover new and backlist writers, and contribute to the development of books and writers. Good examples are the military history, science fiction, and MBS (mind, body, spirit) publisher Osprey (UK), which has used crowdsourcing to suggest topics on which the community would like to see new books commissioned; the enthusiast publisher F+W Media (USA), which for each vertical publishes books, magazines and holds events; and the MBS publisher and associated events organizer Hay House (USA). The Faber Academy (UK) hosts creative writing courses.

MARKET SHARE

If the consolidation of the consumer book publishers in the last quarter of the twentieth century was about the vertical restructuring of an archaic industry, the current consolidation is about gaining market share in the face of ever more powerful retailers and the increasing internationalization of consumer publishing. The market shares of the leading publishing groups in 2012 are shown in Table 2.5 – the top four groups (shortly to be three with the merger of Random House and Penguin) had approaching 50 per cent of the market.

Table 2.5 Market shares (percentages) of publishers for consumer sales 2012 (*source*: Nielsen BookScan)

Publisher	Market share (%)
Random House	14.80
Hachette	12.50
Penguin	11.70
HarperCollins	7.90
Pan Macmillan	3.30
Pearson	2.20
Simon & Schuster	2.00
Bloomsbury	2.00
OUP	1.90
Scholastic	1.60

The long-time pole position of the Bertelsmann companies in the UK (Random House and Transworld, with strengths in fiction) came to be matched by the rapid growth of the French media group Hachette Livre, owned by Lagardère. Hachette had previously acquired Orion, Octopus, Watts and Chambers-Harrap; it then bought Hodder Headline from WHSmith. In 2006 it bought the book publishing businesses of the US company Time Warner (whose imprints included Little, Brown), taking the number one spot in the UK and for the first time giving it access to the US market. In 2007, Bertelsmann responded with its own purchase of BBC Books, which it merged into Ebury.

In a market increasingly dominated by powerful retailers and bestsellers, publisher size is crucial, especially in the largest market segment – fiction. This is one factor behind the merger of Random House and Penguin, alongside the search for cost savings in back office operations including production and distribution. In 2009, the big four (Hachette, Random House, HarperCollins and Penguin) took nearly 90 per cent of the fiction market by value, and the top 10 over 95 per cent. Non-fiction publishing is less concentrated with many smaller players. In the adult non-fiction market, the same big four took 48 per cent by value and the top 10 around 58 per cent (Richardson and Taylor, 2nd edition, page 36).

Both Bertelsmann and Hachette adopt a decentralized approach to the management of their publishing groups. Literary agents are encouraged to submit projects to editors across their imprints, even to the extent that their constituent publishing companies may be in direct competition against one another.

There is a notable polarization between the big players and a large number of much smaller firms – in between there is only a small number of medium-sized companies. The middle-ranking publishers lack the scale of operation and deep backlists of the large players and are sometimes too small to resist the pressures from the large retailers for improved terms of trade, at the expense of their margins. They also face greater risks in publishing brand-named authors on which they depend to give them access to the main retailers. If for example they are in competition to buy a potentially huge book, they may be outbid by an advance on royalties from a larger publisher. Alternatively if they won the book and its sales were disappointing, the failure of their prime investment would have severe consequences on their profitability. In contrast, a major publisher could afford to purchase six potentially huge books, of which the chances are that three or four turn out winners. The biggest authors migrate to the largest publishers – even those who achieve their early success with a smaller publisher, or start out by self-publishing, are likely to be tempted away by larger advances. The smaller publishers, which cannot compete against the large corporations in terms of advances, concentrate on bringing forward new writers, or those overlooked writers who may not have agents or have been rejected by larger publishers. They may opt to build a stable of authors who will work for one-off fees instead of royalties – common in the field of highly illustrated books.

Although consumer book publishing is dominated by the existing majors, there are other large publishers, including Bloomsbury, Macmillan (owned by Holtzbrinck), Simon & Schuster (owned by CBS Corporation), and Oxford University Press. Quarto is a sizeable player in the international illustrated book field. Medium-sized independents include Anova, Atlantic, Canongate (in Edinburgh), Faber & Faber, History Press, John Blake, Michael O'Mara, Profile Books, Quadrille, and the art publishers Phaidon, Thames & Hudson and the Tate Gallery. There are many smaller specialist publishers producing adult or children's books.

Faced with the power of the mass market retailers, leading independent publishers responded in 2005 by forming the Independent Alliance of publishers. The Alliance, led and sales managed by Faber & Faber, offered more favourable terms to independent booksellers, comparable to those received by the chains, and has provided better access for the publishers into the major retailers. The Alliance subsequently became the fifth or six largest publisher in the UK home market. In 2011, Faber & Faber (UK) and Perseus (USA) formed a joint venture, Faber Factory, to provide digital publishing services to more than 70 independent publishers in the UK, Ireland and the Commonwealth.

The recession associated with the financial crisis of 2007 onwards had an impact on consumer spending in many countries, and led to redundancies at publishers, tight control on costs, and reduced advances to authors. This latter effect to some extent levelled the playing field for smaller publishers, priced out of the major auctions. As the larger publishers lowered their level of risk, agents could see advantages for their authors from being published by smaller, fleet-footed companies with an adventurous streak. The recession also led to new categories of publishing such as thrift lit alongside interest in serious political and economic titles about the causes of the financial crisis. An example of the former was the title *Cold Meat and How To Disguise It: A history of advice on how to survive hard times – a hundred years of belt tightening* (2009).

CHILDREN'S AND YOUNG ADULT PUBLISHING

By the late 1970s the outlook for publishers of children's books, especially those producing quality hardbacks, appeared grim in the UK. Many bookshops, other than WHSmith, were hardly enthusiastic buyers, public and school libraries were cutting back their expenditure, and the birth rate was forecast to fall. In that the vitality of children's publishing creates the book buyers of the future, there were serious worries about the demise of book reading, foreshadowing the end of publishing itself. Between 1981 and 1990 the population of 5- to 14-year-olds did indeed fall by 13 per cent but the inventiveness of authors and illustrators, of existing publishers, of new publishers such as Walker Books, and book packagers transformed children's publishing into arguably the most dynamic sector of the industry. Retail sales per child rose by nearly three times, and the number of new titles doubled to around 6,000. Between 1985 and 1990, the sales of children's publishers rose in real terms by 26 per cent while their adult general publishing counterparts achieved growth of only 7 per cent.

The publishers found new ways of reaching the home market via supermarkets (often titles appeared under a supermarket's own brand label), toyshops and direct sales – including book clubs and school book fairs. They sold international co-editions to US and European publishing partners, enabling picture books and highly-illustrated non-fiction or information books to be published at low and affordable prices worldwide. Paperback sales grew enormously and in volume terms came to dominate the market. Teenage fiction lists were established.

The recession of the early 1990s saw a reversal in sales of around 13 per cent yet the publishers continued to increase their title output through to 1995 when it stabilized at around 8,000 titles. The UK market for children's books declined from 1990 through to 1997, as other new products competed for children's attention and parents' spending. However, in 1998–99 the market staged a substantial recovery. Government policy to give greater emphasis to literacy in primary schools was a fillip to some children's publishers, encouraging school and library sales. Some titles became more answerable to the needs of the National Curriculum, although this did create a tension between the book as entertainment and as a learning aid. It is important to note that the children's publishers sell their books through many different distribution channels beyond booksellers, such as direct to schools.

Mark Haddon's *The Curious Incident of the Dog in the Night-Time* was published in separate editions for adults (*left*) and children (*right*)

By the end of the twentieth century an explosion in new children's fiction was apparent. This was led by J. K. Rowling's Harry Potter series, which not only rocketed the independent publisher Bloomsbury up the charts for retail sales in the UK, but also the books became international bestsellers and widely translated. They were attractive to a crossover market – read by children and adults – and stimulated consumer interest in children's books across the board (and interest from film companies in children's book properties). In fiction, the importance of the branding of authors, such as Jacqueline Wilson, Philip Pullman and Francesca Simon, strengthened. Publishers were keen to develop series based around the fictional characters, which could lead to sales of associated merchandise. In the early years of the new century, children's publishing became a vibrant sector with publishers willing to invest in both authors and marketing in search of the next bestseller.

Also notable is the spectacular success of the YA (young adult) category of fiction, spurred on by the success of Harry Potter and then the vampire romance Twilight series of books from Stephanie Meyer. Next came dystopian fiction and in 2012, the year the film was released, around 3 m copies of the Hunger Games trilogy were sold in the UK – both print and ebook (*The Bookseller*, 11 January 2013). A further fiction genre developed called New Adult, as described by John Walsh: 'NA novels are written about (and often by) 18 to 25-year-olds, charting the lives of post-school, university-age friends as they encounter the world of work, offices, money, identity, rented flats and dates with people they've met online' (*Independent*, 28 July 2013).

The major children's publishers include the children's imprints of Puffin, Ladybird and Dorling Kindersley (all in the Penguin group) and of the other adult consumer publishers such as Hachette UK, HarperCollins, the Bertelsmann companies of Random House and Transworld, Pan Macmillan, Simon & Schuster, Bloomsbury, and Oxford University Press. There are other specialist children's publishers, which are not part of adult book publishing groups. The magazine and book publisher Egmont (majoring in licensed character publishing) is in the top rank of children's publishing. Others include Scholastic, Templar, Usborne and Walker Books. Parragon, which began as a packager, has expanded rapidly by publishing books for supermarkets, and extended its reach into high street retail by becoming the licensed publishing partner of Disney.

In the present multimedia age there has been a decline in the market for picture books and booksellers have reduced their range in this area. Publishers have to be more innovative in their pricing and how they combine books with digital offerings. The start-up Nosy Crow grew its sales for young children in both print and digital, producing some successful apps in the early days of the iPad. Ebook sales of YA titles have become a significant part of the market.

Table 2.6 Carnegie Medal winners 2003 to 2013. The medal is awarded by children's librarians for an outstanding book for children and young people. The date of the award was adjusted from 2007 to the year of the award rather than of publication

Year of award	Author	Title	Publisher
2013	Sally Gardner	*Maggot Moon*	Hot Key Books
2012	Patrick Ness	*A Monster Calls*	Walker Books
2011	Patrick Ness	*Monsters of Men*	Walker Books
2010	Neil Gaiman	*The Graveyard Book*	Bloomsbury
2009	Siobhan Dowd	*Bog Child*	David Fickling
2008	Philip Reeve	*Here Lies Arthur*	Scholastic
2007	Meg Rosoff	*Just in Case*	Penguin
2005	Mal Peet	*Tamar*	Walker Books
2004	Frank Cottrell Boyce	*Millions*	Macmillan
2003	Jennifer Donnelly	*A Gathering Light*	Bloomsbury

Now read this

Angus Phillips, *Turning the Page: The evolution of the book*, Routledge, 2014.
John B. Thompson, *Merchants of Culture: The publishing business in the twenty-first century*, 2nd edition, Polity, 2012.

Sources

Diana Athill, *Stet*, Granta, 2000.
Alan Bartram, *Making Books: Design in British publishing since 1945*, British Library, 1999.
Eric de Bellaigue, *British Book Publishing as a Business since the 1960s*, British Library Publishing, 2004.
Simon Eliot and Jonathan Rose, *A Companion to the History of the Book*, Blackwell, 2007.
Jason Epstein, *Book Business: Publishing Past, Present, and Future*, Norton, 2002.
Jeremy Lewis, *Penguin Special: The life and times of Allen Lane*, Viking, 2005.
Tom Maschler, *Publisher*, Picador, 2005.
Daniel Menaker, *My Mistake: A memoir*, Houghton Mifflin, 2013.
Ian Norrie, *Mumby's Publishing and Bookselling in the Twentieth Century*, 6th edition, Bell & Hyman, 1982.
Paul Richardson and Graham Taylor, *PA Guide to the UK Publishing Industry*, Publishers Association, 3rd edition, 2014.
Claire Squires, *Marketing Literature: The making of contemporary writing in Britain*, Palgrave Macmillan, 2007.
Iain Stevenson, *Book Makers: British Publishing in the Twentieth Century*, British Library, 2010.
Rayner Unwin, *George Allen & Unwin: A remembrancer*, Merlin Unwin Books, 1999.

Web resources

www.carnegiegreenaway.org.uk Carnegie and Kate Greenaway Children's Book Awards.
http://blogs.guardian.co.uk/books/ *Guardian* blog about books and the book trade.

CHAPTER 3

Publishing for educational, academic and professional markets

Non-consumer publishing encompasses the educational, academic, STM (scientific, technical and medical), and professional publishing sectors, including the publication of learned journals. The major publishers strive to dominate the sectors in which they specialize – across the world. The companies producing high-level books and information services for professionals (such as in business or law), or publishing the premier journals, are highly profitable and strongly cash generative.

These markets are open to disruption from the large technology players, and Steve Jobs expressed his aim to crack open the school textbook market: 'Jobs had his sights set on textbooks as the next business he wanted to transform. He believed it was an $8 billion a year industry ripe for digital destruction' (Isaacson, Chapter 38). However, publishers have made significant advances themselves in terms of the creation of digital materials and the move from product to service. Sectors such as journal publishing have been in the advance of digital developments, with over 90 per cent of journals now available online. Content has been both aggregated into large searchable databases, and disaggregated so that individual articles can be purchased. Whilst governments around the world continue to experiment with the introduction of digital content in schools, some publishers are looking to own the whole value chain in educational and academic markets by providing learning, testing and examination services.

Increases in government funding for UK schools in the 1960s and 1970s aided the expansion of the educational publishers. The academic publishers similarly responded to the growth in higher education in the same period. Expansion in student numbers, and the ample funding of UK and US university libraries, stimulated the publishing of high-priced academic monographs and learned journals.

The British publishers enjoyed their traditional export markets: the USA, Commonwealth and northern Europe. The American publishers had a much larger home market and so gave little emphasis to exports, the major exception being the college textbook publishers. The US government's Marshall Plan after the Second World War, designed to aid the reconstruction of post-war Europe, helped the US publishers to export college textbooks, which were sold in the UK at very low prices. The publishers opened subsidiaries in the UK and came to dominate college textbook adoption markets worldwide, Commonwealth countries included, by issuing international editions, not for sale in the US.

In terms of ownership, consolidation has continued apace in the twenty-first century and European publishers have acquired US publishers. Private equity groups have played a significant role in reassembling publishing imprints and assets, both by purchasing them and selling them on in new forms. A major driver for consolidation has been the migration to digital formats and services, and the high costs involved in making the transition.

CONSOLIDATION

Pearson, well known for its Longman imprint purchased in 1968, acquired the US publisher Addison-Wesley in 1988, and then in 1998 acquired Simon & Schuster's educational operations – including Prentice Hall and Allyn & Bacon – and the US Macmillan Publishing from its parent Viacom. It created the world's largest educational (textbook) publisher. Pearson led the way in its purchase of companies which offered to educational organizations services in assessment, elearning, and student recruitment and support. Its many acquisitions included: in 2007, Harcourt Assessment from Reed Elsevier, and eCollege, a US provider of elearning, enrolment and student support services to higher education; in 2009, Wall Street English, a provider of English language training in China; and in 2010, a division of Sistema Educacional Brasileiro (SEB), giving it a strong presence in *sistemas* ('learning systems') for preschool, primary and secondary schools in Brazil.

A significant shake-up of publishers occurred around the turn of the century. In 1995 the Macmillan family had sold a majority stake in Macmillan Publishers (whose interests included the journal *Nature*) to the German publisher Holtzbrinck. The remaining shares were purchased by Holtzbrinck in 1999. Taylor & Francis floated on the London Stock Exchange in 1998 and shortly after more than doubled in size with the acquisition of the Routledge group of publishers. It has acquired numerous academic and STM publishers on both sides of the Atlantic, enabling it to enjoy both economies of scale and synergies in areas such as marketing.

In 1999, the German and family-owned Bertelsmann – primarily a consumer-focused media group – bought the German and family-owned STM publisher Springer. In turn, in 2003, British private equity bought Springer, and the academic and STM publishing operations of the Dutch publisher Kluwer. The companies were merged in 2004 and the enlarged Springer became the second largest STM publisher behind the Anglo-Dutch leader Elsevier, and the largest STM book publisher.

In 2002, a private equity consortium bought the large US educational publisher Houghton Mifflin, which then in 2006 underwent a reverse takeover by the smaller Irish educational software company Riverdeep. In 2007 Reed Elsevier, the world's biggest publisher of information for professional users operating in the markets of science, medical and legal, having previously bought the US publisher Harcourt in 2001, decided to sell its school educational imprints outside of the US (including Heinemann in the UK) to Pearson, while keeping the higher education and medical publishing businesses. Likewise the other major information and professional publishers decided to concentrate on providing digital content and services to professionals, rather than compete in education against Pearson. In 2007 the Dutch information and health publisher Wolters Kluwer sold its school publishing assets (including Nelson Thornes) to private equity, in order to concentrate on its professional businesses. In the same year, the Canadian family-owned Thomson Corporation sold Thomson Learning, a division focused on higher education (second only to Pearson in the US college market), again to private equity, to form Cengage, and bought Reuters. In 2008 Cengage Learning was combined with the College Division of Houghton Mifflin. This left McGraw-Hill as the last remaining major US publisher with major shares in US school and college markets. Educational markets (school and college) have been slower than professional markets to take up digital content and services, but there have been significant initiatives undertaken by governments – for example in Turkey the aim is to provide every secondary school pupil with their own tablet computer (the Fatih project).

Running against the trend of European purchases of US publishers, in 2007 the family-controlled US publisher John Wiley purchased the family-owned Blackwell, based in Oxford, which published books and journals for STM, humanities and social science markets. Following the financial crisis beginning in 2008, major merger and acquisition activity in the industry was subdued until 2013 when McGraw-Hill sold its Education division to private equity. In a rare move by a university press, Oxford University Press purchased in 2013 the UK curriculum publisher Nelson Thornes.

The migration to digital formats drives consolidation, not least in the ability enabled by size to invest in technology. The big players can afford to make the necessary large investments in online scientific journals and accompanying tools to aid researchers, and in building ebook collections for libraries. The larger the publisher's content and the greater their control over the intellectual property, the greater is the leverage of the aggregation. It is argued by the large publishers that it is easier for academic libraries and purchasing consortia to deal with just a few publishers and to use their platforms providing online content and services – rather than have to negotiate with dozens of publishers and intermediaries.

EDUCATIONAL PUBLISHING

Schools publishing

Educational markets worldwide are subject to the influence of government, politics and regulations at the state, regional and local levels more than any other publishing sector. Generally speaking, the greater the amount of content prescription and regulatory control, the narrower the range of published material and that tends to favour large publishers over smaller publishers. The UK market is mainly affected by National Curriculum and assessment strategies, the vagaries of government expenditure, organizational and funding changes to the state school system, performance metrics of schools, teachers and students, and more recently the government's emphasis on vocational training. The main educational publishers usually cover schools and further education colleges. Changes in demographics over time affect market size, and for example the UK saw its birth

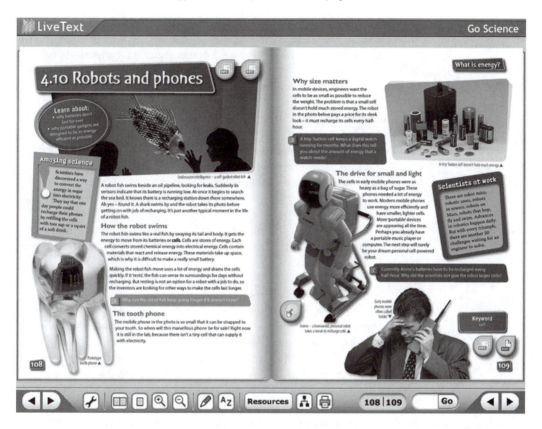

rate at its highest for 40 years in 2013, which will feed through into school enrolments.

Go Science! from Heinemann features an interactive pupil book

In comparison to the consumer book publishers, the UK educational publishers (sometimes referred to as 'curriculum publishers') are less affected by the powerful retailers since many sales are direct to schools (typically more than 50 per cent; it can be more than 80 per cent in the case of primary schools). But they are impacted by the technology companies, increased use of tablets and of free internet content (including supply-side funded Open Educational Resources), and teacher-generated content. For example, lesson plans or activities can be easily downloaded from the internet. Publishers' lists of books, learning resources and services can take longer to build and their sales, though more steady and generally more profitable than in consumer publishing, are subject to periodic downturns. Overall, educational content has become progressively localized and therefore less exportable to overseas countries than hitherto. However, the major companies invest in local publishing and apply their technologies and approaches across their international operations.

The first overseas subsidiaries of UK companies were opened in the late-nineteenth and early-twentieth centuries in Australia and Canada, and in the 1960s the educational and academic houses opened subsidiaries in the newly formed African Commonwealth countries and exported large quantities of UK-based textbooks. The educational systems there were based on UK curricula or examinations.

The UK Bribery Act, which came into force in 2011, holds UK firms accountable for bribery, whether committed directly and on their behalf, in the UK or overseas. Publishers have to take care how they regulate their international businesses in order not to fall foul of this legislation. There have been unfortunate incidents and in 2011, Macmillan was

> ordered to pay £11.3m for 'unlawful conduct' related to its education division in East and West Africa. The High Court order was made after the Serious Fraud Office (SFO) began an inquiry last year following a report from the World Bank. The report said Macmillan had made 'bribery payments' to secure a deal to print textbooks in South Sudan.
>
> (bbc.co.uk, accessed 14 September 2013)

This initiated a significant retreat by the publisher from a number of African countries. OUP faced similar charges in Kenya and Tanzania, and was fined nearly £2 million in 2012.

The first wave of publisher consolidation occurred during the 1980s when UK school pupil rolls declined, and the number of significant educational publishers decreased from around 30 to 15. Sales volumes fell from 1986 to 1990 reflecting in part the underfunding of UK state schools. Export sales were affected by the poverty of some Commonwealth countries and a more nationalist approach around the world to the school curriculum. By the early 1990s, the top three publishers commanded 50 per cent of sales to schools; and the top seven over 75 per cent. The remaining publishers concentrated in specialist areas or subjects.

Consolidation amongst publishers proceeded more slowly until 2007, when Reed Elsevier decided to sell its UK education interests (Harcourt, including Heinemann) to Pearson; and Wolters Kluwer decided to divest its educational publishing assets (Nelson Thornes and other European publishers) to private equity. Then in 2013 the company was sold to Oxford University Press. In 2010 the acquisition by HarperCollins of Letts, Lonsdale and Leckie & Leckie took it to third position in the schools market. The main players are:

- Pearson,
- Oxford University Press (including Nelson Thornes),
- Collins Education (News Corporation),
- Hodder Education (Hachette).

There are other significant players such as Cambridge University Press, which publishes materials for international qualifications, such as the IGCSE (International General Certificate of Secondary Education) and IB (International Baccalaureate); and there are independent publishers such as Rising Stars and Jolly Learning concentrating on niche markets. A range of publishers serve primary schools and the school library market, including children's publishers such as Scholastic.

In addition to producing products and services for schools, publishers also help teachers to use them, for example through holding free seminars. Paid-for training courses and consultancy services may also be provided to schools.

Digital content in UK schools

Although the UK educational system was an early adopter of information and communication technologies (ICT), the take-up of digital content and services has proved difficult and slow (still at only around 5 per cent of publishers' sales in 2012), whilst still ahead of many other countries.

From the early 1990s there were government initiatives to increase the use of ICT in schools, including hardware and software provision, teacher training and digitally delivered curriculum resources. At the start the market was filled by US imports which were not designed for UK curricula and cultural needs. Amongst UK multimedia publishers, many went bust or recorded severe losses, and when Pearson purchased Dorling Kindersley, the multimedia division there was closed. Granada Learning was acquired by private equity in 2006, and subsequently became part of the testing company GL Assessment. The curriculum publishers restricted themselves to modest experiments, preferring the business model of book publishing. In 2002, the government introduced elearning credits (eLCs) which ringfenced funds for the purchase by schools of digital content. However, this pump-priming of the market did not guarantee future spending and use. School spending on hardware did have an impact and by 2009 the average number of interactive whiteboards in a school had reached 8.6 in primary schools and 25.2 in secondary schools (BESA, 2009). The prevalence and success of interactive whiteboards enabled publishers to produce digital resources (online and on disk) for that medium which complemented their texts and aided teachers.

Schools have seen the application of technologies and business models first developed in higher education, such as the introduction of virtual learning environments (VLEs), testing linked to learning resources, the growth of online resources, and the use of subscription sales models. There is also significant use of free resources available online, from both publishers and other sources, and by 2009 nearly two-thirds of schools were making 'significant use of the internet for free downloads of online curriculum software or content products' (BESA, 2009). The first generation of interactive textbooks were published for the iPad in 2012. By the end of 2013 there were around 260,000 tablets for use by pupils in classrooms across the UK state sector, and it was forecast that the number would more than double by 2015 – with a further increase to 1.8 million by the end of 2020 (BESA, 2013).

FOCUS

Government

The UK market, up to the late part of the twentieth century, used to be characterized by little central government intervention and a variety of examination boards setting curricula. A diversity of books and ancillary materials were published by a variety of publishers. The books were purchased through local education authorities and supplied to schools via specialist suppliers, local authority purchasing organizations and bookshops. However, the effects of the 1988 Education Reform Act were profound. The new National Curriculum was far more prescriptive and defined, rendering many backlist textbooks (from which publishers earned most of their profits) largely redundant. The race was on to produce new materials, especially schemes or programmes of study in core subjects, quickly and at great cost. This favoured the large publishers. Speed and quality were of the essence as each school had to be locked into the publisher's programme ideally for say three to five years. Slow publishers risked being knocked out, as indeed some were.

In the late 1990s, there were successive changes to the National Curriculum, and the examination boards in England were merged down to three: the treatment of subjects narrowed further. The boards, which receive a fee per candidate, compete vigorously to secure schools' choice of their syllabus and accreditation (secondary schools usually pay a greater sum to the boards than they spend on textbooks). In the USA, Pearson took the strategic step of acquiring service companies which provided testing and other software for schools, a growth market on both sides of the Atlantic. In the UK, the company controversially bought the examination board Edexcel in 2003. This was seen by some as creating a conflict of interest for the board, which lends its endorsement to textbooks written by its examiners. In 2013, the government regulator Ofqual investigated and approved the separation by Pearson of the examination business from its publishing operations.

A further UK government reform was the weakening of the local education authorities and the transfer of local management to schools. This enabled state schools to order books directly from publishers rather than through their local education authorities. Many intermediaries in the former supply chain (specialist suppliers, local authority purchasing organizations and bookshops), which were receiving discounts of 17–20 per cent from the publishers, were cut out. The increasing autonomy of UK state funded schools and the further weakening of local education authorities continues to this day. By 2013 around half of secondary schools had opted for academy status, independent of local authority control (education.gov.uk, accessed 18 September 2013).

Trade education

An important subsector of educational publishing is referred to as 'trade' or 'consumer' education. This area embraces study and revision guides aimed at students for home study and the parental anxiety market, and self-study products, some of which are published online. It is referred to as 'trade' since historically such product lines were purchased by parents through booksellers and not by schools for class use, although they may be used in schools. The independent Cumbria-based publisher Coordination Group Publications challenges the major publishers in this area. In 2009 Richard Parsons, the founder of CGP, was highlighted as one of the top selling authors of the previous decade alongside J. K. Rowling, Dan Brown and John Grisham.

F O C U S

ELT publishing

The publishing of English Language Teaching (ELT) course materials engages
very large investments and a worldwide marketing strength for this predominantly
export-orientated field. The publishers enjoyed strong growth from export sales
through the 1990s but in 1997 it began to falter. Although the quantity of books
exported rose, prices fell in sterling terms and the real value of turnover decreased.
The strength of sterling, the Asian economic crisis, and the problems in Brazil
and Argentina (important ELT markets) took their toll. Then in the years following
the financial crash of 2008, publishers experienced difficulties in traditional
European markets such as Greece and Spain. The adoption of tablets is helping to
push digital sales in markets in Asia and the Middle East. The main publishers
include:

- Oxford University Press,
- Pearson,
- Macmillan Education,
- Cambridge University Press,
- Richmond Publishing.

Oxford University Press (OUP) is the largest international ELT publisher (by
volume) and this part of the business accounts for a significant part of its sales
and profit. It maintains a market leadership in British English (especially in
Europe) while also publishing in American English. Pearson is the biggest player
in the American English market. It added the important American English lists of
Addison-Wesley (in 1988) and Prentice Hall (1998) – thereby leading the markets
in Latin America and Asia – to its original mainly British English Longman
imprint. Cambridge University Press (CUP) has built its business without
acquisition, and benefits from its close association with the University of
Cambridge Local Examination Syndicate (UCLES), which operates the
internationally recognized examination English for Speakers of Other Languages
(ESOL). Macmillan Education developed its ELT business through the purchase of
Heinemann ELT in 1998. Some overseas ELT publishers have taken advantage of
UK expertise and have established UK operations, for example Richmond
Publishing owned by the Spanish publisher Santillana. Founded in 1992, it has a
strong emphasis on materials for Spanish and Portuguese markets including
Mexico and Brazil. Other major publishers, such as Cengage, have ELT lists, and
there are smaller, niche publishers in the UK, and also packagers which offer
editorial, design and production services to the major players – often their former
employers.

From the standpoint of the major players, ELT publishing is a distinct field of
publishing needing its own publishing operations, typically based in the UK and
the US to produce British and American English materials; plus other publishing
centres, such as those in Spain, the Far East, Latin America and Eastern Europe,
to commission or adapt the courses to national or regional markets; and
marketing sales offices elsewhere. In some countries, ministries of education have
to approve the courses. Part of the strategic importance of ELT is that as a growing
market worldwide it provides the publisher with a local or regional foothold in

non-English areas of the world, through the opening of local companies or marketing offices, or through the acquisition of local publishers. Although the major publishers dominate the international provision of course materials – with high market shares in some countries – they have faced increasing competition from indigenous local publishers (which in many European countries are the national market leaders in schools); private language school chains with publishing operations; newer entrants and online providers.

The convention that children learn their native language and subsequently learn English as a foreign language (EFL) or second language is challenged in some countries where children learn their local language and English simultaneously. English is being taught from primary school in many countries, offering significant new opportunities to the international players and local companies.

OVERVIEW OF ACADEMIC, STM AND PROFESSIONAL PUBLISHING

The internationalization of academic, STM and professional book publishing occurred earlier than in consumer book publishing, and is far more extensive. High-level books and journals in English, especially in STM, have an international currency throughout the world. Such publishers do not have to contend with literary agents' retention of territorial and other rights: they invariably acquire all rights in authors' works, including electronic rights worldwide. The journal and reference publishers were the first to embark on the transition from print to digital publishing in the last century. As in the area of educational publishing, the larger players have looked to move away from the supply of discrete products towards the provision of services and solutions.

The fortunes of academic publishers and the kinds of books and other products they produce are inextricably linked to institutional spending on research worldwide, especially in relation to library budgets in the developed world, to the numbers and wealth of full-time and part-time students (an important factor in the UK), and to the behaviour of librarians, researchers, teachers and students.

Professional publishing in the areas of law or finance has traditionally been highly profitable. The trend has been towards online content and services and, for example, Lexis-Nexis, part of Reed Elsevier, offers access 'across the globe ... to billions of searchable documents from more than 45,000 legal, news and business sources' (lexisnexis.com, accessed 15 September 2013).

Major publishers dominate these fields on a world-wide scale. The market sectors are diverse in respect of the character of the publishing operations. Two giant publishers occupy either end of the spectrum. Pearson Education (part of the UK listed company Pearson) is the world's leading higher education publisher, primarily focused on teaching and learning (textbook publishing with technology support). Elsevier (part of the Anglo-Dutch listed company Reed Elsevier) is the world's leading STM publisher, with a focus on scientific journals and the supply of information to health and pharma markets, with associated book businesses, including some textbook, academic and professional book publishing.

Some leading publishers are quite diverse in their discipline span and the character of their operations. The operations of Wiley-Blackwell, another leading STM publisher with important journals, include the area of humanities and social sciences (HSS) and textbook, academic and professional/trade book publishing. Springer, which embraces the former Kluwer academic publishing businesses, majors on STM journals and books. Wolters Kluwer offers information and services to professionals in the areas of law, taxation, finance and healthcare.

The global STM market is led by four big players:

- Elsevier,
- Wolters Kluwer,
- John Wiley,
- Springer.

Other important academic publishers in the UK are Macmillan Science and Education (which includes Palgrave and the Nature Publishing Group) and the US privately owned SAGE Publications (which began as a social science publisher but has since diversified). Taylor & Francis (part of Informa, and including the imprints of Routledge, CRC Press, and Garland) has a broad spread of journal and book publishing and a large book title output. Big US players with some UK commissioning are represented by McGraw-Hill (which includes the Open University Press, previously the subject of a management buy-out from the university), and Cengage Learning. Smaller UK companies include Ashgate, Bloomsbury Academic (as part of its diversification from trade into academic), Edward Elgar, Emerald, Jessica Kingsley, Pluto, I.B. Tauris, Zed Books and other specialists, such as the professional publisher Kogan Page, and start-ups such as Rowman & Littlefield International.

The university presses are significant book and journal publishers. Oxford University Press, which publishes more than 6,000 titles per year, is by far the largest university press in the world and competes alongside the leading private-sector publishers. It supports financially the university whereas most university presses, especially in the US, are supported *by* their universities. OUP spans most academic disciplines at the higher level of academic and scholarly publishing, and includes textbook, reference and journal publishing. Sometimes described as the 800-pound gorilla of the world of university presses, it has an annual turnover (including trade, reference, educational and ELT publishing) which exceeds the combined turnover of the UK and US university presses – and more than three times the size of the other leading university press, Cambridge University Press, which has a similar spread of activities. The other UK university presses operate on a very much smaller scale and are far more specialist, and include the presses of Edinburgh, Liverpool, Manchester and Nottingham. The Policy Press is based at the University of Bristol. The US university presses are also represented in the UK, notably Yale and Princeton, which have local commissioning operations. Other US publishers may have UK marketing and sales offices to import their books, usually into Europe, the Middle East and Africa (EMEA or EMA).

All publishers specialize in publishing books or journals in particular academic disciplines or groups of allied disciplines. Not even the largest would claim to publish in all disciplines. Their output can be divided into three broad categories:

- textbooks,
- HSS, STM and professional publishing,
- journals.

TEXTBOOKS

UK teaching differs from US practices. However, the US core textbook model best exemplified by Pearson, McGraw-Hill, Cengage Learning, Wiley (and Elsevier in health science) is instructive and offers pointers as to the way publishing is changing. This model is applied to the arguably more defined and quantifiable subjects: mainly the hard sciences, mathematics, psychology, business and economics. The very high cost of the model limits it to a very small number of major existing titles and new titles with high sales forecasts, mainly at the first and second year levels. Such subjects are international. The publisher's aim is to create scalable learning and teaching solutions worldwide.

In the US, textbook publishers analyse and synthesize curriculum needs across the continent, and create printed textbooks of up to 1,000 pages with high design values and special learning features. The US professors adopt one book per course, from which they, or their instructors, usually teach chapter by chapter. In view of the large class sizes and the high value of adoptions generated from sales to students, US core textbook publishing became a very large and competitive business, a market estimated at more than \$7 bn. The publishers invest millions of dollars in such texts, priced highly in the US market but cheaper overseas. The worldwide annual revenue from some of these bestselling titles may dwarf the annual turnover of some medium-sized UK consumer book publishers.

The publishers became engaged in a virtual arms race. In order to secure adoptions of their books they competed to offer the instructors additional and free supplementary material to help them teach the course, such as an instructor's guide. This material started out in the late twentieth century as a marketing device to persuade the instructor to use the publisher's book. It grew in scale and complexity. As part of these supplements, the publishers built test banks of thousands of multiple choice questions to support their big texts. The delivery of the supplementary packages has gone through every development of technology: print, video tape to disk, overhead projection to PowerPoint. With the advent of online delivery and connectivity, the supplements were renamed 'resources' or 'bonus content' and from around the turn of the century they came to embrace publisher technology support.

Textbook publishers have moved beyond their provision of teaching content to the supply of services, especially in assessment and personalized learning. For example, by building on their archives of question test banks, they have developed assessment software, held on their servers. It enables instructors to set and customize assessments for their students. These are marked automatically and downloaded into their students' gradebooks. It saves time for the instructor and lowers the university's cost of delivering teaching. The assessment software has become more sophisticated and has developed beyond simplistic multiple choice. It is sensitive to the students' responses and offers them help (for example links to the pertinent section in the ebook of the textbook, sometimes enhanced with animations and video) and at the top end automated tutorial support. McGraw-Hill led initially in the application of adaptive learning technologies to college products. Publishers claim that their online packages aid student performance and retention.

Institutions use a virtual learning environment (VLE) or learning management system (LMS), such as Blackboard or the open source Moodle. Some publishers offer institutions their own VLEs, providing a distribution channel for online content and services. Publishers are taking their services further in the area of analytics. For example, in 2013 Pearson acquired Learning Analytics, a platform which helps teachers understand better how their students are learning:

> by allowing faculty to ask questions and view feedback in realtime in a graphical representation of their students' comprehension of the material, Pearson is adding an important new service layer for in-class feedback and communication. Pearson's mission at this point is to become a service provider of customized tools and learning packages for teachers and for the changing profile of today's student in higher education. (techcrunch.com, accessed 15 September 2013)

A long-term problem facing the US college textbook publishers, to a far more limited extent affecting the UK, has been the used book market. A high proportion of US students typically invest in the purchase of the textbook and then sell it at the end of their course, affecting the income of publishers and their authors. For instance, the adoption sales of a book on campus may fall 10 per cent after one year, 50 per cent in year 2 and 75 per cent in year 3. To counter this trend, publishers have issued new editions at more frequent intervals, say after 3 years, sometimes irritating the instructors, who are forced to check the extent of the changes, and the students who complain about high new book prices. In effect the US used book market, which may account for nearly a third of sales, increases the price of new books as the high cost of developing such texts is spread over shorter sales lives and lower quantities. Furthermore from around 2006/07, textbook rental through third-party companies such as Chegg and BookRenter, and through campus bookstores, grew quickly, placing more pressure on the publishers' margins. In the USA, rental companies buy a printed book, rent it at a lower cost repeatedly, and do not recompense the publisher and author. Such unlicensed renting is prohibited in the UK where copyright legislation differs. In 2012 Amazon – which may have around 30 per cent of US textbook sales, overtaking sales through campus bookstores – launched its own printed textbook rental offer. Previously in 2011, it had opened a Kindle store for renting textbooks licensed from publishers. Whilst the revenue from printed textbook sales remained flat, the publishers looked to increase their revenue from the licensing of associated digital resources and services.

Another big issue for the US college textbook publishers is the re-importation of the foreign editions of their printed texts by third party arbitrage traders who take advantage of the price differential between high US prices and the lower prices set by the publishers in Europe, Asia and Australia. In 2013, the US Supreme Court ruled in favour of the trader in the Kirtsaeng vs. John Wiley case. Such parallel importation affects all kinds of publishing and has occurred for decades in the print world wherever significant price differentials exist between nation states. By contrast publishers are more able to control digital content through the use of site licences with institutions, and can rely on contract law for protection rather than trying to detect abuses of copyright.

Although some of the online resources from publishers are freely available on companion websites for marketing purposes, the rich material is restricted to password or unique pin code access. The instructor is initially given time limited access to review the book's adoption potential. Once adopted, the instructor is given access to their area, and each student is supplied with a pin code on purchase of the book, giving them access to their area on the publisher's server, plus the ebook (sometimes enhanced). The business model of bundling print and ebook editions of the same book is slow to be applied outside this specific context. Alternatively etextbooks, without print, may be sold to keep, or at a lower price for the duration of the semester. The publishers, for so long separated from students by intermediaries (for example campus bookstores), can now make the direct link with them and derive rich data from how the students use the content. Students may be offered access to additional content and services beyond the textbook itself. Publishers are trying to make the transition from the free supply of online content and services (on condition of textbook adoption) to licensing premium content and services.

An example of a higher education textbook from Palgrave Macmillan

In the UK the teaching tradition differs, and lecturers are far less likely to adopt only one book for a course, or even if they do, to teach from it chapter by chapter. The blockbuster textbooks may be criticized as being too long, exhaustive and expensive, and UK-originated books are cheaper. However, the US-originated core texts are still used extensively. Texts in management studies and the social sciences are usually versioned or localized in the UK for the European or EMEA market, and by other publishing centres elsewhere, not least to deter importation into the USA.

UK-originated publishing largely avoids competing directly against the US core textbooks, but none the less is extensive in title output. The major texts developed in the UK also deploy online resources and assessment. Covering a variety of subjects, they take account of the different approaches of UK academia, and extend up through the undergraduate levels to the very specialist graduate courses. Although rarely finding a significant US market, some UK-originated textbooks are highly exportable elsewhere. There is innovation and enormous diversity in UK teaching that finds expression through publishers.

The uptake of custom publishing and of associated technology, which was pioneered in the USA, enables instructors to tailor a publisher's textbooks for their specific teaching. It is growing in the UK and mainland Europe. Academics can view the database of the publisher's content and pick and mix the content for their course, include their own material and have their name on the cover or digital edition. The physical book is digitally printed and sold to students via bookstores, or directly to the university and supplied to students as part of their course tuition fee. Website material may also be customized.

While students may complain about the high cost of textbooks, their purchase cost is a fraction of the cost of the tuition fees, which have been increasing at a rapid rate. There is a small but growing trend for universities to purchase texts (print and ebook) at bulk discounts directly from publishers, the cost of which is embedded in the fee. Student purchases of etextbooks have not grown fast, despite the publication of interactive texts for Apple and Android devices. However, CourseSmart, founded in the USA in 2007 by the main college textbooks publishers (Cengage Learning, Macmillan, McGraw-Hill, Pearson and Wiley) initially offered an etext inspection service to academics for choosing texts. It has since developed into the world's largest library of etextbooks and digital resources from many publishers which are available to students to rent, to use online and offline, under licence rather than through ownership. Its international operation was opened in the UK in 2012 (where a partnership with Blackwell's was established) and extended to Europe, and then to the Middle East and Africa. Data analytics generated from student online use of textbooks can help teachers monitor their work and publishers the effectiveness of their products. Ingram's VitalSource – with its own ebook software and platform – purchased CourseSmart in 2014. Other companies producing complex etextbooks or platforms for publishers include Aptara and Inkling.

Supply funded Open Educational Resources (OER), available for free on the internet under Creative Commons licences (see Chapter 5), were pioneered by MIT in 2002. Subsequently many universities (including The Open University in the UK) and other agencies invested millions in producing OER, either funded by philanthropy or endowments, or indirectly by tuition fees or taxpayers. OER are seen as disruptive to the business model of universities generally but not necessarily to individual courses or institutions. MIT content was available for free, but MIT certification and participation inside its premium branded ecosystem remained paramount. Publishers, too, initially feared that OER would disrupt their textbook business. However, OER while benefiting many informal learners worldwide have had little impact on campus teaching thus far. OER producers lack the publishers' market and sales knowledge of formal education, and the marketing and sales systems of the publishers and distributors driven by sales and profit targets. The difficulty of discovering suitable quality assured OER content (partly caused by the lack of standardized metadata) prompted Pearson in 2013 to offer a service blending both OER and paid for content and services.

The term MOOC (Massive Open Online Course) was coined in 2008 by Dave Cormier and Bryan Alexander

More recently, massive open online courses (MOOCs), pioneered by premier US universities and backed by venture capitalists, have captured the disruptive imagination of competitive university administrations. Universities may use the freemium business model on both MOOCs and OER. MOOCs provide another channel through which publishers may market and sell their content. A prominent example of a MOOC start-up is the San Francisco company Coursera, 'an education company that partners with the top universities and organizations in the world to offer courses online for anyone to take, for free' (coursera.org, accessed 15 September 2013).

At a more fundamental level, coursepacks developed by teachers themselves have and continue to pose a challenge to textbook publishing. Photocopied packs (or equivalent electronic copies) contain chapters from books, journal articles, and other content. Some publishers partner with AcademicPub which provides digital and print custom books of such material for students. Via Google students have access to a range of free information, and via their university online library an increasing range of HSS and STM books (not designated by publishers as 'textbooks'), journal articles, and reference material licensed by publishers. The former barriers presented to students wanting to access different kinds of printed products are breaking down in the digital era. The continuing challenge for publishers is to aggregate an ever greater range of content into a must-have service.

ACADEMIC AND PROFESSIONAL BOOKS

This title embraces all kinds of books used in academic institutions for teaching and research, and by practitioners in the workplace. These include edited volumes, reference works, handbooks, conference proceedings, and academic monographs (original research) published in hardback and as ebooks at high prices and destined for the libraries mainly in the UK and US, and in other research centres.

Books with some trade sale may be categorized as academic/trade. Some titles are adopted for teaching – from a publisher's standpoint becoming 'accidental textbooks' and bought by students. For many of the smaller academic publishers, including most university presses, printed book sales to libraries and individuals are still likely to account for the great majority of sales revenue. However, ebook sales have increased through etailers (mainly Amazon), and through licences to libraries (via specialist intermediaries, or sold directly). Some publishers are experimenting with the quick publication of short ebooks.

Monographs – peer-reviewed original research in book form – have for a long time been the corner-stone of commercial academic publishing and of the university presses briefed to disseminate works of scholarship. Since the 1980s, their economic viability has been questioned and their demise often predicted. Monograph publication remains especially important to HSS academics for tenure and career progression in the same way that article publication in a prestigious journal is to scientists. Although the supply-side research output has increased worldwide, paid-for institutional demand in the West has declined. Library cutbacks and changing purchasing behaviour, such as the switching of printed book budgets to the subscription of journals and other electronic resources, the greater use of inter-library lending and the growth of library consortia, have progressively reduced print sales quantities. For example, sales of monographs have fallen to very low numbers, from say 1,200 copies in the 1980s down to 200–300 copies by 2012. Some of the commercial academic publishers have now abandoned monograph publishing. However, the remaining publishers (for example OUP, CUP and other university presses, Palgrave and Taylor & Francis, and some of the STM publishers) have maintained their publication by reducing the costs of production (including author royalties, sometimes to zero) and increasing title output. The advent of digital printing and the advent of ebook collections for libraries (such as the pioneering initiatives of OUP, Springer, Taylor & Francis) have aided the continuance of the publication of highly specialist titles. While scholars mostly access journal articles from libraries, they make significant purchases of books for personal use, and this is facilitated further with the availability of ebooks.

Supply-side funded open access (OA) business models, which developed in STM journal publishing, are starting to spread to HSS publishing. Under an OA licence the digital text may be available for free whilst the print or ebook still has to be bought (an example of freemium marketing). Bloomsbury Academic makes some titles available through this route: 'Selected research publications are published on open content licences, meaning that the full text is available online for free in html format. These titles are also available to buy as pbooks and ebooks' (bloomsbury.com, accessed 18 September 2013). One aspect of the push to OA in the UK is that researchers are mandated by their university or funders to deposit their doctoral theses in digital repositories from which they are freely available under a Creative Commons licence, called green OA. Such mandates, apart from impinging on the rights of authors in respect of their control over copyright, also mean that they have to significantly develop and change their work to attract a publisher to invest in and publish a monograph based on their research. The OA publication of professionally produced monographs is sometimes funded by universities and other agencies as part of their primary objective to maximize the dissemination of research. In response commercial publishers came out with an offer to produce OA monographs, and for example in 2013 the charge for publication of a monograph with Palgrave was £11,000 (palgrave.com, accessed 15 September 2013).

In comparison to the consumer book publishers, the HSS and STM publishers have developed a far greater range of demand-side business models for their digital products. In addition to print sales made via booksellers and other intermediaries, and to an increasing extent direct from publishers' websites, ebook sales to libraries are of growing importance. The greater the amount of content offered in terms of aggregation (through titles) and of linked data, the greater the digital opportunity and business value.

The *site licence* business model, applied to licensing online content to universities and other organizations, is fundamental and many other business models stem from it. Site licences were originally applied, for example, to digital reference works and electronic journals used in libraries' local area networks (prior to the widespread use of the internet) – and more recently to ebooks. The licences were first confined to geographical locations, such as a university campus, then to multiple sites and extended to an organization's entire online community, such as the staff and students of a university even when off campus. The university is responsible for the authentication of its members and the security of its network, and thus provides controlled access to the publisher's licensed content. It is a form of digital rights management (DRM). Another important and related feature of a site licence is the way in which tiered pricing may be applied to the licensing of content. For example, a US publisher may categorize institutions, such as between (rich) premier research universities and (poor) teaching community colleges. In the UK, universities are graded into community size bands – the larger the community, the more they pay and vice versa. The terms applying to such site licences are among many negotiated between publishers and library consortia. In the UK, Jisc provides a central role in negotiations with publishers, and facilitates the use of digital resources and services. Throughout the world, libraries join consortia in order to negotiate savings and other benefits from suppliers, but they also buy books independently.

Publishers supply ebooks (in PDF or reflowable ePub formats) to academic aggregators, which in turn offer platform-based services to academic libraries. Such companies include EBSCO/NetLibrary; ebrary/EBL (part of the archive publisher ProQuest); MyiLibrary (Ingram); Dawsonera (Bertrams) and Gardners. The wholesale and library supply market (print and ebook) has consolidated nationally and worldwide in order to derive benefits of scale. Wholesale operations that once specialized in different print market sectors are merging. The one time wholesalers, facing a declining market of physical retailers, are transforming themselves into digital servicing and distribution companies supplying other intermediaries and products directly to end-users.

The content aggregators offer libraries numerous business models that include 'perpetual access' to an ebook (like a printed book purchase); subscription (an ongoing sale); multiple view access; rental; pay per view; and collections of ebooks from multiple publishers. Collections are typically defined by subject and time of publication, and contain monographs, conference proceedings, and edited volumes, but usually exclude textbooks. Collections offer libraries the ability to access large numbers of titles at a discounted price and generate usage even of older titles. Such bundles of content are like the big deals offered much earlier by the journal publishers. Although these once proved popular with librarians and their users, their high cost and lack of flexibility made institutions more cautious when offered ebook bundles (which may contain a range of little-used titles). More recently patron-driven acquisition (PDA), or in the US, user-driven acquisition, is growing. Under this model, the library selects the range of books to be viewed, and usage parameters trigger purchase, thus the library purchases only the books used. It is an example of freemium marketing, the upselling from the consumer to the institution: the consumer samples the product and uses the book for free, but the library pays. The aggregators, dependent on securing titles from publishers, use additional DRM constraints to allay their fears of misuse or loss of sales, such as limiting the number of concurrent users viewing a book, or restricting copy and pasting. Such restrictions irritate users and librarians, and the high prices of some ebooks have reawakened interest at some libraries in holding print copies.

There are also specialist aggregators that operate subscription models, either through site licences to universities and corporates, or directly to individuals. They include Safari Books (operated by O'Reilly Media) for technical and computing books; and Books24/7 (operated by Skillsoft, a cloud based training company) for business, technical and engineering content. The major publishers owning extensive book aggregations have their own platforms and use similar models to the aggregators. Their platforms were originally developed for journals and databases but subsequently they added ebooks during and after the first decade of the century. The larger publishers may offer their platforms and services to smaller publishers. A publisher's platform offers it far more customer data than that supplied by aggregators, and the freedom to control its own business models. For instance, the major publisher Springer abandoned the use of restrictive DRM measures on the use of its ebooks before other majors. The cost of developing platforms used to be prohibitive for smaller publishers: now platform vendors enable them to operate affordably their own customized platforms to sell content directly.

JOURNALS

The publishing of refereed or peer-reviewed learned journals (or serials), sold mainly on the subscription/site licence business models, to libraries and corporates, is a major adjunct to book publishing. In 2012 there were around 28,000 active peer-reviewed journals, publishing upwards of 1.8 m articles (Ware and Mabe, page 5). In STM publishing, the revenues will far outweigh the publishers' subject-related book operations. Historically, the higher net profit of journal publishing (up to 30 per cent) has in effect cross-subsidized book publishing operations, which earned lower profits (say 10–15 per cent). The major international journal publishers are Elsevier, Springer, Wiley-Blackwell, and Taylor & Francis. These publishers combined account for 6,000 to 7,000 journals (Campbell et al., page 149). Other significant publishers include Wolters Kluwer, SAGE, Macmillan, and the university presses of Oxford and Cambridge. Half of all journals are owned or controlled by learned societies. They may have their journals produced and marketed for them under contract by the publishers, or they may publish the titles themselves. Prominent amongst those pursuing the latter approach are, in the USA, the American Chemical Society (ACS) and the American Institute of Physics (AIP), and in the UK, the Institute of Physics (IOP) and the Royal Society of Chemistry (RSC). For many societies, journal publishing has traditionally kept them afloat financially.

STM journal publishing is big business around the world.

Robert Maxwell (1923–91) made a fortune in publishing from learned journals through his Pergamon Press, which he later sold to Elsevier. After his death, having fallen overboard from his yacht, his company Maxwell Communications was found to have substantial debts

> The annual revenues generated from English-language STM journal publishing are estimated at about $9.4 billion in 2011 ... within a broader STM information publishing market worth some $23.5 billion. About 52% of global STM revenues (including non-journal STM products) come from the USA, 32% from Europe/Middle East, 12% from Asia/Pacific and 4% from the rest of the world. (Ware and Mabe, page 5)

Science journal publishing reaches back to the publication in 1665 of both *Le Journal des sçavans* in France and the *Philosophical Transactions of the Royal Society of London*. For the past two centuries, the number of articles published each year and the number of journals have grown by about 3 and 3.5 per cent respectively, along with a similar annual rise in the number of researchers. The USA accounts for 21 per cent of the global output of research papers, followed by China (10 per cent), the UK (7 per cent), Japan (6 per cent), Germany (6 per cent), and France (4 per cent). The reading patterns of researchers are changing: they are reading more (on average 270 articles per year), and that is increasingly driven by search rather than through browsing a publisher's website (Ware and Mabe, pages 5–6). While the journal is the container, the article is the primary object transmitted, via the institution, to the users. The PDF remains an important format for articles but there is experimentation around the form of display of HTML versions with value added. For example, articles are enriched with supplementary datasets and extra functionality to produce graphs or tables.

Broadly speaking a journal's academic editor, or editor-in-chief, backed up by an academic editorial board, with input from the publisher, steers the policy, direction and focus of the journal, which is usually aimed at a well-defined community of researchers. Peer review prior to publication is central to quality control and the selection of articles, readership impact and the branding status of journals across all subjects. The brand value of journals is reflected by their perceived or measured rank in a hierarchy. There are many ways journals are measured to indicate their impact and quality. In science especially, the journal impact factor (IF) – a measure of the average citations to a particular journal over the previous 2–3 years – is of great significance (published annually by Thomson Reuters). The impact factor of a journal is calculated using this formula:

$$2013 \text{ Impact factor} = \frac{\text{Citations in 2013 to articles in the journal from 2011 and 2012}}{\text{Number of 'citable items' in the journal in 2011 and 2012}}$$

It should be appreciated that different disciplines use citations in different ways. Some of the highest-rated journals are published by societies and not-for-profit publishers, not by commercial publishers. Nevertheless, the strength and value of a commercial publisher's business are expressed by the number of leading journals it has created over long periods. Since researchers' career prospects and funding opportunities are often evaluated on the basis of their publication record, they try to be published in the highest-ranked journals in their subject they can attain. Moreover, researchers make a qualitative evaluation of the journals to which they submit their work.

There are many forms of peer review (see chapter 2 of Campbell et al.). To summarize the traditional method: the journal editor determines which of the papers received will be checked for plagiarism (for example through CrossCheck), will be editorially rejected or selected for peer review, and selects the reviewers who assess it. The editor, who also takes into account research novelty and likely impact, assesses the reviews and sends them with recommendations to the author for revision. The revised paper is either rejected or accepted. The article is contracted with the author, produced, published (called the version of record that is citable) and archived. This peer review process is complex and expensive to manage, even though reviewers work for free. The highest ranked journals have the highest rejection rates (up to and sometimes above 90 per cent) and incur the highest peer review management costs for the publisher, which usually pays for the costs of the editorial office. Peer review is pressured by the increasing receipt of articles, worldwide, and faster publication times demanded by authors: timeliness of publication differs across disciplines.

Journals benefit from network effects or positive externalities, a business model on which social media companies are founded. The value of the product or service increases the more it is used, creating a positive feedback loop, a virtuous cycle. For example, the greater the visibility and usage of a journal within its research community, the higher are its citations and IF, and the greater the receipt of better and available papers, which in turn further increases the IF, visibility and readership.

The market imbalance between the ever-increasing supply of articles versus declining library budgets in proportion to total university expenditure, culminated in the serials crisis from the late 1980s to the early 1990s (though some would argue that it is perpetual). The prices for journals were increasing as print circulations fell due to subscription cancellations – in turn caused by the universities coming under increasing financial pressure to reduce costs. It created a negative feedback loop that pushed up publishing costs, increasing prices further. Moreover, the leading journals containing the best research are not substitutable, and are in effect mini monopolies that command high prices – their demand is price inelastic (see Chapter 10). The crisis overlapped with the initial development of electronic journals and led to the development of the *big deal* business model, whereby publishers offered bundles of journal titles in electronic format to library consortia and other major customers at discounts off the catalogue prices. The model gathered momentum from the mid to late 1990s onwards and although initially welcomed by academia – researchers gained access to far more content – it later came under fierce criticism from libraries locked into fixed-term agreements and facing fast-rising prices. In response they formed consortia to negotiate the terms of the deals, giving them greater bargaining power, and began to resist some of the harsher clauses of contracts (such as non-disclosure to third parties of the financial terms).

As the big deals absorbed a higher proportion of their budgets, the libraries had to reduce purchases of HSS book titles. The major publishers, wielding their must-have premier journals bundled up with aggregations of lesser journals, and with their international marketing strength, captured greater visibility for their product, furthering network effects. These companies accrued a range of benefits from purchasing the operations of smaller journal publishers. They could strip out costs, add more value into their journal packages and databases, and increase their revenues and market share (and shareholder value).

Learned societies do collaborate to aggregate their content and create their own big deals – for example, the ALPSP Learned Journals Collection made available through the subscription agent SWETS. Some self-publishing societies outsource their publishing by entering into contracts with publishers which undertake the production, marketing, sales and distribution on their behalf while they retain their editorial independence. There is a migration of society publishing under such contracts to the large university presses and to the commercial publishers that offer them lower in-house costs, more visibility and often higher income.

Journal publishers, especially in STM, have been at the forefront in applying new technologies to digital publishing and the provision of services, either free or sold on subscription. Innovations and investments are made largely by the major commercial publishers, and the larger not-for-profit publishers, for example, the main learned societies, and OUP and CUP. They have not waited for the large technology players to impose their solutions on them. From the mid- to late-1990s, the publishers also developed web-based manuscript submission and peer-review management systems.

Of wider significance to the publishing industry as a whole, the journal publishers pioneered in the 1990s *digital first* production systems: a central concept of which is structured content. It involves tagging the textual elements (such as the article title, author, affiliation, abstract, keywords, headings) enabling the file to be output to multiple file formats. Digital workflows reduce costs and speed publication. Articles can be released when ready rather than waiting for a complete issue to be paginated and published. Journals contain increasing amounts of rich metadata. The addition of the semantic metadata to articles to reveal meaning that computers can understand aids search within databases or through web browsers. The inclusion of data sets alongside journal articles facilitates data mining – the investigation of patterns across large volumes of data. Virtually all journals are published in electronic formats (mainly PDF, HTML and increasingly other screen reflowable formats). Nevertheless, print distribution is still significant, more so in in HSS than in STM, although a large amount of printing has been shifted from the producer to the user.

The major publishers developed their own content delivery platforms. For instance, in 1997 Elsevier launched the first large-scale platform, or full-text scientific database, ScienceDirect, which by 2013 included 2,500 peer-reviewed journals and nearly 20,000 books (sciencedirect.com, accessed 18 September 2013), making available the works of its authors to more than 16 million researchers. Publishers compete on the usability of their platforms, such as reliability, speed, and ease of use, search and linkage to other data. However, the strength – and overall brand – of the platform is based on the brand value of the individual journals and books, and the size of aggregation. The major publishers are large enough to deal directly with the institutional librarians or purchasing consortia (some at state or nation state level), through which the institution's subscriptions to journals and ebook collections are negotiated. Publishers without their own platforms use third-parties for distribution such as HighWire (Stanford University), Metapress and Ingenta (Publishing Technology). The US aggregators of journals and content databases, such as EBSCO and ProQuest, provide library access to the output of publishers. The subscription agents are developing their businesses in many directions.

In the print-only era, the publishing of journals and books were distinct operations, with different systems, channels to market and business models. This was reflected in a publisher's internal organization into book and journal silos for its staff and systems. In the transition to the digital era, the readers (researchers, practitioners, teachers and students) increasingly want to access and use content across former boundaries, and across a range of devices including smartphones and tablets. The channels to market are converging as are the business models. The publishers are reorganizing their systems and staff to reflect the convergence. Researchers also need to demonstrate that their findings are reaching a wider audience, so for example journal articles may be connected up to their presence on social media. Publishers are aiming to occupy more of the value chain within the field of scholarly communication, and this lay behind Elsevier's acquisition in 2013 of the start-up Mendeley: 'founded in 2007 by three PhD students [it] provides academics with a desktop and web program that lets them manage and share research papers via the cloud. It works by extracting the metadata from journal article PDFs and connects users to those with similar interests ... It also provides tools to annotate documents, create citations and bibliographies' (wired.com, 9 April 2013).

Journal publishing benefits from many standards developed through collaboration among the publishers and with the research community. For example, CrossRef (launched 2000) enables readers to link from article references or citations to the cited article. COUNTER (launched 2002) facilitates the recording and reporting on the usage of online content (journals, books, databases) which helps librarians, publishers and intermediaries to operate more efficiently.

The journal publishers use a variety of business models: mainly institutional subscription and site licence; personal subscription (declining); pay per view (article downloads to readers whose institution does not subscribe to the journal); and engage with and sell through online aggregators and subscription agents. Some printed journals attract advertising revenue (for example in health sciences). What publishers cannot ignore are business models based around open access.

Open access

The advent of the internet gave rise to electronic journals and to the concept of open access (OA): the free and unrestricted online access to peer-reviewed research articles in journals, made available under Creative Commons licences. OA was in contrast to the paid for and restricted content, or toll access (TA), provided by the publishers of the time. The OA movement reflects an overall societal trend towards free access, such as open content and data, and OERs and MOOCs. OA and TA publishing is often presented in the media as a conflicting dichotomy which is too simplistic. They are both forms of publishing that overlap and coexist. There are many forms of OA publishing and many forms of TA publishing. Governments are wishing to extend and speed up OA publishing: most recently as proposed in the UK by the Finch Report (2012).

From a business standpoint, however, there is fundamental difference. OA publishing is predominately supply-side funded (for example, currently by a small number of very large governmental research funding agencies, major foundations and universities) whereas TA publishing is predominately demand-side funded by a larger number of market purchasers worldwide (for example, by university libraries, corporates and individuals).

OA publishing has grown considerably over the last decade from a low base, and in 2013 the Directory of Open Access Journals listed approaching 10,000 titles (doaj.org, accessed 18 September 2013). Some former subscription journals have switched to OA entirely, while others incorporate a mix of OA and TA models (hybrid). After initial opposition, the publishers quickly adapted to the new business model, and for instance Springer purchased the pioneering OA publisher BioMed Central in 2008. There is a shift from closed to open content. Furthermore there are degrees of openness in respect of user and author rights. There is also a growth in mandates made by institutions, funding agencies and governments on researchers to make their work available in OA in different ways. OA publishing has become increasingly complex.

Open access publishers adopt many business models to finance their operations. For example, universities may totally subsidize their own publishing through research groups or libraries (usually small scale and especially prevalent in HSS); research funders may finance publishing operations; or universities and OA publishers may form membership organizations to lower and share the cost of publication. However, most OA journals published by commercial and not-for-profit publishers and societies charge a fee to authors (an article processing, or publishing, charge, APC) after peer review and acceptance. It is called *gold OA* or the 'author pays' model. The author's university or the research funder normally pays the charge, say £1,000 to £2,000, and this is the model recommended by the Finch Report. Through the payment of APCs, the entire journal can be fully OA. In 2012–13 the UK health and biosciences research funder the Wellcome Trust paid publishers $6.5 m in APCs. Elsevier netted 25 per cent and the top five publishers 63 per cent (scholarlykitchen.sspnet.org, accessed 21 March 2014).

Hybrid OA is used on many subscription journals: some articles are made OA immediately on publication provided the APC is paid, whilst other articles remain behind a paywall. The *green OA* route is when an article is deposited on publication to a disciplinary or institutional repository. The publisher's concern here is that if the article is made freely available too soon, libraries would cancel their subscription to the relevant journal. Alternatively, authors may choose to publish in a delayed access OA journal, without charge, and deposit their accepted manuscript of the article in a disciplinary or institutional repository, after an embargo period set by the publisher or mandated by the research funder. The embargo periods vary by subject and journal – say 12–24 months – and STM journals usually have shorter embargos than HSS titles. Overall OA publishing has been driven by the interests of the health and biosciences. In STM areas author teams publish numerous articles and have access to large-scale research funding, whereas lone HSS researchers have far less direct access to publication funding. Since the main research universities have the highest output of articles, they are exposed to the greatest costs under the gold OA model while continuing to subscribe to substantial journal collections.

Gold OA publishing favours the large publishers over smaller publishers, such as the societies, and may aid further industry concentration. Supply-side funded publishing businesses are focused primarily on servicing authors (and in this context their funders) rather than the market; and the creation of abundance over content selectivity. There are two main trends in the development of journal publishing, both encouraged by OA: the arrival of mega journals, and the concept of cascade publishing.

In 2006, the not-for-profit US Public Library of Science (PLoS) launched the first gold OA mega journal PLOS ONE. In contrast to the highly selective subscription journals designed to serve small vertical communities, PLOS ONE publishes very large numbers of articles of scientific and medical research submitted from that broad horizontal community. The traditional role of the editor-in-chief to steer and curate for a vertical community is redundant in this context. To speed publication and reduce iterations, it adopts a light peer-review process prior to publication by concentrating on scientific rigour, rather than on novelty and impact that is left to be assessed post-publication. The mega journal concept was emulated subsequently by other publishers, which have also developed the cascade concept. If rejected by a premier journal (with a high rejection rate), an article may be automatically submitted for publication to a lower-ranked journal (with a lower rejection rate) within the same stable of titles, and the peer review process is not repeated leading to cost savings and faster publication for the author.

Such models ensure efficiencies within the ecosystem of journal publishing and enable lower APCs to be charged. Some start-up journals will waive charges altogether. The danger of the supply-side business models is that they diminish quality and allow predatory publishers to take advantage of academics seeking a home for their article, with echoes of the vanity press in consumer publishing. The trend towards gold OA has disappointed those advocates of green open access who view their ideal of content freely available to all as now tainted by compromise. The debates over OA range across business models, the costs and who pays, and sustainability issues; author and user rights, and the licences under which content is made available (for example the Creative Commons Attribution License, CC-BY); increased state control on research (via funding agencies) and the effect on academic freedoms to research and publish; and emerging inequalities between disciplines and individuals. The debates have overshadowed other ways to make research hidden behind paywalls available more widely, for instance through extending licences to public libraries.

Overarching the OA debates are the impact of ever-changing technologies on research, the increased focus on user experience, and the ways in which research and data can be linked and communicated, all of which provide many opportunities for publishers.

Sources

Eric de Bellaigue, 'British Publishing 1970–2000: How deregulation and access to capital changed the rules', *Logos*, 17:3, 2006.

BESA, *ICT in Schools*, 2009.

BESA, *Tablets and Apps in Schools*, May 2013.

Robert Campbell, Ed Pentz and Ian Borthwick (eds), *Academic and Professional Publishing*, Chandos, 2012.

Bill Cope and Angus Phillips, *The Future of the Academic Journal*, 2nd edition, Chandos, 2014.

Finch Report: Working Group on Expanding Access to Published Research Findings, *Accessibility, Sustainability, Excellence: how to expand access to research publications*, 2012.

Walter Isaacson, *Steve Jobs*, Little, Brown, 2011.

Michael A. Mabe, 'Scholarly Publishing', *European Review*, 17, 2009.

Sally Morris, Ed Barnas, Douglas LaFrenier and Margaret Reich, *The Handbook of Journal Publishing*, CUP, 2013.

Ian Rowlands, David Nicholas, Peter Williams, Paul Huntington, Maggie Fieldhouse, Barrie Gunter, Richard Withey, Hamid R. Jamali, Tom Dobrowolski, Carol Tenopir, 'The Google Generation: The information behaviour of the researcher of the future', *Aslib Proceedings*, 60: 4, 2008.

John B. Thompson, *Books in the Digital Age*, Polity Press, 2005.

Mark Ware and Michael Mabe, *The STM Report*, 3rd edition, International Association of Scientific, Technical and Medical Publishers, 2012.

Web resources

http://blog.alpsp.org Blog of Association of Learned & Professional Society Publishers.

www.creativecommons.org Details the licences under which OA content can be published.

www.doaj.org Directory of Open Access Journals.

www.scholarlykitchen.sspnet.org Blog established in 2008 by the Society for Scholarly Publishing.

CHAPTER 4

The characteristics of the main publishing sectors

The previous two chapters have traced the development of the book publishing industry across its various sectors. Themes shared across publishing sectors include the growth of digital publishing, experimentation around business models, changes in publishing processes, and the search for new talent, sometimes from outside the industry.

All kinds of publishers can be described as serving niche markets. Attaining a critical mass in a particular field, right down to a list of books on the narrowest subject area, is vital to publishers of every size. It allows the employment of editors who understand and have contact with authors and associates in a particular field, and who can shape projects for their intended markets. A respected list attracts authors. Furthermore, a list of books needs to generate sufficient turnover to allow effective marketing and selling, which in turn feeds new publishing.

Although common themes can be identified, there remain differences in the ways books are published for different markets. Publishers specialize in reaching particular markets, and each market has a separate dynamic and key drivers. The skills of their staff, the activities they perform and the structure of the business are aligned accordingly.

UK PUBLISHING

Table 4.1, using figures from the Publishers Association, gives the scale of the UK publishing industry in 2012 based on companies' sales. In addition to the sales of £2.9 bn of physical books, there were invoiced sales of over £400 m of digital products (up from £163 m in 2010), giving a combined total of £3.3 bn. Digital sales were 12 per cent of total revenues. The size of the domestic physical market was estimated at £3.1 bn in terms of end-purchaser prices, showing a modest increase of 0.2 per cent on the previous year. There were around 2,115 book publishers registered for VAT (compared to 2,300 in 2006), plus thousands more individuals and organizations publishing a narrow range of titles. The (unadjusted) number of titles published in the UK in 2012 was 170,267. Books in the UK are zero rated for VAT alongside newspapers, magazines published at regular intervals (more than once a year), and printed music. VAT is charged on digital products such as ebooks, online content and CD-ROMs, as they are classified as supplies of services.

Table 4.1 UK publishers' sales in 2012 (*source*: Publishers Association)

	Home	Export	Digital sales	Total
Volume of books sold (m)	416	270		
Sales (£m)	1,721	1,211	411	3,343

Table 4.2 Number of titles published in the UK 2003 to 2012 (*source*: Nielsen BookData)

Year	Number of titles and new editions
2003	131,271
2004	124,027
2005	110,925
2006	115,522
2007	119,465
2008	129,057
2009	157,039
2010	151,969
2011	189,979
2012	170,267

CONSUMER PUBLISHING

The consumer or trade publishers are the most visible part of the industry. Their titles are displayed prominently in high street bookshops and other outlets, receive considerable mass-media coverage and are aimed mainly at the indefinable 'general reader', and sometimes at the enthusiast or specialist reader. They form the mainstay of public libraries, and in some cases penetrate academic markets. In 2012 consumer sales in the UK market totalled £2.1 bn and 269 m books (publishers.org.uk). That is an average selling price (not cover price) of £7.81 per copy (compared to £7.56 in 2006). There were no published figures for sales of ebooks, although bestseller information became available from 2013. *The Bookseller* estimated that the ebook market in June 2013 was worth £17.6 m, 19 per cent of the overall book market.

Most publishers are in London, giving them ready access to authors, agents, other publishers, social venues, journalists and producers of the mass media, and other influential people who decisively affect the life of the nation. The remaining publishers are spread around the country, with concentrations in Oxford and Edinburgh, and tend to be more specialized.

Consumer book publishing is the high-risk end of the business: book failures are frequent but the rewards from 'bestsellers' – some of which are quite unexpected – can be great. The potential readers are varied, spread thinly through the population, expensive to reach, difficult to identify, and have tastes and interests that can be described generally but are not easily matched to a particular book. Publishers bet to a great extent on their judgement of public taste and interests – notoriously unpredictable.

Sometimes the publication of a book creates its own market. And the authors whose work arouses growing interest can develop a personal readership, thereby creating their own markets – perhaps attaining a 'brand name' following, especially in fiction. Publishers compete fiercely for their books. Few other consumer goods industries market products with such a short sales life. Generally speaking for a book to flourish, it is vital for the publisher to secure advance or subscription orders from booksellers before publication and for the response to the book to be good in the opening few weeks post-publication. The peak sales of most new books occur well within a year of publication. Most adult hardback fiction and paperback titles are dead within three months or just weeks, while paperback fiction written by famous authors may endure for long periods. Compared to the non-consumer book publishers, the trade publishers earn a higher proportion of their revenues from their frontlist publishing. With the increasing focus on the lead titles that are part of bookseller promotions and which receive supermarket and etailer exposure, frontlist revenues are increasing in proportion to backlist revenues. Some publishers' lists are very frontlist weighted, while others keep strong backlists alive from their new book programme and by relaunching old books in new covers, reissuing them in different sizes, bindings and as ebooks, or with revisions or new introductions. An energetically promoted backlist provides retailers with staple and more predictable stock, should earn good profits for the publisher, and keeps authors' works alive.

Many readers mistakenly believe that the large price differential between hardbacks and paperbacks is due to the extra cost of binding a book in hardback; it is also argued that ebooks should be cheap since there are no costs of physical production. There are cost differences between editions but the price differentials tend to reflect how publishers traditionally sought to maximize the revenue from a title by segmenting the market through different formats and price points. Furthermore some titles of minority appeal would not recover their investment if first published at lower price ranges meant for books with higher sales potential.

With ebooks in the mix it is harder for publishers to tread the well-worn sequential path of hardback, trade paperback, and then mass-market paperback. A fiction title might still be launched first in hardback at a high price to satisfy eager readers, but there is a market expectation that a lower-priced ebook is available. Over time it has become harder to sell many categories of book in hardback, and some titles may be published first as a paperback or ebook original. In 2012 fiction sales (invoiced to the publisher) totalled £674 m, with £346 m of home and £156 m of export sales, and digital revenues of £172 m – 26 per cent (Publishers Association). The average invoiced value of a physical fiction title was £3.03 (£2.69 in 2008).

The key characteristics of consumer publishing are as follows:

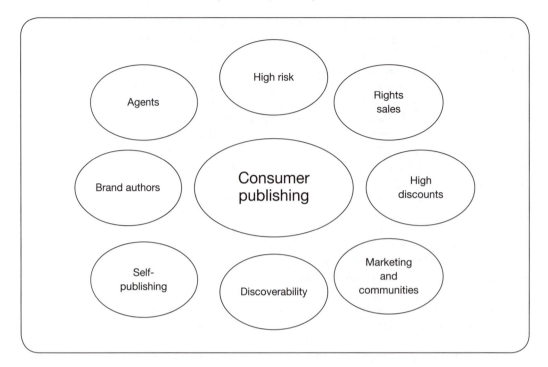

High risk

The business is high risk since it is difficult to forecast the sales potential of new books, and large sums may have to be paid out to authors for advances. The cash return, however, can also be large. The major publishing groups can afford to gamble on a variety of new projects.

Agents

Publishers are squeezed to a far greater extent by agents (on behalf of their authors), who look to negotiate higher royalty rates and advances, compared to non-consumer publishers. The major trade houses may pay out say 30 per cent of their sales revenue to authors (more than twice the percentage paid out by non-consumer publishers). Agents restrict rights granted to publishers to exploit the work in all forms of media, languages and territories.

Brand authors

Consumer publishers give greater emphasis to top authors in terms of advances, promotional expenditure, sales effort and high-profile publication dates – author brands help to sell books.

Self-publishing

Self-published ebook authors erode the market share of publishers but can provide a source of new talent.

Discoverability

Publishers depend to a great extent on retail exposure to aid book discovery and sell their books, and on gift buying for adult and children's books (the pre-Christmas period is of immense importance). The main customers and channels to market for physical books are diverse, including internet retailers, the bookselling chains, supermarkets, independent bookshops and other specialist stores, wholesalers, and direct distribution channels. Rising sales of ebooks and the growth in online retailing (dominated by Amazon) have disrupted the business model of sales through physical stores, and raised the issue of how readers discover books in the online environment.

Marketing and communities

Publicity in the media makes a significant difference to visibility and sales, along with social media marketing. Paid for promotional efforts will boost a book's profile in the retail trade and amongst consumers. A large promotional spend is often necessary to secure large orders from key retailers. Publishers are shifting to direct to consumer (D2C) marketing, and investing in online vertical communities and the provision of services.

Audio publishing

Nicholas Jones, Managing Director, Strathmore Publishing

EXPERT

The UK audiobook market has been recently transformed by technology, specifically the arrival of downloads in the consumer market. In previous decades, the majority of sales were as physical product on CD or cassette, and therefore in an abridged form; today the vast majority of audio listening is on MP3 players, and particularly mobile phones. Almost everyone has the technology to play an audiobook in their pocket, and the ease of adding new titles to a personal library, by download over fast internet connections, has transformed the way in which the medium is regarded. Most books are recorded in full since physical media no longer constrains the running time.

Most of the major general publishing companies run an audio list: Penguin Random House, the Hachette Group, HarperCollins, Pan Macmillan and Canongate Faber are all significant players. Naxos deserves mention as an independent audio publisher for the retail market that acquires rights from diverse sources.

Most audiobook publishers are increasing their output as a direct result of the transfer from physical product to download, with consequently less inventory needed but lower revenue per sale. Some companies which previously marketed only to public libraries welcomed the opportunity to reach a more general market: Isis, Oakhill, and in particular W. F. Howes. The expansion of lists is also a result of the sudden demise of AudioGO, a company set up in 2010 to take over the 'privatized' BBC Audiobooks list, once the largest UK audio publisher. On its closure, the rights held by AudioGO reverted to the book publishers and became available for purchase; some were acquired by Audible, which was founded in the US in 1997, came to the UK in 2006 and became a wholly owned Amazon company in 2008. It increasingly publishes its own material and holds an almost unassailable position as retailer, with a share of up to 90 per cent of the UK download market and 60 per cent in the US.

All publishers welcomed the opportunity to place their recordings on the Audible website, seeing it as additional income in a world where the majority of listening was being done from physical media. But the 'long tail' effect means that whereas audio listeners had perhaps only 3,000 readily available titles to choose from ten years ago, they now have over 100,000, and this has reduced sales of some individual titles to unsustainable levels. The market has thus become self-competitive. The cost of entry into the medium has fallen – home studios can produce recordings as good as some of those done in dedicated studios – and this has led to a sharp reduction in the prices paid by publishers for recordings. At the same time, however, competition has increased the price paid for audio rights. Literary agents, who might previously have bundled the audio rights in with the volume rights, now see them as a valuable separate commodity. As with ebooks, the result of all this disruptive change is a burgeoning in the sheer number of titles (some self-published), but at the expense of consistent quality and discoverability.

A best estimate of sales is that the market is about £100 million at retail in the UK, and about $1 billion in the US. The market is growing in volume terms substantially; the tumbling prices of recordings means that the value is static or growing slowly. The UK internet research group Audiencenet reported for Q2 2013 that 4 per cent of the general UK population over the age of 15 listened to audiobooks, a customer base of at least 2 million. The Publishers Association reported sales up by a third in 2012, with 48 per cent of audio consumed on mobile devices. From figures collected by the RNIB (Royal National Institute of Blind People), in 2012 nearly half (49 per cent) of the top 1,000 selling titles were available in unabridged audio form, up from 13 per cent in 2010. In the US the Wall Street Journal described as an example of the new audio customers a 25-year-old Boston software engineer who read at most two printed books a year but will now get through up to a dozen on audio (5 August 2013). According to the Audiobook Publishers Association, US output increased from 4,602 new titles in 2009 to 13,255 in 2012. Download sales there grew by 29 per cent in 2012.

In book publishing, job opportunities in audio lie in deciding what to publish and acquiring the rights, with perhaps some involvement in the casting of readers. Departments are small, often one or two people (some come from a rights background though most are from editorial); sales and publicity functions are usually shared with the book departments. Production and recording are almost always outsourced to specialist studios. The larger audio-only companies have the full range of functions, and employ some full-time producers.

High discounts

Publishers are squeezed by the large retailers ratcheting up the discounts granted to them. The discounts granted to the book trade, essential to gain exposure in the shops, can reach over 60 per cent of the recommended price of a book in the UK, at least 10 to 20 per cent higher than those granted by the non-consumer publishers. Trade publishers suffer from high returns of unsold books from physical retailers and wholesalers.

Rights sales

There is usually greater scope in consumer publishing to sell rights in the author's work to other firms (for example in translation), and to set up co-edition deals with overseas publishers.

CHILDREN'S AND YOUNG ADULT PUBLISHING

Children's books recorded £318 m of sales in 2012, made up of £233 m home and £77 m export sales of physical books, and £8 m of digital sales (Publishers Association). The top 10 publishers took around 75 per cent of the domestic market, and overall children's and YA books took around 30 per cent of the consumer market (Nielsen Bookscan). Children's books are published by the specialist children's divisions of the major consumer book publishers (for example Penguin Random House and HarperCollins) and independent publishers (for example Usborne and Walker Books). The vitality of children's publishing creates the book buyers of the future. The text and illustrations of children's books must excite, and appeal to, children of different age groups, and at different levels of reading skill and comprehension. They must also appeal to adults in the supply chain (the major non-book and book retailers) and to adults who buy or influence choice (parents, relations, librarians and teachers). Many titles are in full colour yet have to be published at low prices, and these often need co-edition partners in the USA, in Europe and elsewhere in order to attain economies in printing.

The Horrid Henry stories by Francesca Simon are popular with the age group 5 to 9

The books are usually aimed at age bands reflecting the development of reading skill. The bibliographic information supplied by publishers to the book trade is formalized through the Book Industry Communication (BIC) Children's Book Marketing Categories standard which denotes amongst other things, the title's intended age range (bic.org.uk). These are divided up as follows:

A   0 to 5
B   5 to 7
C   7 to 9
D   9 to 11
E   12 upwards

The 0–5 age group from babies to toddlers may be described as the parent pointing stage. Included here are the so-called 'novelty books' (which extend above the age group), a category of ever-widening inventiveness, such as board books and bath books (introducing page turning), colouring and activity books, question and answer books, pop-ups; and the lower end of picture books. Books for the very young need to be durable and often use cloth, plastic or hardback binding. The production departments of children's publishers are particularly concerned with product safety. The apps produced for this age group include reading experiences and games.

The 5–7 age group may be described as the starting to read, as well as reading to children stage. Picture books figure prominently. These books, invariably in full colour, tend to be 32 pages long, display strong narrative and may include just a few words up to possibly several thousand. They may be created by an illustrator or writer (or one controlling mind), and often need co-edition partners. The next stage of young fiction may have from 2,000 to 7,500 words of text, and may be published in paperback in smaller formats; these titles are designed for children reading their first whole novels. There are major series produced by many of the main trade publishers as well as reading schemes by the educational publishers. Moving up, and through, the 9–12 age group, longer length novels of up to 35,000 words come into play as well as the more recent mass-market genre series. Above 11–12, there are the teenage or young adult fiction titles. Much middle and young adult fiction is published straight into paperback and ebook. Non-fiction, sometimes highly illustrated, spans the age groups as do home learning series, reference titles (for example dictionaries), anthologies and character books (some of which are tie-ins to films).

Middle grade novels are aimed at the age group 8 to 12

The seventh volume in the Harry Potter series, *Harry Potter and the Deathly Hallows*, was published in 2007

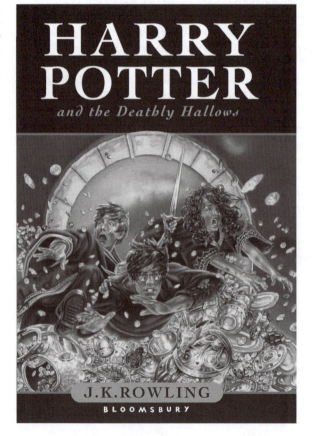

Children's books (but not Harry Potter) receive less window or promotional space in general bookshops; and children's publishers of quality books earn a higher proportion from backlist sales. The children's and young adult (YA) market is subject to crazes for particular authors and series (from Twilight to the Hunger Games), which can be prompted by word of mouth or film releases. Anthony Horowitz said in 2013 that his 'success, and that of at least half-a-dozen other children's fiction writers, rests entirely on J. K. Rowling. We just happened to be around at the right time' (*Guardian*, 14 September 2013). There are also international influences with, for example, manga becoming mainstream in the UK. Whilst the penetration of ebooks across the whole of children's publishing was initially low (around 3 per cent in 2012), there are higher figures for young adult titles. The Hunger Games trilogy sold over 1 m ebooks in 2012 in the UK, around one-third of the total sales.

Some teenage fiction has aroused controversy for its adult content. For example, when *Doing It* by Melvin Burgess was published in the children's imprint Puffin in 2003, the children's laureate Anne Fine attacked the decision:

When *Harry Potter and the Deathly Hallows* was published on 21 July 2007, it sold 2.6 m copies in the UK on that day alone

Some character brands have an international reach: the Turkish edition of *Horrid Henry and the Abominable Snowman*

All of the publishers who have touched this novel should be deeply ashamed of themselves. Astonishingly, they are almost all female. It's time they sat round a table, took a good long look at themselves and decided that it was an indefensible decision to take this book on. They should pulp their own copies now. (*Guardian*, 29 March 2003)

Reference publishing

F O C U S

Reference works (spanning words, pictures, numbers and maps) are sold by all kinds of publisher from consumer book to professional. Although some are ephemeral, reference publishing is usually for the long-term backlist. As consumers now search for their information online and on the go, usually from free resources such as Wikipedia or Google Maps, publishers have increasingly focused on institutional markets. The *Encyclopaedia Britannica* printed its final physical edition in 2012 and is now creating products and services for the schools market.

The reference work *Who's Who* is available both in print and online. It has been published annually by A & C Black since 1849

Major works can take years to compile and can involve investments of millions. *The Oxford Dictionary of National Biography* was published in 2004, both in an online edition and 60 print volumes. Formed in 1992 as a research project of Oxford University, the Dictionary was funded by a £3.5 m subvention from the British Academy and by £22 m from OUP. Reference publishing relies heavily on the application of new technologies, to aid both product development and the publishing of a family of products in different media. The *Oxford English Dictionary* could never have been revised as a complete entity without computerization. Dictionary lexicographers (and in bilingual works, translators) no longer have to rely on the manual identification and retrieval of words in primary sources. Typically they use electronic text corpora holding a vast range of primary and diverse sources from which evidence of word meaning and sentence contextual meaning can be retrieved, manipulated and to an increasing extent analysed electronically. Once the main dictionary database has been built and coded, spin-off shorter or special purpose dictionaries can be subsequently published.

The publishers of online databases, such as in law and business, try continually to enhance their services by expanding the content and the degree of functionality, for example by improving their web interfaces and analytical research tools for users. LexisNexis, owned by Reed Elsevier, pioneered online information in the area of law and taxation, and its services are now used by the top law and accountancy firms, many universities, and local and central government departments.

Echoing developments in adult publishing, children's publishers have little time to build authors slowly. The focus is on promotable first-time authors, established adult authors or celebrities writing for children, and media tie-ins. Author branding and the development of branded series are notable features of children's publishing. As in adult publishing, the gender differentiation of books for male and female markets is evident, in part influenced by consumer advertising of other products to children.

Children's publishing in the UK continues to push out the frontiers of book availability into a wide range of retail outlets, including grocery stores, toy-shops and garden centres, reached via the wholesalers. Such retailers, and some of the book clubs, tend to concentrate on books for the younger age groups. Internationally, the Bologna Book Fair held in the spring is the world's meeting-place of children's publishing. The UK publishers and packagers have long dominated the international trade in the selling of overseas co-edition rights and, like their adult counterparts, they import far fewer.

NON-CONSUMER PUBLISHING

The educational, academic, STM and professional book publishers have a number of advantages by comparison to firms operating in consumer markets:

- Their markets are more defined into vertical communities.
- Their authors and advisers are largely drawn from the same peer groups as their customers.
- Customers can be reached and engaged through their place of work.
- Backlist sales, especially if textbook and reference, account for a major proportion of their business.
- Institutional and business purchasers are far more amenable to buying digital formats.
- Subscription and site licence business models are more prevalent.

EDUCATION

Schools publishing

The total value of school book sales in 2012 was £290 m, comprising £172 m of home and £105 m of export physical sales, and digital sales of £13 m (Publishers Association). Educational publishers provide materials for schools: chiefly textbooks bought in multiple copies, supported by ancillary printed materials and digital media for class use or for teachers, published individually or as a series (for example representing a progressive course of study). Publishers concentrate on the big subject areas. The main publishers are located mainly outside London.

The key characteristics of schools publishing are set out below:

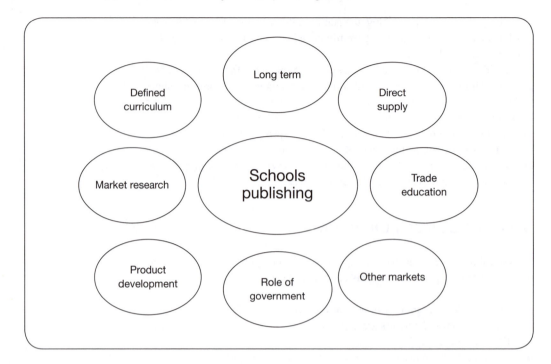

Long term

Compared with consumer book publishing, educational publishing is for the long term. Publishers derive most of their sales revenue from established backlist books. Schools can ill afford to dump adopted texts frequently. New books are published in the hope that they will be reprinted and revised in following years, but in practice they may fail. Curriculum publishing calls for a large amount of working capital – the liquid assets of a company – invested over a long time. The development costs of digital resources are also very high.

Defined curriculum

The books are market-specific (they are precisely tailored to the National Curriculum, examinations, academic levels and age groups). While to some extent the broad content is predetermined, curriculum publishers and their external advisers and authors give great attention to the pedagogy, and also cater for more conservative teachers. They help raise the quality of teaching. Links have been developed between publishers and the examination boards, for example Pearson with Edexcel, and Nelson Thornes with AQA.

Market research

Understanding the market is vital to the creation of a new textbook course for schools. Primary research may include sending out questionnaires to teachers or the use of focus groups.

Product development

Many books are highly illustrated, printed in colour, and involve a publisher in much development work. Yet they must be published at low prices and the cost of developing associated digital materials can be high. Whilst there is a slow uptake of etextbooks, the use of digital resources or of software for interactive whiteboards is growing – to aid homework and exam revision, or to enliven lessons – along with the provision of services to aid the professional development of teachers. The Dynamic Learning online platform from Hodder Education, which enables access to a variety of multimedia content, was used by around half of UK secondary schools in 2012; also popular is Kerboodle from Nelson Thornes. Some schools are experimenting with tablets for all pupils.

Role of government

Publishing is dependent on demographics and school budgets, and influenced by government policies. The latest education minister can have a big impact on the curriculum and how schools are run.

Other markets

Some educational publishers produce books for further education (especially for vocational qualifications) and reference (for home or school library use). In 2012 export accounted for 37 per cent of the sales of school books. Primary school titles in the areas of reading schemes and literacy have an international market. UK-orientated textbooks at secondary level have reduced export potential (other than to the international schools) but there is increasing scope to develop materials for local markets. Lis Tribe of Hodder Education said, 'Most of [our] exported products are designed for specific overseas curricula, and are different from books sold domestically. However, for some books there is a link between the domestic and export markets. For example, books supplied abroad in response to aid-funded tenders will typically be those also sold in domestic markets' (PwC, page 17).

Trade education

With the increased concentration on testing of pupils, there is a healthy trade market for self-study and revision books, sold through bookshops or directly to the more affluent parents and pupils. Personalized online learning materials are at the leading edge. Teachers can influence this parental anxiety market through their recommendations, and there is a growing market for home tuition from specialist companies, often delivered over the internet.

Direct supply

New and backlist titles are promoted directly to teachers and by publishers' sales consultants in schools and at exhibitions. Teachers scrutinize products before adopting them. Textbooks are mainly supplied directly to schools, or via booksellers, specialist school contractors and local authority direct purchasing organizations, and may be stocked by booksellers for parental purchase. The direct supply route to schools provides valuable marketing information to publishers.

ELT publishing

One estimate is that the number of learners of English worldwide could reach 2 bn

Around 600,000 people come to the UK each year to learn English (englishuk. com, accessed 25 September 2013). However, the publishing of English language teaching (ELT) or English as a foreign language (EFL) course materials is export-orientated. In 2012 sales of ELT books were £186 m with £173 m of export and £11 m of home sales of physical books, and £2 m of digital sales.

The traditional main markets have been in Southern Europe (Spain, France, Italy, Greece, Turkey), Eastern Europe, Japan, the Far East and South East Asia (China, Taiwan, Korea, Thailand), Latin America (Argentina, Brazil and Mexico) and the Middle East. The ELT publishers have set up companies, opened offices or acquired publishers in such areas, or have copublishing links with local publishers, or local marketing arrangements. Kevin Taylor of Cambridge University Press said in 2012:

> Our growth markets are India, South Africa and Australia, where there has been substantial public and private investment encouraging ELT over recent years. Through the ELT division, we are able to leverage sales for a number of different product and service lines. The copyright regime of the countries in question is a very important factor in our expansion plans. (PwC, page 17)

The mixed media ELT courses are major investments and may be orientated or versioned to regional cultural distinctiveness and are sometimes produced for ministries. Digital coursebooks may be supplied alongside print, together with the provision of an online environment to support face-to-face tuition. The courses serving primary, secondary and adult sectors are backed up with supplementary materials (such as reading books, dictionaries and grammars) with a broad international appeal. They are sold to the private language schools (PLS), from primary to adult, primary and secondary state schools, and sometimes to universities. In the UK there are specialist booksellers that supply the local and export markets.

Whereas previously UK publishers could rely on the same course to sell well around the world, there are now separate needs for different markets, which raise the costs of product development. The big change has been the growth of the state school market – for example in Italy, Spain, Argentina and Eastern Europe – which has probably overtaken the PLS market. A state syllabus has its own demands, specific to the country, and offers an opportunity for local publishers to enter the market. Some countries, such as Argentina, may insist on using locally produced materials. A key competence in ELT publishing is the ability to network with local schools and educational authorities.

HSS, STM AND PROFESSIONAL PUBLISHING

The terms 'academic' or 'professional' publishing are used loosely and interchangeably. Academic books tend to be associated with the humanities and social sciences (HSS). Research monographs of primary research are described as 'academic' and are vital to career progression. Professional books usually have an applied focus to aid practitioners directly in their work, for example schoolteachers, health care workers, engineers, architects, managers, and those working in law and finance. STM, reference and information books usually fall into the professional book publishing area. Some academic/professional titles may be designed for vocational or continuing professional development courses and be adopted. Their pricing level varies widely, depending on the target audience's ability to pay and whether they are purchased by the individual or the employer. Sales of academic and professional books totalled £1.1 bn in the UK in 2012, with £414 m of home and £479 m of export sales of physical books, and digital sales of £175 m (Publishers Association). The average invoiced price was £15.40 (£12.45 in 2008).

The business models are subject to change. Institutions may want to buy directly from publishers, for example to provide content as part of the tuition fee for a university degree. Dealing direct with customers, and avoiding going through intermediaries, helps to underpin a higher level of profitability by comparison to consumer publishing. The publisher's brand role of quality assurance and accuracy in the supply of information is supplemented by the direct provision of services and tools to end-users. A key added value is to provide users with access tools to the content they need quickly, and in a form they want, at the point they need it in their workflow, be they researchers or lawyers in their offices, or medical practitioners on the move. A good example is the delivery of information to mobile devices.

Not even the largest publisher could claim to be equally strong in all disciplines, or even those in science alone. Publishers concentrate on particular subjects, and vary in the emphasis given to different categories of book. The books for professional or practitioner use which have a wider market beyond teaching institutions tend to be those in the applied sciences for researchers or practitioners in industry and government agencies; and those serving professional sectors (for example law, medicine, management, accounting, finance, architecture). Such high-priced titles are bought by the wealthy (offices, commercial libraries and individuals). Special sales channels include booksellers, aggregators or training companies serving corporations, agencies and individuals; dedicated business, computer and medical book distributors and aggregators reaching end-users directly; conference and exhibition organizers; and companies which take bulk orders of titles as promotional items.

The legal and financial publishers, especially, traditionally used loose-leaf publishing for some of their reference titles. The purchaser, having bought the initial volume, received updated pages. Such publishers, as well as those producing books for business, sell a high proportion of their materials directly to end-users, not via booksellers. Sometimes, reference products (including directories, sometimes dependent on advertising revenue) are written in-house. Publishers have migrated their businesses to digital information services, and their products are usually licensed directly to libraries and businesses on subscription or by use of a site licence. Key abilities of such publishers are to identify information needs and the way that information is used in the workplace, and to translate that knowledge into the creation of products, tools and services using the appropriate media and technologies.

Figures from the Publishers Association show that Europe and North America accounted for 53 per cent of export sales in 2012 (compared to 57 per cent in 2008), followed by 18 per cent in East and South Asia (17 per cent in 2008) and 15 per cent in North Africa and the Middle East (14 per cent in 2008). For many publishers, mainland Europe is the single most important market with the Scandinavian and Benelux countries featuring as significant markets for English language textbook adoptions, and for professional lists. Southern Europe, for example Spain and Italy, is a market for high-level professional texts; undergraduate texts exist in translation or are published locally. The sale of translation rights to Eastern Europe and more recently to China and Korea, for example, has grown.

High-level textbooks, HSS, STM and professional titles are sold to the USA, the largest and richest market, via a sister company. A UK firm without a US presence may develop a copublishing link with a US firm, or license rights to a variety of publishers, or sell directly through importers. Sales to less developed countries tend to be dependent on aid agency funding. Publishers may on their own account arrange for special low-priced editions of some of their textbooks to be published in less developed countries, either through their own local companies or through sublicensing editions to local publishers. At the minimum, such editions have different covers in order to reduce the possibility of their penetrating developed markets through conventional and internet traders.

HSS and STM publishers are mostly outside central London with a high concentration in Oxford, and their output includes major textbooks (often the preserve of the larger publishers); higher-level textbooks for more advanced students through to graduate; edited volumes of reprinted or commissioned articles for students or academics; research monographs; books for professional use; reference titles (mostly online) and learned journals (print and online). These broad categories are not clear cut (for example high-level 'textbooks' may incorporate original research).

Textbooks

There is no commonly accepted definition of what constitutes a 'textbook'. Indeed there are plenty of examples of books of different kinds that are never written or intended as textbooks but which subsequently become adopted by lecturers for teaching and are bought by their students (such as this book first published in 1988). However, from a publishing standpoint, a higher education or 'college' textbook is commissioned, designed, timed and priced at the outset to meet teaching and learning needs in a defined area and at a particular level, and is marketed to lecturers with the intention that they adopt the book for use on a course, resulting in the purchase of multiple copies by students.

There are many factors affecting textbook purchasing in the UK, including student use of the internet, competing financial demands, the rise in published prices above the rate of inflation, changing behaviours about the sharing of books, and the rise of the used book market. Broadly speaking textbooks are published in paperback, though some for professional training (for example medicine, law) may be hardback. The high-level supplementary texts occasionally have a short high-priced print run for libraries, issued simultaneously with the paperback. Conversely, textbooks, printed in larger quantities, may become established and are reprinted for annual student intakes and revised through new editions when appropriate. Competitors constantly attack the market share of successful books. Many of the campus bookshops are owned by the bookselling chains. Nevertheless, academic and professional publishers have been more successful than the consumer book publishers in resisting booksellers' demands for higher discounts, and in containing author royalty rates and advances.

Publishers promote (and sometimes sell directly) their books to lecturers, researchers and practitioners (mainly by mail, email and telephone) and compared with consumer book publishers usually have smaller sales forces calling on a limited range of booksellers, and sometimes campuses, or attending exhibitions. However, some firms publish titles of wider general interest and of bookshop appeal in which case booksellers may be granted higher 'trade' discounts. These include more titles in the humanities, especially history, than the social sciences, some technical books (for example on computing) and medical works (for example personal health) supplied through specialist wholesalers.

Other titles, sometimes referred to as 'supplementary texts', may include the author's original research or commissioned edited collections. These can be priced for student and individual academic purchase, and can be published economically in small quantities – from around 1,500 copies in paperback. Paradoxically, if an author's primary research were to appear in a textbook it could seriously damage saleability through being seen as idiosyncratic or too advanced. The highly saleable textbooks usually reflect a mainstream view of current teaching and assessment. Other kinds of books, such as edited collections and anthologies, may be bought by students and academics. Some publishers continue the practice of publishing dual paperback and hardback editions. Their new books are issued in paperback for personal purchase, and simultaneously as a short-run hardback, say 150 copies, priced at around three times the paperback price, for sale to academic libraries worldwide.

The figure below shows the key characteristics of textbook publishing:

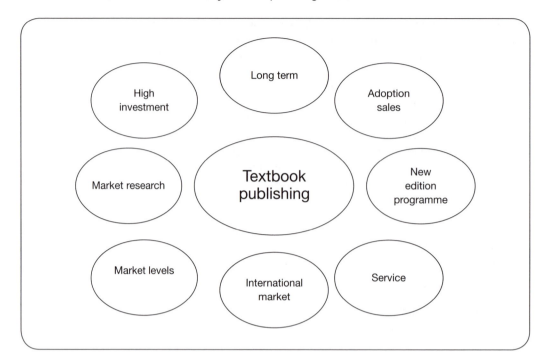

Long term

Initiating and developing a textbook list requires planning and sufficient attention to product development. Textbooks require development editors to control the authoring, schedule and budget.

High investment

Some textbook projects require high levels of investment, and there are growing demands to fund digital content and services.

Market research

Just as in educational publishing, a major investment in a new textbook requires comprehensive research into the market and competition.

Market levels

There will be different levels in the market, from first-year undergraduate through to graduate. Introductory texts may have a larger potential sale but will encounter fiercer competition.

International market

For some subjects there may be a large international market. For example, a business textbook may be used around the world, and some business schools in non-English-speaking countries may teach in English. Successful textbooks may be localized in different markets. For example, Kotler et al.'s *Principles of Marketing* is available in a European edition. The adaptation of textbooks for particular regions of the world aids local sales and inhibits their exportation to other higher-priced regions.

Service

Whilst there has been a slow uptake of e-texts, the publishers producing major textbooks for subjects with high student intakes adopt US practices, such as a periodically updated companion website carrying data, activities, banks of test questions, website links, and lecturers' guides. Used by over 11 m students each year, Pearson's MyLab is a 'collection of online homework, tutorial, and assessment products ... [it] reacts to how students are actually performing, offering data-driven guidance that helps them better absorb course material and understand difficult concepts' (pearsonmylabandmastering.com, accessed 25 September 2013). The large publishers offer lecturers the ability to *customize* – personalize – the book's content to meet their specific teaching needs (assuming sufficient numbers of students). The publisher creates a unique product for the particular institution.

New edition programme

In order to ensure that texts are up to date, and also to minimize lost sales from the used book market, textbooks regularly go into new editions.

Adoption sales

The successful sale of a textbook involves persuading the lecturer to adopt it, the bookseller to stock it and the student to buy it. Most revenue is derived from copy sales, though rental of ebooks is growing.

HSS, STM and professional specialist titles

Specialist titles, including research monographs, are usually high-priced and published mainly for libraries and individual researchers and practitioners. They are printed in small quantities and will be available as ebooks. The trend is towards issuing titles primarily as ebooks, with print orders supplied by short-run digital printing. Publishing books with very low sales forecasts is not risk free – the profit may come from the sale of the last 50 copies. Individual titles or collections of ebook titles are sold directly by publishers to libraries, or via aggregators, using a variety of models based on the site licence. The models include perpetual access, PDA (patron-driven acquisition), short-term loans under rental agreements, pay per view, and subscription. The sale of ebook collections to libraries comes ever closer to the usage and business models of journals.

JOURNAL PUBLISHING

If sales to UK publishers of books total over £3 bn, a further contribution of £1.8 bn comes from journals publishing. Worldwide it is a huge business with sales of several billion dollars just in the area of STM publishing. The content of learned journals, as distinct from magazines, is not predetermined (commissioned or written in-house), and contributors submit papers of original research to an academic editor-in-chief for refereeing and inclusion. Refereed journal articles are a primary information source and serve the research community. The publishing system sorts and assesses the research outputs, and aggregates content in the form of brands – the journal title. It provides quality assurance, visibility and usability. Generally speaking, learned journals are not dependent on advertising for their viability; their revenue is mainly derived from subscriptions, and to a growing extent through various forms of open access (OA) publishing models. Some publishers produce journals for professional use that are supported by advertising.

Journals are published by not-for-profit societies and research institutes (a few of which run substantial journal and book publishing operations), and by divisions of academic and STM publishers including the university presses, and especially in OA by a variety of subsidized publishing operations, usually university and research agencies. The commercial journal publishers initiate journals, or produce and market journals for societies and others under contract. The provision of such services to societies can be a significant proportion of some publishers' business.

Virtually all journals are available electronically though print is maintained for subscription journals. Researchers, students and industry practitioners mostly access journal articles online away from the library. Librarians are able to check the value for money of a subscription from user statistics on articles downloaded. Many authors assign the copyright in their article to the journal publisher or society. Authors and referees are not paid, but academic journal editors may be paid – some only expenses, some handsomely. However, the cost of funding the academic editorial office is considerable. The higher the rejection rate, the higher the cost.

There are more STM journals than in other academic areas. Titles are promoted by mail and at academic conferences, and sold mainly through institutional subscriptions (and those made with consortia), via site licences with academic libraries worldwide (either directly from the publisher's platform or through intermediaries) and to a far lesser extent to individuals. Journals of applied science, management, economics and law also sell to industrial and commercial libraries. Members of societies may receive a journal free as part of their membership fee, or at a reduced rate. Other income arises from pay per view article downloads, advertisements, inserts and reprints (especially in STM). The income from the licensing of back files to institutions and consortia can be significant on long-established journals. The big deal business model (the bundling of content) has become a dominant method of sales. Mailing lists and journals can be used to advertise and sell the publisher's books. There is cross-fertilization of contacts and ideas between book and journal publishers. There is a convergence in reader usage of book, reference and journal articles via platforms. Journal publishing, unlike book publishing, does not require such a complex network of overseas agents. The discounts granted to intermediary subscription agents are very low. The credit risk is also low and there is not the exposure to returns to be found in book publishing.

The impact of OA is felt in a number of ways, including the use of delayed OA (articles are freely available after an initial embargo period), the deposit of articles in disciplinary or institutional repositories on publication (green OA), and the rise of gold OA – whereby authors (or mainly their funders) pay APCs (article processing charges) to have their articles made OA immediately on publication. In 2011, on their publication around 12 per cent of all articles were OA, and by six months after publication 17 per cent (Cope and Phillips). Some subscription journals allowing paid for OA are called hybrid journals. Subscription only journals take a long time to break even – up to five or seven years for some STM journals – and may involve enormous investment. By contrast, journals using the gold OA model can generate income more quickly, provided they attract a sufficient supply of publishable articles. New journals can also be bundled into existing packages to help them gather momentum.

The key characteristics of journal publishing are set out below:

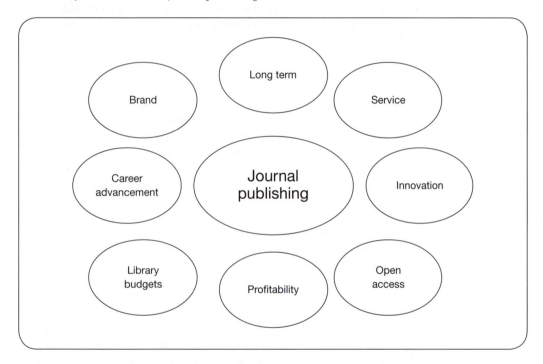

Long term

Journals, especially if subscription, take a long time to establish. Once a journal is established, the sales pattern is more predictable than books, the demand for capital lower (as are staff overheads), and the value of sales per employee is higher.

Brand

Long-established and successful journals, such as *Nature*, become high-profile brands, attracting the best submissions from authors. They are essential purchases in their relevant communities and the curated aggregation benefits from network effects.

Career advancement

Publication in high-ranking journals can establish or enhance the academic standing of authors – counting towards their personal and institutional research funding and their promotion prospects.

Library budgets

Subscription sales are dependent on library budgets in universities, other institutions and corporations. The tendency for publishers to offer the 'big deal' – large collections of journals bundled together – has been attractive to libraries after better value. But some librarians have expressed concern about being tied into longer-term contracts, inflexibility in choice of titles and the price increases applied by publishers.

Profitability

Whereas book publishers operate a business model based on the sales of individual copies, journal publishers have the advantage that annual subscriptions are received in advance of production. Many titles may be bundled up together to form a collection of titles. The profit margins in journals publishing are generally higher than in book publishing, and the business generates cash for its owners.

Open access

The open access movement argues that access to journal articles should be free to the end-user. There are a number of OA models in existence, from 'author pays' to the institutional repository.

Innovation

There are many examples of innovation, some of which reach the other sectors of publishing, from aggregation to the breaking down of content into small chunks. The arrival of OA has prompted a search for efficiencies in the peer review system. Mega journals are not limited by size and will accept articles according to quality standards around the methodology; cascade models allow articles rejected by top-quality journals to be referred to lower-ranked journals within the same stable.

Service

Journal publishing has been at the forefront of online publishing. The large players have invested huge sums in online platforms, enabling them to sell direct to their customers, usability design, and in back file conversion of long-established journals. The migration to digital has meant the transition from a physical product industry to a digital service. Journal publishers constantly strive to improve the service they offer their customers – including access, search facilities, usability and product range.

Now read this

Frania Hall, *The Business of Digital Publishing: An introduction to the digital book and journal industries*, Routledge, 2013.
Paul Richardson and Graham Taylor, *PA Guide to the UK Publishing Industry*, 3rd edition, Publishers Association, 2014.

Sources

Bill Cope and Angus Phillips (eds), *The Future of the Academic Journal*, 2nd edition, Chandos, 2014.
David Graddol, *English Next*, British Council, 2007.
Outsell, *Open Access: Market size, share, forecast, and trends*, 31 January 2013.
Publishers Association, *PA Statistics Yearbook*, 2012.
PwC, *An Economic Analysis of Education Exceptions in Copyright*, a report prepared for the Copyright Licensing Agency, March 2012.
John B. Thompson, *Books in the Digital Age*, Polity Press, 2005.

Web resources

www.publishers.org.uk Publishers Association.

CHAPTER 5

Creating and protecting value in publishing

The aim of a book publisher is to publish and sell at a profit. Even a not-for-profit publisher will want to at least break even, covering their costs, unless they receive a subsidy from their parent organization. A publisher might previously have cross-subsidized less popular titles from the profits of its top sellers. That approach has largely been abandoned although the high-risk element of consumer publishing does mean that bestsellers compensate for titles with poor sales. Of course a book may acquire value as a collectable object or a great literary work to be admired and studied by future generations, but this chapter will concentrate on the creation of monetary value by publishers as commercial enterprises. How publishers add value is of interest to both authors and readers in an age when self-publishing is quick and inexpensive, and consumers expect digital content to be available at lower prices than physical products.

VALUE CHAIN

Taking the raw material – the author's text – the publisher aims to add sufficient value so that it sells the final product at a higher value than the costs that have been incurred. A number of activities are undertaken in order to take the author's text and make it available as an attractive product that consumers will want to buy. These activities are shown below (Cope and Phillips, page 48). Each of the publishing functions is described in more detail in the relevant chapter.

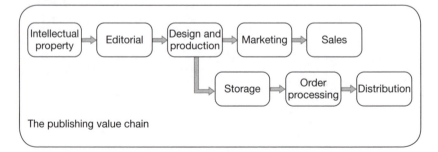

The publishing value chain

Once a book is acquired from an author, it has to be edited, designed, produced, marketed to the book trade and readers, and sold to bookshops or the end-purchaser. Once the book has been produced, it has to be stored in print form or the digital file made available through key intermediaries, orders are taken from retailers or consumers, and the book is then dispatched from the warehouse, downloaded on to a device, or made available through a cloud service. Publishers can choose which elements of the value chain they undertake themselves, and which are outsourced to third parties. For example, while commissioning new titles is usually done in-house, copy-editing and proofreading are typically carried out by freelance editors or by suppliers which provide an entire production service. The key elements of the value chain are the acquisition of intellectual property, editorial, design and production, marketing, and sales, and most publishers will control these functions directly. Publishers can look to combine stages of the value chain and, for example, editorial, design and production may be combined into one function, and the post of production editor is increasingly common.

Publishers seek to gain competitive advantage in the market, and this is done through acquisition and control of the best intellectual property. Having the best possible people in the commissioning roles will be the key to many publishers' success. There is also value to be found in other parts of the value chain. For example, a larger publisher will be able to negotiate from a stronger position with printers and paper suppliers, and with key retailers and wholesalers. 'In the experience of two independent trade publishers, on absorption into large groups they found their print bills reduced by more than 25%' (de Bellaigue, page 192). Some publishers like Dorling Kindersley build up expertise in the area of design. Everyman's Library, owned by Random House, offers editions of literary classics in hardback editions with high production values that contrast with a cheap paperback or free ebook. Giving away high discounts to the bookshop chains has the aim of ensuring that a publisher's stock is widely available, and should increase sales, but it also squeezes a publisher's profit margins. Selling direct, rather than through intermediaries, enables a publisher to keep more of the product's final value. There are economies of scale in production if co-edition orders can be added to the print run. Using digital printing to produce smaller quantities, or selling ebooks, may minimize or eradicate investment in stock. Smaller publishers often benefit from speed to market – commissioning and publishing faster than larger rivals.

There is less competitive advantage to be found for a publisher in the physical distribution of books, since the levels of service are now high across the industry. Nevertheless a larger publisher benefits from economies of scale in distribution in such areas as investment in IT systems, the size of orders, negotiation over carriage costs with shippers, and the collection of money from customers. In electronic distribution the larger publisher benefits from the greater aggregation of its intellectual property, and can spread the costs of their digital platform over a larger range of content.

Adding value

Publishers add value to an author's work in a variety of ways – these reflect both creativity and business acumen. Embedded throughout the book, they are summarized in the figure below.

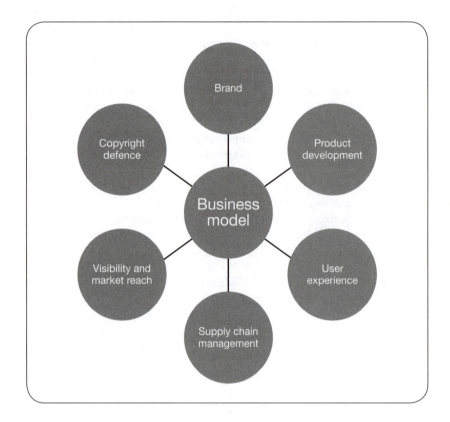

Brand

By lending its brand or imprint, the publisher is making a statement about the value of an author's work – it is worth publication by an investor, in this case the publisher. Emphasis has been placed on the role of the publisher as the curator of excellent content: the brand (or imprint) adds value and endorsement. In trade publishing the payment of an advance (risk capital) gives the author the time and resources to research and write. The flavour or character of an imprint is understood by authors and authors' agents, informed sections of the media, trade buyers in the supply chain in the UK and overseas, and by other media companies and overseas publishers.

Most consumer book publishers run imprints that are called trade brands, recognizable by the trade but not by consumers; they also offer the service of developing and managing an author's brand. However, publishers serving vertical communities (D2C) develop consumer brands which are recognizable by readers.

In non-consumer book publishing, an imprint's status is recognized by associated peer groups (for example teachers) and those in the supply chain, including institutional (such as librarians) and corporate purchasers. Major textbook brands offer authors a platform to show their approach to teaching is better than existing texts, and the advantage of online support services. Highly rated academic and professional publishing brands offer authors peer group recognition worldwide and personal career advancement.

The value of selection and curation by publishers was highlighted by the discovery in 2013 that ebook retailers were selling 'pornographic e-books featuring incest, rape and bestiality on their sites ... Self-published e-books have grown massively in popularity along with the growth in digital e-readers and tablet computers, but retailers have been struggling to filter explicit content that breaches their website guidelines' (bbc.co.uk, 14 October 2013).

Product development

The publisher invests its staff resources and technological infrastructure to produce, market and sell the book on the author's behalf. Their knowledge and judgement of current markets and future trends adds value to those authors who are commissioned and selected by the publisher. Authors are helped through the creative development of the proposal to match market and user needs, including filling gaps in the market (also of course imitating the competition) and realizing opportunities, and through the provision of other guidance and advice. Editorial expertise helps writers craft their work, from advice on structure through to line-by-line editing. The value of editorial intervention is reflected in the purchase of stylistic and other editing by some self-published authors.

User experience

Another creative expertise of the publisher is to design and present the author's work to best effect in a saleable printed book: length, size, format, usability, fitness for purpose, quality and accuracy of content, feel and look (design and production values), especially the cover to sell it. A hardback art book, for example, will be produced to a very high standard and sold at a high price. An inexpensive paperback or ebook will be produced with lower production values. The publisher organizes and manages the workflow to deliver the book. Digital distribution breaks the link between the contents and the physical packaging – for example facilitating the download of a book chapter or journal article. Because readers access digital content through a variety of distribution channels and devices, attention is given to the user experience (UX) of the product and service in their personal context. Brett Sandusky writes that the scope of UX covers

> everything from the first sparks of ideation, guiding product development teams in their endeavors, to marketing practice, through post-launch development, customer service and how end users interact with a company. In short, UX covers a broad range of internal and external curated interactions that collectively have the objective of producing and maintaining a usable product for end users. (McGuire and O'Leary, page 178)

Supply chain management

The publisher orchestrates the production of the book or journal through the procurement and management of a range of external services from individuals – freelance editors, designers – and companies – typesetters, printers, paper suppliers, technology companies. The outsourcing and procurement of services extends to marketing, sales and distribution worldwide. Furthermore the publisher manages the sales channels to market. From a publisher's perspective, authors are critical suppliers and their 'management' is arguably the most vexing.

Visibility and market reach

The publisher sets the time of publication of the author's work in order to maximize sales. It may be related to a specific marketing and sales opportunity or need, to the publication of the publisher's other books, to competitors' publishing schedules, or be subject to the demands of the retailers. The realization of connecting a readership to a book and consequent sales depends largely on the effectiveness of the publisher to promote and publicize the work in a variety of formats to create an audience, to sell it through the numerous channels to market (home and export, including sales of rights), to distribute it, and to collect the money and to account to the author.

Tim O'Reilly argues that the publisher must offer more visibility and sales than the author can get on their own. Specifically, he said that 'your job as a publisher is to do things for authors that they can't do for themselves: things that require special expertise; that require scale; that are expensive, that require marketplace leverage; things that are boring and time-consuming.' (TOC).

Copyright defence

By way of the author contract, the publisher acquires from the author an exclusive licence to exploit the intellectual property rights in the author's work. The publisher's responsibility and expertise are to exploit the rights granted to the fullest in print and electronic forms (and when available to license others to do so), and to protect the author's rights against infringement by others using technical and legal means. The latter is highly important in an age of file-sharing and book piracy.

BUSINESS MODEL

Ultimately a publisher has to operate a profitable business model that delivers sufficient return to enable the publication of authors' works, and offers to authors remuneration in terms of readership, money and status. Changing patterns of authorship, readership and distribution mean that there are a multitude of business models and constant experimentation. Content may be sold as discrete products, bundled into a service sold on subscription, or given free to users to encourage sales of higher value products. Authors may earn a royalty or a share of the profits from a title.

The potential financial worth of the author's work is assessed by the publisher at the outset. The publisher envisages in advance the product package, its price, the potential demand over a time period and the projected sales income, balanced against the estimated costs of production and the payments to the author, resulting in the publisher's forecast profit. The publisher takes the risk decision based on multiple factors as to whether to invest in the author's work or not. When the publisher issues the contract to the author, it confers financial value on the author's work.

Impact of the internet

The internet offers publishers opportunities for value creation. It has speeded up communication and encouraged a global market in design, typesetting and print, which has led to lower costs. There is also a global market of readers to be reached with digital content, and this is an opportunity in particular for English language publishers of many types of book, from educational books to trade fiction. The challenge for publishers is to become direct consumer businesses, rather than simply reaching their markets through intermediaries. As ebooks have become popular, some publishers have been able to save on the costs of distributing the physical book and have established a direct relationship with their readers. The internet provides a means of marketing books – both promoting them and identifying individual consumers. Value can be created through making brands work directly with book readers, through building communities around content, and from involving readers in the creation of content (for example suggesting ideas of new titles). Digital tools such as those used for social networking facilitate the creation of this digital capital (Phillips, 2014, page 93).

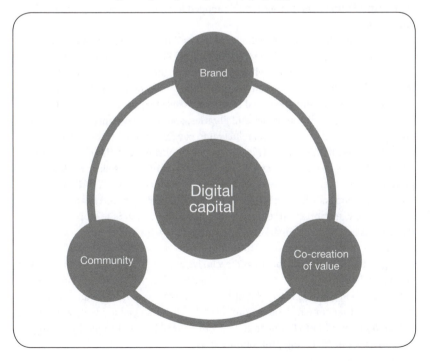

Providers of digital content can also create extra value by adding the element of service. Electronic services can be created using a wide range of content, offering users on demand, up-to-date and searchable content (including pictures, video and animation) from a range of different sources. Such services may be highly profitable once established, but the initial costs can be significant.

The internet also offers a new set of issues. First, there is a vast range of information for free. This has impacted on reference book publishing, for example. Can consumers see the value of publishers' products when there are free sources of 'good enough' information on the web? The coming of Web 2.0 has highlighted the mechanisms available for user-generated content (UGC), such as blogs and wikis. Stephen Fry has described Web 2.0 as

> an idea in people's heads rather than a reality . . . It's an idea that the reciprocity between the user and the provider is what's emphasized . . . People can upload as well as download. (videojug.com, accessed 21 August 2007)

In a relatively short space of time, Wikipedia has come to dominate online searches for information. Founded in 2001, users can write entries and edit the content. In 2013 the English Wikipedia contained over 2.5 bn words. By comparison the 32-volume print set of the *Encyclopaedia Britannica* (2007) had 44 m words. As James Surowiecki comments: 'The enormous gains for consumers in the digital age often come at the expense of workers. Wikipedia is great for readers. It's awful for the people who make encyclopedias' (*New Yorker*, 25 November 2013). User-generated content also covers social networking sites (Facebook, Twitter, Tumblr), video (YouTube) and images (Instagram, Flickr, Pinterest). Wattpad and Scribd have developed large communities around writing and reading.

It becomes difficult to price digital products if there is an expectation that content on the internet should be free. As Andrew Keen writes, 'the more self-created content that gets dumped onto the internet, the harder it becomes to distinguish the good from the bad – and to make money on any of it' (Keen, page 31). Publishers have developed good business models for online services sold to an institutional market of companies and libraries, and have developed strong brands, but how do you sell to consumers reluctant to pay for content? If the advertising market is buoyant, this can provide one model. Publishers can also create additional revenue streams by encouraging click-throughs to companies selling related products – they then receive a percentage on the products' sales. A further issue is how to price ebooks when consumers expect digital content to be cheaper.

If there is a strong market for a particular author, what is to stop the author themselves capturing the market? For example, the wine writer Jancis Robinson runs her own subscription site, offering nearly 10,000 articles, over 80,000 tasting notes, a member's forum and exclusive access to *The Oxford Companion to Wine* (jancisrobinson.com). In 2012 J. K. Rowling launched her own Pottermore site to sell ebooks of the Harry Potter books and create an online experience with games and other content (pottermore.com). Publishers need to identify clearly the service they can offer to brand authors, from editorial work through to running their websites or financing promotional apps.

Dale Dougherty of O'Reilly Media coined the term Web 2.0 – popularized by Tim O'Reilly

In 2013 Wikipedia contained around 4 m articles

Digital products: how to read the map

Henry Volans, Head of Faber Digital

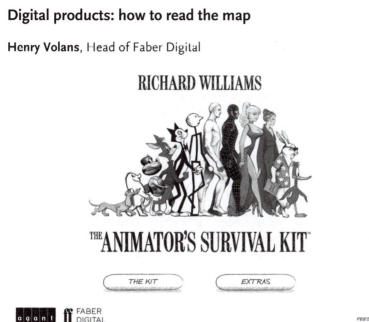

Pressure on the publishing industry is causing the focus of innovation to shift from single products to entire business models (subscription, direct-to-consumer, custom services). Both matter. Hit products drive publishing, and others will learn to build better products if publishers themselves do not.

One problem is that digital products – anything beyond the conventional ebook, such as mobile and tablet apps, websites, and the maligned 'enhanced' ebook – form a hard category to pin down. Devices change all the time in the relentless march to update and upgrade. So do operating systems, browsers and file standards. Then there is the industry debate, which sees fashions come and go with the seasons. New formats are celebrated or written off with vigour.

Behind all this, though, is a steadily maturing expertise and focus. The best digital publishing is brilliant. Unlike print publishing, it is the result of approaches that vary hugely between companies. It is valuable to learn to read this activity on the edge of the publishing comfort zone.

A good start is to think about motive: what was the driving force behind a project? Was it straightforwardly commercial? What would the profit-and-loss estimate have looked like? Although some apps have an element of the lottery about them as they hunt for consumer success, others are more gently effective. At Faber we had ten years of print publishing experience behind *The Animator's Survival Kit* to allow an accurate understanding of its market. Knowing that it would support a premium price (initially £24.49), appeal to a defined audience (professional animators worldwide) and suit the iPad form (finger-scrubbable video) led to a performance on the iTunes App Store in line with our forecast.

Another good motive is to take on the right kind of risk – the kind that breaks new ground. Is a publisher making meaningful partnerships with the games industry? Releasing something that makes TV producers envious? Co-branding intelligently with the world outside? Or just gaining competitive advantage through more imaginative publishing in the round? Despite common talk of risk-taking, experimentation and overcoming the fear of failure, digital projects that take on a big risk for a good reason are rarer than they should be.

This caution can be a factor in less successful digital products, in which minimizing the risk also stifles the potential upside. Projects whose primary aim is to protect existing business can usually be recognized as such. Much fresher and more interesting are projects that have identified a genuine consumer need and which harness the right digital platform to meet it. Put another way, the best digital products do not flatter their makers: they challenge them to compete with the digital world outside: other industries; start-ups; self-publishers. Those who respond to this challenge and build a better digital book are as likely to help reshape the industry as those who seek to dream up a new channel for products that already exist.

There are other issues connected to online publication. Transferring print brands to the internet is not straightforward, which has led some publishers to create new brands for the Web. One example is the EFL teacher's resource onestopenglish operated by Macmillan (onestopenglish.com). Many publishers do not control the full rights to their books, and this can hinder the transfer of illustrations, for example, into digital products and services.

In the world of the printed book, authors and publishers devote a great deal of thought and effort to the creation of a physical entity – the bound volume which is sold as a complete package of information. Readers usually have to buy the entire book, even if they only want part of it. In the digital world, the focus has shifted. As John Thompson writes, publishers have increasingly realized that it is the 'content, and the control of the copyrights that governed what they could do with the content, which was in some respects their key assets, not the books themselves' (Thompson, 2005, page 9). Innovation in style and content is encouraged by digital publishing, from the use of multimedia to new ways of structuring texts. The world of digital content and search unravels the content packaged in printed books. Content may be purchased at different levels of granularity, and consumers may wish to purchase by the chapter or even in smaller chunks such as by the page or illustration. Alongside the fear that consumers will cherry pick the best chapters and sales of the complete work will be cannibalized, there are the potential benefits for publishers – additional purchases may come from those who are not considering buying the whole book. The implications of the digital world for the control of intellectual property are discussed in detail later in the chapter.

Risk

In the traditional business model for book publishing – where transactions are based around the physical copy – there are issues around risk, the power of retailers to ask for high discounts, and the fact that returns of unsold books can take some months to materialize. There are different risk levels according to the publishing sector, and for example consumer publishing is riskier than academic publishing. Paying a large advance to a celebrity whose star may not be shining so brightly when the book is published is a risky venture. The investment in a large print run or a highly illustrated work bears the associated risk that the book will simply not sell. In order to secure the book's availability in the shops, cash will need to be spent on promotion and high discounts will have to be given to retailers. Money is paid out and only recouped some weeks after publication – retailers will demand a period of grace (the credit period) before they have to pay for the stock. By contrast journals publishing has a more secure and profitable model. Subscribers pay money up front to receive a journal, and the evidence is that the market is largely price inelastic – demand for a premium brand title does not drop significantly if prices are raised.

Booksellers have sought a higher share of the value created for trade books, asking for higher discounts off the recommended price. But at the same time price competition has lowered the prices paid for books by consumers. With books sold at up to 50 per cent discount, profit margins have either been squeezed or have disappeared. Just as publishers try to capture more value by selling direct, retailers have been investigating their own publishing operations. The US bookstore Barnes & Noble has done this for a number of years, joined by Amazon from 2009 with a series of imprints.

The sale of ebooks lowers the risk from holding printed stock, and on the face of it margins should be higher without the physical cost of production. But publishers struggled to keep prices as high as they would like when the dominant player in the market, Amazon, was driving the market with competitive pricing. Authors also expect a higher rate of return, and consumers expect that digital products should be cheaper.

New business models abound and, for example, in the UK the publisher Unbound was set up in 2011 around the crowdfunding of new projects. Authors appeal directly to their readers to secure the necessary financial support to go ahead and write and produce their books. 'Unbound puts the power of publishing in the hands of authors and readers. Authors pitch their book ideas directly to you. If you back a project before it reaches its funding target, you get your name printed in the back of every copy and immediate behind-the-scenes access to the author's shed' (unbound.co.uk, accessed 26 June 2013).

Financial performance

From a financial viewpoint, a publisher strives to increase the rate of return on the company's capital, and to improve the profit margin to finance expansion and pay a dividend to the owners. The management aims to:

■   Maximize the income and minimize the production costs.

- Contain royalty rates while keeping competitive. In consumer book publishing it is important to monitor the amount of money and level of risk tied up in authors' advances.
- Control stock levels by selling a high proportion of the print stock on publication or soon after, and storing only adequate stock of backlist titles. Digital printing has changed the management of the backlist.
- Monitor pricing on a regular basis and for key titles almost on a real-time basis for ebooks.
- Re-price backlist titles regularly in line with current prices and exchange rates.
- Exercise tight control over the firm's overheads (for example, staff and office costs) while maintaining effective management. If profits fall, overheads have to be reduced and output increased.
- Take all available credit from suppliers, whether paying printers after a certain period or deferring royalty payments to authors.
- Keep discounts as low as possible and minimize returns while maintaining stock levels in retail outlets.
- Collect debts quickly from customers.
- Obtain the best terms from capital providers such as banks.
- Invest in innovation including the establishment of communities around content, new digital products and services, and experimentation around business models.
- Invest in fixed assets (such as IT systems) only if a favourable return can be shown in comparison with subcontracting or leasing. In the longer term the company will look to minimize any investment in the warehousing of physical products.
- Sell off underused or underperforming assets, whether buildings or publishing lists.
- Buy complementary (or competing) businesses at home and abroad.
- Forecast regularly the cashflow (the flow of money payments to, from, or within the firm) over time; even a profitable publisher can exceed its borrowing requirement before profits are earned and run the risk of going bust.

It is estimated that there are over 130 m titles in print around the world

One key aspect is the compilation of a financial plan showing a profit target for the medium term (say three years). It is built up partly from the historic costs of running the business and from forecasts – the estimated costs of producing the new titles and the revenue from estimated sales of new and backlist titles made through various channels at home and abroad. Departmental managers will prepare budgets for carrying out their activities. Actual performance can be compared with the plan at monthly intervals, and with the performance of the previous year; and the plan itself is updated. Some publishers compile rolling plans for up to five years ahead. The annual profit and loss statement of a publisher reveals the financial performance of the business as a whole. This will differ according to the publisher and the publishing sector. The following figures give an impression.

The total sales revenue is the sum of money the publisher receives from home and export sales after discounts have been deducted from the recommended prices. Taking the revenue as 100 per cent and subtracting from that the production costs of the books (around 20 per cent, plus or minus 5 per cent) plus the write-off of stock unsold (2–10 per cent) and the cost of royalties (10–15 per cent), leaves the publisher with a gross margin of 50 to 60 per cent. High sales of ebooks for a title will reduce the physical cost of production but such sales attract VAT in the UK at a similar level (20 per cent); also the market rate for royalties is 25 per cent to the author. There continue to be editorial and design costs whatever the format. A consumer book publisher may suffer from the write-off of unrecoverable authors' advances, but it may benefit from greater rights sales income. From the gross margin, the publisher's overhead costs are deducted, and will roughly total 30–50 per cent (see Table 5.1). When deducted from the gross margin, this leaves the publisher with a net or operating profit (before interest charges on borrowing and tax are deducted) of 9–12 per cent (compare the accounts shown for Bloomsbury in Table 5.2). After interest and tax, a dividend may be paid to shareholders and the remaining profit re-invested in the business.

Table 5.1 Average overheads of publishers

Overhead costs	Proportion of sales revenue (%)
Editorial	5–7
Production and design	2–4
Marketing and sales staff	5–10
Advertising and promotion	3–6
Order processing and distribution	8–12
General and administrative expenses	7–12

Table 5.2 Bloomsbury Publishing accounts to 28 February 2013

	£000	Proportion of sales revenue (%)
Revenue	98,479	
Cost of sales	41,242	41.8
Gross profit	57,237	58.1
Marketing and distribution costs	12,733	12.9
Administrative expenses and other costs	34,748	35.2
Operating profit	9,756	9.9

Valuing a company

The worth of a publisher can be measured in terms of its physical assets – buildings and stock – but more importantly by the intellectual property it controls. Valuations of publishing companies – how much they are bought and sold for – tend to be based on the revenues of the companies and the sector in which they operate. This is partly because the balance sheets of companies, which show their assets, can be difficult to interpret. Debts owing to the company may include advance payments to authors which will never be earned out, and the value of stock may be inflated by books in the warehouse that will never be sold. Hidden liabilities could include an overseas distributor having the right to return tens of thousands of books for credit. Companies with interests in legal, STM and digital

Selling and valuing publishing assets

E★PERT

William Mitchell, Partner, Bertoli Mitchell LLP

Why are publishing assets sold? Possible triggers for sale include: retirement; or the business requires access to investment and/or skills from a larger organization, for example when a 'legacy' content business is converting to the digital landscape; or, in the case of large publishing organizations, when a strategic review has determined that parts of its publishing portfolio no longer fit with the areas in which it, as an organization, wishes to plant its flag in the long term.

How are publishing businesses sold? Most successful publishing sales are achieved through a discreet competitive process. An information memorandum (IM) is the bedrock of an effective competitive sale process, and must map the intellectual property rights being sold in detail, especially historical sales and margin data by product, likewise the status of the forward programme. The IM is distributed to interested parties who have signed non-disclosure agreements and who are set an 'offers date' by which to submit offers in writing. All prospective buyers must be marched to the same deadlines.

When, after negotiations, a preferred bidder emerges, that party may be granted an exclusivity period in which to complete its investigations and finalize contracts. From start to finish the sale process will typically take four to six months, or more. The process will often be run on behalf of the seller by a specialist advisory firm like Bertoli Mitchell LLP. Of course, not all publishing businesses are saleable and at any given point many will be worth more to hold than to sell.

How are publishing assets valued? The short, and ultimate answer is: 'by the buyer'. Publishing assets are only worth what the market will pay for them. So there is no science of valuation or such, although there are classic drivers of value, and there is a consensus on normal valuation ranges.

The principal driver of value is strategic fit. Buyers will pay a premium price for assets which fit exactly with their own strategic priorities, be they subject priorities (for example medicine), or capability priorities (for example educational assessment software), or be they geographical priorities (for example increased market penetration in BRIC geographies).

Intrinsic drivers of value at the level of publishing sectors include: quality and reliability of revenue streams, patterns of cash flow, typical profitability, market growth potential. Valuations at the level of individual companies will vary according, *inter alia*, to market position, scale (larger businesses command higher multiples), revenue mix, forward pipeline and ownership of intellectual property.

The drivers referred to above are reflected in the different 'sales multiples' paid for assets in different publishing sectors – the sales multiple being what buyers have typically paid to buy a pound (£) of sales in companies they have purchased (e.g. £1.5 m paid for a company with £1 m sales represents a sales multiple of 1.5). Typical ranges by sectors are: consumer publishing 0.5 to 1 × sales; educational and academic publishing 1 to 3 × sales; professional publishing 2 to 5 × sales.

publishing are likely to be bought for a higher multiple of sales than consumer companies. This reflects the varying degree of control over intellectual property – higher in legal and STM publishing with, for example, the easier acquisition of world and subsidiary rights – and the lower levels of risk. There tend also to be higher levels of profitability.

Publishers create value through innovation, coming up with new ideas and variations on existing titles. Larger publishers strive to maintain innovation with the maintenance of small imprints with their own distinctive profile. Smaller publishers may be more likely to try out new authors and formats. Innovation is encouraged by the system of copyright, which creates value in intellectual property and provides a mechanism to protect that value. Reflected in a company's value are the intangible assets, such as their publishing licences and goodwill. Goodwill is the term for those elements which contribute to the company's competitive advantage, including its brand, publishing relationships and employees. It is given a monetary value if the company is taken over when there is an opportunity to value the worth of the company over and above the net assets shown on the balance sheet. The goodwill then appears on the balance sheet of the acquiring company. The publisher's licences and brand will be protected by intellectual property rights.

INTELLECTUAL PROPERTY AND PROTECTING VALUE

The intellectual property (IP) owned or controlled by a publisher includes its copyrights and licences. The publisher may own some copyrights outright, for example in the case of reference works, or have acquired licences from their authors. Other IP may be brands which could be registered as trademarks. Trademarks can cover words, logos, or pictures used as identifiers for goods and services, and must be renewed every 10 years in order for them to stay in force. Examples of trademarks are Penguin and the Penguin logo, Beatrix Potter characters such as Peter Rabbit, and Apple's iBook.

Although copyrights need not be registered in the UK, trademarks need to be protected by registration

Copyright

It is important to examine on what basis publishers control their intellectual property. Book publishing today rests on copyright. In general terms, this is a form of protection, giving authors and other creative artists legal ownership of their work – that is, it establishes their work as their personal, exclusive property; and because it is their property they have the absolute right to sell or license it to others. It is these exclusive rights that make an author's works attractive to publishers. What the publisher wants from authors is the sole, exclusive right to publish their work and sell it as widely as possible. Without copyright protection, authors would not be able to grant this exclusive right and could not demand payment for their efforts; and publishers would not risk issuing a book which, if successful, could be instantly copied or plundered by competitors. Copyright stimulates innovation in a market economy, protects the author's reputation and is the common foundation for publishing and the other cultural industries.

For copyright to subsist in a literary work (one which is written, spoken or sung) it must be 'original'. Some effort, skill or judgement needs to have been

There is no copyright in ideas, or in the title of a work

exercised to attract copyright protection, and it must be recorded in writing or otherwise. Copyright exists in the concrete form of expression, the arrangement of the words, and protection in the UK endures for the author's life plus 70 years from the year end of the author's death. After that period the work enters the public domain. If, for example, an author died on 11 January 1928, their work came out of copyright on 31 December 1998. This is the case with the novelist Thomas Hardy. The previous period of protection was 50 years and under that system the works of Hardy had already come into the public domain at the end of 1978. When, in 1995, following an EU directive, the period in the UK was increased to 70 years, Hardy came briefly back into copyright until the end of 1998 and publishers of new editions of his work had to pay royalties to his estate. Publishers compete fiercely on the pricing of public domain classics, such as Jane Austen, on which no royalties need be paid, and face competition from ebooks which are free to download. The term of copyright in the European Union and the USA is also 70 years. In France there is a special 30-year extension to this term for authors considered to have died for their country – 'mort pour la France': such writers include Irène Némirovsky (1903–42) and Antoine de Saint-Exupéry (1900–44).

Works created by employees in working hours – and covered, as a further safeguard, by their terms and conditions of service – are the copyright of the employer. Publishers who commission freelance editors, technical illustrators, indexers and developers ensure that copyright is assigned in writing to the publisher through an agreement. The publisher's typographical layout of the page is the copyright of the publisher and that lasts for 25 years from publication. Copyright in an index belongs to the compiler, unless assigned to the publisher; copyright in a translation belongs to the translator. Copyright exists in compilations, such as databases, provided that there is an adequate degree of originality in the selection and arrangement of the information.

Moral rights

The moral right of paternity must be asserted by the author

Under the 1988 Copyright, Designs and Patents Act, authors were given additional statutory rights, called moral rights. Deriving from the practice in mainland Europe, and in particular the *droit moral* in France, they are as follows:

Paternity

First, there is the moral right of paternity, which gives the author the right to be credited as the author of the work. This must be asserted by the author before it can be enforced. Often this can be seen on the title verso of a book – the reverse of the title page: 'The right of Giles Clark and Angus Phillips to be identified as the Authors of this Work has been asserted by them in accordance with the Copyright, Designs and Patents Act 1988.'

Integrity

Second is the right of integrity, which is the author's right to be protected from editorial distortion of the work. An author who argues that such distortion has occurred may be asked to give proof of financial loss, and as Mira T. Sundara

Rajan says, 'The case of an author whose artistic integrity is damaged, but whose work actually sells better because of intervention – for example, the addition of erotic scenes to bring excitement to a film adaptation of a novel – might have little hope of success' (page 35).

False attribution

Third is the right to prevent false attribution, which prevents an author from being credited with something that they did not write.

Privacy

A final right gives privacy to individuals in the case of photographs they have commissioned, perhaps for a wedding, from a photographer who owns the copyright.

Moral rights are likely to grow in importance in an era of digital publication, which frequently involves substantial adaptation of the work of authors and illustrators. Manipulation of authors' works is relatively straightforward, increasing the risk of non-attribution and of plagiarism. Moral rights can be waived by an author, and if a publisher owns the copyright in a book, it will probably want to ensure that such a waiver is contained in the contract. The moral rights of paternity and integrity have the same duration as copyright; the right to prevent false attribution lasts for life plus 20 years.

Copyright or licence?

Should a publisher be content to negotiate a licence with an author, or should it take outright the copyright? Theoretically the latter will give it more control over the work. Some journal publishers, for example, still take the copyright in all the articles that they publish. But increasingly book publishers regard a licence as giving them the necessary protection that they require. The licence is a grant by the author of the rights to publish and sell a work, and also the right to stop others from copying the work. If a licence is in place which grants the publisher all the necessary rights, there is usually no need to request that the copyright is assigned by the author. Hugh Jones and Christopher Benson write:

> a sole and exclusive publishing licence, drafted in wide terms if necessary (including a very robust clause allowing the publisher to take legal action if necessary), will probably meet most publishers' needs. It has been likened by a number of commentators to taking a lease of a house rather than buying the freehold – a long lease for all practical purposes will probably be just as valuable. (Jones and Benson, page 76)

The civil law protects copyright holders in the UK, and cases can be brought by them or the exclusive licence holder against individuals or institutions who copy texts without the necessary permission. Under a set of international treaties and conventions, UK copyright works are also protected around the world. These

The copyright symbol © is required under the Universal Copyright Convention

include the Berne Convention, which dates from 1886, and the WIPO Copyright Treaty signed in 1996. Under the Universal Copyright Convention (1952), all copies of a book should carry a copyright notice, and again on the title verso you will find the standard wording – © Giles Clark and Angus Phillips 2014. The date given is the year of publication, and a new edition attracts a new date in the copyright line. Copyright can be held jointly, as is the case with the present book.

Permissions

An author seeking to quote from a work by another author should seek permission from the publisher of the work, which usually holds the anthology and quotation rights on behalf of the author. It is not necessary to ask for permission if the quotation is used for 'criticism or review', allowable as 'fair dealing' under the 1988 Copyright, Designs and Patents Act. The Society of Authors and The Publishers Association have stated that they would usually regard as 'fair dealing' the use of:

■ a single extract of up to 400 words,
■ a series of extracts (of which none exceeds 300 words) to a total of 800 words from a prose work, or
■ a series of extracts to a total of 40 lines from a poem, provided that this did not exceed a quarter of the poem.

The words must be quoted in the context of 'criticism or review' (societyofauthors. net, accessed 26 June 2013).

In order to use an illustration contained in another book, permission should be sought from the publisher or original source of the illustration (this could be a library or gallery). Obtaining permission to use material from websites is fraught with difficulty, since there may not be a satisfactory paper trail to prove who owns the original copyright.

Digital rights management

Digitization has reduced the costs of copying and distribution to next to nothing. Yet the production of ideas and information by authors and publishers is expensive in time and money. Publishers earn their living from selling ideas and information and make efforts to protect it from illicit copying. They are fearful that their work will escape into the wild on the internet from which they receive no payment. The technical means of controlling usage is broadly referred to as digital rights management (DRM), and it 'might be defined as a set of standards and technologies that allow digital content to be distributed whilst also being protected, managed and tracked by content providers' (Owen, 6th edition, page 334).

The software for DRM is problematic. DRM systems are frequently broken into by hackers – not least because of the weakness that each time a proprietary system gives someone a locked item, a secret hidden key is provided to unlock it. Hackers around the world work on discovering such secrets – they may then publish them on the internet for others to access the content. DRM can also be sidestepped by a user scanning a printed book and posting it for free on the internet. The most common forms of DRM for ebooks are those from Amazon, Apple and Adobe.

When a reader buys a printed book, under the 'first sale doctrine' there are few restrictions on its further uses.

> If you read a book, that act is not regulated by copyright law. If you resell a book, that act is not regulated . . . If you sleep on the book or use it to hold up a lamp or let your puppy chew it up, those acts are not regulated by copyright law, because those acts do not make a copy. (Lessig, page 141)

There can, however, be restrictions on the use of an ebook – the reader usually buys the book under a licence. By accessing the book over the internet, a copy is made and copyright law comes into the picture. There may be controls on the number of times the book can be read, whether it can be printed out, or on its transfer to other devices. Since the use by consumers of digital materials is defined by a licence, it may be sufficient in some cases for publishers to take the risk that they are sufficiently honest and trustworthy not to abuse their rights. Social DRM, employed for example by the Pottermore website, simply ensures that ebooks when sold are watermarked rather than subject to strict control. The watermarking allows users to be traced if they post up the books on pirate websites, and also for irresponsible fans to be named and shamed by fellow users. Academic publishers license materials to universities, under site licences via their libraries. The user group is clearly defined – staff and students using their institution's IP address, or users authenticated off-campus through the use of a password system. Authentication reassures publishers that any points of leakage outside the user group may be identified and halted, and helps universities to limit their liability in the case of defamation, obscenity or copyright infringement.

Future of copyright

Without the copyright regime, publishers would be unable to prevent works being copied at will. Books would be photocopied, printed and sold, or passed around in digital form for free, without a return for the copyright holder and their licensee. Publishers are naturally anxious about any threats to the stability of the copyright regime. They can see what has happened in the music industry, for example, and the tendency for music to be downloaded and shared for free, and have become concerned that a change in public attitudes could lead to a similar situation. Will consumers develop a similar attitude to the sharing of content, and how will authors and publishers receive a fair return?

Major digitization projects are carried out by commercial publishers, libraries, or technology companies such as Google. The latter has digitized out-of-copyright works in the collections of major institutions including the New York Public Library and the Bodleian Library in Oxford. Google Print has also digitized books in print from a variety of publishers, enabling searches within the titles. Links then offer ways of purchasing either the printed book or online access.

There are also authors who would like to see their work – text or pictures – more widely disseminated and feel that the present system of copyright does not adequately meet their needs. Self-publishing is relatively straightforward and the author may be looking to garner a wide readership rather than attempt to make their fortune. Founded in 2001, Creative Commons is an initiative to enable authors to offer their work on different terms to the usual publisher's licence. 'Every license helps creators — we call them licensors if they use our tools — retain copyright while allowing others to copy, distribute, and make some uses of their work — at least non-commercially' (creativecommons.org, accessed 26 June 2013). For example, a photographer may choose to publish their work with a Creative Commons licence that enables others to copy, distribute or display the photographs, provided that the work is attributed to them. The objective is for more people to have the opportunity to view their work.

The issue of an *orphan work* (a copyrighted work for which the owner cannot be traced and therefore contacted) came to prominence during Google's scanning of library books in the mid-1990s. An orphan work may have gone out of print but may still be in copyright. The problem of being unable to trace copyright holders hinders creativity, for example when an author wants to seek permission from a third party to use their text or illustrations in a new work but who faces an arduous detective trail in trying to find the owner. Google proposed to establish a 'rights registry' to expedite and automate the permission process. More recently, governments in North America and Europe are focusing on the issue which becomes progressively more important for all of the creative industries in a digital world. There is a volume of text or images available on the web for which the ownership and rights are uncertain or unknown, and this creates an explosive growth in new digital orphans.

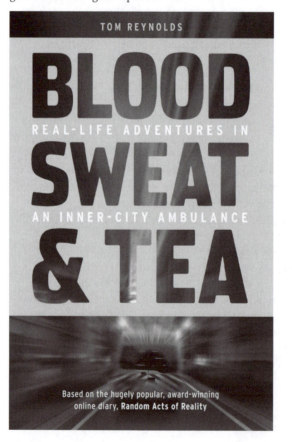

Published by the Friday Project under a Creative Commons licence, *Blood, Sweat and Tea* by Tom Reynolds was given away free online and as an ebook. It went on to sell 300,000 print copies and inspired the TV series *Sirens*

In the area of journals publishing, the open access movement has gathered pace, which argues that publicly funded research, notably in the area of science and medicine, should be freely available. All mainstream publishers now offer an open access option for authors. If the author, their institution or, more usually, the research body that funded the research, provides payment, the article will be freely available from first publication. Open access has also stimulated self-archiving. Journal publishers will usually allow an author to self-archive the preprint of an article on their homepage – the preprint is the unpublished version of the article before it is refereed – and sometimes the final accepted version (after peer review) in their institutional repository. Yet even open content models rely upon the retention of copyright. The initial decision to release open content licences is made by the copyright holder.

An institutional repository is a digital collection of research papers by members of an institution

Digital publishing has added considerable uncertainty as to who controls intellectual property and its financial returns. It is in the interest of a large technology player such as Google that as much content as possible is freely available – their business model is built primarily around the sale of ads. For publishers the key is to build a direct relationship with their end-users, so that they are not solely reliant on intermediaries such as Amazon for their sales income. Fearful of piracy, they are reluctant to relinquish DRM controls but at the same time they do need to ensure that content is readily available through legitimate channels, and that ownership is clearly identifiable to potential licensees.

Sources

Eric de Bellaigue, *British Book Publishing as a Business since the 1960s*, British Library Publishing, 2004.

Michael Bhaskar, *The Content Machine: Towards a theory of publishing from the printing press to the digital network*, Anthem Press, 2013.

Bill Cope and Angus Phillips (eds), *The Future of the Book in the Digital Age*, Chandos, 2006.

Hugh Jones and Christopher Benson, *Publishing Law*, 4th edition, Routledge, 2011.

Andrew Keen, *The Cult of the Amateur*, Nicholas Brealey, 2007.

Lawrence Lessig, *Free Culture*, Penguin, 2004.

Hugh McGuire and Brian O'Leary (eds), *Book: A futurist's manifesto*, O'Reilly Media, 2012.

Nicholas Negroponte, *Being Digital*, Hodder and Stoughton, 1995.

Tim O'Reilly, 'What is Web 2.0?', 30 September 2005, www.oreillynet.com, accessed 28 June 2013.

Tim O'Reilly, 'The Future of Digital Distribution and Ebook Marketing', Tools of Change (TOC), 2010.

Lynette Owen, *Selling Rights*, 7th edition, Routledge, 2014.

Angus Phillips, 'Does the Book Have a Future?', in Simon Eliot and Jonathan Rose (eds), *A Companion to the History of the Book*, Blackwell, 2007.

Angus Phillips, *Turning the Page: The evolution of the book*, Routledge, 2014.

Michael E. Porter, *Competitive Advantage: Creating and sustaining superior performance*, Free Press, 1985.

Michael E. Porter, 'Strategy and the Internet', *Harvard Business Review*, March 2001, pages 63–78.

Mira T. Sundara Rajan, *Moral Rights*, OUP, 2011.

Simon Stokes, *Digital Copyright: Law and practice*, Hart Publishing, 2013.

John B. Thompson, *Books in the Digital Age*, Polity Press, 2005.

John B. Thompson, *Merchants of Culture*, Polity Press, 2012.

Web resources

www.copyrighthub.co.uk Copyright Hub - information about copyright in the UK.

www.creativecommons.org Creative Commons.

www.ipo.gov.uk UK Intellectual Property Office.

www.jisc.ac.uk Jisc – the website provides a briefing paper on open access.

CHAPTER 6

The author

Authors have different motivations for writing, according to the type of book and the individual. Writers of poetry and fiction may be driven to write by an inner force – they just have to write. Academics have to be published in order to advance their career. Professional authors may earn their living from their books, and writing is what they do. The now various routes for self-publishing add a different dimension to authorship, and anyone can post an ebook on Amazon in the hopes of gaining a wide audience, and perhaps attract the interest of a publisher.

The reality for many authors is that the financial returns are low. A survey published in 2007 by the Authors' Licensing and Collecting Society revealed that the average earnings for authors in the UK were £16,531 and the median (or typical) earnings were only £4,000. For those who are successful, the rewards can be very high – the top 10 per cent of authors earned more than 50 per cent of the total income earned by authors – but only 20 per cent of those surveyed earned all their income from writing.

Authors such as Dan Brown are highly organized in their approach. In his witness statement for the 2006 case in the High Court regarding *The Da Vinci Code*, he said:

> Writing is a discipline, much like playing a musical instrument; it requires constant practice and honing of skills. For this reason, I write seven days a week. So, my routine begins at around 4 am every morning, when there are no distractions. By making writing my first order of business every day, I am giving it enormous symbolic importance in my life, which helps keep me motivated. If I'm not at my desk by sunrise, I feel like I'm missing my most productive hours. In addition to starting early, I keep an antique hour glass on my desk and every hour break briefly to do push-ups, sit-ups, and some quick stretches. I find this helps keep the blood (and ideas) flowing. (*The Bookseller*, 31 March 2006)

The Da Vinci Code sold around 40 million copies in its first year, and has made Dan Brown a fortune. Yet for many authors, the income earned is of secondary importance, and the pleasure of seeing their work published is a reward in itself. There is no shortage of authors who would like to be published, and in fact there is an oversupply. How then do authors set about getting published? The

The novelist Jeanette Winterson says about writing: 'It is what I'm for'

'When I finished my first novel, I put it into a brown envelope and sent it to Weidenfeld & Nicolson. Now, I don't imagine they'd even look at it.'
Margaret Drabble (*Guardian*, 6 November 2013)

traditional method was to send your manuscript to a number of publishers, and hope that it caught the eye of the relevant editor.

After all, J. K. Rowling was rejected by a number of publishers before being picked up by Bloomsbury. What is known as the slush pile is a system seldom operated by publishers anymore, and trade publishers will rely on agents to supply them with proposals. Authors look to be signed up by an agent first and many publishers do not accept unsolicited material. Agents can receive hundreds of submissions each month and the chances of being taken on are slim, but first-time authors are still discovered through this route. In recent years agents have relied more on personal contacts and recommendations, and many are also closed to receiving unsolicited typescripts. The slush pile has been moved online, with authors posting their work on community sites for writers such as Wattpad. There they can engage directly with readers and gain feedback:

> Wattpad is the world's largest community for discovering and sharing stories. It's a new form of entertainment connecting readers and writers through storytelling, and best of all, it's entirely free. With thousands of new stories added every day, an incredibly active community of readers, and the ability to read on your computer, phone, or tablet, Wattpad is the only place that offers a truly social, and entirely mobile reading experience. (wattpad.com, accessed 29 June 2013)

The 17-year-old UK novelist Beth Reekles posted her novel *The Kissing Booth* on Wattpad, chapter by chapter, and started to gauge her popularity when she posted a cliffhanger, which led to hundreds of emails from readers.

In between homework assignments, Beth Reekles wrote a novel, *The Kissing Booth*, which centers on a never-been-kissed teenager who comes face-to-face with her secret crush while running a kissing booth for her school carnival. She posted the novel on self-publishing Web site Wattpad, and it caught the attention of Lauren Buckland, senior editor at Random House Children's Publishing UK. (*Publishers Weekly*, 9 April 2013)

The book was taken on by Random House and published (first as an ebook) in 2012.

When celebrities or sports stars come to write their memoirs, they may require the services of ghost writers to turn their words or thoughts into a polished book. Sometimes the writer will remain anonymous, but since such a working relationship has become quite usual their name may even appear on the title page. Most academic theses that are sent direct to editors are unpublishable as they stand, but a fraction can be turned into monographs. It is very unlikely that an unsolicited textbook manuscript would have the right structure to be commercial, but occasionally unsolicited ideas can be developed. In areas such as non-fiction and textbook publishing, publishers will want to see a proposal from the author as the first stage. This is an outline of the proposed book, which sets out the content and gives the publisher a sense of the book's commercial potential. The advantage of this system is that the author need not take the risk of writing the whole book until they have a contract in place.

Donna Tartt says, 'The immediacy of discovery, that's what's interesting to me. Every book is a different country' (*Sunday Times*, 13 October 2013)

Book proposal

The following are the main elements of a book proposal.

Title

This must be eye-catching and can be crucial to the book's success.

Introduction

A summary of the idea for the book and its likely market.

Contents

An outline of the structure of the book, fleshed out to show what each chapter will cover.

Readership and market

Who will buy the book and what is the market? The danger here is to rely on the mythical general reader, and avoid the difficult task of saying who is likely to need, or be interested, in the title. (An equivalent danger is trying to reach too many markets with one book.) For a book on canoes, will it help someone paddle one, or build one? What is the readership for a business textbook – first-year undergraduate or graduate students?

Competition

Successful authors know the market for which they are writing – not just the readership but also competing titles. How will the book differ and improve upon the titles presently available? Existing titles on the same subject may not be a disadvantage, since they can help prove there is a market. Indirect competition could include content on the web, not just published titles.

Marketing ideas

How can the book be marketed? Ideas can include forthcoming events or anniversaries, hooks to arouse media interest, public appearances and connections with influential people.

Author details

Author to Consumer (A2C) marketing is growing in importance

Required are biographical details of the author with relevant information such as previous publications. For non-fiction books it is important for the author to prove their credentials as an expert in the subject area of the book. Publishers may be interested in whether the author is promotable to the media, for example in the case of a first-time novelist. An author can also display a talent for self-promotion, and they are often expected to have their own website, blog, or Twitter account. This is the cause of some disillusion to the writer Jonathan Franzen, who said:

> what happens to the people who became writers because yakking and tweeting and bragging felt to them like intolerably shallow forms of social engagement? What happens to the people who want to communicate in depth, individual to individual, in the quiet and permanence of the printed word, and who were shaped by their love of writers who wrote when publication still assured some kind of quality control and literary reputations were more than a matter of self-promotional decibel levels? (*Guardian*, 13 September 2013)

Additional material may also be attached, such as sample sections or chapters. There should be no spelling or grammatical mistakes in the sample material.

Once completed by the author, the proposal is sent to the relevant in-house editor. An agent may also invest a lot of time in rewriting the proposal to raise its chances of success. If there is interest from the publisher, suggestions for changes may be made before the proposal is circulated to key decision-makers in sales and marketing. The final decision on a proposal is taken at an editorial meeting attended by the relevant staff.

STARTING OUT AND SELF-PUBLISHING

It is tough for authors to get their work published. It is common for authors to begin their published career with smaller publishing houses, which may be less conservative in their approach to commissioning titles. The difficulty for smaller houses is that they may not have the funds to keep authors who have become successful.

There are trends in publishing which may affect what types of books publishers would like to acquire. In 2012 the top categories amongst the bestsellers were romance and sagas (boosted by the huge success of the *Fifty Shades of Grey* trilogy) followed by children's fiction, young adult fiction and crime. Arthur Klebanoff comments that the 'commercial prospects for writers of non-fiction are heavily influenced by choice of subject matter and sometimes by fickle public response to subject matter' (page 91). Sales of ebooks have been dominated by genre fiction, and digital-only imprints have concentrated on areas such as sci-fi, fantasy, crime and romance. Liate Stehlik, a publisher at HarperCollins in New York, said that ebooks are the optimal format

> for people who want to read a lot of books, quickly and frequently. Digital has replaced the paperback, certainly the paperback originals. I think the audience that gravitated to ebooks first really was that voracious reader, reading for entertainment, reading multiple books in a month across multiple genres. (*Wired*, 26 June 2013)

First-time novelists can be offered a two- or three-book deal, which ensures that they are already signed up should their first book prove to be a winner. The advance paid can also be set against all of the books. If an author does hit the big time straight away, this can prove to be a mixed blessing, increasing the pressure on them to deliver another bestseller. Also it is possible they are trapped in their agreement with a smaller publisher, unable to accept the higher terms being offered to move publisher. A midlist author with several modestly successful titles in print in turn runs the risk that they are dropped by their agent or publisher in favour of new authors, perhaps seen as more 'promotable' (viewed by some to mean young and good looking). Francesca Simon describes how it took some time before her Horrid Henry children's books became successful: 'It wasn't until *Horrid Henry's Nits* was published, three years on, that the books started to attract attention. Nowadays, if authors haven't got noticed after two books, they are cast adrift. So had I begun it 10 years later, Horrid Henry would never have had a chance' (*Guardian*, 17 June 2013).

Publishers may look to pick up titles that have originated in blogs or from the large number of creative writing courses that are now available. Blogs offer publishers market testing as to which writers can attract and keep an audience. Christian Lander started a blog, 'Stuff White People Like', in 2008 and within three months he had a book deal with Random House. His blog satirizes the interest of left-leaning, city-dwelling white folk (stuffwhitepeoplelike.com). The blurb for the book categorizes them as follows: 'They love nothing better than sipping free-trade gourmet coffee, leafing through the Sunday *New York Times*, and listening to David Sedaris on NPR [National Public Radio] (ideally all at the same time). Apple products, indie music, food co-ops, and vintage T-shirts make them weak in the knees.'

Creative writing courses have proliferated in the USA and the UK and famously Ian McEwan was the first writer on the MA course at the University of East Anglia, run by Malcolm Bradbury and Angus Wilson. Marina Lewycka's first novel, *A Short History of Tractors in Ukrainian* (2005), was picked up by an agent

George R.R. Martin originally conceived *A Song of Ice and Fire* as a trilogy: 'At the time, in the mid-nineties, fantasy was dominated by trilogies'

In 2010 there were around 150 m blogs worldwide

when she joined the course at Sheffield Hallam University, and was published in 2005 when she was 58. The poet and novelist Andrew Motion is Professor of Creative Writing at Royal Holloway, University of London:

> There was a time when creative writing courses were seen on a par with athletes taking steroids, as if it somehow gave them an unfair advantage. There was this idea that creative writing was something that had to take place in a garret. But aspiring dancers go to the Royal Ballet School, and actors to Rada – why should writing be any different? (*Guardian*, 10 May 2011)

New consultancies have developed in the UK offering writers' services. For a fee, the company offers to give the author an assessment of their manuscript, both the writing and the likely market, and editorial services including rewriting of proposals or full works. Publishers have also developed a range of services including creative writing workshops and self-publishing operations. Novelists such as S. J. Watson and Rachel Joyce are alumni of the Faber Academy, which offers courses for aspiring writers.

Self-publishing has left behind any stigma of vanity publishing – it is inexpensive on the web and cheap in print form. It can take place directly by the author or through a specialized company offering a service. Ambitious authors can take to sites such as Kickstarter to crowdfund a multimedia writing project. As well as posting work on community sites, writers can publish their book as an ebook on Amazon or other platform such as Smashwords. Starting from the Word file, an author can make their book available in a very short space of time. Patrick Barkham wrote that 'It has never been easier to publish your own book. Traditional publishers may take a year to turn your manuscript into print on a page but you can get your own ebook on sale around the world in about four minutes' (*Guardian*, 6 June 2012). A self-published author typically receives a 70 per cent share on ebook sales, whereas through a publisher would receive 25 per cent. However, self-publishing authors have to bear at their risk and expense all the costs, such as editing, cover design, marketing and project management. The chances of bestsellerdom remain slim: most self-published authors sell fewer than 100 or 150 copies (*New York Times*, 15 August 2012). But the success stories are there. In 2012 fifteen of the top one hundred bestselling Kindle titles in the UK were self-published, twelve self-published authors sold more than 100,000 copies, and fifty authors earned at least £50,000 from their self-published books (*Forbes*, 14 January 2013).

The internet has enabled many kinds of self-publishing. For example, in the area of fan fiction – new works written by fans of original fiction – there are now hundreds of thousands of stories available online based on the characters from the Harry Potter books. For print publishing, the growth of print on demand using digital printing means that print runs can be as low as a few or single copies. Companies such as CreateSpace (owned by Amazon), AuthorHouse (owned by Penguin) and Lulu offer authors a low-cost route to publication. Only when a book is ordered from Lulu's website is it then printed and sent to the purchaser. The company was founded by the digital entrepreneur, Bob Young, who saw the need for a way to help authors publish niche items such as poetry or technical manuals. However, self-published authors usually find that booksellers will not stock their print titles.

In 2011 over 235,000 titles were self-published in the USA

AGENTS

Literary agents, now called authors' agents (reflecting the broad range of writers they represent), are mostly located in London or New York, giving them close proximity to their main customers: fiction and non-fiction editors, mainly in adult but also in children's book publishers and other media industries. Their business is selling and licensing rights to a variety of media (not just book publishers) at home and abroad on behalf of their client authors with whom they have a contract on each book for the full term of copyright. Agents receive a commission on authors' earnings, typically 15 per cent on earnings from home sales but rising to 20 per cent on deals made abroad. The commission on film and TV deals tends to be from 15 to 20 per cent. The prevalence, power and influence of agents are very much a feature of the Anglo-American media worlds. In mainland Europe and elsewhere there are still few agents, although the numbers are growing. There are also 'sub-agents' of English language agents or publishers – not of local authors – who may earn half of the 20 per cent commission received by the UK agent. Some Anglo-American agents sell directly into foreign language markets. There are also literary scouts, who tip off agents and publishers about new authors – or established authors in other territories – in return for a fee. Scouts are sometimes described as the 'black ops' of the book business (*Publishing Perspectives*, 13 February 2012).

Agents operate in an increasingly polarized market in which a small number of top-selling authors secure advances against royalties of more than £100,000, compared to the majority of authors receiving advances below £10,000. An agent may spend equal amounts of time on both types of author, but with a very different financial return. For example, if an agent secures an advance of £6,000 and charges 15 per cent commission, their share is just £900.

Agents represent many of the established professional writers: those who derive much of their income from writing. While some agents are prepared to review unsolicited manuscripts from aspiring novelists for which they may charge a reading fee, others discourage this practice and take on new clients only on personal recommendations from credited sources, such as media contacts and their other clients. Agents manage lists of authors and taking on a new writer may mean dropping an established client. Rarely is it worthwhile for an agent to represent academics unless their work appeals to a wide readership. Authors can make multiple submissions – to several agents at once – but this method should be used with caution. Andrew Lownie offers this advice:

> Agents understand that authors need to make multiple submissions to agencies but dislike 'beauty parades'. It is not flattering nor encouraging to be told one is simply one of a hundred approaches. Time is limited and if one suspects the author may go elsewhere then one simply says no at the beginning. Keep quiet about multiple submissions and only send a few at a time so one can adapt the submission in the light of responses. (andrewlownie.co.uk, accessed 29 June 2013)

Once an agent has taken on an author, it is their job to pitch the book to the right editor in the most suitable publishing house. The literary publishing house Jonathan Cape was rarely offered more commercial books, and in his memoir *Publisher*, Tom Maschler recalls being sent the manuscript for *Not a Penny More, Not a Penny Less* by the literary agent Deborah Owen. The author, unknown at the time, was Jeffrey Archer.

> She did not actually say it was a first submission but, in the manner of certain agents content to mislead, this was the implication. The aspect of Archer's book which especially intrigued me was that he himself had been involved in a con and had lost a great deal of money, both his own and others'. And now he had written a thriller about a man similar to himself, and furthermore was doing so in order to earn a large sum so that the money could be repaid . . . I found the conceit intriguing, and although the style was indifferent, decided to offer a contract. I must admit I was motivated, in part, by the feeling that Jeffrey was so obviously ambitious that he would be likely to succeed in almost anything to which he put his mind. (page 200)

In 2012 Neil Gaiman signed a five-book deal to write children's books for HarperCollins

An agent manages a writer's career primarily from a commercial viewpoint, for example by placing the author's work with the right publisher or fuelling competition between publishers (on major books by holding auctions); negotiating deals to secure the best terms; by submitting their own contracts to licensors weighted in the authors' favour; checking or querying both publishers' advance payments against royalties, and royalty statements, and chasing debts.

The example of the author–publisher contract summarized in Chapter 8, and weighted in the publisher's favour, shows the author granting various world rights to the publisher. Because most authors are unable to market the rights in their work worldwide they mainly allow publishers to do so on their behalf. But an agent representing an author may limit the rights granted to a publisher, and their territorial extent, and license the rights retained on behalf of the author to other firms at home and abroad. They do this both to maximize the author's income but also in order to ensure a range of advocates for the author's work. For instance, the UK publisher's licence may apply to the English language only, and the territory (the countries) in which it has the exclusive right to publish (for example the Commonwealth and Europe) are listed, as well as those from which it could be excluded (for example the USA, including/excluding Canada). An agent could then license the book in the English language to a US publisher directly. A UK publisher, within its exclusive territory, could for instance be granted the following rights: the right to publish in hardback, paperback and ebook; and to license to others – book club, reprints, second and subsequent serial (for example extracts appearing in newspapers after the book's publication), quotation and anthology, mechanical and reproduction, broadcast reading rights, etc. An agent would then retain, for example, foreign language translation, first serial rights (extracts appearing before book publication thereby giving a newspaper a scoop), stage/ radio/television/film dramatization, games, merchandising, audio and other electronic rights.

However, there is no clear-cut division of rights or territories covered – each book differs. A publisher which has the idea for the book and contributes much editorial and design effort, or which is investing a large amount, for instance in a new writer on a two-book deal, has a strong case for acquiring wide territorial and language rights and the sharing of other rights. Publishers and packagers producing highly illustrated books for the international market need world rights in all languages. A wider set of rights is needed in order to recoup the initial high costs of these books. Book packagers and some highly illustrated book publishers often try to acquire the copyright outright from authors, enabling subsequent repackaging and recycling of authors' material without further payment or author contract.

UK agents retaining rights may sell them directly to US publishers or mainland European publishers, or use overseas agents with whom they have arrangements. Conversely, UK agents may represent well-known American authors on behalf of US agents, and sometimes US publishers. Agents also sell rights to a range of media, such as to film, TV and game companies. The selling of rights from a publisher's viewpoint is described in Chapter 12; an agent's work is similar except that an agent solely represents the author.

An additional dimension of agents' work falls under an editorial heading. For instance, agents send out synopses and manuscripts for external review, comment on manuscripts and advise authors on what they might write and the media they might write for, and develop ideas with them. Agents might be asked by publishers to supply authors; or they might initiate projects themselves for sale to publishers. In such ways, some agents increasingly take on roles which were once the province of publishers' editors. They can reflect trade realities back to authors, and arbitrate on arguments between their authors and publishers. They may help an author evaluate the publisher's marketing plan and offer support during the book's marketing, such as on the development of the cover. A further role may be to manage the author's backlist, which could include moving titles between publishers or negotiating ebook deals on older titles, or helping them to self-publish ebooks through a scheme such as White Glove from Amazon.

Agents provide a degree of continuity in the face of changing personnel amongst publishers and editors. However, some authors decide to change agents or are poached by them. This famously happened when Martin Amis changed agents to Andrew Wylie, known as the 'Jackal', when selling the rights in his novel *The Information* (1995). The former agent may continue to receive commission on contracts which they negotiated. The long-established agencies manage the literary estates of classic authors whose work remains in copyright.

Agents usually specialize in particular genres, such as adult fiction or non-fiction, or children's books. Some agents operate from home as single-person companies but the trend in recent years has been for agencies to get larger in order to meet the needs of authors with interests across a range of media, including public speaking appearances. They may be in competition against other kinds of agents who represent celebrities and sports stars. There are medium-sized agencies consisting of several agents plus assistants, and major agencies such as Curtis Brown and AP Watt. A large agency has a range of agents, each of whom specializes in broad areas of books or the selling of particular rights, though each agent usually looks after a particular primary group of authors. A specialism is film and TV rights, which involves selecting books for screen adaptation, and submitting them to producers. Some of their assistants show sufficient aptitude to develop their own list of authors, and new agents come from rights and editorial staff of the publishers. The larger agencies usually have agencies on both sides of the Atlantic, and good connections in Hollywood. There are also agencies which specialize in selling particular rights, such as translation, or film and television, on behalf of publishers and authors' agents. Sometimes a package of talent (book, star and director) is offered to a film studio.

Agents may fear disintermediation in an age of self-publishing, and this has led many to broaden their offer. They have followed publishers into the area of creative writing courses (for example Curtis Brown Creative), and some agents offer authors assistance or advice on digital marketing and self-publishing. Diversification has led some into film production or to co-invest in new digital projects. More controversially, others have established their own publishing imprints, leading to questions about a possible conflict of interest – can their advice to authors remain independent?

Now read this

Chapter 7, Commissioning.
Carole Blake, *From Pitch to Publication*, Pan, 1999.

Sources

ALCS, *What are words worth?*, March 2007.
Alison Baverstock, *The Naked Author: A guide to self-publishing*, A&C Black, 2011.
Julia Bell (ed.), *The Creative Writing Coursebook*, Macmillan, 2001.
Alexander Gordon Smith, *Writing Bestselling Children's Books*, Infinite Ideas, 2007.
Arthur M. Klebanoff, *The Agent*, Texere, 2002.
Mandy Little, 'Agenting Now', *Logos*, 22:2, 2011.
Tom Maschler, *Publisher*, Picador, 2005.
Rachael Stock, *The Insider's Guide to Getting Your Book Published*, 2nd edition, Trotman, 2011.

Published annually, the following guides contain useful information about publishers and literary agents:

UK

The Writers' and Artists' Yearbook, A&C Black.

USA

Children's Writer and Illustrator's Market, Writer's Digest.
Guide to Literary Agents, Writer's Digest.
Writer's Market, Writer's Digest.

Web resources

www.agentsassoc.co.uk Association of Authors' Agents.
www.andrewlownie.co.uk/fifteen_tips Useful tips on approaching agents, from Andrew Lownie.
www.authonomy.co.uk Writing community from HarperCollins.
www.bookcountry.com Writing community owned by Penguin.
www.fanfiction.net Thousands of examples of fan fiction, from *Harry Potter* to *The Lord of the Rings*.
www.freakonomics.com/blog/ An example of an author blog – for *Freakonomics* by Steven D. Levitt and Stephen J. Dubner.
www.jeanettewinterson.com This includes a Flash movie profiling her books.
www.publishingcrawl.com Blog from authors and industry professionals.
www.scbwi.org Society of Children's Book Writers and Illustrators.
www.societyofauthors.net Society of Authors.
www.writersandartists.co.uk 'The insider guide to the media'.
www.writersguild.org.uk The Writers' Guild of Great Britain.
www.youwriteon.com Peer review website sponsored by the Arts Council (UK).

Commissioning

The commissioning editor in a publishing house is responsible for coming up with marketable ideas and matching them to good authors. Working for the editorial director or publisher, who manages the editorial team, the editor is a key player in the publishing process. The more senior commissioning editors will take a strategic view of their list or imprint – called list-building – while junior editors may commission within a set brief.

Most editors remain unseen to readers, although the best editors across all types of publishing become known and respected by author communities in their particular fields. The role of editors, especially in consumer book publishing, has been impacted over generations by changes in the publishing environment. After the Second World War, editors had to adapt to the rise of authors' agents, and during the 1960s and 1970s to the impact of corporate accountants instilling financial controls. The rise of the bookselling chains in the 1980s and 1990s affected the types of books published and increased the power of sales and marketing over publishing decisions. The transition to digital publishing is having an enormous impact on editors across all fields of publishing: whether it is how they connect with authors and readers – for example, they may use social media to promote a book long before publication – or in the opportunities presented to publish books in a variety of formats. Digital publication also opens up an international audience, and editors need to be aware of what will work commercially around the world.

EDITORIAL COMMISSIONING

In consumer books, editors may cover different fiction genres or non-fiction areas, or specialize in hardback, paperback or digital lists, or children's/YA books. In educational, academic and STM houses, an editor may concentrate on several subjects, spanning a variety of academic levels and markets, or on product types, such as journals or textbooks. The style and identity of each list are the outcome of the editor's attitudes and effort.

A publisher depends on its editors to provide a sufficient flow of publishable projects to maintain the planned level of activity, for example 15 to 30 new books annually per editor, sometimes far fewer or three times more (depending on the market sector). Editors are assessed on the revenue they bring in or the overall profit, or contribution, of their books. They are seen by some publishers as business managers. Publishers have electronic systems in which editors record their output in terms of titles commissioned and forecast revenue. Editors out of tune with senior management regarding the character of the books, or who fail to produce a profit, leave voluntarily or are fired. The job is high risk and exposed, especially in consumer publishing.

With some exceptions, such as in the area of fiction, editors do not assess titles for publication on their thorough reading of complete manuscripts. Most books (including some fiction) are commissioned from authors on the basis of a proposal or specimen material, or are bought from agents. Editors generally do not edit the author's work in detail – that is done by freelancers or junior in-house staff. However, the senior editors may structurally edit by giving authors substantive criticisms and suggestions to help them produce their best work and to shape it for the intended market.

A distinction can be made between books *acquired* from agents or authors, where the idea often comes from the author, and those books that are *commissioned* from scratch by the editor. In the case of the latter books, the idea comes from the editor, who then goes in search of a suitable author. In textbook publishing, for example, this is the typical process for commissioning.

List-building

Publishing lists have their own identity and even within the larger groups there has been a conscious decision to keep separate imprints, each with their own distinctive flavour. In consumer publishing, imprints assist the trade to make sense of the large number of new and existing titles. Lists may be built around fiction genres and authors (in fiction, for example), subjects (the Yellow Jersey list of sports books), brands (for example the *Teach Yourself* and *For Dummies* titles span a large range of subjects), or design character (text only or highly illustrated). A set of titles that presents a defined genre or subject to a specific audience will have a greater value than one which simply aggregates disparate titles. Successful lists attract both authors and readers, and marketing a list is often more cost-effective with cross-marketing opportunities between titles. Lists are assets which can be bought and sold between publishers. List-builders may be asked to create a new imprint from scratch – reflecting changes in the market or strategic ambition – or to expand and strengthen an existing list. They will be on the look-out for new authors and projects, bearing in mind their list's identity, and focus, future direction and changing boundaries.

A programme of new editions is important in non-fiction and essential in textbook publishing, in order to refresh the list and keep titles up-to-date. Rebranding the list in new covers can also achieve this. A strategic view includes planning digital developments, for example in the areas of travel or textbook publishing.

Yellow Jersey Press, an imprint of Random House, was founded in 1998 by Rachel Cugnoni: 'Then followed the two most terrifying years of my life. I'd never commissioned a book before, let alone edited one, but somehow or other it was successful, and hallelujah'

Editorial contacts and market research

Good personal contacts are paramount for commissioning. An editor's in-house contacts are the members of senior management who accept or veto projects; the people who produce the books; and those who market and sell them. But more significant are the editor's external contacts. Prime sources of new books are the firm's previously published authors – they often have new ideas, or editors suggest ideas to them which are developed jointly.

Consumer books

In consumer book publishing, editors try to establish a mutual trust with authors and their agents (often over lunch). Agents may send fiction manuscripts or non-fiction proposals to selected editors one at a time, or sometimes conduct auctions amongst several publishers on highly saleable titles. Conversely an editor may contact an agent if they are pursuing one of their stable of authors, or have an idea and want the agent to find an author. Fiction editors may find new talent by spotting people who can write well, not necessarily fiction. They may be journalists or writers who are being published poorly or in an uncommercial medium, or who have generated a following for their blog. Editors may look to pick up authors from community sites or from the pool of self-published authors – the writers come already market tested. Celebrity authors may have to be wooed, sometimes in an unusual fashion:

> In the summer of 2010, the Oscar-winning actress and writer Emma Thompson received an intriguing package in the post. Inside was a small cardboard box with a half-eaten radish leaf and a letter from Peter Rabbit. The letter said Thompson's 'certain mischievous twinkle' in her eye made her the perfect person to write another adventure for the rabbit – a sequel to Beatrix Potter's beloved children's story. (*Daily Telegraph*, 5 September 2012)

Non-fiction editors develop contacts in a variety of fields, constantly keep an ear to the ground, notice people's enthusiasms, or review the media or blogosphere for topical subjects. They try to predict trends or events which will be in the public's interest, monitor successful book categories and authors by understanding what makes them good and why are they selling, and either avoid the competition, imitate it, or attempt to find unfilled niches by developing a new twist. They write speculatively to those who have the potential to capture the public's imagination – as do agents. They could be an up-and-coming celebrity or sports star, or an academic with a talent for popularization. Editors interested in television and film tie-ins keep abreast of new productions and monitor audience ratings.

Editors forge links with other firms from whom they might buy or sell to, for example at the Frankfurt Book Fair or, in the case of highly illustrated books, with packagers. UK editors are in contact with US editors and rights sales managers in order to gather market intelligence on new projects. Children's book editors have contact with agents, packagers, teachers and librarians, and if producing illustrated colour books know US and foreign language publishers with whom they might trade.

Nielsen BookScan provides the publishers with sales data on their own and competitors' titles

Working with authors

Simon Winder, Publishing Director at Penguin Press

EXPERT

Working with authors is a delicate and complex business. There is a constant need for the editor to balance between the needs of the business and the sensibilities of the author. Sometimes these are simply not reconcilable – there are deadlines to be met, jacket designs to be approved, ruthless decisions about acceptable length, costs and schedule. But it is too easy for the editor to slip into the role of an incompetent sort of slave-driver. Somehow corporate timetables and demands have to be balanced with a much more delicate and private world.

Authors who are driven along will, at a point invisible to the editor, suddenly realize that their relationship with their publisher is no longer enjoyable and, however regretfully, will simply run away, moving on to a fresh publisher. An author sometimes spends years working on a project, often in considerable isolation: the smallest thing can take on a huge importance, whether it is a specific phrase or a way of laying out the page or placing an image. The tension between an editor and an author is inevitable, but editors must not ever lose sight of the fact that one of the reasons they are being paid by their employer is to act as a reliable and truthful conduit for an author's feelings. If, for example, an author really hates a jacket design, the editor has to balance corporate needs (the deadline approaches, the art director is adamant) with an imperative to be the author's advocate. If an important manuscript is really not ready, then the editor has to act accordingly and break the bad news to colleagues and as early as possible.

All departments in publishing have important relationships which are *outside* the office and which are largely invisible to those they work with – Production with printers, Publicity with literary editors, Design with freelancers. For the editor those invisible relationships are with agents and their authors, and in the end those relationships are based around trust, reliability and availability. Other editors are always prowling around and each has nightmares about that party or dinner, to which they are not invited, at which a competitor successfully turns an agent's or author's head. A lot can be done to head this off just by remembering to keep in touch – even if a manuscript is not due to deliver for another three years, it is really easy with a short email or an occasional lunch or drink to remind a writer, who may be having a terrible time battling with an intractable script, that you are to hand and can be talked to, shouted at, cried over pretty much any time day or night. This thoughtfulness can feel like an intolerable burden, as it sits to one side from the day-to-day rain of emails and office deadlines and is invisible to colleagues, but for some writers it can be a real life-line – they have someone to talk to and a real incentive to hit often very difficult targets – any worthwhile book is a triumph of exertion and focus. If the editor has done a good job at this stage in the process, then the editor is also much more likely to be believed and trusted by the author when the final, tricky stages of deadlines, blurbs, jackets and so on march into view, making these a lot less grim, and making the slave-driver editor a thing of the past.

Non-consumer publishing

The educational, academic, STM and professional book editors publish for more defined markets about which more statistical information is available. This includes student enrolments, and the numbers of researchers or professionals working in specific fields. These editors, apart from reading school and college syllabuses, and the relevant journals, are engaged in direct market research and product development, especially in textbook publishing.

Quantitative research can include:

- student numbers,
- number of courses in a subject,
- sales figures of similar titles, and
- market share of the leading titles and publishers (indicated by data from Amazon).

Qualitative research covers:

- trends in the subject area,
- analysis of competing titles – their extent, features, authors, strengths and weaknesses,
- questionnaire results on products used and future needs,
- focus group data – from students, teachers or librarians, and
- visiting schools or universities.

The academic and STM publishers may retain for each discipline exclusive advisers who direct new writers to their publishers. They could be senior academics or professionals with worldwide contacts. Expert general or series editors may be employed by publishers, especially in non-consumer sectors. Their task is to help editors develop and edit the books, and they usually receive a small royalty.

It is vital for editors to understand the current and future market on the ground. Educational editors see local education subject advisers, inspectors, examiners and lecturers on teacher training courses; school heads, and teachers using the materials in the classroom; and attend conferences. They need to understand forthcoming changes to the curriculum (and the opportunities they offer), and the trajectory within subjects stimulated by the views of the latest education minister. ELT editors, in addition to using UK contacts, will travel abroad and visit ministries and institutes of education, private language schools, offices of the British Council, and local publishers and distributors to meet key contacts and decision-makers. College textbook editors spend several days a week visiting universities and will meet teaching staff in order to discover subject trends, find out their views on the books currently available, and flush out ideas and contacts they have and to sell the firm's books. Academic editors may forge links with institutions, societies and industry organizations for which they could publish or distribute books or journals. They will visit academic conferences to network and become known amongst the relevant academic communities. Organizations and societies issue publishers with invitations to tender to publish their materials (such as journals), and competing editors will submit bids on behalf of their companies. When large US sales are anticipated, editors shape the material in conjunction with their US counterparts and visit their sister companies. All editors receive in-house feedback from the marketing and sales departments.

The editor in educational publishing

Brenda Stones, Author, editor and lecturer on educational publishing

What is special about educational publishing?

Because both the content and the size of market are fixed, UK educational publishing is fiercely competitive, and the areas in which publishers can compete are often less to do with the products and more to do with the services offered to the customer. The content is prescribed by the National Curriculum and exam syllabuses, with little opportunity for different interpretations. The size of the market is fixed in terms of the number of students in a year group or for a particular subject or syllabus, and of the funding delivered to schools by the government. So the only opportunities for expanding the market are, for example, in export territories and from parental spending. The publisher usually sells directly to teachers, rather than through the intermediary of bookshops or distributors, and this gives the opportunity for direct contact with the purchasers.

What are the key tasks of the educational editor?

The editor has to research their markets thoroughly, in order to gain familiarity with the curriculum and anticipate its future changes. They have to study their competitors – their market shares, and how their products compete – and their audience, meaning both the teachers who make the purchasing decisions and the students who are the ultimate consumers. Each editor has to make a forward plan of print or digital products to be published in a range of subjects and levels, to meet the revenue targets expected by the company. With the choice of technology platforms, in particular, the editor has to be sure that sufficient revenue is being generated by single-copy digital resources, by comparison with the multi-copy print-based sales. Appropriate authors or author teams are then commissioned to write materials to the editor's specification, and the editor maintains communication on progress throughout the development of the project.

Additional tasks include briefing the design of the products, so that they are easy to teach from, easy to read, and appealing to teachers and students. There is always hands-on editing in educational publishing, to ensure that the text covers the curriculum requirements, is factually accurate, and is at an appropriate language level for the particular students. The editor writes promotional copy and briefs the promotion and sales staff on the benefits of

E★PERT

the new publications. Finally the editor monitors the sales of their educational list against targets for revenue, profitability and market share.

What experience and skills do educational editors need?

- Teaching experience, especially if this involved writing teaching materials,
- the ability to write and edit to different language levels,
- a sense of accuracy and eye for detail,
- numeracy, and the ability to interpret numerical data,
- familiarity with technologies and how they are used in the classroom,
- visual awareness, and the ability to organize visual information,
- sympathy for children and their interests at different ages,
- a deep interest in the importance of education and how children learn.

The decision to publish

Many factors influence an editor's decision to pursue a new project.

Suitability for list

A title has to fit the style and aims of the list it will join, so that it is compatible with the firm's particular marketing systems and its sales channels to market. Taking on a book in a new subject area has implications for marketing and sales, not just editorial. Editors assessing new titles are also concerned with the list's overall balance, direction and degree of innovation.

Content

The editor's judgement of the quality and appropriateness of the content is aided by others. Fiction editors may use junior editors, or external readers, to supply plot synopses or to offer first or second opinions. Non-fiction editors may ask specialist external readers to comment on specialist titles. Other publishers rely heavily on experts – teachers, academics, professionals – sometimes worldwide to comment on material. All these external readers are paid small fees and remain mostly anonymous to the author. The management of the peer review process is critically important in academic and journals publishing.

Author assessment

This covers the author's qualifications, writing ability, motivation and time available to write the book, public standing, reliability to deliver on time, responsiveness to suggestions and connectivity with the intended audience. Whether the author is 'promotable' is a key question for some types of consumer books. This can be interpreted as – is the author personable? – although the more cynical will say it is also a question about age and looks. There is also a growing expectation that an author has developed a social media presence – an author with 75,000 followers on Twitter will be attractive to a publisher.

Unique sales proposition (USP)

What will make this book different from others (its competitive advantage), or what makes it special – the quality of the author, a new treatment of the subject, or some differentiation by price or format? What are the special marketing opportunities through which the book could be promoted? This could be a tie-in with a TV series, taking advantage of a special sporting event for a sports autobiography, or the author's status and celebrity.

> The USP defines what makes a book stand out from competing titles

Market

Understanding the main audience for which the book is intended, who would buy it, and the possible take-up at home and overseas. The sales records for the author's previous books or those of similar books may be used as a guide, along with market research regarding interest level and trends. Sometimes the rights sales potential is assessed, such as likely translation and co-edition sales. This is most relevant to trade titles. The likely international market is important now that an ebook can reach all parts of the globe before any print distribution.

Competition

The title's features and benefits compared with competing titles are evaluated. This is important for textbooks and reference titles, and for a variety of non-fiction. The strengths of competing titles should be acknowledged, not just their weaknesses. Consideration should also be given to indirect competition, such as content freely available on the internet.

Frontlist/backlist potential

Is the book expected to have a short life on the frontlist, or does it have the potential to 'backlist' for a long period? If the former, the commercial opportunity needs to be sizeable.

> New titles are the frontlist; established titles the backlist

Packaging and price

What is the best combination of packaging and price for the project? This covers word length, illustration content, size, binding style (if print) and production quality, the likely cost and the price ranges within which it could be sold in different physical and digital formats. *Digital first* could be considered for books which should reach the market quickly; *digital only* might suit a short text or a journalistic approach.

Investment and return

How much time and money needs to be expended on acquiring the book, such as the size of advance expected by the agent, and on developing and marketing it through to publication, in relation to its expected earnings and profitability? Would its earning power justify its place on the list? Sometimes a project may be too small in scale to be worth pursuing. Alternatively it may be worth investing in a new market where the number of readers is likely to grow.

Risk and innovation

What are the external factors at play affecting the risk investment, such as the timing of publication in relation to the optimum time to publish, the link to topical events and their perceived popularity, and the actions of competitors? What is the downside if the expectations are not realized? To what extent is the project experimental in terms of taking on a new author, or publishing in a new area or format (print or digital), or price? Without taking risks and innovating, the publisher is overtaken by competitors.

Approval process

Some ideas are rejected by the editor, especially after unfavourable reports. Some authors are asked to resubmit in the light of the editor's suggestions. If an editor wants to take forward a project, they cannot offer a contract without the agreement of senior management. Editors sound out and lobby senior colleagues, such as the marketing and sales managers, over possible prices and sales forecasts, and the production manager over production costs. For a major investment, such as a large advance, the finance director will be consulted. The editor prepares a publishing proposal form, which covers the scope of the book, its format, its market and competition, readers' reports, publication date, and the reasons for publication. A costing or financial statement sets out the expected sales revenue, the costs of producing the book and the proposed royalties to the author, in order to show the hoped-for profit margin – provided the book sells out. For standard formats there may be a set of production scales that feeds into the costing form. Different combinations of prices and sales forecasts, and of production costs and royalties may be tried – they will reveal differing margins.

Many publishers hold formal editorial meetings at which the senior management hear editors' proposals – a lot are accepted, but some are referred back or rejected. Editors have to be prepared to defend their proposal and demonstrate their wholehearted commitment. Tom Maschler writes: 'To publish well the publisher must be passionate about the book for its own sake. . . . Once the choice is made the task begins. It is to transmit one's conviction first within the publishing house and then to the outside world' (page 282).

If given the green light, the editor negotiates the contract with the author or agent (see the next chapter), agrees or invents the book's title, and on commissioned books ensures that the author appreciates what is expected (for example content, length, deadline). Titling is an important skill. In a crowded book market, unusual titles can attract attention, for example that for the novel

Salmon Fishing in the Yemen (2007) by Paul Torday, or *The Hundred-Year-Old Man Who Climbed Out of the Window and Disappeared* by Jonas Jonasson (English edition, 2012). Stephen Hawking's 1988 popular science bestseller was originally going to be called *From the Big Bang to Black Holes: A Short History of Time* until 'his editor at Bantam, Peter Guzzardi, turned it round and changed "Short" to "Brief". It was a moment of inspiration that surely helped Hawking amass record sales' (*Guardian*, 14 September 2013). Internet searches drive the need for clear and explanatory titles for specialist titles. Sometimes the book 'does exactly what it says on the tin', such as Andrew Marr's *A History of the World* (2012). Some titles work at more than one level: the footballer Frank Lampard's autobiography was called *Totally Frank* (2006); and Steven Norris, the former Conservative transport minister, used the title *Changing Trains* (1996).

When signing up a new fiction writer, the editor may decide on a two- or three-book deal – if the first novel is a hit, the author is already safely under contract for the second novel. There may be an optimum publication date which would maximize sales. The book may be topical or need to be published for the Christmas market. In the case of textbooks, bound copies will be needed for inspection by teachers in time for the details to be added to the relevant reading lists – ideally they should be published by March to May at the latest.

The Bookseller's Diagram Prize is awarded each year to the oddest title for a book. Past winners include *Bombproof your Horse*, *How to Avoid Huge Ships*, *The Joy of Chickens*, and *The Joy of Sex: Pocket edition*

NEW TITLE COSTING

Successful publishing is founded on contracting good books that sell, and each new book is a business in its own right contributing to the business as a whole. The decision to publish is the crux of the whole enterprise. If mistakes are made here, all efforts of management to control overheads will come to nothing. Books which fail to achieve their target sales and profitability must be counterbalanced by equal profits from other books which exceed their target.

We said earlier that in order to gain approval for a project, editors must prepare a costing – a profit and loss form – to prove the book's profitability. There are varying degrees of sophistication in this process, and electronic templates are now in widespread use. What is important, however, is to understand the principles behind a new title costing. The editor is not simply finding out a cost for the book, but comparing revenue and costs to maximize profitability, while working within the price constraints of the market and the formats chosen.

Net sales revenue

The publisher's net sales revenue (NSR) – also called the net receipts – is the sum of money the publisher receives after the trade discounts have been deducted. For example, a book with a recommended price of £20.00 may be sold to bookshops by the publisher at an average discount of 50 per cent. The bookshop will pay the publisher £10.00 for the book, and this is the net sales revenue for one copy.

Price:	£20.00
Average discount:	50 per cent
Net sales revenue:	£10.00

In order to calculate the total revenue for a book, a sales forecast needs to be made. If a book is overpriced, few copies will be sold and the total revenue will be low. If a book is priced too low, the opportunity will be missed to maximize the income for a title. The art is to price the book competitively within the market, thereby maximizing sales and the total revenue. There is a more detailed discussion of pricing in Chapter 10.

The sales forecast is related to a time period. Publishers print stock sufficient for a limited period only (six to 12 months, or for mass-market paperbacks only a few months) in order to minimize the cash outlay, costs of storage and the risk of overprinting. The planned life of a hardback may only be one sales season before the book goes into paperback – it will simply stop selling when the paperback appears. Judging the print run is a difficult art. Keeping the run low may lead to lost sales if a title is selling fast; raising the run may lead to overstocks which cannot be sold. The latter approach runs the higher risk. Ebooks offer a flexible option for satisfying the market, and when in 2013 the author of the recently published *The Cuckoo's Calling*, Robert Galbraith, was unmasked as J. K. Rowling, the immediate spike in sales was of the ebook (only a few thousand print copies had been manufactured). A US bookstore owner said: 'People who can't get it as a book are going to run and get it as an ebook. By the time the [print] books are back, two weeks from now, most people are going to have read it on some device' (*New York Times*, 16 July 2013).

While each book is sold at many discounts, according to the customer and sales channel, an average discount can be derived by working out the likely orders from different types of customer or territory. Estimates may be gathered from the sales departments or overseas branches. The ways in which an international publisher trades within the constituent parts of its group vary and depend upon in which territory it is advantageous to declare profits for taxation and shareholder benefit. For instance, by transfer pricing they may sell internally a UK-originated book to their sister US firm at a very high discount thereby increasing the profit in the US.

Costs

The costs of producing a book usually come under two headings. The fixed costs are incurred before the printing presses roll and do not change whatever the quantity of books ordered. They may include:

- sums paid to external readers, translators, or contributors,
- legal fees – for example, if the book needs to be read for libel,
- permission fees for the use of third-party copyright material (text and illustrations), unless paid for by the author,
- payments to freelance copy-editors, proofreaders, illustrators, and designers (for both text and the cover),
- indexing, if not done by the author, although this charge may be put against the author's royalties, and
- payments to suppliers for typesetting, file conversion, origination of illustrations, proofing, corrections.

The *variable* costs occur after the presses start to roll and depend on the quantity of books ordered. They include the costs of printing and binding, and the paper consumed. The quantity ordered would be the sales estimate plus an allowance for copies wasted or gratis copies given away, for example for review purposes. The total production costs are the sum of the fixed costs and the variable costs. Ebooks incur little by way of direct variable costs, and the cost of a digital copy approaches zero, but there are still the fixed costs to be covered (and any relevant sales tax to be paid). Publishers may regard the income from ebook sales as additional revenue, or try and work out what share of fixed costs should be borne by the digital edition.

The average cost of producing each print copy, the unit cost, is calculated by dividing the total costs by the print quantity. The unit cost diminishes with increasing print quantities, falling rapidly on short printings of between, say, 500 to 2,500 copies and then more slowly. The rapid decline in unit cost results from the fixed costs being spread over larger quantities. Although the per copy cost of producing the book becomes progressively lower with increasing quantities, the total cost still increases. Therein lies the danger for editors preparing a costing.

The temptation is to reduce the unit cost by increasing the print quantity – but if the books are not sold the publisher has sunk an even greater amount of cash into the book's production.

The author's royalties are calculated by applying the different royalty rates to the sales forecasts for home and export markets. A costing prepared before a contract has been signed with the author will show suggested royalty rates for the title. The royalty may be based on the book's price or on the net sales revenue – the sums actually received by the publisher. To carry on with the earlier example:

Recommended price:	£20.00
Average discount:	50 per cent
Net sales revenue:	£10.00

If the royalty is 10 per cent of the published price, the author would receive 10 per cent of £20.00: £2.00 on each copy sold. If the royalty is 10 per cent of the net sales revenue, the author would receive 10 per cent of £10.00: £1.00 on each copy sold. A publisher looking to reduce their costs would work with royalties based on the net sales revenue. The author may not necessarily agree with this approach or even understand the difference between the two methods of calculating royalty payments. A good agent would push hard for the best deal.

Gross and net profit

The gross profit is what is left after the unit cost and royalty have been deducted from the net sales revenue.

Net sales revenue:	£10.00
Unit cost:	£4.00
Royalty to the author (10 per cent of NSR):	£1.00
Gross profit:	£5.00
Gross margin:	50 per cent

The gross margin is the percentage of the net sales revenue that forms the gross profit. In the above example, the gross profit forms 50 per cent of the revenue (this calculation for all products gives the gross profit in the company accounts in Chapter 5, page 117). The management may say to their editors, 'We want to see each publishing proposal attaining a minimum gross margin of 55 to 60 per cent'. That percentage represents the sum of money the publisher would have left after the production costs and royalties have been deducted from the NSR, provided all the copies were sold. The sum would, in theory, be sufficient to recover the overheads and expenses and to provide a net profit. The publisher's overall net profit is the sum left after all the costs of running the business have been deducted (again see the company accounts). Overheads for a publisher would include the costs of salaries, marketing and sales, warehouse and fulfilment, online platforms, general administration, office space, heating, lighting and other items such as bank interest and bad debt.

The editor strives to balance the income and costs so that the desired gross profit is attained. This is called *value engineering*. If the gross profit is too low, the production costs could be trimmed (fewer pages, fewer illustrations, cheaper paper) or the author's proposed royalties reduced. Conversely the price and/or sales estimate could be increased. But while the publisher worries about costs and margins, the end-user is concerned with price and perceived value, and does not care about the costs, the number printed or the author's effort. Reducing the production values on a book, for example by using cheaper paper or fewer colours for the cover, may harm the book's sales. It will depend on the type of publishing and the expectations of the market – which are high in some markets like art or cookery books. For an editor publishing a book with a limited market, there remains the fatal temptation to imagine a non-existent larger market and to increase the print-run in order to lower the unit cost.

In the late 1990s Dorling Kindersley printed 13 m copies of its *Star Wars* titles – sales only reached around 3 m

When the publisher takes the final decision on fixing the price and print quantity, the fixed costs have already been incurred and cannot be changed. On account of the uncertainties of estimating demand, a prudent publisher favours a higher price and a lower quantity rather than a lower price and a higher quantity. If the actual demand for the book is less than expected, a price on the high side may still return a profit, whereas too low a price could lead to substantial loss. The great dangers are underestimating costs, overestimating demand, and underpricing. This leads not only to a loss on the individual book, but also can wipe out the profit on others. Successful books can always be reprinted, but at a price and quantity which again are chosen to avoid loss. Ebook editions can soak up surplus demand, and their prices can be adjusted almost in real time. If a book is likely to be added to the backlist, there may be an argument for accepting a lower than usual gross margin on the first printing, on the grounds that a reprint will have a much healthier margin. The first printing of a school textbook may attain no profit, but the hoped-for second and subsequent printings should move it into profitability. Also hardbacks can perhaps tolerate a lower gross margin, since the ebook or follow-on paperback will not have the production fixed costs to bear. A quirky trade title with no certainty of making the backlist, such as *The Book of Bunny Suicides* or *Fifty Sheds of Grey*, has to make its money straight away.

Other factors affecting the pre-publication decision concern the level of investment at risk, for example very high authors' advances or a large investment in a major textbook, and its duration. Several combinations of price and sales forecast print run may be tried out, including 'worst case scenarios', and the *break-even* may be calculated. A project's break-even point is the minimum quantity that must be sold to cover the production costs and the author's advance or royalty. Also included might be a proportion of the company's overheads. On some proposals, if the break-even is considered attainable, that may inspire sufficient confidence to go ahead. Some publishers calculate a project's cashflow and the interest incurred over time. From the outset to after publication, the publisher usually endures a net loss before the income surpasses the outlay. The estimated income is derived from the sales forecasts broken down over time (for example, monthly, quarterly and yearly). Possible rights sales income, other than that from co-edition deals, usually does not enter into the early costings and thus can be regarded as extra profit. However, it may be included, especially when needed to justify paying the author a large advance.

Some publishers stop their calculations at the gross profit line while others continue and deduct direct overheads expressed as overall percentages (for example for editorial and marketing or sales and distribution) to reach the *net profit*. The way in which overheads are apportioned, either as actual sums or percentages, varies (see the indicative percentages in Chapter 5, page 117). To continue with our example:

Net sales revenue:	£10.00
Unit cost:	£4.00
Royalty to the author:	£1.00
Gross profit:	£5.00
Gross margin:	50 per cent
Editorial and marketing overheads (15%):	£1.50
Sales, platform and distribution overheads (15%):	£1.50
Net profit (Gross profit less overheads):	£2.00
Net profit margin (as percentage of NSR):	20 per cent

The problems with the method as outlined above are that titles are allocated overheads in proportion to expected revenue (which may not accord with reality). It also focuses attention on a desired percentage rather than money – for example a title with a 25 per cent gross margin may yet deliver much more cash than one with a 55 per cent gross margin. It is important therefore to look at the total sums involved, and not just concentrate on the percentages. A costing should also include a column showing the totals received and paid out: revenue, costs and royalties.

Recommended price:	£20.00
Average discount:	50 per cent
Net sales revenue:	£10.00
Unit cost:	£4.00
Royalty to the author:	£1.00
Gross profit:	£5.00
Gross margin:	50 per cent

Total number of copies required:	10,000
Copies sold:	9,500
Total NSR:	£95,000
Total production costs:	£40,000
Royalties due to the author:	£9,500
Gross profit:	£45,500

In the above example, the royalties are calculated on the sales, but in order to secure the book a much larger advance might have to be paid to the author. This sum is paid even if the book's sales are disappointing. If the advance paid to the author against royalties was £15,000, the overall cash surplus would be reduced by £5,500. A costing should allow provision for copies given away free or gratis, and for returns from booksellers, and so should not assume that all copies are sold. A fuller costing would show income from the ebook or paperback edition and projected rights income. Preparing a separate costing for an ebook is possible since they are mostly sold on the same wholesale model as for print (a discount is given against the recommended price), and there is broad agreement that royalties are paid on the net sales revenue. But the calculation is complicated by the payment of VAT and the question of what costs to apply – the marginal cost of an ebook is close to zero.

Mark-up method

An alternative costing approach is the mark-up method. This traditional and simple method is severely criticized but can be used as a ready-reckoner. The unit cost is derived from dividing the quantity of books to be ordered or expected to be sold into the total production costs. This is then multiplied by a factor (say 5–8 for a trade title) to arrive at the published price. The accounts department calculate for editors the factors pertaining to different kinds of books (for example consumer or academic) with different royalty rates and discounts. Provided the copies sell out, the factor accommodates the firm's costs and profit. But if the published price is thought too high, the editor is tempted to increase the sales forecast print run to lower the unit cost in order to arrive, by multiplication, at a reasonable price. Conversely, the publisher may print the number it believes it can sell but fixes the price too high to absorb that number. Unless careful the publisher ends up with unsold copies or loss-makers. The method, based on a predetermined level of activity, disregards the fact that costs do not act alike as output increases or decreases. It encourages rigid pricing and conceals assumptions. Worse, it focuses attention on the unit cost and away from the market and price elasticities.

The method can be used in reverse. The gross retail value (price multiplied by sales estimate) is divided by the factor to arrive at the desired unit cost. The book's specification could then be adjusted to match.

The use of a mark-up factor often occurs when consumer book publishers buy books from packagers. A mark-up factor (say 6 to 7) is applied to the packager's all-in, royalty-inclusive, price per copy to arrive at a published price. If the publisher is translating and resetting a title, the mark-up factor could be 5 or 6.

CASE STUDY: *INSIDE BOOK PUBLISHING*

New books, or new editions, are costed at the time of signature of the contract with the author. Publishers rarely show their confidential costing of a book to authors. But Routledge, part of Taylor & Francis (T&F), provides here their estimate for this book. The costing was compiled by the development editor of the Media and Cultural Studies list. Prepared in advance of the authors' handover of the manuscript to the publisher, it is revised during the course of production to take account of the inevitable changes to the book's specification and sales prospects.

The estimate is reproduced here in three parts (there are other costing spreadsheets lying behind these figures):

- product specification of the paperback edition,
- estimated production costs for the paperback edition, and
- income and expenditure showing the book's estimated gross and net profit across all editions.

The estimate is for a new edition of a textbook, the sales history of which stretches back 26 years. It is, however, costed as a new book with the advantage that the likely demand can be informed from its recent past history. Six years after the publication of the fourth edition, annual paperback sales are around 450 copies. An active used book market for previous editions is all too evident on the internet. Its medium is classified as a 'printed product', based on a copy sales business model. The various other ways it may be licensed, for example, in translation, are not shown. It has been translated into German (second edition), Vietnamese (third edition), Romanian, Chinese Simplified and Korean (fourth edition). For the fifth edition, the publisher required the authors to write chapter abstracts to encourage sales of individual chapters.

The book is published simultaneously in three editions: paperback, hardback and ebook, each of which is allocated an ISBN. The plan is to print 1,600 copies of the paperback edition to meet the sales expectation over the first 18 months, and to reprint 1,000 copies to meet demand from 18–36 months. The calculation is thus three years, typical for a textbook adopted annually on courses. The paperback and ebook editions are priced at £25.99 in the UK, and at $46.95 in the US – a parity dollar price on the exchange rate at the time of estimate (£1: $1.60). The hardback edition is priced at £80 in the UK and $130 in the US, and the 70 copies to be printed are destined for libraries (mainly academic) in the first 18 months.

The estimate starts by locating the product within the organization, part of the international group of T&F. It summarizes the book's paperback specification – for brevity details of the hardback edition have been deleted here. The 'extent' is stated at 360 pages (fourth edition 320 pages). The production method is digital from a PDF file (the fourth edition was litho printed). The format (or page size) is pinched crown quarto; the interior (the text) is printed in one colour (black) on

Preliminary estimate – INSIDE BOOK PUBLISHING ED5

ISBN: 978-0-415-53717-9

Extent: 360   **Lifecycle calculation**

Production project/Product

Publisher:	Humanities
Division:	Media & Cultural Studies
Medium:	Printed Product
Version:	Paperback
Binding style:	Limp
MS type:	Disk
Copy-editing level:	Simple
Pages Roman/Arabic:	360
Production method:	Digital
Binding Method:	Notch
Format:	Pinched Crown Quarto
Interior colours:	1 colour
Print file format:	PDF
Typesetting difficulty:	Medium
Font:	Scala
Typesetting format:	MSWord

Binding	**Finishing**	**Paper quality**	**Colours exterior**	**Colours interior**
New design	Matt laminate	240 gsm 1-sided	CMYK	

Sections	**Paper quality**	**Colours**	**Bleed**	**Paper weight**
TEXT	Matt Blade 90 gsm	1 colour	No	90 gsm

Illustrations	**Colours**	**Qty**	**Tables**	**Formulas**
Positioning only	1 colour	50	**B/w** 10	**Math.:**
Redraw (line)	1 colour		**Colour:**	**Chem.:**
			Difficulty: Basic	**Difficulty:**

Paperback edition

Cost element		1st printing	2nd printing
Currency: GBP		**1,600**	**1,000**
F	Author/series editor fee		0.00	0.00
F	Contributors' fee		0.00	0.00
F	Subsidies and grants		0.00	0.00
F	Illustrations permissions		383.23	0.00
F	Legal fees		0.00	0.00
F	Translation fees		0.00	0.00
F	Text permissions		0.00	0.00
F	Cover design	350.00	350.00	0.00
F	Illustration fee		0.00	0.00
F	Additional design fee	150.00	150.00	0.00
F	Copy-editing	862.28	862.28	0.00
F	Proofreading	424.24	424.24	0.00
F	In-house	365.60	365.60	0.00
F	Typesetting	1,398.80	1,398.80	0.00
F	Typesetting corrections	248.34	248.34	0.00
F	Proof sets	86.23	86.23	0.00
F	Tables	47.90	47.90	0.00
F	Relabelling a/w		0.00	0.00
F	Redraw line a/w		0.00	0.00
F	Redraw maps		0.00	0.00
F	Artist drawings		0.00	0.00
F	A/w positioning	95.81	95.81	0.00
F	Retouch a/w		0.00	0.00
F	A/w origination		0.00	0.00
F	Scan line		0.00	0.00
V	Print and Paper	1.55	2,474.01	1,886.22
F	Other manufacturing contingency	479.04	479.04	100.00
	Prod. Costs total fixed		4,891.47	100.00
	Prod. costs (total) variable		2,474.01	1,886.22
	Prod. costs (total)		7,365.48	1,986.22
	Prod. costs fixed per unit		3.06	0.10
	Prod. costs variable per unit		1.55	1.88
	Production costs per unit		4.61	1.98

Handover costing - Inside Book Publishing 5e

Version Type	ISBN	Project No.	Prod. Project No.	Calc No.	Price UK£	Price US$
Hardback	978-0-415-53716-2	93266		225731	£80.00	$130.00
Paperback	978-0-415-53717-9	93388		225732	£25.99	$46.95
eBook	978-1-315-77776-4	93268		225733	£25.99	$46.95

Initial royalty rate 7.5% HB   7.5% PB
Premium Text

3-YEAR SALES PROJECTION

	1st Printing Sales (18 months)			2nd Printing Sales (18-36 months)			3-year sales projection		
	Qty	£	%sale	Qty	£	%sale	Qty	£	%sale
Hardback	70	3,145	10.00%				70	3,145	10.00%
Paperback	1,600	24,094	70.00%	1000	17,265	100.00%	2600	41,360	80.00%
eBook	300	5,068	20.00%				300	5,068	10.00%
Total	1,970	32,308	100.00%	1,000	17,265	100.00%	2,970	49,573	100.00%

GROSS PROFIT	20,109	62.2%	13,132	76.1%	33,241	67.1%

DIRECT VARIABLE COSTS	£	%sale	£	%sale	£	%sale
Manufacturing	7,874	24.37%	1,990	11.53%	9,864	19.90%
Royalty	2,709	8.39%	1,280	7.41%	3,989	8.05%
Contingency	1,615	5.00%	863	5.00%	2,479	5.00%
Total	12,199	37.76%	4,133	23.94%	16,332	32.95%

OVERHEADS	£	%sale	£	%sale	£	%sale
Distribution	3,554	11.00%	1,899	11.00%	5,453	11.00%
Allocated Costs	15,000	46.43%			15,000	30.26%
Total	18,554	57.43%	1,899	11.00%	20,453	41.26%

NET PROFIT/CONTRIBUTIO	£	%sale	£	%sale	£	%sale
	1,555	4.81%	11,233	65.06%	12,788	25.80%

RETURN ON INVESTMENT	%sale	%sale	%sale
	5.06%	186.20%	34.76%

90 gsm paper. The binding (or cover) is a new design, printed in CMYK (four colours) on a heavier paper of 240 gsm, with a matt laminated finish. The binding method is notch – the spine folds are glued together but not cut off. The numbers of illustrations and tables are estimated. An assessment is made of the amount of work required – copy-editing level is classified as 'simple' – or of the difficulty in typesetting (medium). The automated costing system applies the current costs of T&F suppliers to the specification.

Costing

Lying behind the estimated figures is a mass of actual cost information built up by a publisher producing more than 1,600 new books per year in the UK alone. The page extent is an important factor in determining costs and for some production categories, the publisher would have worked out a set per page cost. Following the product specification is a table of estimated production costs for the paperback edition, stated in GBP (Great Britain Pounds). Each row has the prefix F (fixed costs which do not depend on the quantity produced) or V (variable costs which change with the quantity produced). The costs given for the F rows are set against the first printing of 1,600 paperback copies, and are not carried over to the second printing, the straight reprint of 1,000 copies. The variable costs of print and paper relate to the quantities of the first and second printings. The fixed costs represent 66 per cent of the total production cost of producing 1,600 paperback copies. The impact of setting the fixed costs against the first printing becomes very evident in the totalled production costs:

- £7,365 for the first printing of 1,600 paperback copies – unit cost of £4.61,
- £1,986 for the second printing of 1,000 copies – unit cost of £1.98.

The estimates above are called direct costs in that the publisher can identify the labour related to the production of this book, payable to external suppliers. For under £5,000 the publisher can produce this book economically up to and including the source file from which it is printed or published as an ebook.

Sales

We now turn to the all important forecast of sales over the first 18 months, broken down by territory, as follows:

Table 7.1 Sales forecast for *Inside Book Publishing*, fifth edition

	Hardback	Paperback	Ebook
UK	15	1,000	
US	15	100	
Rest of world	30	300	
Frees	10	200	
Total	70	1,600	300

Export of the hardback represents 75 per cent of sales, while that of the paperback 28 per cent. The paperback UK sales forecast is 1,000 copies, up from 700 copies for the previous edition. Frees are copies given to the authors and contributors, and for review. Teachers considering adopting the book for student purchase may now receive an e-inspection copy instead of a printed copy. The sales of the ebook edition are growing and are estimated at 300 copies.

The copy sales forecasts are converted to sales revenue in the section headed '3-year sales projection: first printing sales (18 months)'. The hardback edition (70 copies printed; 60 to sell) is forecast to deliver a net sales revenue (NSR) of £3,145 (or 10 per cent of the total NSR £32,308). The paperback edition (1,600 copies printed; 1,400 to sell) is forecast to deliver a NSR of £24,094 (or 70 per cent of the total NSR). The ebook edition (300 copies to sell) is forecast to deliver a NSR of £5,068 (or 20 per cent of the total NSR).

How has the publisher arrived at these NSR figures? The system, using the sales forecasts, has deducted the average book trade discounts from the local published price in the given territories. Overall the average discount granted to resellers for the paperback and ebook editions is around 35 per cent: the publisher receives around £17 (or 65 per cent) per copy for these editions priced at a recommended published price of £25.99. Since the authors' royalty (initially set at 7.5 per cent) is based on the publisher's net receipts, the lower the discount granted by the publisher to resellers, the greater the sum they receive, as does the publisher. Larger publishers, such as T&F, have stronger leverage with resellers than smaller publishers.

The revenue from the hardback edition accounts for 10 per cent of sales, an apparently disproportionate amount in view of a sale of just 60 copies. The argument here is that the libraries buy one copy at triple the price in a more durable binding for multiple and free use by readers. There is also an element of cross-subsidy. If there were no hardback edition, the price of the paperback (sold mainly to students) would increase. The hardback is printed once only and is intended to sell out within 18 months.

Gross profit

Beneath the total NSR of £32,308 from the first printing is the gross profit line. The gross profit is calculated by first summing the direct fixed and variable costs paid out to suppliers and shown here under manufacturing (the total production costs of both the hardback and paperback editions: £7,874) and the authors' royalty of £2,709 (calculated by applying the authors' royalty percentage to the publisher's net receipts). A contingency budget of £1,615 is included for stock write-off, such as books too damaged to dispatch again after returning unsold from booksellers. These direct variable costs totalling £12,199 are deducted from the total NSR of £32,308, to give the gross profit of £20,109, which when expressed as a percentage of the NSR, gives a gross margin of 62.2 per cent:

$$\frac{£20,109}{£32,308} = 62.2 \text{ per cent}$$

The gross profit on the second printing of 1,000 paperback copies for the period 18–36 months, reflecting the expected decline in the rate of sales, is £13,132. However, when expressed as a percentage of NSR, the gross margin jumps to 76.1 per cent because the fixed costs of developing the book were only applied to the first printing sales period. On the three-year view, the gross profit totals £33,241, which at 67.1 per cent achieves the gross margin target of 60 per cent or more so often set to editors by their senior management.

Contribution

To reach the net profit or contribution (the so-called bottom line), the publisher's overheads have to be deducted. These are sometimes referred to as indirect costs because they cannot easily be attributed directly to the individual book. The overheads of operating different areas in the company are aggregated and expressed as overall percentages. These percentages are applied to the NSR and then deducted from the NSR. Publishers treat overheads in different ways. In this particular example, T&F applies two areas of overheads to the title:

- distribution at 11 per cent of NSR, and
- allocated costs at 46.43 per cent of NSR.

Distribution includes storage, order fulfilment and shipping costs (Taylor & Francis outsources its distribution to third parties around the world). The allocated costs or overheads cover all the other internal costs of running the business and are related to the type of product published. The distribution costs are incurred for as long as the book remains in print. But the allocated costs are set against the first printing only and once again are not carried over to subsequent printings of a book, which may never occur. In reality, much of the staff time devoted to developing and marketing the book occurs in the 12-month period before and around publication.

The net profit/contribution line shown here is calculated by deducting the overheads from the gross profit. Thus on the first printing, the total overheads – set at 57.43 per cent on sales of £32,308 – work out at £18,554, which when deducted from the gross profit of £20,109, leaves a contribution or net profit of £1,555. When expressed as a percentage of NSR this gives:

$$\frac{£1,555}{£32,308} = 4.81 \text{ per cent}$$

The publisher's net profit from the first printing is below the amount paid out in royalties to the authors. If sales of the book struggle to attain the first printing estimate, the publisher would incur a potential loss or at best record a very low level of profitability. But on the second sales period printing, the contribution rises dramatically to £11,233 and leaps to 65.06 per cent. On the three-year view, it is estimated that the contribution would be £12,788: a 25.8 per cent net profit. If the sales forecast is cautious, not least to avoid tying up too much cash in stock and storage, and sales exceed expectations, the net profit would nudge up further and be attained earlier.

Return on investment

There is another percentage measure to assess the book. The return on investment (ROI) line in the estimate shows the ratio of money gained, expressed as a percentage, on the publisher's investment in the book for the first and second printings over the given time periods, and over the three-year view. For instance, if a publisher invested £10,000 in a book and got back £15,000 in revenue, the ROI would be 50 per cent. This is calculated by expressing the profit of £5,000 as a percentage of the investment:

$$\frac{£5,000}{£10,000} = 50 \text{ per cent}$$

For *Inside Book Publishing*, on the first printing sales period, the publisher's investment is the direct variable costs of £12,199 and the overheads of £18,554. These total £30,753. The NSR is £32,308 from which is deducted the total costs of £30,753 leaving a net profit of £1,555. Expressing £1,555 as a percentage of the investment of £30,753 gives the ROI of 5.06 per cent:

$$\frac{£1,555}{£30,753} = 5.06 \text{ per cent}$$

However, on the three-year view, the ROI is 34.76 per cent:

$$\frac{£12,788}{£36,785} = 34.76 \text{ per cent}$$

which exceeds the ROI target set at 30 per cent, sufficient to cover all the overheads of the publisher and to provide a reasonable profit.

Market effects on costing

A publisher's costing software has to be periodically updated in response to changes in publishing methods and markets. For example, on the fourth edition of this book, costed in 2007/08, the editor needed to make it an even working of 10 × 32-page printed sections in order to enable economic printing by litho. This edition is produced on a digital press and its planned extent of 360 pages does not need to be so defined by the multiples pertaining to litho presses. Moreover, while the costing gives the set print quantities, in reality the publisher may digitally print smaller or larger quantities according to actual demand.

Since the fourth edition in 2008, there have been even more significant changes in the market. The print estimate for the hardback edition has fallen from 100 copies (fourth edition) to 70 copies (fifth edition) reflecting changes in library acquisition. For the fifth edition, an ebook is included in the costing from the outset. The fourth edition had no planned ebook edition, though the ebook was issued soon after publication.

T&F is maintaining the value of the work by pricing the paperback and ebook editions at the same price. Furthermore, some libraries, instead of purchasing the hardback, will buy the ebook at the institutional price – the same as the hardback

Commissioning

S K I L L S

No editor can simply sit back and expect marketable ideas and authors to flow in. Editors need to be creative in that they encourage and develop received ideas – or initiate ideas themselves and match them to authors. Inevitably these lead to false trails, so editors have to be agile enough to hunt the front-runners, ruthless enough to weed out the wrong projects, and tough enough to withstand their exposed position within the publishing house. Editors need a knowledge of production methods (limitations and costs), digital opportunities, and contracts, and the skill to negotiate with authors, agents and others. As the book's champion, the editor must display infectious enthusiasm and superb persuasive skills. An editor's strength in marketing the book, in-house and externally, is imperative, and today extends to creating an audience for a book ahead of publication through the use of social media.

Publishing is a business, and it is vital that editors have financial acumen. Profitable publishing also depends on a perception of trends in markets and timing. Good editors pre-empt competitors – in textbook publishing the lead time can easily be three years. In specialist fields the work involves asking experts the right questions and being able to talk to them intelligently. The skill lies in choosing the right advisers and readers. The consumer book editors, who face great difficulty in ascertaining market needs, base their judgements on a combination of experience of what sells, having a finger on the pulse, and intuition. Backing one's own hunches takes considerable audacity and confidence, and the stakes can be high. Without a reasonable hit rate, they run the risk of losing their job.

Fundamental to book and author selection is the editor's ability to assess the quality of the proposal and of the author's writing and purpose. This critical faculty is underpinned by skills in speed reading and sampling sections of writing. Most editors will be able to assess a manuscript from the first few pages, and this skill develops with experience. Editors should be able to contribute to structural improvements, and in specialist areas appear to the author not merely as a cipher for expert readers' comments.

Authors are engaged in long spells of isolation when writing with little else to draw on but experience, knowledge and imagination. In their books rest their hopes and dreams. In their eyes the editor is exclusive to them; to the editor an author is one of many. Authors expect editors to represent their interests in-house, to get things done and so judge editors on their level of clout. Conversely editors must represent the best interests of the publisher to authors – at times a fine juggling act. Good editors persuade authors to write, often plead with them to deliver, and foster author loyalty to the house. Authors need encouragement, reassurance and praise – that, and the editor's diplomacy, are vital. Those authors who rely on their books for income (unlike teachers, or academics) centre their whole life around their writing. To some, an editor becomes inseparable from their private lives.

edition – which allows multiple users simultaneous access to the content. Although readers are switching from print to ebook, the sale of the printed editions is still forecast to deliver most of the revenue, and as such the print editions carry most of the costs in publishing the work. The ebook edition has no printing or physical distribution cost thus its gross margin will be higher than on the print editions. There are, however, costs in ebook distribution, such as that of maintaining the T&F platform, but these are not shown currently. The costing methodology for the sixth edition will look different again.

SUCCESS AND FAILURE

Generally speaking, publishers make very little net profit from their new book publishing programme over the first year. Their profits stem from the titles that continue to sell strongly. That said, a Christmas bestseller can still make a large sum of money, as can a title timed to coincide with a sporting event or anniversary. If a book continues to sell and the publisher has recovered all its development and marketing costs from the first printing, the gross margin and net profit increase dramatically. With the advent of digital printing and ebooks, publishers are able to lower their level of risk around stock. They can keep an extensive list of titles in print and respond to demand without incurring significant warehousing costs.

A vigorous and profitable publisher is in a strong position to publish books which, it is estimated at the outset, will not show a profit; indeed there may be good publishing reasons for doing so. A book could be published for prestige purposes. A fiction publisher may believe in a novelist's long-term ultimate success, or want the author's next, more desirable book. A textbook publisher may want to enter a new area and undercut competitors. A university press may be obliged to publish a great scholarly work – sometimes supported by a subsidy or grant.

Publishing is a high margin business and can be immensely profitable, but for many publishers those profits prove to be a mirage. Some authors fail to deliver their manuscripts or submit unacceptable material. Publishers have forecast budgets and if a proposed book is not published, the estimated contribution needs to be recouped from elsewhere. It is relatively easier for a consumer book publisher to fill its list more quickly, for example by buying from agents or from another company abroad, than a school textbook publisher. However, the consumer publishers, which pay significant sums on signature of contract, will find the advances impossible to recover if the level of sales is disappointing. All the decisions regarding the quality of a book, its market, price and sales potential are based on advance subjective judgements. Amongst the new books there inevitably lurk those that will fail to recover their production costs or the author's advance, let alone make a contribution to overheads.

With the growth of digital printing, small numbers can be reprinted much more easily and this model has spread across all sectors of book publishing

Now read this

Gill Davies, *Book Commissioning and Acquisition*, 2nd edition, Routledge, 2004.

Sources

Diana Athill, *Stet*, Granta, 2000.

Eric de Bellaigue, *British Book Publishing as a Business since the 1960s*, British Library Publishing, 2004.

Ros Jay, *The White Ladder Diaries*, White Ladder Press, 2004.

Tom Maschler, *Publisher*, Picador, 2005.

Daniel Menaker, *My Mistake*, Houghton Mifflin Harcourt, 2013.

Angus Phillips, Mark Saunders, Sue Pandit and Deshini Chetty, 'The Nature of the Relationship between Authors and Editors', *Publishing Research Quarterly*, 21:2 (Summer 2005).

Christopher Potter, 'Evolving into Something', *Publishing Research Quarterly*, 16:1 (2000), pages 20–5.

'Refreshing that Vintage Appeal', interview with Rachel Cugnoni, *The Bookseller*, 24 May 2007.

Thomas Woll, *Publishing for Profit*, 4th edition, Chicago Review Press, 2010.

CHAPTER 8

The author contract and editorial development

Once the costing for a new title has been agreed and the book receives the green light, a contract is drawn up with the author. This chapter examines the author contract and the editor's continuing role in shaping and developing the project.

AUTHOR CONTRACT

Each publisher – as the buyer of rights from an author – draws up its own contract, also called the agreement. The contract differs according to the book and the author, but most publishers operate with standard contracts. Commissioning editors negotiate contracts with authors or their agents, and can then adjust the standard contract to fit the final terms agreed. The publisher is usually in a position to weight the contract in their favour. Some authors sign the contract that is offered; others, or their agents or lawyers, will try to improve the royalty rates and advance offered, or ask for changes to particular clauses, which may have to be reviewed by the publisher's legal department or outsourced to a contract specialist. Alternatively the agent will present their own contract to the editor.

The contract formally defines the relationship between author and publisher. Today's publishing contract can be a lengthy document as the publisher seeks to secure as many rights as possible, and the obligations of both parties are set out in detail. The full acquisition of rights will prevent problems that may occur whether in selling a book around the world or its exploitation as a digital product. It will also maximize the income from licensing a range of rights to third parties. Although it is unlikely that a book will be turned into merchandized goods such as tea towels and duvet covers, it did happen with Edith Holden's *The Country Diary of an Edwardian Lady* and Flora Thompson's *Lark Rise to Candleford* – many years after they were first written or published.

A contract is usually a legal document signed by both parties – the author and the representative of the publisher. The requirements seen as important for an enforceable contract (Jones and Benson, page 64) are:

■ a clear agreement,
■ an intention to be legally bound by it, and
■ some valuable consideration to seal the bargain.

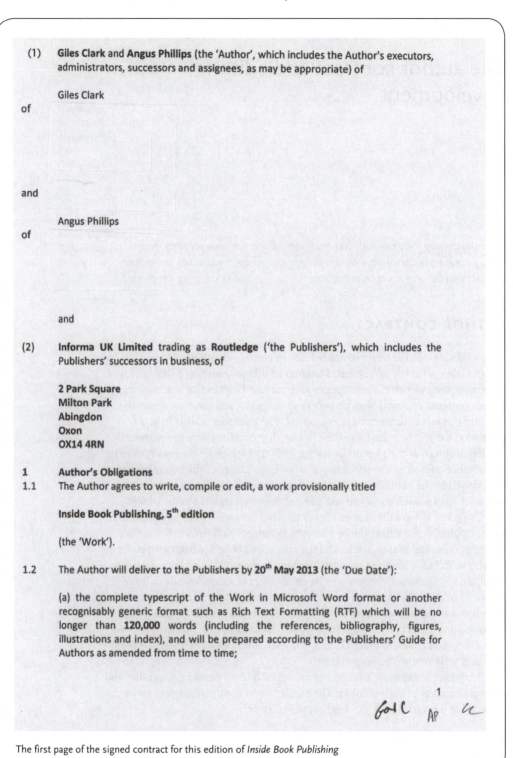

(1)   **Giles Clark** and **Angus Phillips** (the 'Author', which includes the Author's executors, administrators, successors and assignees, as may be appropriate) of

of   Giles Clark

and

of   Angus Phillips

and

(2)   **Informa UK Limited** trading as **Routledge** ('the Publishers'), which includes the Publishers' successors in business, of

2 Park Square
Milton Park
Abingdon
Oxon
OX14 4RN

1   Author's Obligations
1.1   The Author agrees to write, compile or edit, a work provisionally titled

Inside Book Publishing, 5th edition

(the 'Work').

1.2   The Author will deliver to the Publishers by **20th May 2013** (the 'Due Date'):

(a) the complete typescript of the Work in Microsoft Word format or another recognisably generic format such as Rich Text Formatting (RTF) which will be no longer than **120,000** words (including the references, bibliography, figures, illustrations and index), and will be prepared according to the Publishers' Guide for Authors as amended from time to time;

1

The first page of the signed contract for this edition of *Inside Book Publishing*

If these requirements are in place, a verbal agreement may be enough to form a contract. This was highlighted by the case of Malcolm vs. OUP (1991), when an editor offered assurances over the telephone to the author that they would publish his book. The book was later turned down by the publisher, but in court it was revealed that the author was tape recording the conversations. The court ruled in favour of the author, who was awarded significant compensation. Since that case, editors have been cautious about giving verbal agreement to publish, and most companies have tightened up their procedures so that deals are subject to a final written contract. It is rare, however, for disputes between the author and their publisher to reach court, and there is little case law in existence.

A verbal agreement can be sufficient to form a contract

Main elements of the contract

The following are the items covered in a typical contract between the author and the publisher. Of main interest to the author will be the level of the royalty and any advance. Other clauses open to argument or negotiation include any option on the author's next work, royalties for new editions (should they be increased?), payment for illustrations (does the author or publisher bear the cost?), and the number of free copies for the author.

Preamble

The date, names of the parties (their assigns and successors in business) to the contract, and the title of the 'Work' (the book's provisional title) are stated.

Author's grant

The author usually grants to the publisher the sole and exclusive licence and right to publish the book (the 'Work') in volume form (print and electronic), in all languages, for the full term of copyright (author's life plus 70 years), throughout the world. By granting a licence, the author retains ownership of the copyright. Sometimes authors, such as contributors to multi-authored books or to highly illustrated general books, assign their copyright, thereby passing ownership and all control to the publisher. The grant of electronic rights may include 'the right to publish or license the publication of the Work in all formats now known or later invented', or other similar phrase, to cover the publisher against future technological developments.

Author's warranty

The author warrants that they control the rights granted, that the work is original (not plagiarism), does not contain defamatory, libellous or unlawful matter; and will indemnify the publisher for any loss or damages.

Competing works

The author agrees not to write a directly competing work for another publisher.

Typescript

The contract will detail the length of the typescript (preferably in words not pages), the delivery date and form (typically double spaced, in Microsoft Word, and electronically). It will also cover the author's responsibility for supplying illustrations and the index, and for obtaining and paying for third-party copyright material (unless otherwise agreed). The publisher reserves the right not to publish if the delivered manuscript is overdue or does not conform to a previously agreed brief.

Corrections

The author is constrained from making extensive corrections to the proofs – other than those attributable to the publisher or printer – and is charged if author's corrections exceed a specified percentage (say 15 per cent) of the cost of typesetting. The author must return proofs within a certain period, usually two to three weeks.

Publication

The publisher solely controls the publication – production, design, publicity, price, methods and conditions of sale. In practice authors may be consulted on matters such as the cover design. The author is given a number of free or gratis copies (typically six) and may purchase more at a discount.

Payments to the author

On the publisher's own editions, the author is normally paid a royalty expressed either as a percentage of an edition's recommended published price on all copies sold; or as a percentage of the publisher's net receipts: the sum of money received by the publisher after discounts have been deducted. The author's earnings are thus proportional to price (or net receipts) and sales. Royalty rates are quoted for each of the publisher's own-produced editions: hardback; paperback (generally lower); sales made in the traditional home market (the UK and Ireland), and in export markets. Export rates are usually lower to take account of the higher discounts involved. Royalty rates on the publisher's own digital editions are also given.

A scale of royalties rising by steps of 2 to 2.5 per cent when certain quantities have been sold may be included, especially on home market sales. Royalty rates on the published price can range from 5 to 15 per cent (many authors never surpass the lower base rates). If an author has reached a higher rate on a scale (whether based on the published price or net receipts), and a new edition is produced, the royalty reverts to the base rate. When the book is remaindered (surplus stock is sold off cheaply), no royalties may be paid. Other provisos where lower royalties apply are stated. If royalties are based on the published price, for example, the rate applied may be reduced or based on net receipts if the publisher sells the book to a large retail chain at a high discount of say 52.5 per cent or above. A lower royalty rate may also apply to small reprints.

Subsidiary rights

The contract lists further rights granted to the publisher, which it could license to other firms, and the percentages payable (from 50 up to 90 per cent) to the author on the publisher's net receipts from the sales of those subsidiary rights. If the publisher is granted, for example, US and translation rights, the firms to which these rights could be licensed may print their own editions and pay royalties to the publisher to be shared with the author. However, the publisher may print bulk quantities, for example for a co-edition partner. The publisher sells such copies at a high discount (up to 80 per cent) and the author's royalty may be based on the actual sums received (a common rate is 10 per cent). There are many other rights such as serial and extract rights; dramatization rights on stage, film, television and radio; broadcast reading rights; audiobook; quotation and anthology; large print; digest condensation; mechanical reproduction rights (for example on CD); and digital publishing rights, including games. There is a fuller discussion of rights in Chapter 12.

Accounting

The publisher's accounting period to the author is usually six months for general books and a year for educational and academic books, with settlement up to three to four months after. Consumer book publishers normally withhold a proportion of royalties payable in an accounting period as a reserve against subsequent returns of unsold books from retailers.

Revisions and new editions

The author agrees to revise the book when requested or to permit others to do so at the author's expense.

Reversion

The rights may revert to the author if on request the publisher fails to keep the work in print. The reversion of rights has become more complicated – print on demand and the ebook mean that a book need never go out of print. Many agents would insert a clause to ensure that the level of sale should be the determinant of whether rights can be reverted. For example, a novelist may wish to revert the rights for their older books from the publisher in order to self-publish. By contrast many academic authors are only too pleased to have their works available indefinitely through a respected publisher.

Arbitration

Arbitration may be necessary in the case of a dispute between the author and the publisher.

Option

The author may give the publisher the right of first refusal on their next book.

Moral rights

These are covered in Chapter 5, page 120.

Advance

An advance, if paid, is set against the author's future royalties. It is important to note that the advance has to be earned out before the author receives further payments for the book. Most authors receive either a small advance – up to £10,000 for a two-book deal in the case of a first-time novelist – or none at all. Big advances tend to make the headlines in the trade and sometimes the national press, for example when Lena Dunham accepted an offer of $3.5m in 2010 for her debut book: 'The publisher is presumably shelling out mega bucks because Dunham, thanks to *Girls* (the TV show she writes and directs), has become an emissary from Generation Z, polarising and transfixing in equal measure with her painfully acute observations of twentysomething behaviour.' (*Guardian*, 10 December 2012.) Advance payments may be staged, with separate payments on signature of the contract, delivery of an acceptable manuscript, and on publication.

In 1996 Random House in New York sued Joan Collins in an attempt to retrieve an advance paid to her of $1.3 m for two novels. It alleged that the manuscripts she delivered were unpublishable. The star of Dynasty won the case since the original contract only said that the manuscript should be 'complete' not satisfactory.

Signatures of the parties

The author and the nominated representative of the publisher will sign at least two copies of the agreement, and one copy will be kept by the author. The signature of the contract is the trigger for allocating an ISBN to the title, and the editor's dispatch to the author of the author questionnaire for marketing purposes.

Electronic rights

The publisher's 'volume rights' or 'primary rights' encompass print and electronic. Some of the far-sighted educational, academic and STM book publishers included electronic rights in their contracts with authors during the 1990s, even in the 1980s. By the twenty-first century many of the main publishers had secured electronic rights from authors on tens of thousands of old contracts which had made no previous provision. The learned journal publishers are also free to publish electronically since contributing authors often assign their rights to the publisher, or society. Similarly, many of the book packagers and highly illustrated publishers own the copyright in the texts they publish, and in the commissioned artwork and photography, through assignments.

It is generally accepted by authors and agents that trade publishers should hold the electronic rights in new and backlist titles, especially since the proportion of ebook sales on some titles can be very high. The royalties paid on ebook sales range from the rate payable on the printed book up to the industry norm for trade books of 25 per cent of net receipts.

This issue of who owns electronic rights in backlist titles was highlighted in the USA by the case of Random House, Inc. vs. Rosetta Books (2001), in which it was ruled that the publisher did not automatically hold ebook rights, even if it was granted the right to publish a work in book form, and if the rights were not specifically granted in the contract they were retained by the author. The inclusion of third-party material – text extracts and photographs – in many books across most sectors of publishing is sometimes an impediment to the epublishing of the backlist and of new books. The rights holders, both printed book publishers and picture agencies, can be resistant to granting electronic rights or charge exorbitant fees – in effect a refusal.

Impact of agents

Where the author has an agent, the contract used may be provided by the agent weighted in their client's favour. The agent's contract typically is shorter than one from a publisher, reflecting the more limited grant of rights by the author. So-called boilerplate agreements – standard contracts – are used with the leading publishers, avoiding wrangles over the wording of standard clauses. Agents may opt to withhold many of the subsidiary rights (to them they are not subsidiary), such as serial and translation, preferring either to sell the rights themselves or to negotiate if the publisher proposes a deal later. The decision may also be taken to divide up the English language territories, selling UK and US rights separately. For sought-after books this can yield a higher income for the author.

The death of territoriality?

Traditionally, the UK and US publishers (especially consumer) were in separate ownership and divided the world English book market between them. For books published on both sides of the Atlantic, the UK and US publishers sought exclusive market areas (closed markets) from which the other's competing editions of the same book are excluded. The US publisher's exclusive territory was essentially the USA; the UK publisher's the Commonwealth, Ireland and South Africa and a few others. The remaining areas were then non-exclusive to either – called the open market, such as mainland Europe – where UK and US editions of the same book are in direct competition. Canadian rights were exclusively retained by UK publishers on their own originated books, and by US publishers on theirs. For some books this broad division persists and can affect the way agents and packagers grant rights to publishers, and how publishers trade books between themselves. For example, the two separate arms of a large consumer publisher, in London and New York, may bid separately for the same title, since the rights have been divided up by the agent. A UK publisher that holds world rights can either sell its own edition into the USA through its related US firm, or license the rights to a US publisher, in which case the US publisher's exclusive, non-exclusive, and excluded territories would be negotiated. Conversely a UK publisher may buy a US-originated book from a US publisher or author represented by an agent, and its rights and territories would also be carefully defined.

This traditional territorial split in English language publishing of exclusive, non-exclusive (open market) and excluded territories is threatened by actions of governments, consumer pressure groups and internet traders. For example, Singapore legislated itself into the open market in the mid-1980s. In 1991 Australia required local publication to occur within 30 days of first publication anywhere in the world, if the local edition is to preserve its exclusivity. This measure was designed to encourage domestic publishing and boost the earnings of local authors. In 1998 New Zealand declared itself an open market. Meanwhile the availability of books from online booksellers is breaking down the influence of territoriality, with competing international editions visible to consumers.

The major college textbook and academic publishers holding world rights face the problem of maintaining differential prices across territories. Third-party traders may look to transfer products from low-priced territories, such as parts of Asia, to high-priced territories, such as the USA. A case before the US Supreme Court in 2013, Kirtsaeng vs. John Wiley, tested the principle of whether cheaper international editions could be brought by third parties into higher value markets. A student imported hundreds of textbooks, bought by his family in Thailand, and resold them in the United States, and it was ruled that the first sale doctrine (see Chapter 5, page 123) should take precedence over the publisher's wish to keep markets separate. Such arbitrage trading is a feature of printed books; for ebooks, sold under a licence, territorial and payment restrictions may limit the ability of consumers to shop around.

The advent in 1993 of the EU single market principle of free movement of goods is in conflict with the traditional UK/US publishers' contracts whereby the UK is an exclusive territory and mainland Europe is open. The greatest fear of UK publishers is that the UK itself might potentially become flooded with cheaper US editions imported from mainland Europe, negating the UK publishers' exclusive contractual and territorial rights. Such 'parallel' importation is unlikely to occur from direct breaches of contracts by US publishers, but instead at the hands of third-party traders in the USA or mainland Europe.

UK publishers argue that the European Union and additional countries joining it should be treated as a single market and that it should be the exclusive territory of UK publishers, in the same way as the US unified market is treated. Projects originated in the UK tend to be sold by agents with exclusive rights in Europe; and UK publishers may offer Canadian rights to US publishers in exchange for exclusivity in Europe.

The development of internet bookselling in the late 1990s enabled UK consumers to purchase books relatively easily from US-based booksellers. The major internet booksellers in the UK have agreed to list only the UK edition, based on territorial rights information from the bibliographic database supplied by Nielsen BookData. One answer to the thorny issue of territorial rights is for the publisher to acquire world rights from the author. This is easier to do in some sectors of publishing, such as educational and academic. Most of the major UK and US consumer book publishers are in common ownership and aim to be strong enough to acquire exclusive world English language rights in authors' works. This enables them to overcome legislative difficulties anywhere in the world and ameliorates any 'buying around' practices of third-party traders. However, the authors' agents still believe that they can secure better offers from different international publishers by dividing exclusive territorial rights amongst competing publishers.

In 2011 Richard Charkin, executive director of Bloomsbury, was reported as saying that 'the publisher had moved to a global alignment and now tried to buy world English rights in all cases, adding that the ability provided by digital to publish globally meant territorial restrictions based on countries were "obsolete"' (*The Bookseller*, 22 June 2011). The collapse of territorial rights is not a foregone conclusion given the opposition from many agents. Furthermore if territoriality is in the interests of the US media corporations, the US government would defend its continuance. The major power blocks of the USA and European Union also have to grapple with the related issue of the potential loss of tax revenues from offshore internet traders escaping the conventional tax nets. On the internet, the consumers' choice of bookseller is affected by the cost of shipping a physical book and the timing. The growing importance of ebooks, often available instantaneously at a lower price, changes the equation and the consumer will also be choosing on format and device.

Apart from price differentials between competing editions (which are influenced by £–$ exchange rates with the Euro and other currencies), there is also an issue around the date of release of different editions of the same title. US and UK consumer book publishers deploy the strategy of maximizing earnings through the sequential publication of a particular book in different formats and prices. For example, first publication would be in a higher priced hardback, followed by a trade paperback and a smaller-format, mass-market paperback edition. In export markets, especially the growing mainland European market, UK and US publishers will aim to pre-empt the other's competing edition in paperback while maintaining their home markets for a period exclusively in hardback. Hence UK export editions of paperbacks are available earlier on mainland Europe than in the UK, and can be bought on the air-side of UK airports. Mainland European paperback importers may hedge their bets by simultaneously ordering their stock from both US and UK publishers to ensure they receive stock from whichever is the earliest. Importers also compare the prices of competing editions, and scout around for bargain-priced editions. Ebooks can quickly penetrate markets across Europe and their low prices impact on the sale of print and local translations.

In the UK printed books do not attract VAT, whereas digital products are classified as a service and are subject to the tax

PRODUCT DEVELOPMENT

Once a book has been commissioned from an author and the contract has been signed, it needs to be monitored while it is being written, and planning begins for the editing, design and production stages that are interlinked with the book's marketing. Books need differing levels of care and attention during their development. Commissioning editors may await the completed text of a novel or biography. Some authors would like editors to read chapter drafts while the writing is in progress. For textbook and reference projects especially, attention will be paid to word length, any co-ordination necessary if there are a number of contributors, and the use of templates during the writing process, which can help with the tagging vital for digital editions. Authors may deliver the complete manuscript on time or later, an inherent trait of many authors. The non-deliverer may have their contract cancelled. The delivered manuscript is checked for length, completeness and quality – and for any sensitivities around libel or third party content. It may be returned for revision, or accepted and passed on for production. The author may be reminded to complete the author's questionnaire which is used for marketing purposes.

Commissioning editors brief and liaise with junior editors, designers, production, promotion and sales staff. Editors may write the blurb for the cover and catalogue entry, and may seek endorsements from experts or opinion formers. The copy may also be used as the basis for the book's AI – advance information sheet – which is needed six to nine months ahead of publication. Although editors have no managerial control over other departments, they endeavour to ensure their books receive due attention. Commissioning editors may present their books to the publisher's sales force at the regular sales conferences.

Some editors, especially those involved with complex and highly illustrated books, or major textbook projects involving digital resources, get very involved in the product research and development stages. Commissioning editors may undertake development work themselves, or hand on the work to junior editors, whose job titles could be Editor, Development Editor, Production Editor, Assistant Editor, or Editorial Assistant. Those working across print and electronic products are sometimes called Content Managers or Editors, and the word digital is now added to some traditional job titles. The editor maintains contact with the author so as to plan backwards from the proposed publication date, trying to ensure that the manuscript is delivered in good time to make smooth progress through the production process. A development editor in textbook publishing carries out survey research in association with the marketing department, organizes the external review of drafts, and helps shape the project with the authorial team from conception to completion.

At the page-proof stage, the book's price is fixed across formats, as well as the number of physical copies to be printed and bound. The number printed may differ from that envisaged at the outset, and changes may have been made to the format and pricing. This could reflect feedback from major retailers, changes in the market, or a new view on ebook sales or the best way to publish the book. Editors may also make decisions on reprints and have to manage stock for their lists. In some larger companies this work is handled by sales and inventory control specialists.

Particular times of year can be good for the publication of trade books, and the publisher has to make sure the book appears at the time of the relevant sporting event, anniversary (for the subject of a biography), or the relevant season (Christmas for cookery, spring for gardening titles). Publicity opportunities such as media exposure or festivals (for example Valentine's Day) may influence the date of publication. The new year, and its associated resolutions, offers opportunities for publishers of health and personal improvement titles; beach reads are out for the summer months. Hardbacks tend to get the most media coverage in the spring (when many of the literary festivals take place) and autumn (in the run-up to Christmas). Apps may appear after Christmas when consumers have just acquired new tablets or other devices. New college textbooks should appear early enough in the adoption cycle (in the spring) so that lecturers can view them ahead of preparing their reading lists.

Illustrations can add value and this continues to be reviewed during product development. Are illustrations necessary to aid the explanation in the text – for example in a school textbook? Are they essential in a particular market – art publishing or cookery? Can you charge more if there are many illustrations – will you sell more copies? A balance needs to be struck between the cost of illustrations and their likely added value.

> The New Year is a good time to publish self-improvement titles

Editorial project management

Planning tasks as part of the product development process include:

- a schedule for the editing, design and production stages,
- the necessary clearance for permissions for both text and illustrations,
- a brief for the text and cover design,
- copy written for the cover, and
- a budget.

Schedule

This is preferably drawn up in advance of the delivery of the typescript from the author. A copy-editor can be booked in advance, and the design and production stages can be planned around the proposed publication date. Schedules can be more or less complicated, and can be done using software or simply a single sheet

June to December	Picture research/clearance of permissions
January	Delivery of the typescript
	Copy-editing (six weeks)
	Cover and marketing copy written
March	Handover of typescript/illustrations to design department
	Cover proofs
April	Typesetting
May	First page proofs (three weeks for checking)
	Index preparation
June	Revised proofs and index proofs (one week for checking)
	Passed for press
July	Advance copies from the printer
	Copies into warehouse (six weeks before publication)
September	Publication (print and ebook)

of A4. There may be a standard set of weeks allowed for different stages, but there is no formula set in stone. If a competing title is to be beaten to market, or if revenue is required within a particular financial year, the schedule may be severely shortened. If this was done with every title, however, there would be the risk that quality would suffer and there would be tremendous pressure on the staff involved. A sample schedule is shown on the previous page.

Permissions

Permission may need to be sought for the use of text and illustrations in the book. Longer quotations not covered by fair usage will need to be cleared, and for anthologies of poetry or prose some detective work may be required to track down the relevant copyright holders. A freelancer may take on the work of clearing permissions for an anthology. Usually the first approach is to the originating publisher, who may control subsidiary rights. Occasionally you will see a line in a book saying that 'every effort has been made to contact the copyright holder', and the extract will appear without permission having been granted. The publisher has made a risk assessment before going ahead.

Under the contract the author may have to clear and pay for the permissions, and the publisher may request copies of relevant correspondence. The publisher may still have to undertake picture research or brief a researcher, putting the cost of the permissions against the author's royalty. If the publisher is responsible for obtaining copyright permission, the editor or researcher writes to the copyright holders. Each illustration or table is labelled and compared against the accompanying text and caption. Caption and source copy are prepared.

Drawn illustrations are prepared from copies of those previously published, if suitably amended, or from the author's original line work, roughs or ideas. They are edited for sense and consistency before being passed to the designer or illustrator. The desired position of the illustrations is indicated in the text.

Design brief

Standard forms or memos may be used to brief the cover and page designers. The cover designer will be briefed on the market for the book and its contents. For the page design, the brief may be to follow the design of another title (copy enclosed) or to create something new and distinctive. A sample chapter or two enables the design to be started on before the book's delivery. For key titles, sample spreads may be needed to help sell rights or to assist the author in writing to the correct length.

A design brief may contain the following elements, and separate consideration may need to be given to digital products:

- *the market for the book* – in the case of fiction, age and sex,
- *the content* – synopsis or contents list,
- *some text elements* – with sample text (to show content, heading structure) and illustrations,
- *single or double column format* – double column format can accommodate smaller type and is often used for reference works,

Blurb writing

The blurb is the copy, describing a book's content, printed on the back cover of a paperback or displayed in an ebook. It remains highly important as an influence on the purchase of print books (along with an arresting front cover), and it may well be used as the basis for the description on sites such as Amazon. There it is perhaps less important now that potential purchasers can read customer reviews and assess the star ratings given to a book.

No blurb should be longer than 120 words – for fiction probably no more than 100 – and all must be:

- impactful,
- intriguing,
- relevant, and
- short.

Paperbacks often make generous use of review quotes, and many new books appear with specially solicited quotes from opinion-formers. Non-fiction blurbs need to be concise but complete – in other words, answer all the questions you would want to ask a salesperson if you were buying the product in a shop. Bullet points can help put across the key benefits of the book; jargon should be avoided, and time taken to choose the right word. Short sentences can be highly effective.

Fiction blurbs are more emotional: you must think yourself into the story. Try to engage potential readers with the first few sentences. The first line in the blurb for Anne Tyler's *The Accidental Tourist* shows how to draw you in: 'How does a man addicted to routine – a man who flosses his teeth before love-making – cope with the chaos of everyday life?' A shoutline on the front cover can give the story in a nutshell, as with 'Twenty Years, Two People' for *One Day* by David Nicholls, or make use of tried and tested angles: 'Now a compelling film starring ...'; 'The no. 1 international bestseller'; or 'By the award-winning author of ...'

- *the style of the running heads* – chapter heads are more informative than simply the book title, and
- *a similar title* – if the book is to follow that more or less closely in style.

Cover copy

The cover is needed well in advance of the printed book for promotion and sales purposes, and is an important part of the metadata which helps sell the book online. Cover copy (for example title, author, blurb and ISBN) may be prepared before the book's delivery by the author. Blurb writing is an important skill. In the case of fiction, it must grip the potential reader without giving away too much of the plot. Review quotes or advance puffs from prominent names may be used. Editors may

Short sentences can be highly effective in a blurb

ask sales or marketing to review the blurb copy for important titles, and the copy should also be written with an eye to online searches by potential customers.

Budget

The title costing will have estimates for the first costs of the book, including editorial and design work, and permission costs. The budget may be reviewed in the light of real costs or any change in the book's specification – page extent, number and type of illustrations.

Editorial

SKILLS

Crucial editorial skills include the ability to get on with authors and close colleagues, and to communicate well with those in other parts of the company. Agreeing changes with authors and getting them to return proofs on time takes tact, self-confidence, persuasion, tenacity and negotiation. Editing manuscripts and proofreading demand a meticulous eye for detail, a retentive memory, sustained concentration, patience, commonsense detective work and an ability to check one's own and others' work consistently. Authors often have great loyalty to both commissioning and more junior editors, and this loyalty binds them to the company.

Copy-editing and proofreading skills can to some extent be learnt from books, but added to that must be an editor's sound grasp of grammar and spelling, and preparedness to look things up. Editors should be able to place themselves in the reader's mind whatever subject knowledge they themselves hold. Good copy-editors and proofreaders are prized and valued.

The enhancement of an author's work involves not only a knowledge of current stylistic conventions and language, but also judgement on the desirability and extent of their application, recognizing when it is necessary or unnecessary to make changes. Breaking the rules for effect is not restricted to fiction. Appreciating the intangible quality of the author's voice can be important, especially in children's books.

Although an editor needs an enormous capacity to soak up detail, the ability to examine the text's overall sense is equally important. Visual awareness is valuable, especially in highly illustrated adult and children's publishing and packaging, and low-level textbook publishing. Knowledge and understanding of production processes and ways of minimizing costs at all stages are essential, as is clear marking of the text for structure. An understanding of publishing software is also important as the range of editorial duties expands.

A publisher's office is hardly conducive to concentration. Editors dealing with many books (all at different stages) are pressed by production to meet deadlines, and are constantly interrupted by colleagues wanting instant information. Good editors are unflappable, they set priorities, manage time efficiently, juggle projects, switch quickly from one activity to another, and expect crises.

Editorial work

Although a commissioning editor or junior editor may copy-edit manuscripts in detail, this work is usually done by freelance copy-editors. There are also packagers and offshore companies which undertake the entire editorial and production process (including project management) up to the delivery of the digital files ready for manufacturing and digital publication, although the publisher still retains direct control of the cover.

Junior editors supervise the progress of books from manuscripts to bound copies, working closely with the production/design department, and giving information to marketing and sales people. They may copy-edit manuscripts and organize illustrations themselves; they may edit manuscripts for overall clarity and pass them to freelance copy-editors for the detailed work. They subsequently send proofs to authors and to freelance proofreaders, collate corrections and generally oversee the book's production from an editorial standpoint. Some book and journal publishers employ production editors, who are also responsible for the design and production stages, and the management of suppliers. The production department may organize freelance editing and proofreading. In illustrated book publishers and packagers, editors work alongside designers to create the book spread by spread.

In firms where job demarcations are drawn not too tightly, and where junior editors work specifically for sympathetic commissioning editors, there is sometimes also the opportunity to gain commissioning experience, usually without responsibility. This may depend on the size of the company. A common job role is that of editorial assistant, whose work ranges from administrative support to editorial work under supervision, such as proofreading, collating corrections, finding pictures for the text, applying for the clearance of third-party copyright material, and handling reprints. In consumer book publishing, junior editorial staff may write reports on new book proposals. In textbook publishing, development editors may look after the commissioning of new editions.

Copy-editing

The aim of the copy-editor, who may be the only person other than the author who reads the book before publication, is to ensure that the text and illustrations are clear, correct and consistent for both the printer and the ultimate readers. 'Good copy-editing is invisible: it aims to present the book the author would have written if he or she had had more time or experience – not, as some new copy-editors think, their own improved version' (Butcher et al., page 32).

The copy-editor is also usually expected to look out for passages that may be libellous:

> Any statement in a book or journal or newspaper, or any other published matter (an advertisement, e-mail or website, blog, message board for example), runs the risk of being defamatory if it contains an untrue allegation or imputation which disparages the reputation of another. (Jones and Benson, page 168)

The novelist Iris Murdoch (1919–99) refused to have her work edited, even resisting changes to her punctuation

In the case of an unauthorized biography of a leading celebrity, a read by a lawyer may be required alongside evidence from the author to back up any controversial claims. Investigative reporting and publishing were given a boost in 2007 with the case of Graeme McLagan's book *Bent Coppers* (2003), 'The inside story of Scotland Yard's battle against police corruption'. The UK court of appeal decided that the author had acted responsibly when writing and researching the book. 'The court upheld the so-called "Reynolds defence" of qualified privilege, under which journalists can claim the right to publish material in the public interest even if they cannot prove its accuracy or it turns out to be untrue' (*Guardian*, 11 October 2007). This was the first time the Reynolds defence had been applied to a book.

The copy-editor, who is briefed on the nature and market of the book, first needs to check that all the manuscript items handed over are indeed present and that they have been clearly labelled and numbered by the author. The author is asked for any outstanding items, otherwise the book will be held up.

The work of copy-editing falls into three related processes:

- consistency,
- substantive editing, and
- structural mark-up.

House style

R. M. Ritter, Author of *The Oxford Style Manual*

E★PERT

In its broadest sense, 'house style' is the way a publisher or printer typically produces its work: it encompasses every aspect of how a publication is presented, including its spelling, grammar, punctuation, typography, hyphenation, references, and layout. This definition can extend beyond print to such physical features as uniform bindings, paper, format, or dust jackets, and even specific colours and presentation of logos or colophons. In practical terms, the purpose of house style is to establish guidelines for everyone involved in creating a publication to follow, in order to ensure accuracy and consistency. Nowadays it is usually imposed by a publisher's copy-editors and proofreaders as part of the editing process.

While the vast majority of these guidelines are unremarkable – good grammar, standard spelling, sensible punctuation – people who are not involved in producing texts (and some who are) tend to think of house style as concentrating on those elements that are either contentious or arbitrary. For example,

"She said she liked the colors 'red, white and blue.'"

is nearly identical to

'She said she liked the colours "red, white, and blue".'

and the minor differences in spelling, punctuation, and quotation marks do not affect its meaning. So why go to all the trouble to impose such seemingly whimsical alterations?

Since the birth of printing, printers recognized that authors are notoriously inconsistent. This is hardly surprising: when writing we are concerned for the most part with what we are saying, not how we are saying it, or what it looks like thereafter. And a text of any length is likely to have variations in style that are inconsequential to the writer, who is concentrating on substance over style. Nevertheless, readers do pick up on irregularities, though they might not be looking for them. Even if such variations do not actually muddle the sense, they can diminish the ease or pleasure of reading; and if there are enough of them, they can actually cast doubt on the quality or reliability of the writer or publisher.

One might think the most sensible course is simply to mirror a writer's preferred usage, and iron out the differences. Unfortunately, such a task is time-consuming, expensive, and inexact, since it is by no means certain that a writer's usage on page 1 will reflect the style that carries through – barring lapses – to the end. To do this accurately would require compiling a list of all style preferences as they crop up, deciding which are most common, and then starting over to impose them properly – a process that would need to begin afresh for each work. So, to avoid the effort of reinventing the wheel with each text, publishers impose their own styles, which are familiar to them, to ensure that consistency is followed from the very first.

These days, publishers rely on style guides that are considered to reflect established standards in their own countries or, in the case of academic work, their own disciplines or fields. They might disagree with those guides in some respects: variations are often listed on a publisher's website. If a work is to be published quickly, or is to be collected with similar works, or is non-fiction, a publisher's house style is more likely to be imposed unilaterally during editing. In the case of fiction or larger works, publishers tend to seek authors' preferences, and establish a happy medium.

Consistency

The most basic task is to ensure that the author's text is consistent in such matters as spelling, hyphenation, capitalization, agreement of verbs and subjects, beginning and ending of quotation marks and parentheses, and many other points sometimes included in the firm's editorial house style. The house style may be based on a particular reference work, for example *The Oxford Style Manual*, or may have been developed internally. In the USA most editors use *The Chicago Manual of Style*. One advantage of following a house style is that proofreaders and other staff working on the text will have a set policy to help resolve problems later on in the production process.

Working on-screen, the editor can use tools such as the search facility to help with the enforcement of consistency in spelling and hyphenation. There are also software programs used by freelancers and at typesetters; and publishers may provide macros to editors that will help incorporate basic elements of house style. The danger is that some words, such as in quotations or references, are also changed by mistake. The editor must check the accuracy and relationship of parts of the text to others, such as in-text cross-references to illustrations, captions, chapters and notes; the matching of headings on the contents page to those in the text; and of citations to the reference list. The arrangement and preparation of pages about which authors may be unsure (for example the preliminary pages) are also the editor's concern. Each new book presents its own problems in the detailed handling of stylistic points, and decisions have to be made in regard to alternative ways of applying the rules.

Substantive editing

While some publishers restrict copy-editing to work on consistency, others expect editors to engage in the second parallel editorial process, which may be termed substantive or content editing. This calls for clear perception of the author's intent and sometimes restraint from the copy-editor. Where appropriate, attention is paid to discordant notes, such as obscure, incoherent, misleading or ambiguous sentences, or non sequiturs in factual passages; unintentional use of mixed metaphors or of repetition; unusual punctuation in sentence construction; paragraphing; and over or under use of headings. Furthermore, errors of fact, and inconsistencies, omissions, contradictions and illogicality in the argument or plot may be found. Substantive editing may entail the rewriting of sentences, reorganization, or suggesting other ways to present material. It is important, however, not to annoy the author by making unnecessary changes.

Editors look out for abbreviations and terms unfamiliar to readers. The avoidance of parochialisms or culturally specific UK examples is especially important in books aimed for overseas markets. Books can be edited in British English, American English or even mid-Atlantic English. The avoidance of offensive – for example, sexist or racist – language or values and of corresponding stereotypes are issues which confront editors, designers and illustrators, particularly those in educational and children's publishing. These staff also try to ensure that the level of language and the illustrations are appropriate for the intended age group.

Structural mark-up

The parallel editorial process carried out, whether the second substantive form is done or not, is to indicate to the designer or typesetter the structural elements of the text. Items so tagged or coded include the heading hierarchy (chapter headings, section and sub-section headings) and other elements (long quotations, lists, notes, captions, tables). The following shows Extensible Markup Language (XML) tagging for a chapter opening. Each opening tag must be completed with a closing tag.

<ch>40 Does the Book Have a Future?<chx>

<au>Angus Phillips<aux>

<epig>Old media don't die; they just have to grow old gracefully. (Douglas Adams 2001)<epigx>

<number>2

<title>Slow books

<rhr>Slow books

<rhl>Slow books

<text>Just as the prospects for books look limited without authors, the same applies without readers. Paul Auster says, 'If you write a story or a poem, you hope there will be a reader,'[1] although of course there are a good many titles read by very few people. There is a received wisdom that reading is good in itself, and offers personal and social benefits beyond those for the economy of having an educated and literate population. If studies show that readership of books is in decline, does this matter? What is at stake here? Are there other ways of learning and developing our intelligence, and how can we expect books to compete with the range of other media which compete for our attention?

Surveys suggest a fall in reading over time, in many countries, and this chapter will examine the evidence and the reasons put forward. These include the loss of time to read, in an often frenetic world of competing demands, and declining interest amongst newer generations. Is the reading of books being replaced by other forms of reading, for examplee.g. blogs and websites? The science of reading tells us what is happening inside our brains, and suggests that the pace of reading is faster with some digital devices.

<head1>Decline in reading

<text>The statistics regarding reading have to be treated with some caution. There is no satisfactory set of data over a long period, and none certainly none which can provide

A sample page from a typescript showing marks and tags inserted by the copy-editor

Text that is structurally tagged is platform independent and can be published in different formats (ebook, online) or readily licensed to third parties. A further impetus on publishers (especially educational firms) to make books available in structured, digital formats is the Disability Discrimination Act (1995). There is demand from the reading impaired (not just the visually impaired) and their institutions. Text in digital form can be adjusted by the user in size, style and colour contrasts. Functionality includes the ability to have the text read out loud using a screen reader, or the provision of extra navigational information – such as whether a line is a heading or a short sentence. Publishers can also produce audio files for download.

Working method

Individuals differ in their approach to copy-editing. A common method involves the editor quickly looking through the manuscript to gain a measure of the author and the book. Ideally, decisions regarding the handling of stylistic points (for example spelling, hyphenation, capitalization, terminology) are taken at the outset. A style sheet is developed to aid consistency and memory, and helps the proofreading, which will be done by a separate freelancer.

To a varying extent, house style editing and substantive editing conflict, in that concentration on one may lead to neglect of the other. Good editors may go through the copy several times at different speeds, focusing attention at various levels, moving back and forth during each examination. Editors may work on hard copy – a typical example is shown opposite – or on screen (using software tools), or both.

> Skilled on-screen copy-editors, making good use of their computer's tools such as find and replace and macros, can work quickly and efficiently; and if they are able to present the typesetter with fully corrected and coded files that can be simply passed through the typesetting system and run out as pages, there can be genuine savings in the schedule. (Butcher et al., page 15)

During each examination editors make alterations on matters – especially those of house style – they believe to be right and defensible, but even so authors may disagree. Queries to the author are marked on the copy in the electronic file using track changes, listed separately or scanned to make a portable document format (PDF) file. Those that affect the design or production of the book are addressed to the design or production department.

If the author is contacted by telephone, email or in writing, editors need to be particularly tactful, explaining the kind of editing that has been done – perhaps by mentioning representative samples – raising matters needing assistance, and reaching agreement on matters of concern. Best practice is that the edited copy is returned to the author for checking (although some publishers are reluctant to do so if a large amount of tagging is visible), as this reduces costly and time-consuming changes at proof stage. Sometimes a meeting is held with the author – or the editor or lead author in the case of a multi-author work. By adopting the reader's viewpoint, and suggesting solutions, the editor sets out to persuade the author to make necessary changes. If the text has been edited on-screen, the edited copy may form an early proof.

103

impulse is a short signal comprising a single value followed by zeroes. The nature of the filter's

response, called the *impulse response*, will characterise the filter. The simplest form of filter is

called a Finite Impulse Response FIR filter, in which 'taps' are taken from successive samples,

which are then multiplied by a coefficient (a multiplicative factor) and the results are added

together to form the output of the filter. This is called 'finite' because there are a fixed number of

taps. An IIR filter, by contrast, allows feedback between the output and the input, which can

create some long-lasting results, including growth of decay over time. This is particularly useful

please give in full

for effects such as reverberation. Where the impulse-response of a physical space may be

recorded by, for example, firing a gun or bursting a balloon, the IIR filter may be used to model

the same digitally. However, IIR filters are often unstable and somewhat inaccurate, owing to the

complexity of their operation, and can easily produce feedback and other such unwanted results.

This makes digital reverberation one of the most difficult things to achieve sucessfully, and the

range of commercially available solutions can be quite variable in quality.

Creative uses of such filters include interpolation, in which sounds of two different types are

apparently fused together over time, and convolution, which combines two soundfiles / an input

and an impulse response by multiplying their spectra together to produce a new sound file.

Frequencies that are common to both sound files will tend to be reinforced and resonate together.

The filter will try to match bin content across the two spectrum. Where there is a match, the data

is preserved. Where there is no match, it is discarded (or, strictly, multiplied by zero). Among other

things, this enables the application of the reverberant properties of resonance to FFT windows

over time and thus the superimposition of the reverberant characteristics of one sound upon

another.

Where digital filters find the most direct parallel with analogue equipment is in the field of EQ,

or Equalisation. Both analogue and digital EQ are designed to make the final recorded sound

equal to the original source, by correcting inadequacies of both equipment and the recording

environment. However, it can also be a highly creative tool when used skilfully. EQ adjusts the

A sample page from a typescript copy-edited by hand

Prelims and end-matter

The editor usually drafts the preliminary material – 'prelims' or 'front matter' – the first few pages of the book. These include the pages giving the book title and author, the name of the publishing house, the copyright notice, and the International Standard Book Number (ISBN) – a unique number identifying the book. Other pages are the contents page, list of illustrations and acknowledgements – for advice and support to the author, or for copyright material used. The author writes a Preface; a third party provides a Foreword. The cataloguing in publication (CIP) data (supplied by the British Library and Library of Congress) has to be applied for.

The usual order of the prelim pages is as follows, with variations according to the book. A right-hand facing page is called a recto; a left-hand facing page a verso. Recto pages are visually more important, but the advent of ebooks has diminished the impact of such distinctions.

- *Half-title page* (recto) – the main title without the subtitle and author's name.
- *Half-title verso* – often blank, or a list of the author's previous works.
- *Title page* (recto) – full title and author's name, with the publisher's imprint.
- *Title verso* – copyright page with the publication history and ISBN.

The other prelim pages follow. These include the dedication, acknowledgements, preface, contents page and the list of illustrations. The prelim pages are paginated using roman numbers, switching to Arabic numerals for the introduction or the first chapter. The advantage of this system is that changes can be made to the prelims at proof stage without affecting the main pagination (which could have knock-on effects for the index). If pages need to be saved to achieve a set extent, the prelim pages can be adjusted. The pages at the end of the book, or 'end matter', can include appendices, notes, bibliography and the index.

Proofreading

Most unillustrated books, or those with only a few illustrations which are easily placed, go straight to page proofs following copy-editing. The typesetter arranges the page breaks, inserts any illustrations, and returns proofs of pages numbered as they will finally appear. Proofs are usually sent as PDF files by email. Proofs are normally read by the author and publisher (most commonly by a freelancer). They can be checked *against copy* (compared to the original), which is more expensive, or simply read *by eye* for obvious errors. The corrections and improvements are collated by the editor and inserted using standard symbols – proof marks are set by the British Standards Institution – on one master set in paper form (the marked set) or marked electronically in the PDF. Correction marks have traditionally been colour-coded (red for typesetter's errors, blue or black for author's and publisher's) so that costs can be apportioned, but this practice is not always followed. Publishers are likely to charge authors for excessive corrections. The marked set or file is returned to the typesetter for correction, and second page or revised page proofs are produced to check the author's and proofreader's corrections have been correctly implemented. Books with many illustrations integrated with the text may follow a different path. The designer may supply a page layout to the typesetter or work on the pages themselves. A sequence of page proofs is checked by the author and publisher.

Most manuscripts arrive on disk or by email, and there is no necessity to have them rekeyed. This minimizes errors at proof and if the copy-editor works on screen a high-quality version of the text is passed to the typesetter. In some companies production editors or designers prepare the digital file from which the book is published.

Index

Serious non-fiction books should have reliable indexes that anticipate readers' needs and expectations. The author is often responsible for index preparation and the cost, and either compiles it themselves or is supplied with a freelance indexer, found by the editor, sometimes from the Society of Indexers. Typesetters can prepare simple indexes using standard software. Indexes are prepared from a page proof and have to be edited and typeset at great speed because the publication date is close. The professional indexers have usually passed their Society's course exams, use specialist indexing software, and may wish to retain copyright. The index may be missed out of ebook editions given the complexity of flowable text without fixed pagination, and the availability of a search function.

'Should not the Society of Indexers be known as Indexers, Society of, The?', from the play *Bookends* by Keith Waterhouse, 1990

Now read this

Judith Butcher, Caroline Drake and Maureen Leach, *Copy-Editing: The Cambridge handbook for editors, copy-editors and proofreaders*, 4th edition, 2006.

Hugh Jones and Christopher Benson, *Publishing Law*, 4th edition, Routledge, 2011.

Sources

Rick Gekoski, 'The Importance of Good Editing', *Guardian*, 14 June 2012.

Barbara Horn, *Editorial Project Management*, Horn Editorial Books, 2006.

Barbara Horn, *Copy-editing*, Horn Editorial Books and Publishing Training Centre, 2008.

Blake Morrison, 'Black Day for the Blue Pencil', *Observer*, 6 August 2005.

The Chicago Manual of Style, 16th edition, University of Chicago Press, 2010.

Lynette Owen (ed.), *Clark's Publishing Agreements: A book of precedents*, 9th edition, Bloomsbury, 2013.

New Oxford Style Manual, 2012.

Katharine Rushton, 'A Time to Publish', *The Bookseller*, 29 June 2007.

Web resources

www.bsigroup.com The British Standards Institution maintains the standard proofreading marks and symbols.

www.indexers.org.uk Society of Indexers.

www.nuj.org.uk National Union of Journalists; see its Freelance Directory.

www.sfep.org.uk Society for Editors and Proofreaders.

CHAPTER 9

Design and production

Alongside the work of the editor in product development, the contributions from the design and production staff are equally critical. Good design sells books – whether it is the cover of a novel attracting an impulse buyer in a shop, or the effective use of typography and illustrations in a school textbook. Some publishers, especially in the highly illustrated book and art book markets, are actively design-led. Their design standards are used as a marketing and sales tool internationally. In the transition to digital publishing, production managers make crucial decisions about quality which affect how a book is perceived in a market of multiple p and e formats. Through effective purchasing of services from freelancers, trade suppliers and project management companies, they ensure that work is kept to budget and schedule.

Authors primarily want publishers to market and distribute their books effectively, but they also want publishers to produce them efficiently and attractively. Some new competitors to the more established companies offer speed to market and more flexible operations. Author service companies will bring books to market in a matter of a few weeks, whilst digital only publishers and distributors are free of print-first production systems. They can offer authors faster publication and are less constrained by the economics and physical restrictions of print.

The previous boundaries in the design and production process have been broken down so that authors, editors and designers are much more involved in producing the final text. On highly illustrated books, designers, not typesetters, may produce the final file for the printer; at the same time the increasing sophistication of pagination software reduces the need to employ designers to hand craft the layout of illustrated texts. The requirements of digital publishing mean that the file of a book will be rendered to several outputs: print and digital formats. There is now an imperative to hold a properly archived version of a book so that it can be published across formats and repurposed as necessary. Publishers making the transition to digital publishing are re-engineering the workflow and that is one of their biggest challenges.

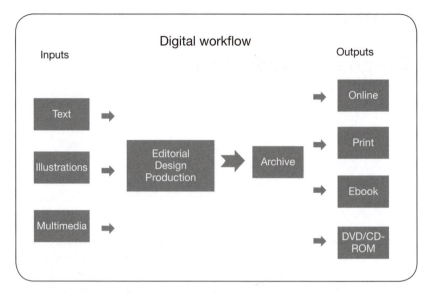

Re-engineering the workflow

Publishers are changing, and have changed, the work and system processes of publishing content in order to move from a print only world to a mixed print and digital world. The growing use of XML is an important part of the transition, and in the previous chapter structural mark-up was introduced – the tagging that aids the searching and linking of content. STM, professional, and reference publishers were early adopters, but trade and educational publishers are catching up. Within each sector, publishers vary in the extent to which they have changed the workflow.

At first, publishers adopted the least disruptive approach. The publisher's typesetter produced the XML file after the printed book was printed. As that could delay ebook publication, progressive efforts were made to introduce structural tagging earlier and earlier. For example, the typesetter may produce the tagged file from an application such as InDesign, or before that from the copy-edited manuscript. In an 'XML first' workflow the content is tagged in Word by the copy-editor – or even the author – and then exported to XML. Underlying the XML approach is the drive towards greater standardization in the production process in order to lower costs and quicken lead times, to publish in various formats through different channels to market, and to future-proof the business. Publishers are moving from a 'cottage industry approach', where the production of each book differs, to scalable production approaches and systems. This is not to say that handcrafted books do not have importance in some markets, and building value into print products is one response to the rise of digital.

The publisher's suppliers have kept in step with the moves towards standardization and modernization of the workflow. Whilst publishers in the period after the Second World War used printers which offered a complete service from re-keying and typesetting of manuscripts through to printing and binding, by the last quarter of the twentieth century, publishers' production managers found it cheaper and more flexible to use specialist typesetters to produce the film of the finished book, which they then sent to a printer for printing and binding.

UK publishers also used overseas printers in continental Europe and the Far East which offered lower prices, especially for the manufacture of colour books. The UK printers facing a static, if not declining market, consolidated, or became part of pan-European groups (such as CPI), and more recently added digital services (such as St Ives, which owns the book printer Clays). Some, however, went bust in the face of continued downward pressure on manufacturing prices, the internationalization of the publishing and retailing industries, and new technologies. They had to contend with new competitors from different sectors exploiting digital printing technologies which enabled short-run printing or print on demand (POD). Lightning Source created by the US wholesaler Ingram pioneered POD in the late 1990s, and Amazon acquired the POD printer BookSurge in 2005. Printers were forced to diversify by offering supply chain management and distribution services (including direct delivery to intermediaries and end-users), to supplement their conventional practice of delivering stock to publishers' warehouses. Advances in digital printing allowed publishers to reduce their printed book inventory and switch part of their backlist to just-in-time fulfilment of orders. Printing for local markets now saves shipping and environmental costs. Distributors serving publishers are aligning themselves with digital printers, and the growth in self-publishing offers digital printers new business.

The pre-press supplier market evolved too from the 1980s. Typesetters made greater use of computers for the pre-press production processes of printed books, and this led to a dramatic fall in the cost of typesetting per page. As digital publishing developed at the turn of the century, the typesetters, mostly based overseas, adapted and consolidated. New firms arose offering publishing solutions and they made large investments in technology to process content and data. Some of the largest, for example global companies such as SPi Global, Aptara and Techset, employ large and well-educated workforces in offshore locations, such as India and the Philippines. From the late 1990s they digitized the printed back issues of journals into fully coded and thus searchable content. The digitization of saleable journal back issues is nearly complete; by comparison the backlists of many book publishers have yet to be digitized in a systematic way, and the concentration has been on file conversion to ebook formats. In any case trade publishers have less control over their IP, which is often agented and includes third-party content such as illustrations.

The academic publishers in particular have looked to strip out costs from their organization through outsourcing to service providers, which now offer a range of higher value services, including copy-editing and proofreading, permission clearance, technical drawing, design, outputs to all formats, project management, and the development of enhanced ebooks. The client base of these companies is broadening out from the academic and professional publishers to include educational and trade houses. There are also specialist companies to supply content management systems within which workflow is managed and content is stored – examples are Librios in the UK, and RSI in the USA; and others which focus on the development of e-learning solutions and digital textbooks, such as Hurix in India, and Inkling in the USA. In the area of apps, digital directors within publishing houses will usually work with third-party developers, either in a partnership which shares the financial risk – and any profit – or by commissioning the project against a budget. Such multimedia projects will typically use a team approach, involving the author alongside a software developer, designer and producer. Examples of app developers in the UK include Touch Press (also a publisher) and Inkle.

The major trends of the adoption of a digital workflow, the output to a range of formats, standardization in processes, outsourcing to service providers (rather than to freelance copy-editors and designers), and the use of digital printing to manage the backlist of printed books, are having a major impact on the production departments of publishers. Some of the tasks (and job roles) of the print-only world are eliminated. On the other hand, the management of pre-press services, an awareness of constantly changing technologies, sound project management skills, and expertise in print buying remain vitally important.

DESIGN

With regard to the text design, the basis of the book designer's job is visual planning. They operate within technical, cost and time constraints, and take into account the views of the editor, and the production and sales departments. Their task is to transform and enhance the author's raw material, text and illustrations. The printed book should have aesthetical appeal and meet the practical needs of its users – whether for leisure, information or education. The drawing element of the job, if any, usually extends to providing blueprints or rough visuals for others (technical illustrators, artists, typesetters, image originators or printers) to execute. Design work can vary greatly according to the nature of the content.

The use of freelancers or agencies to design books or websites is widespread. They are commonly commissioned by editors, production staff, or in-house designers. Small publishers, without in-house staff, may ask a good printer to help with the design; and in some large firms issuing relatively straightforward books, editors or production controllers may design the books while commissioning the covers from freelance designers. Many titles – for example fiction, lightly illustrated non-fiction, academic and professional books – follow pre-set typographic templates.

In-house staff tend to be employed by medium to large houses, designing covers or more complex illustrated books (from illustrated adult and children's non-fiction to textbooks), and by the more established book packagers. They will work in a design or production department, reporting directly to the manager. The design manager, responsible for the overall brand of all the firm's books, is concerned with the deployment of in-house and external services, budgets, scheduling and administration. Senior designers may co-ordinate the work of junior designers; there may be design assistants; and some in-house designers specialize in particular lists. The design of book covers for most kinds of books, other than the most utilitarian, requires specific design attention which is carried out by in-house cover designers, or freelancers under the supervision of the art director. For the production of complex digital and print products, multi-disciplinary teams may be set up, consisting of editors, designers, interactive media designers, developers and project managers.

Touch Press sold more than 250,000 downloads of its app *The Elements*

The cover design is usually carried out separately from the text design

The preparation of artwork is mainly outsourced, and some publishers and packagers employ illustrators and designers on short-term contracts. Photography is normally commissioned. The design of promotional material may be the responsibility of in-house designers in marketing, or freelance designers or agencies commissioned by that department.

Design brief

The point at which a designer is first involved with a new book varies. It may occur before or after the author has completed the manuscript, the designer receiving either an edited or unedited copy. By then the book's overall parameters (for example format, extent, illustrations, binding, paper) have been planned. In some firms, editors personally brief designers while in others design meetings are organized, attended by the production team and sometimes the sales staff. The outcome may be a production specification, a budget and the schedule. It is vital for the designer to be given a clear brief by the editor at the outset. A designer may be able to suggest alternative ideas to save money or to improve sales potential. Assuming the book is not part of a fixed format series or that a pre-existing design cannot be adapted to suit it, the designer's opening tasks are to prepare the type specification and page layout which are supplementary to the book's overall production specification.

Type specification and page layout

The type specification sets out how the main text elements should be typeset in respect of typefaces, sizes, page depth, and line lengths, and of the positioning and spacing of the elements. The elements include:

- body text,
- headings – the hierarchy of chapter heads and subheadings,
- displayed quotations – broken off from the main text,
- tables,
- captions for illustrations,
- running heads at the top of the page, and
- page numbers.

The page layout is a graphic representation of the printed page – invariably of two facing pages. Layouts are based on a grid – the underlying framework within which text and illustrations are placed on the page.

> A grid is the graphic design equivalent of a building's foundations. As we read from left to right and top to bottom, a grid is generally a series of vertical and horizontal lines. The vertical lines will relate to the column widths, while the horizontal will be determined by the space that a line of type occupies. (Roberts and Thrift, page 18)

Layout and typographic style considerably affect the readers' perception of a book. The two are interdependent and should, if well designed, allow the author's work

The main text of this book is typeset in Scala and is unjustified (it has no fixed margin on the right-hand side); the boxed panels are in Scala Sans

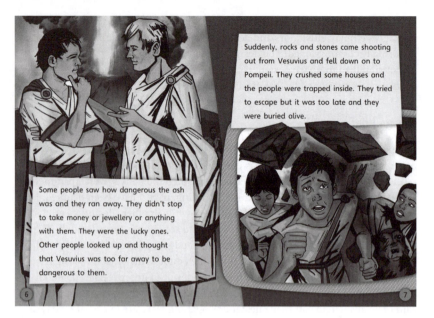

Suddenly, rocks and stones came shooting out from Vesuvius and fell down on to Pompeii. They crushed some houses and the people were trapped inside. They tried to escape but it was too late and they were buried alive.

Some people saw how dangerous the ash was and they ran away. They didn't stop to take money or jewellery or anything with them. They were the lucky ones. Other people looked up and thought that Vesuvius was too far away to be dangerous to them.

A double-page spread from the *Rapid* reading programme from Heinemann

to be presented consistently and flexibly, taking into account the content, aims, character, market and technical and cost constraints of the book. Book typography has four main functions (Mitchell and Wightman):

- readability – the text should be comfortable to read,
- organization – the structure of the text should be clearly communicated,
- navigation – information in the book should be easy to find, and
- consistency – the overall effect is to create a unified whole.

Factors that should be taken into account are the fitting of the author's manuscript into the desired extent; the ability of certain typefaces to cope with mathematics or foreign languages, or to ease reading by early or poor-sighted readers; and the typefaces available from a supplier. The designer presents one or more designs in the form of mock-ups to the editorial and production staff for their comments and approval – usually specimen pages are produced.

Typefaces popular for blogs and web pages are Arial, Georgia and Verdana

There are a variety of typefaces commonly used in books, ranging from traditional faces, such as Bembo, Garamond, or Times New Roman, to sans serif fonts (without the finishing strokes at the ends of letters) including Frutiger, Helvetica and Univers.

Typographic mark-up

Once the complete manuscript is edited, the designer may carry out the typographic mark-up, that is the addition of typesetting instructions to the manuscript or disk. Some instructions, such as the mark-up of the heading hierarchy and use of italic or bold within the text, may have been marked in copy-editing. The copy-editor may also have implemented a system of coding to mark the different text elements. The designer checks, for instance, the editor's

Adobe Caslon Pro

abcdefghijklmnopqrstuvwxyz 1234567890 1234567890

ABCDEFGHIJKLMNOPQRSTUVWXYZ fiflffiffl ½ ¼ ¾

At endre magna faccum velessis ad eu feuguercin henit lore et, vulla at, sequat,
consenibh et wisl iustie erosto odolessequat in vel utatue duis aliquam, quatem exeriure
vel ullam. Con utate te velit illumsan ullandre corperat alit nonsenim adit lutatie dunt
utpatie conse facipit at velesse quismol orperci tisi. Pit veliquate dolortie molutatem
ipsum vel do consenqu ipsustisi. El doloborem velis autet ad te ter luptatue ming estrud
esse modit laor aci tin hent dolortissi.

Adobe Garamond Pro

abcdefghijklmnopqrstuvwxyz 1234567890 1234567890

ABCDEFGHIJKLMNOPQRSTUVWXYZ fiflffiffl ½ ¼ ¾

At endre magna faccum velessis ad eu feuguercin henit lore et, vulla at, sequat, consenibh
et wisl iustie erosto odolessequat in vel utatue duis aliquam, quatem exeriure vel ullam.
Con utate te velit illumsan ullandre corperat alit nonsenim adit lutatie dunt utpatie conse
facipit at velesse quismol orperci tisi. Pit veliquate dolortie molutatem ipsum vel do
consenqu ipsustisi. El doloborem velis autet ad te ter luptatue ming estrud esse modit laor
aci tin hent dolortissi.

Adobe Jenson Pro

abcdefghijklmnopqrstuvwxyz 1234567890 1234567890

ABCDEFGHIJKLMNOPQRSTUVWXYZ fiflffiffl ½ ¼ ¾

At endre magna faccum velessis ad eu feuguercin henit lore et, vulla at, sequat, consenibh et
wisl iustie erosto odolessequat in vel utatue duis aliquam, quatem exeriure vel ullam. Con
utate te velit illumsan ullandre corperat alit nonsenim adit lutatie dunt utpatie conse facipit
at velesse quismol orperci tisi. Pit veliquate dolortie molutatem ipsum vel do consenqu
ipsustisi. El doloborem velis autet ad te ter luptatue ming estrud esse modit laor aci tin hent
dolortissi.

hierarchy of headings to ensure they conform to the agreed type specification, and
may want them modified. The typesetter follows the specification or style coding.
However, depending on the complexity of the material, the designer may indicate
the design treatment of recurring text matter which, though covered by the
specification, may still need to be marked by using abbreviations or codes.
Complex text (including tables) as well as displayed text, such as that of the
prelims, may require specific mark-up.

SKILLS

Design

Designers have technical proficiency and usually a vocational qualification. Underpinning design is a thorough knowledge of typography and the ways in which books and covers are put together. Mastery of software such as Adobe InDesign and Photoshop is essential, and an understanding of the capabilities of XML and HTML, and the different ebook formats. Designers need perception, clarity of thought, an ability to take a raw manuscript (perhaps badly presented), to analyse it, and come up with an effective design within financial and technical constraints. They should be able to anticipate the problems of readers. It calls for a combination of imagination, knowledge and understanding of current technical processes and current software, and an awareness of the work of leading freelancers and of trends and fashions in book design. For cover design a creative mind is pre-eminent, combined with a gut feeling of what sells.

Designers must develop the ability to extract a brief – tactfully overcoming some editors' quirks and preconceptions. They must be able to explain to authors, editors and sales staff, who rarely think in shape, colour and form, how they arrived at a solution, and why it is the best. They must be able to give clear and unambiguous briefs and instructions to other designers, illustrators, production staff and printers.

Highly illustrated work requires designers to get under the skin of a subject, to undertake research if necessary, to ask probing questions of experts and to pay due regard to ethnic or cultural sensitivities. The establishment of the all-important rapport with in-house staff and external suppliers takes time and experience to develop. The handling of artists, illustrators and photographers, some of whom can be awkward, calls for a special mixture of tact, pleading or coercion to induce them to produce their best work. Most designers work on many projects simultaneously, all at different stages in production. Thus, like editors, they need to be flexible and self-organizing.

Illustrations

The illustrations may reach the designer before the author has handed over the manuscript to the publisher. The designer may have briefed the author or supplied the editor with guidelines to help the author prepare drawn illustrations. Designers are usually responsible for commissioning the technical illustrators or graphic artists who execute the final artwork – often prepared on-screen in software such as Adobe Illustrator. In children's books, more traditional techniques of illustration may still be used. When many complex diagrams need to be drawn, the designer prepares an artwork specification to serve as a technical reference for illustrators.

Chosen freelance illustrators or artists are contacted directly, or are recruited from artist's agents, art colleges, or commercial studios. The designer, who may have developed or sometimes revisualized the author's roughs, briefs the contact about the purpose of each illustration and the style of execution (including the final size) and gives a deadline for completion; the cost is estimated in advance. Roughs may be prepared as the first stage and the designer checks that the brief has been followed; they will also want to confirm with the illustrator that the technical standard is suitable for processing and reproduction by the printer. The designer ensures that mistakes attributable to the illustrator are not charged to the publisher.

Proofing stages

With unillustrated books that go straight to page proofs, the edited and coded file (together with the type specification and grid) is sent off to the typesetter or pre-press supplier. For a book with illustrations grouped on pages, the designer provides a layout. When illustrations are interspersed with the text, the sized artwork and photographs are sent off with the text, or the designer instructs the typesetter to leave specified spaces for the illustrations to be inserted later. The designer may fine-tune the typography and correct any bad page breaks or layouts at page-proof stage.

With more complex illustrated books, the designer controls and plans completely the book's layout by means of a manual layout on screen, using Adobe InDesign or QuarkXPress. The designer may be involved with the final selection of photographs and advises whether they will reproduce well. The layout of a page can affect the choice, and the integration of text and illustration influences the sizes of photographs – these may need to be adjusted or cropped. At this stage the designer may work with low-resolution scans of the images, which enables proofs to be generated showing the illustrations. The designer tunes the ensuing page proofs and any illustration proofs, spotting visual errors which authors, editors and proofreaders may fail to recognize.

It is important to establish the correct final version of the text of a book, and this issue was highlighted when the UK edition of *The Corrections* by Jonathan Franzen appeared in 2010 with hundreds of mistakes. The typesetter had apparently sent the 'last but one' version of the book file to the printer. When the book is all correct and ready for printing, the typesetter produces the digital file of the book in one or more formats such as a high-resolution portable document format (PDF) file used by the printer, a low-resolution PDF file (perhaps for use on the web), an XML file, and ebook formats such as ePub or Kindle. There may be further stages undertaken by the printer to ensure the supplied PDF is reproducible by their system (a pre-flight check), and on colour books various kinds of proofs to verify the colour reproduction. All file conversions to the different ebook formats need checking.

Ebooks

Ebook file formats can be produced from many types of source file formats, such as InDesign or PDF, and are not dependent on an XML-early workflow. Backlist titles can be converted at relatively low cost by specialist companies or suppliers of publishing solutions. The greatest disruption to traditional book design has been the introduction of reflowable text enabling ebooks to be read on a variety of

EXPERT

XML

Meg Barton, Project Editor, Multimedia – Health Sciences, Wiley

XML (extensible markup language) is a method of tagging text so that it can be used not just by typesetting systems but also by the programs used to build electronic products like ebooks. Tagging is a way of adding invisible labels to words in your text. For example, HTML tags are used to impose some basic formatting on the web. The example below shows the tags for italic in HTML:

Did you enjoy the film of <i>Pride and Prejudice</i> yesterday?

Yes, but I liked the version with Colin Firth <i>much</i> better.

The opening tag switches on the italic and the closing one switches it off. HTML has a single set of tag names. Here is the same sentence tagged in XML:

<question> Did you enjoy the film of <filmtitle>Pride and Prejudice</filmtitle>yesterday?</question>

<answer> Yes, but I liked the version with <forename>Colin</forename><surname>   Firth</surname><emphasis>much</emphasis> better.</answer>

There are some important differences to note:

- XML tags identify items according to their meaning, rather than just specifying typography or layout.
- Unlike HTML, which has a single set of tag names, the naming for XML tags is not standard or universal. For example it would be equally valid to have named your tag <movietitle> rather than <filmtitle> or <query> rather than <question>.
- Anyone can make up their own XML tag names (depending on the sort of items they want to tag), and can devise and use any number of them – which is why XML is called extensible. In the above example you could add more tags to Colin Firth, for example <namegroup> to identify his two names as a group, and maybe <filmstar> to distinguish him further:

<filmstar><namegroup><forename>Colin</forename><surname>Firth</surname></namegroup></filmstar>

Apart from a few basic rules about consistency – for example each opening tag must have a closing tag – the only other requirement is to keep a reference list of the tags you have used – this list is called a DTD (Document Type

Definition). Any piece of text that obeys these rules is a 'valid' XML document. Different publishers (and other industries) have different names for their tags and develop their own DTDs.

Tagging of the text can be done by the typesetter as part of the typesetting process (or earlier by the author or copy-editor). The typesetter just needs to be supplied with a copy of the publisher's DTD. The typesetter will supply the publisher with XML files at the same time as the print files for the book, or can run off the XML files at some later date when requested by the publisher. Publishers are able to use the tagged XML text for a variety of electronic products: for example, ebooks, online databases, or textbook question banks. Most importantly, the XML-tagged text can also be stored by the publisher to use not just for these things, but for any other electronic medium that might be invented in the future. Production editors increasingly need to have a working knowledge of XML (just as they need to be familiar with the typesetting process without having hands-on experience of it). In-house programmers and technical staff will have a detailed knowledge of XML.

It is hoped that XML is the solution that publishers have long been looking for – a way of storing and reusing future-proof content.

screen sizes. As Chris Jennings says: 'Designers who work within publishing companies are often frustrated with the results when their beautifully crafted print books are converted to eBooks. Particularly if they are flowable eBooks, that can have their layout and fonts changed by the user' (Jennings, page 7). Designers of printed books concentrate on positioning and sizing text and illustrations on fixed pages in an attractive way. The typography conveys functionality and aesthetics, and it differentiates the character of one book from another. Reproduction as a PDF enables the design to be preserved when read digitally, but most ebook consumers are now happily choosing their own font and type size, and seeing the text reflow accordingly. Reflowable text makes it hard for designers to control set proportions, or the placement of illustrations and captions. The concept of the page spread, across two pages, often becomes redundant, and text and illustrations flow in a linear single column. The producers of ereading devices may also strip out formatting by the publisher to impose their own styles, reducing product differentiation.

Designers can, however, work to ensure that the text design is flexible and capable of display on a variety of devices. They can adjust the ebook design to ameliorate features of printed books, which if carried over to an ebook would irritate readers, such as omitting blank pages or adjusting spaces around chapter headings. Usability is aided by providing navigational hyperlinks between the content page headings and the relevant point in the text, or between note cues and end-notes. The design limitations of most published ebooks are partly due to technical and commercial reasons.

There are many ebook formats in existence and publishers will rarely wish to publish for just one format or retailer. The most universal format is ePub, which is a free and open XML standard, backed by the International Digital Publishing

Forum (idpf.org). EPub supports both reflowable content and fixed-layout content, and the needs of visually disabled readers. Although the format is supported by the publishing industry worldwide, and by most ebook resellers and device manufacturers, Amazon still uses its own proprietary formats derived originally from the Mobi format.

The most popular form of ePub is version 2 which is sufficient for many books other than the most complex. Although ePub 3 was launched in 2011, its uptake by reading device manufacturers and publishers has been slow. It is based on HTML5, supports rich media (audio and video), global languages, improved accessibility features, typographical and layout enhancements, user navigation and interactivity. The format offers the prospect of enhanced ebooks with features formerly restricted to apps. Publishers could potentially find out information on reader behaviour; and through the use of embedded JavaScript gain interactivity with them for marketing and sales. It also allows publishers to embed metadata within the file of the book, which intermediaries can then extract and use as they wish. In 2012, Apple launched iBooks Author and introduced its own fixed layout ePub (suitable for highly illustrated titles) for its devices. With iBooks Author it took the initial lead in enabling the design of interactive books for tablets, especially for use in education: 'If you're looking to create books that are digital first, use dynamic page designs, and are truly interactive, there is no better tool for the job' (McKesson and Witwer).

Alongside the numerous ebook formats, HTML5 (the next generation language for the Web) is seen as another ebook publishing medium offering great potential for so-called 'browser books'. HTML5 is especially designed for low-powered tablets and smart phones. Since HTML sits at the heart of the ePub and Mobi formats, O'Reilly Media advocates that authoring and production should take place in (X)HTML5. Such a workflow would obviate the numerous file conversions from Word to InDesign to ebook output formats (which incur costs and errors) and facilitate digital first publication. Pearson too has developed the Pearson XHTML5/ePub 3 workflow (PXW) for enhanced educational products: content is tagged semantically (by meaning) for delivery to multiple formats, platforms and devices. The future, however, is far from set on any one technology, platform, format, application or device.

Some publishers have the capability themselves of converting source files into ebook formats. There is a large variation in the time taken (and the ensuing cost) between working on straightforward books, such as fiction (very quick and cheap), and highly illustrated titles (slow and expensive). In practice most publishers use conversion houses to produce ebooks of their backlist – or of frontlist titles created using conventional workflows. The ebook files produced have to be verified for each format and tested on the most-used reading devices to ensure they work.

Highly illustrated colour books

Some print books are sold on the quality of their design and pictorial content, such as colour illustrated, non-fiction titles and textbooks. The approach to the design of these titles is closer to that of quality magazine publishing – the designer's role is more central. The interrelationship of the text and illustrations,

CPI Group's first
colour Quantum,
installed at Antony
Rowe in Chippenham
in 2012: an HP T360
inkjet press coupled
with a Timson T Fold
finishing line

and the positioning of colour within the book is planned and controlled, page by page, right from the outset. Sample spreads are produced to aid the writing by the authors or contributors. Such material (supplemented with the cover and a dummy) is used to interest overseas publishers in copublication. The designer normally has a greater say over the format, appearance, art direction and creation of the book, which allows more scope to vary its grid and pace, and to provide surprise elements. Some books, including school and ELT texts, use double-page spreads on topics. The strong headlines, dramatic illustrations and extended captions (often read first) capture the interest of a bookshop browser or learner.

Books for international copublication have special design needs. To gain economies in coprinting (printing two or more editions simultaneously), the colour illustrations should remain unaltered in position, whereas the translations of the text are changed on the presses. The typographic design allows for the greater length of translations (into German, for example); chosen typefaces have the full range of accents; type is only printed in black; type running around illustrations is avoided; type is not reversed out of blocks or colour or illustrations; and illustrations are not culturally specific to the UK.

Cover design

The cover or jacket protects the book, identifies the author and title, and carries the blurb. The ISBN and bar code enable ordering. The cover's main purpose is to sell. The design should inform as well as attract, be true to the contents, and be tuned to the market. The sales objective of the image is more significant in consumer book publishing (especially paperbacks) than other areas because of the importance of impulse purchase; and covers are used by the sales department to sell books well in advance of publication to wholesalers and retailers. The image must be powerful enough to attract a browser to pick the book up within a few seconds, and be typographically clear enough to be reproduced in reduced form on websites, and in the catalogues of the publisher, overseas publishers or agents.

Cover images are usually needed at least six months ahead of publication. The designer is briefed by the commissioning editor and generates rough visuals for approval by the editorial, marketing and sales departments. The chosen treatment is developed, and illustrators, photographers and picture researchers commissioned as necessary. Designers will typeset the copy and the cover will be proofed. The author may be consulted over the cover, or need to be persuaded by the editor of the merits of the publisher's choice. Covers arouse strong passions amongst all participants, and at worst may be revised right up to publication.

PICTURE RESEARCH

Picture research is the selection, procurement and collection of illustrations of all kinds. The number of in-house picture researchers is very small. They are concentrated in some of the large consumer and children's book publishers (where they may create a picture library), and educational houses. More commonly a publisher or packager will use expert freelance researchers, who specialize in particular subjects and serve a range of media. Otherwise, picture research for the text or cover may be just part of an assistant's work in an editorial or design department.

A general working specification for a book is drawn up in the editorial department. This covers the title, author, publication date, print run, book's market and its territorial extent, number of pictures required, ratio of colour to black and white, page size and picture budget. The picture researcher will be briefed by the editor or designer usually before the author has completed the manuscript, to ensure that the pictures are ready for the design stage. The brief can range from being very specific (the author or editor supplying a complete picture list citing most sources), less specific (just listing the subjects), to very vague (requesting pictures to fit the manuscript). It is vital for the researcher to clarify the brief.

The researcher may read the outline or manuscript in order to generate a list of ideas for approval by the editor and the author, or amend the picture list supplied by the author to something more feasible. An estimate of cost is produced, based on the researcher's experience, and the researcher advises whether the time and budget allocated are realistic; and potential sources are listed. The researcher cannot progress quickly with selection without knowing where to look for an image, and without a relevant set of contacts.

Sourcing pictures

The possible sources, both home and abroad, are varied and include:

- museums,
- libraries,
- archives,
- commercial picture agencies,
- photographers,
- PR departments,

- professional and tourist organizations,
- charities, and
- private individuals.

Some major collections are accessible on the web in low resolution, and there are low-cost banks of images which can be obtained under licence. Researchers consult print and online directories and picture source books, museum and library catalogues, guidebooks, brochures, magazines, acknowledgement lists in books and forage in reference libraries. They build up personal contacts with picture libraries and agencies, interview photographers, visit photographic exhibitions, and form contacts abroad. They compile their own records, indexes and address books. Their knowledge accumulates with each assignment.

Photographs can be commissioned for a project from photographers. Working to a brief, they will set up a shoot specially for the publisher. This can be expensive, with fees sometimes payable to the subject as well, but it should provide high-quality images. Often the relatives or friends of staff are called upon to act as subjects. Images may be put online during the shoot to ensure the right images have been taken.

The criteria for selecting picture sources include the nature of the material required, such as the subject range, type of material, quality, and the service offered – accessibility, speed and reliability, terms and conditions restricting borrowing or use of material, and cost. The use of stock images will lower the cost but is likely to look cheap alongside higher-quality pictures used in competing titles. Researchers will know which picture libraries are more expensive and from

Picture research

Picture researchers require the ability to interpret the message the book is trying to convey and, during selection, to make critical judgements on technical possibilities and costs as well as on aesthetic values. An understanding of the complexities of copyright and permission fees backs up their knowledge of sources; and allied to budget consciousness are the skills of negotiation especially with commercial picture agencies. Researchers must be highly organized in their work. As one art director puts it, 'It's a fascinating job – creative as well as administrative and business-like.'

Picture researchers are only as good as their source address books and accurate visual memories. They must keep up-to-date and use imagination in research, not just in visualizing fresh uses for remembered pictures but almost instinctively knowing where to start looking for pictures on any subject. Also necessary are methodical thinking, the knack of finding cheap sources, and a dogged persistence to get into new areas, getting behind closed doors. It is vital to forge good relations with sources – on the telephone, in writing and face to face. Some picture researchers have a degree in fine art or the history of art; knowledge of foreign languages eases contact with overseas sources; and IT skills are essential.

which ones special terms may be sought, perhaps when selecting a number from the same source. Linda Royles, then CEO of the British Association of Picture Libraries and Agencies (BAPLA), said:

> If you are doing a book about a specific subject, you are advised to go to an expert – a professor or someone with the world's largest collection on that subject. But if you are just looking for a picture of someone taking a phone call for a design brochure, a search on the web may be sufficient. (Harriet Dennys, *The Bookseller*, 25 August 2006)

With the list of potential sources compiled, the next task is to request and collect the pictures by telephoning, emailing or visiting. The web has made it much easier to view sample images, and today most images are received from agencies electronically. Under a limited licence, digital files can be used to prepare sample pages, but a full licence must be agreed in order to include the images in the final publication. For non-digital images, replies are reviewed, and the incoming material is logged and labelled with sources' names. The researcher is responsible for the good care of the material, so they select suitable items and quickly return the rejects to avoid paying holding fees and reduce the risk of loss.

The researcher does the initial selection and rejection of the pictures from a large assortment. The criteria for selection include the picture's editorial content – for example does the picture make the points or convey the impression or mood the author intended? Also important are the picture's composition, which should give the content clarity and impact, and reproducibility (tonal range, colour range and definition), bearing in mind the quality of paper and reproduction method to be used. The costs are assessed – reproduction fees, fees for digital use, print fees if buying prints, and search and loss/damage fees. Some pictures may be rejected on the grounds of cost.

Once the researcher has sufficient suitable illustrations, the cost is estimated again and a meeting held with the editor and designer to make the next selection. It might be that the researcher has to find more pictures very quickly before the final selection is made. Photographs must be ready by first proof stage to enable the designer to start the page layout. The researcher organizes the pictures for handover to the designer, and supplies the picture credit copy and information for the captions (provided by the sources of the photographs) to the editor.

The next task is to write to the sources for copyright permission to reproduce pictures, and to negotiate the fees. These will depend upon the territories and languages, print and digital formats required, the sales forecast, and the size (whole page, half page or quarter page), and whether the image is for a cover/jacket or the inside of the book. Some ebooks appear without the illustrations from the print edition in order to save on cost – the fees requested reflect the continuing anxieties of agencies about the use of images in digital publications (can the publisher control copying of the whole book or the image?).The researcher passes the suppliers' invoices for payment and calculates the total picture costs. After checking the page proofs (some sources want copies), the book is printed, and the final responsibility, if required, is to return the pictures to the sources.

PRODUCTION

The publisher's production department is the link between editors and designers and external suppliers. As the publisher's big spender, it buys the services of the pre-press suppliers and the printers which manufacture the books – and also raw materials, such as paper, if purchased separately. As publishers move further into digital publishing, the department increasingly deals with technology providers and developers, and has the responsibility for reorganizing workflows. The production department manages the pre-press technologies and the digital archive of the publisher's products for print and digital publication. In this respect, 'production' broadly defined concerns content management and is highly technical. Overall the job of production is 'to manage the conversion of inputs into outputs using a series of processes (usually provided by outside suppliers) so that the required number of books is available at the right time and to the right standard ... Production management is about project management' (Bullock, page 25).

Organization of the production department

Within a production department, there are commonly three main levels of job.

Production manager or director

They are responsible for the purchasing policy on sources of supply; establishing standard book sizes and papers; controlling the flow of work and maintaining quality standards; contributing to the preparation of the publishing programme by planning schedules and cost budgets for forthcoming books; and responding to major technical changes such as managing the pre-publication workflow. This manager contributes to the firm's profitability by buying materials and services at the most economic cost, by conserving the firm's cash by influencing the timing of major items of expenditure and by obtaining the longest possible credit periods from suppliers. The manager also handles the production of certain important books.

Production controller

This role is responsible for seeing books through the production stages from manuscript to receipt of bound copies and ebook publication. They may specialize in whole imprints or just part of the list, for example working alongside certain editors. This role may also be called a production editor or project manager when the job includes a wider remit of overseeing the editing and typesetting.

Production assistant

Some people start their production careers at this level. The production assistant gives clerical or administrative support to the department. They monitor proofs and production schedules, chase editors and suppliers, and record production costings.

In some publishers, production activities are split. One section deals with the pre-press process: essentially concerned with originating the products with external suppliers, or creating them in-house; and with the maintenance of the digital archive and its internal and external connections. Another section organizes and purchases the manufacturing of printed books and journals: essentially from printers and paper suppliers; and sometimes of other non-print items, such as CD-ROMs and DVDs and their packaging.

Production and book design go hand in hand. Production staff may design the books or hire freelance designers, or in-house book designers report to the head of production – if there is not a separate design department. The production department gives the accounts department information on anticipated costs and their likely timing, details of work in progress, and materials held in stock. In a small firm an editor may carry out production duties or use freelancers or external companies which provide a project management/production service; but with increasing size a firm will employ its own production, IT and data management professionals.

Provisional estimates

The production manager, or an automated costing system, supplies the commissioning editor with estimates of the costs of producing a proposed new title, and may suggest alternative production options. The book is envisaged in broad terms, for example its format, extent, illustrative content, the quality of paper desired, and the binding style. The estimate itemizes the costs across different sales forecasts. Some costs, such as for editorial and design work, will not change with the sales forecast, and overall the unit cost will decrease as these fixed costs are spread over higher forecasts. They include:

- the origination of illustrations,
- illustration and text permissions,
- design costs,
- editorial costs (including copy-editing and proofreading),
- typesetting and proofing,
- printing and binding,
- paper, and
- cover printing.

Once the author has signed the contract, production may advise the author, directly or via the editor, on how the text should be keyed – some publishers issue authors with style sheets in Word, or XML templates. The production controller, who gathers information from the editor or from pre-production meetings, prepares a specification – a detailed technical description of the book. The book's desired physical attributes, the amount of money and time available for its production, and any special market needs (particular typefaces, a subsequent paperback edition or co-edition) are taken into account, and the choice of production processes and materials is made. In children's publishing, ensuring physical product safety is vital.

Print and paper buying

The specification is sent to one or more suppliers so that they submit an estimate or quotation. Although there are printers that carry out all the processes, they may not do all economically or well. The typesetting and printing specifications may be sent to different specialist firms, known as trade suppliers. A publisher usually deals with a core of regular and trusted suppliers whose technology, machinery, staff, strengths and weaknesses are known; but new ones are tried. Sometimes fixed price schedules are negotiated with major print suppliers for standard types of work, which reduces the need for quotations and simplifies estimating. Suppliers may offer discounts on titles processed in batches or during slack periods. Moreover, the long time (for example six to 18 months) books take to produce gives publishers and packagers the option of using overseas suppliers (for example in Europe, the Far East or the USA). Whilst the printing of monochrome books is largely carried out in the UK, most colour book printing now goes abroad. The competitiveness of overseas suppliers is affected greatly by exchange rates, but other factors such as freight, communication, and environmental costs, longer timescales, and the location of the book's main markets are considered.

Suppliers are assessed on five main criteria:

- price,
- quality of work,
- service – the ability to keep to dates, or to make up for slippage, and communication,
- capability – skills and machinery, and
- capacity – the ability to handle larger jobs/reprint quickly.

The priority given to each varies according to the type of work. For example, a small saving from the cheapest source may be outweighed if that supplier produces inferior work or misses dates. Cost savings can be achieved by sending work abroad, but other considerations may keep the work in the UK. For example a quick reprint may be needed during the run-up to Christmas, and the domestic printer may be more amenable if they had carried out the original job.

The quotations are assessed, prices sometimes negotiated downwards and the work awarded. From the quoted prices, another in-house estimate is prepared. Paper is a major cost item and is bought either by the printer, or by the publisher from a paper merchant or directly from a mill. Pulp and paper are a world commodity subject to exchange rates and to price instability. During periods of price fluctuations or of real or imagined shortages, publishers may peg the price by buying forward, or store paper as an insurance against non-availability for quick reprints, even though that ties up the publisher's cash and incurs storage costs. Some publishers are responsive to environmental concerns, for example by choosing to purchase paper derived from sustainable forests and made with minimum pollutants; others use acid-free materials to ensure that their books and journals will last. There is a fine balance between using newly sourced paper from forests certified by the Forest Stewardship Council (FSC) or paper which has been recycled. Each has its merits and some paper will in fact have both types of content. The print run for the final Harry Potter volume, *Harry Potter and the Deathly Hallows* (2007), was printed on recycled paper, blended with virgin pulp from FSC certified forests.

Paper

Adrian Bullock, Principal Lecturer, Oxford International Centre for Publishing Studies

Paper is a versatile material which is strong enough to be used in a car, and soft enough to wipe your mouth with. It can trace its origins back to China at the beginning of the second century (105 AD), when it was made from rags, hemp, and old fishing nets. However, since the 1860s, most paper has been made from wood pulp, predominantly from softwood, coniferous trees, such as pine and spruce. These trees are used because of their longer fibres, which give paper its strength; and, because they grow best in temperate climates, most of the world's wood pulp is produced in northern countries like Canada or Finland. Pulp can be produced from broad-leaved, hardwood trees like oak or beech, but this is not generally done – their fibres are too short. This is also true of tropical hardwoods which grow in the rainforests of South America and Africa. The threat here does not come from papermaking: the rainforests are being cleared, and the trees burned, to make way for cattle ranching, agriculture and mining.

Trees for papermaking are planted as a crop, just like rice or wheat; and, like a crop, they are harvested at a later date – sometimes 25 to 30 years later, or even longer. Only part of the felled tree ends up as paper: the trunk, for example, is usually turned into timber for the furniture and construction industries. For every tree cut down, at least three seedlings are planted to ensure that the paper and the timber industries do not run out of their basic raw material – wood.

Despite the predictions of a paperless world, paper consumption has, if anything, increased over the past 15 years, bringing with it growing pressure on the forests as the need for pulp intensifies.

In 1993 the Forest Stewardship Council (FSC) was established 'to promote environmentally appropriate, socially beneficial, and economically viable management of the world's forests.'

Publishers, as major consumers of printing papers, are increasingly aware of the need to source their paper responsibly; and more and more books now carry the FSC logo with the statement that the publisher 'makes every effort to ensure that the paper used in its books is made from trees that are legally sourced from well managed and credibly certified forests'. Publishers also use recycled papers to print their books on, though evidence indicates that they still prefer papers made from virgin rather than waste pulp.

Paper comes in many qualities, from newsprint to coated art paper. The product determines the quality of the paper, as much as the paper determines the quality of the product. The publisher's skill lies in being able to match the paper to the product. Paper, as a natural product, has properties which are critical to the publisher, as well as the printer, and binder. In addition to a paper's colour (shade), roughness/smoothness (finish), and the quality of the pulp used to make it (furnish), the publisher needs to give careful thought to the following:

Weight

Measured in grammes per square metre (gsm/gm²); in the US, paper is measured in pounds per 500 sheets of a certain size. Heavy papers make heavy books. This can be a problem for the reader, who might get tired holding it; and for the publisher, because heavy books cost more to distribute by post than light ones. Book papers range between 70 and 115 gsm.

Bulk

The thickness of a sheet of paper is its bulk, measured in microns. A more useful way of measuring bulk is by volume basis, which makes it possible to calculate the bulk of a complete book, and not just one sheet of paper. Bulky papers are thick, and can be relatively light: for example, a tissue.

Opacity

This is a paper's lack of transparency. Matter printed on high opacity paper (90 per cent plus) cannot be seen from the other side of the sheet. Opacity is not really an issue in work where lines of text are printed back to back on each side of the sheet, such as a novel. However, in highly illustrated work, like an art book, with pictures appearing anywhere on the page, high opacity paper is essential. Opacity comes more from the paper's finish and its furnish, than from its weight or thickness. Increasing a paper's weight does not necessarily make it more opaque.

Grain direction

This is the direction in which the fibres lie as they are made into paper. Good bookmaking requires the grain direction to run parallel with the spine (right grain), though this is not always possible, especially with books printed on a web press. Books bound with the grain running from side to side (wrong grain) handle less well, and may develop a wave along the foredge. Covers printed wrong grain often bow.

Getting the paper right is the first step to getting the product right.

Paper has both weight and thickness (or bulk). Short books can be bulked out with a thicker paper; long books may need to have thinner and lighter paper. Recycled paper tends to be thinner than virgin papers. Paper may also be judged on its opacity – the degree to which image or text shows through to the other side of the page – and its colour or shade – from white through to cream or ivory. Coated papers are used for highly illustrated titles such as art books. Acid-free papers have a longer life.

There is also a range of sizes in which books can be printed. A trade paperback is 198 × 129 mm (also called B format) and the mass-market paperback size is 178 × 110 mm (A format). Popular formats for hardbacks are demy octavo (216 × 138 mm) and royal octavo (234 × 156 mm). The dimension head to tail is given first in the UK, but in the rest of Europe and the USA the convention is to give the width dimension first (the US dimensions are also in inches).

Table 9.1 Standard book formats (UK)

Format	Dimensions (H x W)
A4	297 × 210 mm
Demy quarto	276 × 219 mm
Crown quarto	246 × 189 mm
Pinched crown quarto	Up to 248 × 175 mm
Royal octavo	234 × 156 mm
Demy octavo (C format)	216 × 138 mm
A5	210 × 148 mm
B format	198 × 129 mm
A format	178 × 110 mm

The format of *Inside Book Publishing* is Pinched Crown quarto

Scheduling and project management

The production controller is usually responsible for all stages in the production of the book, following receipt of the approved manuscript from the editor. The stages include typesetting and cover development through to the final outputs; a production editor will also supervise the copy-editing, proofreading, and index preparation. All of these activities are usually outsourced to specialist freelancers or companies. The controller draws up the schedule of the internal and external operations that end with the output of the PDF file and ebook formats, and delivery of bound copies to the warehouse a few weeks ahead of the publication date. The schedule, related to those of other books, takes account of any optimum publication date, cashflow demands, the time needed for the tasks and to route material to and from suppliers. Alternatively, if the project management is outsourced to a full service supplier, the controller liaises with the supplier.

Production staff monitor progress and chase editors, designers and external suppliers to keep to agreed dates. As all the book's material passes between editor and designer, and between publisher and suppliers, it is handled by production at every stage, as are any problems with suppliers. Outgoing material is accompanied by documentation and orders; incoming material is logged, sent on to editors and designers, and return dates agreed. If the return dates are not adhered to, the machine time booked at the printers will be missed and the book unduly delayed.

Content management systems

In some publishers, the pre-press processes are carried out in-house and the documents progress through the stages and staff entirely in digital form. Content management systems (CMS) were first used by journal and reference publishers faced with processing and reusing large amounts of text data. They are designed to manage the creation, handling, storage and delivery of content for publication, and subsequent re-purposing. Content is stored without print-specific formatting, and typically XML is used to tag the content using standardized templates. As digital publishing has become more important, workflows are adapted to hold content in properly archived files, which can then be used to publish products on different platforms. Journals publishers have led the way in creating a production route that enables articles to be published rapidly online.

Additional functionality includes workflow management and access control. Such systems monitor the movement of jobs through the stages, and the workloads and performance of staff. Automated alerts track the progress of files as manual or automated sequences are applied. Users of the system are given differing levels of access. Authors may be part of the process – for example journal authors may be asked to write using an XML template supplied by the publisher; they can also track their articles online through the production process via journals management systems.

Production

Fundamental to production is a thorough understanding of current technical processes and digital developments, of machinery and materials, and of freight systems and methods of payment. More senior roles require strategic thinking as digital workflows are configured or adjusted. Most production staff have a degree or vocational qualification, or equivalent professional background. Knowledge of languages is useful in a department handling international co-editions. Numeracy, computer literacy skills, the ability to see alternative options and the consideration of all components are necessary in costing titles. Project management skills cover planning and progress chasing skills – ascertaining and clarifying objectives, setting priorities, assessing strengths and weaknesses of suppliers, foreseeing crunch points, and the development of specifications and schedules. Strong negotiations skills are required to deal with a range of suppliers.

Effective and fluent communication with in-house staff and external suppliers is crucial. Production staff must be able to work with editors and designers as a team even though their priorities of tight cost control and the maintenance of dates may conflict with those of editors and designers. Much of the work is highly administrative, requiring a good memory and meticulous attention to detail and record keeping. While friendly working relationships are formed with suppliers, production staff must never get too close to suppliers otherwise the negotiating edge is lost. Sometimes they have to be very tough, and they must have the integrity to reject any inducements.

Production staff come under great pressure. As the buffer between publisher and suppliers they receive kicks from all sides. They must buy competitively, conserve the cash, meet the deadlines and not make mistakes, which can be expensive to correct. Much time is spent troubleshooting and trying to keep everyone happy. They need to resolve problems, to think laterally and find the best solution, to switch quickly from one thing to another, and thrive under the strain.

SKILLS

Monitoring costs and quality

Many books, especially if illustrated, may change from their original concept during the writing and design stages. A new format may be chosen or the number of illustrations varied. Deviations from the original estimate and specification are monitored and costed. There is a constant risk that the estimate of costs made at the outset will be exceeded. Substantial proof corrections quickly erode a title's profitability. Costs incurred to date are recorded and revised estimates of total costs produced, particularly at the page-proof stage. Then the publisher normally fixes the book's price and the balance of print/digital sales, influenced, for example, by the actual advance orders from booksellers. Suppliers' invoices are subsequently checked, passed for payment, or queried.

The production controller checks the completeness of material at every stage as well as the accuracy of the instructions from the editor and designer, the quality of illustration originals sent to suppliers, and the quality of material returned. Technical advice is given to editors and designers to help them in their work. Constant contact with suppliers' representatives, and visits to suppliers maintain relationships.

Highly illustrated quality colour books may involve the production manager or controller in approving the sheets of each section run off the press – whether in the UK or abroad – and taking responsibility for the quality on behalf of the publisher or packager. The printing is compared against the final proof to ensure that corrections have been made, and that the colour quality matches the values agreed at the contract proof stage.

Advance copies of the bound stock are checked to ensure that the specified materials have been used, and that the binding, as well as the overall quality of the product, meets the publisher's standards. Exceptionally if a major error is discovered, an enquiry is held to determine who is responsible and has to pay. Finally, all the costs of producing the book are compiled. Controllers also cost and organize reprints and new editions; some large publishers employ staff solely for this task. The publisher or packager owning the digital file does not always use the original printer in which case the job is moved to the new supplier.

The printing of editions for other firms (for example English and foreign language co-editions) involves supplying the rights department with estimates of costs. The costs will include printing the bulk order – or if the buyer does the printing, the cost of supplying digital files – and costs of imprint changes – for example, the name of the co-publisher will have to appear on the title page instead of the original publisher's and the details on the copyright page will change; all of this makes a halt in the printing and costs money. When the publisher or packager prints foreign language editions, the overseas publishers supply the file of the translated text which is checked by production to ensure it fits the layout of the colour illustrations. Production staff may also be concerned with the purchasing of the manufacturing of non-print items and their special retail or mail-order packaging requirements.

Suppliers are chosen according to cost, technology and quality. Significant cost savings can be achieved by outsourcing typesetting and printing to countries in the Far East. Companies in India, for example, not only offer typesetting but also IT services (digitization and tagging) and editorial and design work. The whole process from receipt of the author's text through to the digital file for the printer can be outsourced.

PRODUCTION PROCESSES

Typesetting

The core business of a typesetter is text and data processing, plus other services. This could range from cleaning up authors' Word files prior to editing, XML tagging, pagination and proofing, through to production of outputs for printing copies, and for ebook and web distribution. They may digitize the backlist in whatever formats the books exist. There is a reduced role for typesetters when designers supply the finished files.

> The typesetters that remain specialize in the larger, more complex jobs, such as legal and science or medical reference books, and, being labor intensive, much of this work is carried out in countries such as India. Some publishers supply authors with templates, however, and so for text books the authors essentially typeset the book as they write. (Bann, page 48)

Some firms offer additional editorial and design services while others concentrate on highly technical material or text database management. The vast number of titles with no or minimal illustrations do not require designers to lay out the pages – the typesetters' largely automated pagination systems do it for the publishers. They can generally take a 100,000-word manuscript and submit page proofs to a publisher within two weeks – much faster if supplied with coded disks.

Typesetters use a variety of applications, such as Adobe InDesign and QuarkXPress. Only typesetters who have specialist-trained staff operate the very expensive and sophisticated programs designed especially for academic books and journals (such as Arbortext Advanced Print Publisher – formerly 3B2). LaTeX, pronounced 'laytek', is an open source program with many variants, designed by mathematicians in Chicago for authors of physics and mathematics to present their papers and books full of equations in an attractive way; or they may use MathML. Writers and publishers of technical and computing books may use DocBook – an open source XML vocabulary that allows them to create documents in a presentation-neutral form that captures the logical structure of the content. Using free tools along with the style sheets, content can be published as HTML pages and PDF files, and in many other formats, such as ePub (docbook. sourceforge.net, accessed 11 October 2013).

The typesetter will supply proofs as PDF files for checking by the publisher and author. The publisher will usually ask the typesetter to convert the output of its pagination systems into PostScript (PS) files or PDF files. Where PostScript is a page description language, a programming language, PDF can

> also contain information not only related to how a page looks, but also can describe how it behaves and what kind of information is contained in the file. So PDF is a file format that is smarter than EPS. A PDF file can contain fonts,

images, printing instructions, keywords for searching and indexing, job
tickets, interactive hyperlinks, and movies. (adobe.com, accessed 16 October
2013)

From such files printers are able to output text and graphics straight to plate or
press.

Reproduction of illustrations

Illustrations may be prepared or sourced in digital form and can be provided to
the typesetter as EPS (encapsulated PostScript) files – from a drawing program
– or as TIFFs (tagged image file format) or JPEGs (joint photographic experts
group) – for half-tones. Non-digital originals of illustrations are converted to
digital form. This can be done in-house, using a scanner and an application such
as Adobe Photoshop – or by a professional repro (reproduction) house, the
typesetter or the printer – to sizes specified by the designer.

Book printing presses cannot reproduce directly the continuous shades or
tones of colour appearing in photographs or pencil drawings, thus 'the half-tone
process' is used. The image of the black and white or colour original is 'screened'.
It is broken into a series of dots of varying size with larger, closer or adjoining
dots in dark areas; and smaller, further apart, or no dots at all in light areas. When
printed, the dots create the illusion of continuous shades.

Printing a full colour image requires a four-colour process. The image needs
to be broken down into four basic colours: cyan (blue), magenta (red), yellow, and
black (known as key). These colours, used to put ink on to paper, are called
'CMYK', or process colours, and are subtractive primaries. Red, green and blue
(RGB) are the additive primaries, used in TV screens and computer monitors.
They cannot be used on a printing press. Colour separation can be done using a
scanner, or a digital image can be saved as CMYK in an application such as Adobe
Photoshop. In order to print a four-colour image, you ideally need a four-colour
press, capable of printing all four colours in one impression. It is possible to print
a four-colour image on a two-colour press, but this is less efficient and can cause
quality problems. Various kinds of proofs are submitted to the publisher before
the final digital file of the illustrations is accepted. If necessary, books can be
printed in six colours. This process was used, for example, for Kevin McCloud's
Choosing Colours (2007), where orange and green inks were printed after the
CMYK to create a six-colour job.

Litho printing: imposition and platemaking

The printing plates on a litho press do not print one page at a time. Rather each
sheet of paper, printed both sides, carries 8, 16 or 32 pages (or multiples of these),
and is subsequently folded several times and cut to make a section (or signature)
of the bound book. Since printers have different sized presses and different
binding machinery, each printer is responsible for its own imposition: the
arrangement of the pages that will be printed on each side of the sheet so that
once the sheet is printed and folded the pages will be in the right sequence and
position. The publisher will supply the printer with PS or PDF files that have been

prepared by the designer or typesetter. The printer then imposes the pages on to each plate – this is called computer to plate (CTP).

Online content

Low-resolution PDF files can be conveniently put on the web for either downloading or viewing within a browser. The user sees a replica of the final printed page. Journal articles are often presented in PDF for the ease of librarians and others wanting a common standard, and for publishers who are working with print-designed documents.

Structured mark-up of the text using XML, independent of any typographic mark-up, allows the text to be published in different ways. From a source XML file, the content can be published as a book, an ebook, an HTML (HyperText Markup Language) file for the web, or on a mobile device. Publishers also find it easier to sell XML data to third parties for electronic publication. Its use facilitates the online linking of elements such as bibliographic references and illustrations. The growing use of Adobe InDesign by publishers facilitates the origination of XML.

Publishers or content aggregators look to add value online by generating keywords for content, enabling online searches, and also by identifying text elements or chunks by metadata. For example, a journal publisher can use a DOI (digital object identifier) to identify an article or an illustration within the article. A DOI name can apply to any form of intellectual property expressed in any digital environment. DOI names have been called 'the bar code for intellectual property'; like the physical bar code, they are enabling tools for use all through the supply chain to add value and save cost (doi.org). Industry-wide initiatives such as CrossRef enable the linking from references in online journals to the cited article (crossref.org).

Publishers with websites or online services which need regular updating or additions may opt to use a content management system (CMS) – software for managing websites. For some publishers the web is a different medium needing different design approaches, which are not based on linear textual organization and print-derived typographic design. Web pages may be prepared using HTML and supplementary content, such as animations, video clips, and sound recordings. Tricia Austin and Richard Doust write:

> there is no reason why a website should look like the printed page, and a new generation of new-media designers are seizing the opportunity to throw away the rule book and break new ground . . . Designers can introduce sound and movement into their new-media designs. (pages 89–90)

Printing

Many books are still printed by offset lithography (abbreviated to offset or litho), but there has been a rapid growth in the use of digital printing. Offset metal plates have a flat surface which is treated so that the areas to be printed attract grease (ink) and repel water; and the non-printing areas attract water and repel ink. A plate is clamped around a cylinder on the press, dampened and inked by rollers.

This is a T-48 Timson press, built for Clays in 2007. The conventional Timson presses are web-offset, fixed format machines – this one is for royal format books

The plate rotates against a rubber coated cylinder (or blanket) on to which the inked image is offset and from which the ink is transferred to the paper.

Many offset presses are sheet-fed and vary in plate size and in capabilities. There are also offset presses – known as web presses – that print on to a reel of paper. Sheet-fed presses would be the usual choice for standard printings of black-and-white books. Web presses produce a folded signature at the end of the operation. This, and their high running speeds, make them attractive for long print runs.

Digital printing

High-speed digital printing has begun to challenge litho printing. Digital printers do not use printing plates – instead they create the impression on the paper with an ink jet or by using toner and electrostatic charge (like in a photocopier). A number of single copy orders can be printed one after the other without the disruption of having to set up the press each time – the computer lines up the next titles. The quality of digital printing has been variable, but is now perfectly acceptable for most monochrome books and much colour work.

This book was printed using a digital press

The choice of litho or digital printing comes down to economics. Manfred Breede writes: 'Conventional printing processes remain unsurpassed in their ability to reproduce large print runs cost effectively . . . In comparison, the cost per unit of operating a digital printing device is always the same regardless of the run length' (Cope and Phillips, page 35). Depending on the equipment operated by the printer, litho runs are increasingly rare below 1,000 copies, and digital runs would not generally exceed 2,500 copies. For runs in between, other factors may come into play such as the quality, page extent, or format required. Digital printing facilitates the viability of printing a book with a very short run – for example five copies – but also genuine print on demand – where just one copy is ordered by a customer.

Timson Prosper: a complete book line at Clays, comprising a digital Timson T-Press with a T-Book transfer system creating cut pages in book block form that feed into a Muller Martini binding line. The 'sweet spot' for the line is print runs of between 1,000 and 3,000 copies in multiple formats

Digital printing is suitable for use by publishers of specialist books or for backlist titles more generally. After the initial printing (litho or digital), publishers face continuing demand. They could reprint a short run by digital printing, either to hold in stock or to supply a major customer, or print one copy in response to a firm order. Once the title moves to 'on-demand' status it need never go out of print. The manufacturing time from the receipt of an order for one book is measured in hours, rather than in the weeks taken by litho print-runs, with immediate dispatch. The automated workflow batches together different titles sharing common specifications, configures the production machinery accordingly, manufactures the batch and then reconfigures the machinery to the next shared specification.

There are now also automated stock-replenishment systems using short-run printing, whereby printers receive direct feeds from the publisher's warehouses and produce in quantities of anything from 20 to 500. Digital printers, however, offer a more limited range of book sizes compared to the litho printers. In order to work cost effectively and quickly, they standardize sizes, paper, cover finishes and binding.

Digital printing has generated new ways of working beyond the management by publishers of the backlist and single copy orders. Wholesalers can use it to produce copies for end-users from digital files supplied by publishers. The printing of hard copies becomes 'distributed' as opposed to being centralized by publishers through their own print suppliers. Publishers can customize for a teacher a pack of teaching resources drawn from a variety of titles for student purchase. Smaller digital presses are now commercially available, and these have the potential to be placed anywhere in the world, in bookshops, libraries and universities, with access to an unlimited catalogue of titles over the internet. The Espresso Book Machine, which can print and bind a 300-page paperback in three minutes, was launched in 2006 but has been slow to take off.

Binding

After printing, the sheets are folded by the printer or possibly by a trade binder. The folded 8-, 16- or 32-page sections are gathered in sequence to make up every book. Some hardbacks and some quality paperbacks, especially those printed on coated papers (including some textbooks) have their sections sewn together. With quality hardbacks, the sewn sections are trimmed on three sides (leaving the sewn spine folds intact), end papers are glued to the first and last sections (unless the text paper is sufficiently strong), any decorative head or tail bands added, strong material glued to the spine to reinforce the hinge with the case, and the spine sometimes rounded. Meanwhile the case is made by gluing the front and back boards (and paper backstrip of the spine) to the 'cloth' which in turn is blocked with the title, author and imprint in gold, silver or a range of different colours. The outer sides of the end papers are pasted, the finished case dropped over the book (spine-side up), and the book squeezed. The jacket is printed on a small colour press, sometimes by another firm. This is often laminated with clear plastic film and wraps the finished book. Sometimes the printed cover is glued to the case before binding to produce a *printed paper case* (PPC) or *cover to board* book.

Sewn bindings are stronger but more expensive. Adhesive binding methods are commonly used for paperbacks and some hardbacks. *Perfect* binding is used typically for cheap paperbacks – the spine folds of the sections are cut off and the spine edge of the now individual leaves roughened. Glue is applied to hold the leaves together and to stick the printed cover to the book, which is then trimmed on three sides. The cover may have been varnished (on a printing press or special machine) or laminated. Another method, cheaper than sewing but stronger and more expensive than perfect binding, is known variously as *slotted*, *notch* or *burst* binding. The spine folds of the sections are not cut off. Instead they are perforated during sheet folding. The binding machine merely injects the adhesive to hold together the folded sections, applies the cover and trims the book.

Packing and distribution

The printer or binder packs quantities of the book by shrink wrapping, parcelling or in cartons and delivers them on pallets to the publisher's specified warehouse. Printers have traditionally delivered the bulk stock of new titles to the publisher's warehouse, which in turn ships them out to the main retailers and wholesalers. However, printers competing on service may deliver stock directly to key customers and to individuals. In the case of print journals, for example, they may deliver to subscribers.

Now read this

Adrian Bullock, *Book Production*, Routledge, 2012.

Sources

Tricia Austin and Richard Doust, *New Media Design*, Laurence King, 2007.

Phil Baines and Andrew Haslam, *Type and Typography*, Laurence King, 2005.

David Bann, *The All New Print Production Handbook*, RotoVision, 2006.

Alan Bartram, *Making Books: Design in British publishing since 1945*, British Library and Oak Knoll Press, 1999.

Linda Bennett, *PA Guide to Going Digital*, Publishers Association, 2010.

Manfred Breede, 'Plus ça change: Print on demand reverts book publishing to its pre-industrial beginnings', in Bill Cope and Angus Phillips (eds), *The Future of the Book in the Digital Age*, 2006.

Robert Bringhurst, *The Elements of Typographic Style*, version 3.1, Hartley & Marks, 2005.

Adrian Bullock and Meredith Walsh, *The Green Design and Print Production Handbook*, Ilex, 2013.

Elizabeth Castro, *EPUB Straight to the Point*, Peachpit Press, 2011.

Harriet Dennys, 'Picture This', *The Bookseller*, 25 August 2006.

Simon Garfield, *Just my Type*, Profile, 2010.

Chris Jennings, *eBook Typography for Flowable eBooks*, PagetoScreen ebook, 2012.

Marshall Lee, *Bookmaking*, 3rd edition, Norton, 2004.

Nellie McKesson and Adam Witwer, *Publishing with iBooks Author: An introduction to creating ebooks for the iPad*, O'Reilly, 2012.

Ruari McLean, *The Thames and Hudson Manual of Typography*, Thames and Hudson, 1980.

Michael Mitchell and Susan Wightman, *Book Typography: A designer's manual*, Libanus Press, 2005.

David Alan Rech, 'Instituting an XML-First Workflow', *Publishing Research Quarterly*, September, 2012.

Lucienne Roberts and Julia Thrift, *The Designer and the Grid*, RotoVision, 2002.

Web resources

www.bapla.org British Association of Picture Libraries and Agencies.

www.britishprint.com British Printing Industries Federation (BPIF) provides information on book printing.

www.crossref.org CrossRef operates a cross-publisher citation linking system.

www.digitalbookworld.com Digital Book World.

www.doi.org International DOI Foundation.

www.futurebook.net FutureBook blog of *The Bookseller*.

http://goodereader.com Good E-Reader – ebook and digital publishing news.
www.idpf.org International Digital Publishing Forum.
www.mashable.com Mashable – news site for digital technology.
www.mobileread.com Mobileread.
www.radar.oreilly.com O'Reilly Radar blog.
www.tasi.org.uk Technical Advisory Service for Images.
www.techcrunch.com Techcrunch.

CHAPTER 10

Marketing

Marketing within the publishing industry used to be regarded as primarily the promotion of new books. In trade publishing, this would involve talking to the literary editors on the national newspapers, securing coverage in the print and broadcast media, placing relevant advertisements, creating point-of-sale material, and organizing tours for selected authors. While marketing was about generating public interest in new books, its other main objective was to persuade the book stores to display frontlist titles on their shelves, thereby giving visibility to new books to drive sales. Whilst some marketing practices developed for print books carry over to the digital world, marketing has undergone a radical change in emphasis from the physical to the internet and mobile. Also marketing has a much broader role and marketers play a pivotal role in many aspects of a book's publication. In an age of self-publishing, consumer publishers in particular have to be able to demonstrate to authors the efficacy of their marketing efforts and their ability to develop and manage an author's brand.

The effects of the internet and associated technologies continue to have major implications on the ways in which books are marketed and sold. The growth of internet retailing has hit hard physical book stores, reducing the opportunities for in-store impulse purchases. Readers can see thousands of titles in a bookshop, and on screen they see very few. The challenge for publishers is to help readers to discover, and buy, their books in a digital world of content abundance, much of it available for free.

Whilst it has diminished print newspapers and the amount of review space for books, the web has opened up many new marketing opportunities, often at low direct cost. Internet retailing has broadened and deepened book availability worldwide. The rapid rise of social media has fostered word-of-mouth recommendation – hitherto restricted to family and close friends – and the influence of bloggers and book recommendation sites has grown. The web enables the development of vertical communities, sharing interests, who can be attracted to a publisher's books, and publishers themselves can develop such communities around their titles. Publishers commission online book trailers, author video chats and podcasts to supplement author tours. Technology reduces the cost of formerly print-based marketing and extends its reach. For example, trade publishers send digital proofs to reviewers; academic publishers send e-inspection copies of textbooks to teachers. Trade publishers produce online newsletters and academic and STM publishers conduct targeted email campaigns when formerly they were restricted to posting out printed items. The power of search has given prominence to SEO (search engine optimization) and the importance of metadata (information about content from a book's cover through to chapter abstracts).

Most significantly, technology facilitates direct to consumer (D2C) marketing and a dialogue with readers and users. Publishers can connect with individuals within the audience, to inform publishing decisions and increase marketing cost-effectiveness. The use of analytics increases the understanding of consumer behaviour. This direct connection with individuals offers the prospect of being able to customize and personalize the content they wish to consume, and helps to predict which authors and books will succeed. Book marketers play a vital role in the changing business models of publishers. 'Every large house has a consumer insight or consumer research department, as publishers realize how important it is to find out about the consumer and how relatively easy it is to have direct contact' (*The Bookseller*, 26 July 2013).

Marketing staff in large publishing groups may be attached to particular companies, imprints or lists in the group. Many marketing departments consist of just one or two people who do everything, but in medium to large firms there are usually at least three levels: marketing director; marketing, brand or product manager; and marketing executive or assistant. Marketing encompasses numerous, diverse activities. Large companies employ specialists in key areas, such as public relations and publicity (sometimes called 'communications'); market research and analytics; website and social media; sales support; events and exhibitions; and product, mailing and customer databases. The collection and management of data in all its forms and its effective application are increasingly important across all activities.

Senior marketing staff may first become involved at the publishing proposal stage. They will advise on product development, especially when the project is a large investment. They will be involved in a range of discussions about the book's pricing, cover, target market and the ways this can be reached. From discussions with editors and sales staff, each book is evaluated and decisions made on the promotional material required – to support sales and for the target readership – and what publicity and media coverage should be sought. The marketing budget may be proportional to the expected sales revenue or set separately for key titles. It is impossible to promote all books equally and, especially in consumer book and textbook publishing, the lead titles receive by far the largest budgets. The key judgement for every title is deciding how much to spend to generate profitable sales that more than recoup the outlay.

A company will develop an overall strategy for a list or set of products and services. This will involve targeting particular market segments, positioning the product or brand in the minds of customers, settling on the relevant marketing mix for those customers, and establishing a budget for marketing expenditure. For significant new products or series an individual marketing plan may be prepared.

Marketing plan

There is no fixed template but a marketing plan will contain the following elements.

Executive summary

Target market and marketing environment

Market segments, market drivers, and the results of market research. Analytical tools to be used include PEST (political, economic, social and technological) and SWOT (strengths, weaknesses, opportunities and threats). Research into reader demographics and social media analytics may be used.

Product overview

Information about the current situation regarding the company's products and competitor activity.

Marketing objectives

These should be SMART: specific, measurable, achievable, realistic, and time-bound. For example, to achieve a market share within the secondary school mathematics market of 15 per cent within three years.

Marketing strategy

Outlines the target markets, key influencers, positioning, the readers the publisher wants to reach, where they can be found, what kinds of marketing they respond to best, and what it will cost to reach them. Analysis of what size of response rate is required in order to make the campaign viable is also essential.

Specific strategies for each area of the marketing mix

The marketing mix is the 4Ps – product, price, place and promotion. This is covered in detail later in the chapter.

Schedule and budget

Set out are the actions within a time-scale, costed through in detail.

Controls

How will progress be monitored and analysed?

Follow-up plans

What are the possible next stages?

FOCUS

THE MARKET FOR BOOKS

The first step in marketing a product is to understand the nature of the market. A range of data is available on the purchasing behaviour and demographics of the consumer book market. Table 10.1 reveals the factors that influence consumer book purchases in the UK. For marketers it shows the importance of having a book in stock in a shop, the value of building author brands, and the impact of recommendation on a book's sales.

Table 10.1 Purchase prompts for UK consumers (*source*: 2009 data from Book Facts Online)

Purchase prompt	Percentage of books bought
Saw browsing	28.7
Subject-matter	23.6
Read author/series before	21.2
Gift request	7.7
Review/recommended	7.7
Low price/offer	5.6
Cover design/info	3.3
Saw film/TV adaptation	1.8
Prize win/nominated	0.3
Not specified	0.1

There is variation across the population in terms of the number of books bought. First, around 30 per cent of adults do not buy a book at all – how can publishers reach this part of the population? (Mintel, 2012) Generic initiatives to encourage reading are important for the industry. A prominent example is World Book Day, and in 2013 UK schoolchildren received a £1 book token to spend on a specially created £1 book; or they could put it towards the cost of any book. Quick Reads was launched on World Book Day in 2006 to provide 'fast-paced, bite-sized books by bestselling writers for emergent readers, anyone who had lost the reading habit or simply wanted a short, fast read' (delni.gov.uk/quick-reads). There is also World Book Night, when free books are handed out on the international day of the book (23 April, also Shakespeare's birth and death date), with a focus on giving to those who do not normally read for pleasure. City Reads, which began in Seattle in 1998, encourages a whole city to read the same book. In September 2013, everyone in Brighton was invited to read the Discworld novel *Guards! Guards!* by Terry Pratchett.

Organizations such as the National Literacy Trust and Booktrust (UK) are involved in the promotion of reading and literacy. Reading for pleasure amongst both adults and children is under pressure in a rich media environment of TV, the internet, games and social media. Examining reading amongst children in the UK in 2011, the National Literacy Trust found that:

> In 2005 we found that four young people in 10 read daily outside of class. This research carried out at the end of 2011 found that only three young people in 10 now read daily in their own time. However, the number of

children and young people who enjoy reading very much or quite a lot has remained static since 2005 (50% today vs 51% in 2005). These findings together suggest a clear issue with children's and young people's leisure time with many children and young people enjoying reading but pushing it out in favour of other activities. (National Literacy Trust, page 11)

Publishers consistently talk of the challenge of getting teenage boys interested in books, especially fiction, and the research discovered that more girls than boys said they enjoyed reading very much (27.6 per cent compared to 18.3 per cent). Can reading books on an electronic device encourage more boys to become active readers?

Libraries play an important part in promoting reading and the use of books, and librarians promote books in a variety of ways, from personal recommendations to working with children and schools to champion reading. Despite this, there has been a noticeable decline in library borrowings, falling from 376.9 m in 2001/2 to 287.5 m in 2011/12, a drop of 24 per cent (LISU issue statistics).

The temptation for publishers is to concentrate on selling to the heavy book buyers, those who purchase a lot of books. If they are regular visitors to bookshops, they can be reached by ensuring that the books are in stock and promoted there. If frequent purchasers online, they can perhaps be reached through social media or word of mouth.

The average UK household has 138 books, less than half of which have been read (World Book Day research, 2014)

Demographics

Table 10.2 shows book buying by gender, age and socio-economic group. The overall picture is that book purchasing tends to increase with age and income.

Table 10.2 Book buying in the UK – demographics (*source*: 2009 data from Book Facts Online)

	Proportion of all books (%)	Proportion of adult books (%)
Female	58	52
Male	42	48
12–16	2	1
17–24	4	4
25–34	15	12
35–44	18	16
45–54	15	16
55–64	21	24
65–79	26	27
AB	24	25
C1	32	31
C2	22	21
DE	20	22

Travelling by public transport encourages reading, as can most readily be seen on the Underground in London. The age at which the person left education is also an important factor – those who leave later are bigger consumers of books. When it comes to ebooks:

> The demographic characteristics of e-book buyers are quite similar to all book buyers, the main difference being that men are almost as likely to have bought ebooks in the past year as women, suggesting that the anonymity of reading with e-readers, the convenience of the ebook and the technology are all factors which have served to engage men where print books have previously failed. (Mintel, 2012)

Targeting

With a clear view of the market segments amongst book consumers, publishers can decide whether to target a particular audience, say single young women for chick lit fiction. The same principles apply in textbook publishing, where first-year undergraduates may be chosen as the segment for an introductory marketing textbook.

Decisions around targeting have implications in consumer publishing for the cover design, where any advertising is placed, and what type of media coverage (including social) is planned. When in 2010 Orion published the first YA novel by Carlos Ruiz Zafon, *The Prince of Mist*, they decided to target both a children's and adult audience. Marketing included advertising in London Underground stations and a targeted digital marketing campaign, based around the author website run by Orion, with teasers sent to the author's existing fans. Other ways of segmenting the market include by retail channel: there are different demographics for those purchasing books at Waterstones or in supermarkets. A book may be seen as ideal for promotion through a particular channel.

Positioning

Once the target market has been selected, it must be decided how the product will be positioned in the mind of the consumer. Marketers can prepare positioning maps which show how their product or brand will fit into the market. Will this be a high-value item with an air of quality, or a cheaper product with an emphasis on value? 'More for more' positioning involves creating an upmarket product or service at a relatively high price; 'the same for much less' offers a basic product at a competitive price. An example of the former would be electronic access to the *Oxford English Dictionary*, and an example of the latter would be a low-priced ebook in genre fiction. In the reference market the Dummies brand offers simplified information across a whole range of subjects, and Marcel Knobil, founder of consultancy Superbrands, said: 'Wiley has built an ownership of the idea that you can become an expert from a beginner' (*The Bookseller*, 6 December 2007).

MARKETING MIX

For lead titles, marketers will prepare full marketing plans which assess the target market for the title and lay out strategies for reaching that market both through online and offline activities. Marketing activities can be placed under the four general headings of what is known as the marketing mix:

- product,
- price,
- place, and
- promotion.

Product

Marketing plays a full role in the development of new projects, from coming up with new ideas and commenting on editors' proposals to market testing new projects during their development. Marketing will also be involved in commenting on the book's title (including any subtitle) and other textual elements to maximize search engine optimization (SEO) and discoverability; its genre or subject classification; cross-marketing opportunities with other titles; and the cover design and how it works with the target market.

When the Osprey Group ventured into the area of science fiction publishing, it was as a result of market research which showed that this would fit with the interests of their existing audience in the area of military history. Market research can inform decisions about new projects, covers and marketing ideas, and research into the book market can be commissioned from specialist organizations such as Bowker Market Research (purchased by Nielsen in 2013). Regular data on the sales of individual print titles, their demand curves, and books by category is available from Nielsen BookScan – sales rankings on Amazon are a free alternative. By 2013 bestseller data for ebooks was becoming available in the UK. Publishers would dearly love access to the data held by Amazon and Apple – not only on sales but also on consumer behaviour and profiles. Those publishers able to build a direct relationship with their customers can collect their own information, enabling them to target new customers and design appropriate products and services. They can also stimulate the co-creation of value, with readers perhaps suggesting commissioning ideas, titles for translation, or classic books to reissue (see Chapter 5, page 111).

Educational publishers developing a new textbook will want to assess market trends in terms of student numbers in that subject, and evaluate the competition. They will also conduct primary research in schools, and major new textbooks and digital media will be concept tested using focus groups. An academic publisher may seek the views of librarians on a proposed online database of key texts and journal articles. Data analytics may show how content is being used by learners in schools or academic researchers.

Publisher branding

It used to be said that the brand names of publishers and those of their imprints have little impact on sales – readers do not select books on the name of the publisher. It is true that the general public's recognition of publishers is generally weak, apart from notable exceptions such as Penguin. Trade brand names are, however, important to publishers' business connections – to agents, authors and book trade intermediaries – and to media relations. The success of *Eats, Shoots and Leaves* by Lynne Truss (2003), which sold half a million copies within six months of publication, will have persuaded bookshops to take seriously future titles from Profile Books. Teachers in schools recognize publisher brands and this may influence their purchasing decisions or recommendations. Consumer branding is used to good effect for book series, for instance in language learning, reference, travel and computing guides, and in children's publishing; and for vertical communities interested in some fiction genres and non-fiction subjects. In ELT publishing, publisher brands will be an important guarantee of quality in overseas markets. In an internet world that is oversupplied with information of uncertain provenance, publisher branding should assume greater significance in conveying quality assured products and services. The risk for publishers is that users will head for content on the web that is free – perceived as 'good enough'.

> Palgrave Macmillan and SAGE are noteworthy examples of branding in academic publishing – the brand helps attract new authors to the publisher

As we saw in Chapter 5, consumer publishers have to direct their attention towards the creation of communities and brands which will work with consumers. Does the publisher have existing brands which will work as consumer brands, or does it need to create a new identity? Part of that effort will involve the management of key author brands.

> Brands are more than just names and symbols. They are a key element in the company's relationship with consumers. Brands represent consumers' perceptions and feelings about a product and its performance – everything that a product or a service *means* to consumers. (Kotler et al., page 257)

Brands and travel publishing

Stephen Mesquita, Travel publishing consultant

EXPERT

Travel is a fertile area in which to study the effect of brands in publishing. The sales of printed travel guides have fallen in most of the major world markets. For example, the UK sales of world travel guides (the international series) fell by 44 per cent in the eight years between 2006 and 2013; and the US sales of this type of guide fell by 45 per cent (Nielsen Bookscan). It is a sector that has proved particularly vulnerable to the growth of free online information.

In the pre-internet world, the marketing efforts of many travel publishers focused on vying for in-store visibility, rather than building their brands. Most guides were bought through retail bookshops, and guides were the primary source of information for most travellers – all that has changed. With the rise of Amazon and with the competition of user-generated content (UGC) available on websites such as Trip Advisor, the emphasis for the traditional travel publisher has changed from visibility to discoverability. To be discoverable, you need to be known – you need a brand.

In the eight years that saw such a steep decline in the sales of world travel guides, the two largest publishers worldwide in that category were Lonely Planet and Dorling Kindersley (with their Eyewitness books). They consistently outperformed the market (UK sales down 25 per cent) and both have strong brands – but brands which function in very different ways.

Lonely Planet (LP) has invested heavily, particularly in the last twenty years, in creating a worldwide brand. The company recognized early on the importance of digital information, even creating in Thorn Tree a very early example of a community. LP built its name worldwide with, amongst other moves, a series of licensing deals with powerful publishers in key European markets. The strength of the brand has also made it easier for LP to diversify into new areas such as magazines and TV – and to exploit the digital market for their content. The value of the brand was a major factor in persuading BBC Worldwide to pay £130 m for the company in 2007 (but it was since sold again in 2013, to NC2 Media, for only £51 m).

The DK Eyewitness guides are a brand with very different characteristics. The design – which was ground-breaking when the guides were launched over 20 years ago – functions as the brand. It is a global brand which has made the guides desirable and collectable, as well as usable. They still rely on visibility in-store – so may be vulnerable in the longer term – but, for the moment they continue to outperform the market.

There are other smaller, niche brands which continue to be competitive. For example, the Bradt guides remain first choice for visitors to super-adventurous destinations. But the whole sector has seen a major shakeout, in which brands such as the AA and Thomas Cook – household names in the UK – have thrown in the towel and stopped publishing world travel guides. The vacuum left by these – and other publishers – pulling out of the market has only served to strengthen the sales of the printed guides of LP and DK. The next few years will tell whether even those travel publishers with strong brands are strong enough to resist the rise of online travel information.

Author branding

Since one of the factors that influences book purchases is familiarity with the author, much attention is paid to the branding of authors (and sometimes the characters they have created), whether on author websites, social media, book recommendation sites or through their covers. Publishers build author brands but do not own those assets. Once authors develop a fan base, those readers are targeted early in the promotion of the author's next book, and are emissaries who spread word-of-mouth recommendations worldwide. All the covers for an author may receive a similar treatment, encouraging the reader to look out for and buy the next book by one of their favourite authors. Brands also affect gift purchases. David Cooke, formerly category manager at Tesco, said of women's purchasing behaviour: 'If you're thinking of buying a book for your husband you go for a safe name' (*The Bookseller*, 17 August 2007).

Covers

Covers are still seen as important in a world of ebooks, and books without covers on Amazon will not sell as well. The challenge is to reinvent the book cover for an online world and publishers have experimented with moving covers such as animated gifs. Titling is ever important when sometimes a cover may only appear at a small scale. Attention must also be paid to the design of icons for apps and successful approaches combine creativity with simplicity in order to gain recognizability – examples include Hipstamatic and Flipboard.

48 per cent of women can be considered to be Page Turners, or avid readers, compared with only 26 per cent of men (*Guardian*, 22 March 2009)

Covers can give off messages about a book's target audience, and they help to position the book in the mind of the consumer. Research carried out for the Orange Prize for Fiction in 2000 found that the front cover and title of a book are taken by readers to be strong indicators of the kind of fiction, and whether the book is intended to be a male or female read. A novel was regarded as a female read based on the author's gender, the colour and general look of the cover, and its title. Women are far more likely to read books regarded as male reads (40 per cent of the women in the survey), with only a quarter of men interested in a book if they regarded it as a female read. Ian McEwan's *Enduring Love* was seen as a book which sent out signals from the look of its cover (including the use of pink) and from its title (using the word love) that it was a female read.

A good cover will encourage the consumer to pick up a book, and the consumer is then five times more likely to buy (Phillips, 2007, page 28). Mostly publishers target heavy buyers, who provide the bulk of their sales, and design the covers accordingly. Women are more likely to be heavy buyers of books, purchasing for their children, gifts, or themselves. Purchases can be classified by occasion – when the book will be read – and benefits – what the book offers to the reader. Covers can suggest a light read for the beach, an air of mystery, or a mood of passion. In general, hardback novels, which may become collectables, have elegant and restrained jackets, aimed at older groups. Fiction aimed at younger readers may go straight into paperback.

Research may be commissioned into the readers of an author and a new cover look may reflect the results. For example, research by Anita Shreve's publisher, Time Warner, found that readers associated her books with emotions and human feelings. They then made sure that a new cover design put people on her covers. Sometimes a book is issued with two cover designs to capture different market segments. This happened with the Harry Potter books when it was found that they had a crossover adult market. Four designs were produced for Mark Haddon's *The Curious Incident of the Dog in the Night-Time*: adult and children's editions in both hardback and paperback. When Bloomsbury first published *The Little Friend* by Donna Tartt, it appeared with a disturbing image on the cover of a doll's face with a cutout eye. Two years later the book was reissued with a new cover image – a child on a swing – aimed at a summer reading market. Cover research can also take advantage of eye tracking and other technology to detect the most effective design.

Add-ons

Extra value can be created with digital add-ons to the printed book, internet or augmented reality links in the text, or the bundling of print and ebook editions together. Amazon launched its Matchbook service in the USA in 2013, allowing customers to buy inexpensive ebooks of print titles they had already purchased. Games can be created for consumer books and in 2013 the fantasy series for children, Spirit Animals, was launched by Scholastic linked to an online game. It would now be unusual to publish a major textbook without an associated website offering extra resources. Videos, tests, quizzes and games may be available for educational texts, with lesson plans for the teachers. For academic textbooks, lecturers may be provided with a full course of lecture slides and, for major texts, a full range of resources including student assessment. Ebooks can contain rich media features such as videos, animations and quizzes.

Price

Marketing will be involved in setting the prices for new books. Factors affecting the book's possible published price include its perceived value to end-users; their ability to pay low or high prices (for example high-earning professionals); and the price of competitors' books, especially if the book can be easily compared against similar books. Sometimes a book has a uniqueness that can let it command a premium price. Other factors include whether the book will be bought primarily by end-users or by libraries or businesses; and whether there are established price norms in the market which, if ignored, could reduce sales (for example to an impulse buyer, gift buyer, student or school). Trade publishers have to price with a view to the discounts offered by retailers to consumers. Christmas bestsellers will have their recommended price set in the full knowledge that retailers will reduce the price considerably. A hardback priced by the publisher at £25 may be sold at up to half price by retailers if a price war develops in the market.

Pricing strategies include 'skimming' – pricing high a hardback before moving into paperback – through to 'penetration' pricing – capturing market share for a new series through aggressive low pricing. 'Competition-based' pricing is common and it is essential to review the prices of competitors' products. Sometimes this can lead to counter-intuitive outcomes, as in the case of the independent bookseller Daunt Books:

Daunt Books, an independent bookseller in London, UK, isn't likely to win a price war against Amazon or Barnes & Noble; it doesn't even try. Instead, the shop relies on its personal approach, cosy atmosphere and friendly and knowledgeable staff to turn local book lovers into loyal patrons, even if they have to pay a little more. (Kotler et al., page 313)

The raising of the recommended retail price for a book would usually lead to a fall in demand, whereas lowering the price would usually (but not always) lead to a rise in the quantity sold. Products which are thought to be 'price inelastic' – changing the price has only a limited effect on the level of demand – tend to be highly specialist and professional titles. A book or database may convey need-to-know information for which an organization or professional is happy to pay a high price. Top science journals command premium subscription rates. Consumer books, especially paperbacks or ebooks, which may be bought on impulse, and many textbooks tend to be 'price elastic' – changing the price has a greater effect on the level of demand. Price elasticities vary according to the type of book and product. It can be difficult, for example, for an editor to persuade an academic or professional book author that lowering the price will not open the gates to a flood of eager readers.

Digital products can be difficult to price when there are no set price points in the market. Publishers may resort to cost-based approaches in order to recoup their investment, or keep prices low initially in order to encourage early momentum. Apps have to be priced in line with market expectations, and face stiff competition from products issued by other media sectors such as games.

The demand for consumer ebooks is price elastic

The prices of ebooks may match those of printed books or be lower, say two-thirds or a half. The pricing of consumer ebooks is in constant flux as they have proved to be highly price elastic, and their prices can be altered almost in real time. When the price of *The Hundred-Year-Old Man Who Climbed Out of the Window and Disappeared*, by Jonas Jonasson, was reduced in 2012 as part of a Sony promotion to only 20p, it sold nearly 150,000 copies. Occasional flash sales are used by retailers to capture market share. Publishers and self-publishing authors too may use 'pulse' pricing, dropping the title's price drastically over a short period to increase demand. Larger publishers may employ analysts to work out pricing policies which maximize unit sales or revenue per sales channel. Such 'dynamic' pricing is automated through the use of algorithms, pioneered by Amazon. Simon Johnson of HarperCollins said in 2013: 'We have well over 10,000 ebooks in our catalogue and a significant proportion are re-priced every week. It varies from market to market and partner to partner' (*The Bookseller*, 26 July 2013).

A cost-based approach to pricing is now much less common – this involves a standard mark-up from the unit cost of the book. Instead publishers will price to the market with a keen eye on the relevant competition. For trade fiction, pricing to market will override considerations such as the book's length. There are common price points in the market for given categories of books, such as general hardbacks, trade and mass-market paperbacks. This is also true for academic textbooks: for example, the price points for humanities and social sciences paperback texts are lower than those for management and STM titles. Periodically brave publishers break the prevailing price points, by lifting the price or lowering it to undercut competitors. Educational and college textbook publishers take account of the context the textbook plays in the total offer of digital resources and services.

Publishers of all types price their books primarily on their biggest market (usually but not always the home market) and that sets the basis for pricing in export markets. However, if an overseas country, such as the USA, is the main market, then the book is priced primarily on that territory. Pricing for export markets is complex and requires constant review as exchange rates (and rates of VAT) vary. Pricing a printed book to make it affordable and saleable in a poorer overseas market runs the risk that arbitrage traders will sell it in higher priced market, including the home market.

The level of discounts given by publishers to booksellers is a marketing cost to the publisher. It determines the amount of money the publisher actually receives from sales made by the retailer. The trade publishers, highly dependent on retail exposure, give booksellers the highest discounts. Most sales in a bookshop are made within the first 20 to 30 feet of the entrance, and this is the prime location where offers to consumers are displayed, such as 'buy one get one half price'. Retailers ask publishers for especially high discounts to participate in their promotions, and for additional sums (co-op payments) to secure window or table displays and prominence in catalogues. Co-op payments are also demanded by some internet retailers to increase a book's visibility:

> While the case can be made that co-op in a bricks-and-mortar store is a worthwhile investment – money is spent on getting books to physical areas of the store, such as front tables, where consumers will see those books first – it's much less logical on a Web site. Does having a video or an author Q&A on a book's page on Amazon really encourage a customer who has already clicked on that book to make a purchase? (*Publishers Weekly*, 15 December 2011)

Academic and STM publishers offer individual titles at different prices. A title may be published simultaneously as a high priced hardback for multiple reader use in libraries and at a lower price in paperback for personal purchase. Digital publication affords many further options. The bundling of journals as part of a big deal allows libraries to access the journals at a lower aggregate price than if subscribed to individually. Librarians seek the lowest price of printed books offered by different sources. The use of site licences, however, enables publishers (directly or via aggregators) the ability to set different prices for each title depending on the ways in which it is licensed. For example, the ebook may be acquired under a perpetual access licence, or it may be licensed as part of a collection (in effect at a discount per title), or made available through a subscription package or through Patron (user or demand) Driven Acquisition, or through short term rental. Digital textbooks may be rented to students at lower prices for set periods. Different user rights are granted in the different licences.

Printed books and journals are free from VAT in the UK, but the tax is payable on digital products such as ebooks, ejournals, CD-ROMs, DVDs and online content. That has the effect that publishers have to absorb the tax cost in their digital pricing of an ebook or subscription journal.

Place

A full view of a book's distribution and the different channels through which books are sold is provided in later chapters. From the point of view of the marketer, they need to understand fully the markets into which books are sold, both the needs of consumers and the different sales channels. The movement of sales away from physical stores to internet retailers is a key trend which has affected the marketing of books. Marketers need to assess the likely audience for a book and work out, with the sales department, how it can be made available through the relevant physical and digital channels, as well as promoted to the relevant decision-makers and consumers.

Given the importance of search and discovery in the purchasing and accessing of many books online, marketers must ensure that full and correct metadata is available to all the relevant sales channels and libraries. This includes the book's cover (vital to drive online browsing and sales), description of the content, product details, and reviews. Metadata in the virtual space substitutes for the bookshelf in a physical bookstore or the former printed library catalogues. For example, books are classified by subject category (a metadata field), originally developed to help booksellers and librarians shelve them. For specialist books, assigning an incorrect subject category can be fatal to sales and library usage. Conversely assigning several relevant subject categories from the specific to the more general aids a title's online visibility. A choice of subject category in which fewer books are published increases the chance that a book would achieve a higher sales ranking.

Copy for web pages needs to be written with an eye to achieving a favourable page ranking on Google searches. Relevant keywords need to be identified and used as part of the copy, and links encouraged from other sites with good reputations. Consumer reviews – whether on a site such as Goodreads or on Amazon's own website – are increasingly important and encourage sales (Phillips, 2014, page 81). Investment in paid search or SEO helps to direct consumers towards community websites or social media (for example Facebook pages) set up by the publisher. There has been controversy about paid-for rave reviews on Amazon, commissioned by self-published authors, and click farms which will generate automatically likes on Facebook pages.

Promotion

The aim of promotion is to make the media, the book trade and consumers conscious of the company and the products it offers; and to stimulate demand. The work may be divided by task. In some publishers, especially consumer, specialists deal solely with public relations and publicity, or with the development of promotional and point-of-sale (POS) material for retailers, or with catalogues, or with space or outdoor advertising or copywriting; or with online marketing and community development through a presence in social media. In some academic and professional publishers, the work may be divided by product type, for example between textbooks or journals promotion. Publishers of all kinds may also hire advertising agencies (especially for major projects or authors), freelance publicists and specialists in direct mail, SEO and website design. While in-house designers and production staff are sometimes used, marketing staff often make extensive use of InDesign. They may commission freelance designers and buy print themselves because the relevant suppliers are different to those producing the books. Some major publishers have adopted content management systems to facilitate catalogue and website production. The use of XML workflows that allow content to be repurposed is growing.

The promotional material produced and the interest generated help sales staff to sell to the book trade, or to schools or colleges, and also rights staff in their work. Details of the promotional spend and activities will help pre-publication orders from booksellers. Home and overseas customers use the promotional material as a reference source for ordering.

Online marketing

The development of online marketing has revolutionized promotion and the whole marketing function, offering a cost-effective means of reaching a wider international audience. At the start of the century many publishers' websites were in early stages of development and were beginning to perform a range of functions. For most book publishers, however, their sites at the outset performed the direct marketing function of providing information on their titles – in effect an extension of their print-based catalogues.

Today publishers in the consumer field embellish their web pages, for example with author interviews and interactive material, such as activities or games linked to particular books or children's characters and newsletters. Efforts are made to persuade readers to register through offering, for example, discounts and competitions with prizes and they are encouraged to share content. Community sites around content by imprint or genre will encourage sales – usually from the main retailers but sometimes direct. This has become ever more important as internet and ebook sales have grown, and physical retail diminishes, and the challenge is to help consumers discover a publisher's titles. Publishers of consumer books written by brand-name authors face the reality that their imprint name is a sub-brand to that of their authors in the public's mind. In order to co-ordinate the promotion, publishers may advise authors on the use of websites and social media, or offer to host their websites.

The full benefits of the use of social media have not yet been established, and there remains some scepticism about its effectiveness. Yet the number of opportunities continue to multiply – from Google+ and LinkedIn to Tumblr and Vine. Publishers recognize they must have an active presence (with the minimum of Facebook or Twitter) in order to drive book discoverability and encourage word-of-mouth recommendations – and ensure their authors are equally active. A trailer for a book may be uploaded to YouTube, a viral video posted on Vine, a book club started on Twitter, or a cover pinned to a board on Pinterest.

Pinterest is a popular place to showcase book covers

For significant new products or services, it is important to engage in online communities either through the creation of one from scratch or by making use of those already well established. Book publishers can gain network effects through developing their own community sites around their books. Community sites may be built around different levels of content aggregation: imprints, genres, series or individual bestsellers or long enduring titles, such as the *Writers' & Artists' Yearbook*

E★PERT

Online communities in publishing

Alastair Horne, Social Media and Communities Manager at Cambridge University Press

The first phase of publishing's digital transformation centred on distribution: making content available in digital formats – mostly the same books that had previously been available as print. The second phase, which has already begun, focuses on data and the reader.

Historically, publishers have been perfectly happy to delegate the relationship with book buyers to bookshops, but that no longer works in a world where data about customer habits is a vital source of business intelligence. Retailers such as Amazon can gather immense amounts of data during both the purchasing and reading processes; since they are unwilling to share it, publishers have to find other ways to engage with their audience, to find out what readers want and how they want it.

Social media provides one means of building this relationship. Most publishers now have Facebook pages and Twitter accounts, where they share free content and prizes in exchange for attention and engagement: offering fans an opportunity to win an iPad mini – and it's so often an iPad mini – in return for their email address and their thoughts on a possible new product line.

Though social media can often be viewed as a cheap alternative to conventional marketing, creating this content can be labour-intensive, and most publishers tend to limit the amount of overt product promotion anyway, since a click on the 'unfollow' button is only ever one annoying post away. The better accounts focus more on building longer-term relationships with customers, establishing trust in the brand so that the consumer will actively seek out their content when the need arises.

The biggest problem for publishers with social media is their dependence on third parties. It can be difficult to extract data from such platforms in useful quantities, and the ability to reach an audience is often dependent upon the latest version of the algorithm that governs precisely who sees your content – only a small proportion of the people who 'like' your page on Facebook will actually see your latest post, for instance.

Consequently, some publishers are building their own online communities, undertaking the considerable expense involved in return for greater control over the data created. The most successful of these communities offer members something they won't get elsewhere – professional development, or access to an exhaustive encyclopedia for their favourite fiction genre – while gathering data that can be more easily aggregated and interpreted than the information obtained from social media. Where the value to the consumer is easily demonstrable, these communities may ultimately become financially self-sustaining, funding themselves from user subscriptions. For most publishers, however, they currently remain a marketing expense, a costly but rewarding exercise in gathering market intelligence and building brand loyalty.

(Bloomsbury). The community has to have a purpose that matters to the people who the publisher is trying to reach. Sharing control is important. On the one hand publishers create content for and about the community, and on the other, value and stimulate the contributions and lively debates from community members. Sites are designed to attract new registrants and customers, and to retain membership. Many techniques are used, such as the marketing of events, special offers, and membership and subscription schemes. Community sites may offer new revenue streams and innovatory opportunities for content sales, and offline and online services.

Designed partly to aid discoverability of content, a community can range from a Facebook page for an academic journal through to an online game which can be played alongside other fans of a character or series from around the world. In 2011 Orion Publishing launched the SF Gateway as a community site for sci-fi fans whilst making available ebooks of classic sci-fi and fantasy titles. A social media curator encouraged visits to the site using Twitter and Facebook. In 2013 Random House announced the launch of The Happy Foodie – its first 'cookery vertical and responsive design website that aims to bring cookery books to life and help readers get happy in the kitchen'(randomhouse.co.uk). 'Most major book publishers now maintain active podcast streams, featuring interviews with authors, extracts from forthcoming novels and occasional promotional features' (*Daily Telegraph*, 16 February 2013), and one example is BookD from HarperCollins: 'The majority of the time BookD airs its author interviews either on or just before publication because "the buzz generated on Twitter just makes so much more sense"' (*The Bookseller*, 2 August 2013). Some YA publishers develop community sites which include writing forums.

The presence of Amazon, Apple and Google in the marketplace offers both opportunities and threats to publishers. Academic publishers have welcomed the opportunity to display their books through Google Book Search, since they believe their titles have exposure they would not otherwise receive. Readers can view sample pages and then click through to buy the book. Amazon has such a service with Search Inside, and some major publishers and distributors have similar schemes.

Internet marketing does have huge potential for niche publishers. Specialist and academic titles are not widely stocked in high street bookstores. Publishers can establish special interest communities around their publications to whom they can directly sell their titles. For some of the well-known academic and specialist publishers, direct sales of their books from their websites grew quickly, along with sales via internet booksellers. The internet means they can keep in touch with their market, and mail to a highly relevant audience in a cost-effective way. In academic publishing, email marketing to lecturers is a key activity.

Word-of-mouth recommendations

Publishers have long recognized that an important influence on sales is the elusive word of mouth (WOM). Sales are generated by trusted recommendations from friends, family or booksellers. Sometimes bestsellers can appear from nowhere, such as *Captain Corelli's Mandolin* (1994) by Louis de Bernières and *Eats, Shoots and Leaves* by Lynne Truss (2003). Publishers cannot guarantee a buzz around a book, but they are constantly trying to encourage it through obtaining

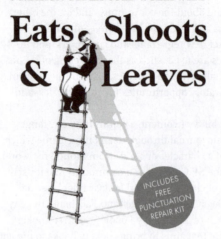

Eats, Shoots and Leaves by Lynne Truss (Profile) is an example of a title that sold by word of mouth

coverage in the media (TV, radio, newspapers), spreading the word on social media, placing extracts pre-publication, or making sure the book is stocked prominently in bookshops. A long-standing method is to give books away, a tactic used to generate interest in Stieg Larsson by his UK publisher: 'Mark Smith, who founded Quercus in 2004, became so desperate to shift copies, which some retailers refused to stock, he gave them away to people reading in parks – and planted dozens more on the back seats of taxis and on Tube trains. "At that stage we were giving away more than we sold," Smith says. "It was getting pretty nerve-racking"' (*Independent*, 6 August 2010).

Editors and marketers may tweet about a book whilst it is still in development in order to attract early attention. Publishers will send print or digital proofs to key influencers in the Twittersphere or blogosphere in order to stimulate a conversation around a new title. For example, a book aimed at a female audience could be sent to the UK community site for parents, Mumsnet, which in 2013 had 9 million visits per month (mumsnet.com). Bloggers on children's/YA books are especially active. A viral marketing campaign may be planned – to spread an idea, a joke, or information.

> Viral marketing involves creating a website plus a video, e-mail, mobile phone message, advertisement or other marketing event that is so infectious that customers will want to pass it along to their friends. Because customers pass the message or promotion along to others, viral marketing can be very inexpensive. And when the information comes from a friend, the recipient is much more likely to view or read it. (Kotler et al., page 523)

The Five Readers Book Group from Newbury. It is estimated that there are 50,000 people in reading groups in the UK

Deckchairs for the Hay Festival, Hay-on-Wye, Wales. Held annually the festival attracts both writers and celebrities, and was described by Bill Clinton as the 'Woodstock of the mind'. The town boasts over 20 bookshops selling both new and second-hand books

The success of local reading groups represents an opportunity to influence book sales. Publishers produce information packs and web resources around leading authors to encourage reading groups to adopt their titles. The Oprah Book Club in the USA and the Richard and Judy Book Club in the UK have given exposure, first on TV and later online, to books and authors, and have had a considerable impact on sales. Other influences on book sales can include winning a major literary prize such as the Booker (Table 10.3) or adaptation for film or TV. Classic as well as contemporary authors receive a boost to their sales when the latest adaptation makes it on to the screen.

The author plays a prominent part in promoting their books, from appearances at book signings or literary festivals to sending out flyers with their Christmas cards and adding a link to the relevant Amazon page to their website or email signature. Amongst the largest literary festivals are the ones held at Edinburgh, Hay-on-Wye and Cheltenham. A conservative estimate in 2011 put the total number of literary festivals in the UK as around 250 (*The Bookseller*, 18 March 2011). Lionel Shriver commented on this phenomenon: 'If you really want to write, the last thing you want to be is a success. Now that every village in the United

The Booker Prize for Fiction was first awarded in 1969, and Man Group became the sponsor of the prize in 2002

Hilary Mantel became only the third person to win the Booker Prize twice, following on from Peter Carey and J. M. Coetzee

Table 10.3 Man Booker Prize for fiction winners 2004 to 2013

Year	Author	Title	Publisher
2004	Alan Hollinghurst	*The Line of Beauty*	Picador
2005	John Banville	*The Sea*	Picador
2006	Kiran Desai	*The Inheritance of Loss*	Hamish Hamilton
2007	Anne Enright	*The Gathering*	Jonathan Cape
2008	Aravind Adiga	*The White Tiger*	Atlantic
2009	Hilary Mantel	*Wolf Hall*	4th Estate
2010	Howard Jacobson	*The Finkler Question*	Bloomsbury
2011	Julian Barnes	*The Sense of an Ending*	Jonathan Cape
2012	Hilary Mantel	*Bring Up the Bodies*	4th Estate
2013	Eleanor Catton	*The Luminaries*	Granta

The top-selling title out of all the Booker winners is *Life of Pi* by Yann Martel

Kingdom has its own literary festival, I could credibly spend my entire year, every year, flitting from Swindon to Peterborough to Aberdeen, jawing interminably about what I've already written – at the modest price of scalding self-disgust' (*New Republic*, 24 October 2013).

As the novelist Jane Rogers writes:

> Books are promoted to us endlessly, through adverts, reviews, adaptations, through glossy attention-grabbing covers in bookshops, and wild claims on jacket sleeves. They are set texts for exams; they are hyped by prizes and awards; or they are written by celebrities. But in the end, every reader knows, probably the most compelling reason for picking up a book which is new to you, is when a friend tells you, 'Read this, it's really good.' (page vii)

Marketing fiction

Professor Claire Squires, Author of *Marketing Literature: The making of contemporary writing in Britain* and Director of the Stirling Centre for International Publishing and Communication at the University of Stirling

Publishers have always made efforts to promote, distribute and sell fiction, but the late twentieth and early twenty-first centuries were a period of marketing intensification. Campaigns for potential bestsellers combine a range of generic marketing materials (catalogues, point-of-sale, bound proofs) and targeted marketing strategies to support the journey of novels from the author to the eventual reader.

The traditional marketing method for fiction – literary journalism and press coverage – still has its place, but doubts about the impact of reviews on book sales, and the diminution of review space in most national newspapers have prompted publishers to attract customers in other ways. In 1969, the Booker Prize was established by the Publishers Association, and since this date, literary prizes have had a crucial impact on book sales. Alongside the rise of literary prizes, there has been a growing meet-the-author culture, through events in bookshops, libraries and literary festivals. The expansion of reading groups has also presented publishers with opportunities to interact with consumers, and print, broadcast and new media-based reading groups have pushed book sales.

The collapse of the Net Book Agreement in the UK and more recently of agency pricing in the USA, and competitive forces among retailers, drove heavy discounting practices, with fiction featuring prominently. Branding, however, is difficult in fiction – titles by market-leading authors may sell immediately, with the help of the brand identity of cover design – but for most novels publishers have to work hard to differentiate their products in a very crowded marketplace.

Online selling and social media are now an integral part of marketing fiction. Amazon's use of customer reviews, bestseller charts, and time-limited sales promotions, underpin sophisticated algorithmic marketing activity. Metadata and data analytics are crucial tools in this environment. Shared online reading practices, via reading communities such as Shelfari and Goodreads, offer the potential for rich information to be gathered on customer behaviour.

Social media sites such as Facebook, Twitter and Pinterest provide opportunities for authors and publishers to interact directly with readers. New job roles, such as communities and web content managers, cross over editorial and marketing functions. A website such as Canongate.tv attempts to draw in readers direct to the publisher by providing additional multimedia content. Opportunities for crowdfunding (for example via Unbound) and crowdsourcing of taste-making functions (for example through sites such as HarperCollins's Authonomy, and fan fiction sites) bring readers themselves into editorial and marketing roles, fulfilling the role of 'prosumers'. Much remains of traditional marketing models, but – as with all other sectors of publishing – the digital environment is seeing the rapid evolution of literary marketing.

PROMOTION AND PUBLICITY TECHNIQUES

Before running through the promotion and publicity techniques that are applicable to many books, we will take a quick look at the way the marketing department of a consumer book publisher would set about promoting a major lead title. Most of the promotion budget and staff time goes on titles envisaged as bestsellers.

Lead consumer titles

New authors may be positioned in terms of established writers – for example, the 'new Catherine Cookson'

The first priority of marketing – many months in advance of publication – is to plan and undertake trade-focused promotion. The aim is to persuade the book trade that the book will deliver a flood of customers to their stores during the set publication slot; that they will need to display it prominently and order large quantities. The central buyers of the retailers are courted. They might be invited to meet the famous author or visit the exotic location of the book. They are sent early reading copies and other devices to captivate their attention, from free gifts to DVDs with author interviews.

Much of the marketing budget that is directed at the book trade is spent on the main retailers to ensure they place the book in the prime spots in their stores and take it as part of their promotions (for example a summer reading campaign). Other techniques designed to increase their order quantities are developed, such as bespoke competitions for each retail chain and point of sale material to maximize the book's presence in their stores. Marketing then follows through with their consumer-focused promotion – the big bang advertising campaign to potential readers occurring closer to the book's publication. The publisher's consumer marketing spend, which is known to the book trade in advance of their ordering, demonstrates that the publisher is backing the title to the hilt and reinforces the book trade's confidence to order large quantities. Meanwhile, the publisher's publicist has been imaginatively engineering media interest in the book and author, which manifests itself around publication, alongside personal appearances at literary festivals and other events. A social media strategy is developed which it is hoped will stimulate debate about the book and its subject-matter, or cause word-of-mouth recommendations to ripple through the population. The editor may have been tweeting about the development of the book, and this is followed by regular updates from the author and the publisher on the book's content and associated promotional activities.

Children's/YA books

Children's books, reaching a general retail market, libraries and schools, combine the techniques of trade and educational publishing. The marketer creates and mails the catalogue, generates free publicity, organizes exhibitions, attends conferences and liaises with schools and libraries; and, occasionally, may dress up as a large, ungainly character for a delighted audience. YA titles are additionally marketed to adult audiences.

We now turn to the variety of techniques used more generally.

General marketing activity

Author questionnaire

Around the time of the delivery of the manuscript, the author completes a questionnaire, which is returned via the editor. The author supplies personal information, a biography, a blurb, a short synopsis, and the book's main selling-points and intended readership or applicability to courses. In addition they may supply lists of their affiliations to membership organizations and online forums; details of blogs or websites to which they contribute; and lists of print, digital and broadcast media (and individuals) that might review or publicize the book. Well-connected authors may need to be contacted in person to gain information on media and other contacts. Other information could include relevant festivals, conferences and exhibitions.

Keywords and analytics

The identification and use of keywords in all marketing activities (such as in descriptive copy about the book, press releases and social media activity) has grown in importance to aid the discovery of books through the main search engines, social media, and retail sites such as Amazon and Waterstones. Google Keyword Planner can help marketers to build lists of words which attract relevant traffic. Words used by authors and publishers internally may not be those used by potential readers searching for a book. There is also a growing use of analytical tools, such as Google Trends, which shows interest in topics over time and the correlation with search terms, Facebook Analytics, and proprietary tools.

Metadata and bibliographic information

The book's metadata is updated throughout the book's sales life. It encompasses all the information associated with the publishing of the book, such as the title, author, formats, cover, description, subject classification, territorial rights, price, availability and reviews. It is used by search engines, social media and all intermediaries that help sell the book. It is essential for findability (when a reader already knows of the title) and greatly aids discoverability (when a reader happens upon it). The signature of the book contract with the author usually triggers the publisher to assign to the book the product identifier, the International Standard Book Number (ISBN), from the batch of numbers assigned to it by the national ISBN agency. An ISBN is normally given to each tradable format – in print (for example hardback, paperback) and digital (for example ebook) – although not every intermediary requires that an ebook should have an ISBN.

Supplying the main bibliographers and resellers with accurate information in the standard format (in the UK, BIC BASIC new title record) on each new title is essential. This can be done by using an agreed electronic format such as ONIX (Online Information Exchange).

> ONIX is a family of electronic messaging standards for the communication of book industry product information, that share common elements. ONIX is

both a data dictionary of the elements which go to make up a product record and a standard means by which product data can be transmitted electronically by publishers to data aggregators, wholesalers, booksellers and anyone else involved in the sale of their publications. (internationalpublishers.org/, accessed 2 August 2013)

Each of the main publishing nations has its own, and different, book subject classification system. In 2013, the standards body EDItEUR launched a new system called Thema, designed to be a 'single, international subject classification scheme for the global trade, initially alongside purely national schemes and perhaps eventually superseding them' (editeur.org, accessed 8 November 2013).

The supply of rich information about a book is a low-cost means of promoting the title worldwide, and facilitates its ordering through the supply chain. Information given to the bibliographers – the main ones are Nielsen BookData (UK) and Bowker (USA) – nine to six months ahead of publication lists the new title on their electronic databases. There are differing levels of service from a free listing of basic bibliographic information through to a fuller (paid for) description with author biographies, covers and reviews. The classification of books into subject categories differs around the world (US publishers use BISAC categories published by BISG), and major retailers may use their own.

Bibliographic Data Services in the UK is a leading supplier of bibliographic information (data and information – rich metadata) about print books and ebooks to libraries and suppliers. It specializes in the promotion of new title information in MARC (Machine Readable Catalogue Format), a data standard used by libraries to store and exchange information. It also supplies the Cataloguing in Publication (CIP) data to the British Library's weekly addition to the definitive British National Bibliography (BNB) and other products, accessed worldwide. You sometimes see the CIP data (and similar from the Library of Congress, USA) for an academic book on its title-verso page.

Legal deposit is the act of depositing published material in designated libraries. Publishers in the United Kingdom and Ireland have an obligation to deposit published material in the six legal deposit libraries, which collectively maintain the national published archive of the British Isles. The six libraries are:

- British Library,
- Bodleian Library, Oxford University,
- Cambridge University Library,
- National Library of Scotland in Edinburgh,
- National Library of Wales in Aberystwyth, and
- Library of Trinity College, Dublin.

The publisher's in-house metadata includes each title's current status (future or actual publication dates), current prices by format, production specifications, covers, its coding by product category or subject, related products and additional information on each title built up over time (such as long and short promotional and contents copy, reviews received and association with other media releases). More extensive metadata will cover contractual matters, such as the rights held and the rights available for sale or licensed to others. The advantage of such a database is that it is a central repository of definitive information about the publisher's titles. It allows the publisher to retrieve and manipulate information in forms most suited to the intermediaries and end-users, in print and online (especially for the web catalogue).

Advance information sheet

Marketing will prepare the book's advance information (AI) sheet, and its electronic equivalent, which contains bibliographic information (title, author, format, extent, illustrative content, hardback/paperback, ISBN, planned price and publication date); a synopsis, the cover blurb, and a contents list; and a biography of the author. The above are the book's features, and it is important that the AI also sets out the book's benefits – i.e. what it will do for the purchaser or reader in the context of the book's use. A dictionary will help someone with their studies or to work more effectively in business. A travel guide will enable someone to make the best of their weekend away, giving them the key information and guidance they need. Is there a key benefit – the book's unique selling proposition (USP)? For example, for a non-fiction title, is it written by the leading expert in the field; for an educational title, does it match the latest curriculum requirements? The key benefits can be difficult to identify when a book is coming into a crowded market, but the exercise is even more crucial. If there is any doubt, the editor can be consulted on why they commissioned the book.

The book's description or synopsis is re-purposed in style and in length for different audiences and the places where it is read. In various forms it appears as the cover blurb read in bookshops; or web copy on the publisher's or retailer's site; or reduced for inclusion in an email campaign, advertisement or catalogue for end-users; or is versioned for the media or trade buyers, or for audiences in different countries such as the UK or USA etc. Use is made of bullet points and lists, feature structures and summary first techniques, and keywords may be tested for SEO.

The AI is sent well ahead of publication (preferably around nine months before) to all the people who help sell the book: the publisher's sales force and overseas agents, booksellers, wholesalers and aggregators.

Cover

The cover is another promotional item used by the publisher's home and export sales departments, wholesalers, library suppliers, internet booksellers and overseas agents. Produced well ahead of publication – preferably six to 12 months – it will be used to secure advance orders from bookshops. Publishers find that books sell better on Amazon if they appear with a cover, and dummy front covers may be used when the book is first listed, ahead of the completion of the final version. The cover blurb is written by the editor, marketer, or an in-house or freelance copywriter.

Catalogue

Catalogue preparation is a major task: it involves gathering book information from all round the firm, updating it, collecting illustrations, copywriting, briefing a designer, sometimes print buying, and carrying through all the production stages, as well as database management. Publishers have experimented with the abolition of printed catalogues and stocklists, on the basis that the information can be accessed online. This has met with mixed success and most publishers have retained print versions in some form.

The twin aims of a catalogue are to present the firm and its products attractively to buyers – the book trade and consumers; and to act as an informative, readily understandable and accurate reference so that products can be ordered easily through the supply chain at home and abroad. Consumer book publishers normally produce imprint catalogues announcing their forthcoming books geared to their six-monthly selling cycles. The autumn/ winter catalogue appears in time for the preceding mid-summer sales conference; the spring/ summer catalogue appears for the preceding Christmas sales conference. Catalogues are distributed to all members of the supply chain and to main libraries, to the public (via booksellers to account customers), and to review editors and relevant contacts in other media.

Educational, academic, STM and professional publishers usually arrange their new book catalogues (and selected backlist) by subject or subject groupings. Different subject catalogues may be produced for different levels of the education system, and books within a textbook catalogue (which includes selected backlist) may be arranged or classified by the age group, or examination or academic level served. Catalogues are produced annually to cover the following year's publications, or six-monthly or more frequently. Although the catalogues are mailed to selected booksellers, wholesalers, library suppliers and exporters, they are aimed primarily at teachers, academics, and professionals – those who decide to purchase or adopt the books. They are distributed to schools, academic libraries, institutions, departments; and, where appropriate, to targeted subject specialists or professionals, and to industry.

Reviews

It is essential to maintain an up-to-date and comprehensive database of suitable reviewers. Then for each title a review list is prepared, tailor-made, taking account of the author's ideas and contacts. Review copies may be bound, uncorrected proofs, digital proofs, or printed books. They are sent out with a review slip, press release or email which gives the details of the title and its publication date, and requests a review. Any review clippings received are circulated in-house and to the author. Reviews have declined in importance in their influence on trade book sales, and greater attention has been directed to book recommendation sites, bloggers, social media and PR for a title. John Sutherland writes:

> Old hands will hark back nostalgically to the days when Arnold Bennett could clear a whole edition with an enthusiastic epithet in the London *Evening Standard*. Now the literary editor, David Sexton, could disembowel himself, Mishima-style, on the roof of his building and it would not generate a ripple of interest among book buyers. (*Financial Times*, 9 October 2004)

Reviews can still be crucial for biographies or academic works, for example, where potential readers may want to gauge the quality of the work ahead of their purchase. Reviews on Amazon may be written by enthusiastic readers or friends of the author. There has been controversy over 'sock puppets', fake personas used by publishers and authors to write reviews both good and bad. In 2012 the crime writer Stephen Leather announced that he used sock puppets to write positive reviews of his own books; and another crime author, R. J. Ellory, admitted giving rival authors poor reviews and low ratings.

Public relations

Public relations (PR) include generating free publicity and furthering a company's brand image with authors and the media. By comparison to the big budgets elsewhere in the marketing department, publicists operate with little direct expenditure. Engineering free publicity in the print and broadcast media is vital in consumer book publishing, and spreads word-of-mouth knowledge about the book. This can also come from encouraging debate and discussion in the blogosphere or on Twitter. For titles which do not receive marketing expenditure, PR can propel sales, and smaller publishers will use it to compete effectively with the major players. On some major titles prior to contract, the publisher's innovatory publicity ideas (and promotional spend) may persuade the author to write for their particular company, rather than for competitors. Publicists can develop strong bonds with authors, and become close friends.

The publicist, also called the press and PR officer, is in constant contact with press and magazine editors, journalists, radio and television producers. Their credibility with these contacts is crucial and will be lost if an author is pitched who then turns out to be poor or inappropriate. With so many books and authors competing for media space, a book or author has to be carefully positioned in the marketplace. At the manuscript stage, the publicist targets the market, and formulates a publicity plan to commence six months before publication. A key part of the task is to meet with the author and discuss their book, interests and promotional ideas. The publicist identifies the appropriate media that would be interested in the book, and helps them come to a decision to cover the title by suggesting suitable angles. The stimulated coverage should occur around publication. Coverage is gained from features, author promotions which authors may be contractually obliged to fulfil – tours, literary festivals, signing sessions, radio and television appearances, accompanied by the publicist – press releases and launch parties. New authors may need coaching in media awareness and interview techniques. Around the time of publication, authors will appear in newspapers and magazines outlining their typical day or answering questionnaires about their likes and dislikes.

In 2013 Facebook had 1.1 bn active users

A digital campaign is planned using the author's own online presence or specially created social media. For the launch of *A Street Cat Named Bob* by James Bowen in 2012, a Twitter account was set up for the ginger street cat with the starring role in the book, as well as a Facebook page for the book. Authors themselves may come up with innovative ways to promote books. For her collection of stories *No One belongs Here More than You* (2007), Miranda July created a website with messages written on the top of her refrigerator – the site was viewed more than three million times in just one week (mirandajuly.com).

Signing sessions, competitions for booksellers and joint promotions with booksellers, especially the main chains, are arranged in close conjunction with the sales department. Sales staff are warned about any impending coverage so that they can inform the booksellers who are thus more likely to stock the book, which in turn sells more copies. Major TV or film tie-in titles receive cross-media promotion involving the link-up between the publisher and the media company for mutual benefit. Film and TV adaptations work wonders for the sales of classic authors as well, increasing their sales by three or four times.

In 2013 1 bn tweets were sent every 2.5 days

Other PR involves informing the trade press (in print or online) about the company and forthcoming titles, distributing proofs or finished copies to influential people (this includes opinion formers with a huge following on Twitter), entering titles for literary prizes, helping to plan and attend exhibitions (including the publisher's own sales conferences), maintaining contact in the UK with the Publishers Association, Booktrust and the British Council (all of which promote books) and sometimes answering queries from the public, teachers, librarians and booksellers.

News stories can be a good way of getting books on to the front page, or into the radio or television. For a major dictionary, for example, stories will be given to the press about the latest words to enter the language:

> The Twitter-centric meaning of the term 'tweet' has been added to the *Oxford English Dictionary* as part of its annual revisions process. ... Standalone

Marketing

For all roles in marketing an interest in the firm's books and the ability to identify the editorial reasoning and sales potential are necessary. Creativity is important in the area of promotional ideas, as well as an understanding of the relationships between costs and expected sales in maximizing the profit potential of each title, within budget. Marketing is a strategic activity, and knowledge is required of competitive behaviour and the market environment. Familiarity with social media and how it can be used to best effect is required, and web and IT skills are desirable. There are now specialist digital roles in the areas of website management, online publicity and community development. Good personal relations inside the company (particularly with editors) and outside the company (for example with authors or the media) are vital, as are administrative and planning skills. Qualifications can be obtained through the Chartered Institute of Marketing (CIM).

The development of promotional material and online content engages copywriting (which can be learnt by literate people who appreciate the different styles demanded for different platforms and audiences), editorial, production and InDesign skills. PR work involves living on one's wits, exchanging favours with the media, establishing a rapport and trust with all kinds of media and authors, knowing when to hype and when to hold back, being able to talk oneself in and out of situations fast, having supreme self-confidence and a high tolerance of rude people and working anti-social hours.

SKILLS

additions tend to revolve around pop culture, tech and current affairs. They include: dad dancing, epic, fiscal cliff, flash mob, follow, geekery, pay day lending and the silent treatment. Other notable newcomers are: fracking, tray bake, eggy bread, BDSM, and search engine optimisation. (*Wired*, 17 June 2013)

Serial rights

In consumer book publishing, publicity staff instead of the rights department may sell serial rights to their contacts in the press and magazines. Extracts or serials should appear around book publication and produce income and publicity. (See also Chapter 12.)

Paid-for promotion

Point-of-sale (POS) material

Eye-catching material – posters, display kits, copy holders, presenters, brochures, badges, etc. – is designed to focus booksellers' and readers' attention on major books, series or brand imprints; to make shops more enticing; and to capture display space both at home and abroad. Produced mainly for consumer books (but sometimes for major reference books and textbooks), most is declined or thrown away by booksellers. Nevertheless, it shows the publisher's commitment to the book and assists advance selling to the book trade and customers abroad. Sometimes a publisher may provide major retailers with spinners or special shelving for a series, but books are usually displayed on tables or standard shelving in the larger shops within the retailer's set of categories.

Media advertising

For most books, the high cost of advertising in the press, magazines, online, or on television or radio, or by poster would not be recouped by the sales generated. It has to be used very selectively, and short-lived, large-scale consumer advertising is restricted to major consumer books. In times of budget restrictions, advertising spend is often readily cut. The large publishers spend most of their budget on press and outdoor advertising, especially adverts on the London Underground and buses. Although its effectiveness is intangible, it encourages the book trade to buy and display the book and pleases authors and agents. Non-fiction, academic and STM publishers advertise selectively in specialist magazines and websites, and journals (especially their own) – ostensibly to sell books, but also to please authors and attract new ones.

Outdoor advertising for books includes ads on London buses

The main tasks involved in advertising are conceiving selling ideas from editorial concepts, relating advertising to the other promotions, copywriting and working with the designer or agency, negotiating the best rates and positions, and maintaining tight budgetary control. In 2011 the top five consumer publishers all spent over £1 m on advertising, with Random House spending over £2 m.

Table 10.4 Media spend in 2011 by consumer publishers (*source*: Mintel, 2012)

Media type	Marketing spend £000	Proportion of total marketing spend (%)
Outdoor	6,911	40
Press	4,933	29
Direct mail	2,717	16
TV	1,304	8
Internet	848	5
Radio	398	2
Cinema	48	
Total	17,159	

Marketing on social media is sometimes called marketing by consent. It aims to attract attention while not interrupting the conversation. However, paid for advertising on social media is another tool to aid discoverability and word of mouth. It aims to increase visibility on search rankings, or on Twitter to resonate tweets.

Direct marketing

The preparation and mailing of brochures or email campaigns direct to targeted specialist audiences forms large part of the work of promotion staff in educational, academic, STM and professional publishers. The relevant audience could be teachers in schools, university lecturers and librarians, or business and legal professionals. Alongside mailed subject catalogues (and to some extent reviews) it is the main promotional means by which these groups can learn about new and related backlist titles (monographs are normally promoted only once). Together with the editor, the marketer works out the scope of the market, the best approach, what kind of mailing piece is appropriate including email, the time it should be distributed (usually around publication) and to whom, deciding which mailing list to use – all within the allocated budget.

The marketer writes the copy, often designs it, and carries through the production stages. Depending on the export arrangements, material may be sent direct to libraries, teachers, academics and booksellers in selected countries. Other promotional material includes flyers or showcards which authors can distribute or display at conferences, exhibitions or other events.

In order to write effective copy, a useful acronym to remember is AIDA: attention, interest, desire, action

Textbook promotion

Teachers and academics are unlikely to prescribe a book for student use unless they have examined a copy first. Titles that are expected to be ordered in bulk for schools or placed on a reading list of books which students should buy (excluding monographs and professional reference titles) are displayed in catalogues or emails inviting a request to view. Inspection copies can be ordered or downloaded from the publisher's website. The teacher, having placed the order, is asked to supply comments on the suitability of the book. If the book is adopted for student purchase, the lecturer is asked whether it is the core text or to be used alongside other titles, or merely recommended, and to fill in the number of students on the course and the name of the supplier. If adopted, the recipient keeps the book for free; if not, they pay for it or return it – although policies differ according to the publisher. Some publishers will send unsolicited free desk copies of textbooks to influential teachers; or access may be given to the digital version. The feedback and response rates are used for market research. In academic publishing the information is passed to the sales staff, who contact lecturers directly and alert the campus booksellers through which the books are purchased and the library, which may order copies. Textbook publishers of all levels build databases of adoptions (institution, course, student numbers) for subsequent follow-up and targeting. In school textbook publishing the schools ordering class sets directly are recorded.

Lecturers' reading lists, which may be available on the internet, are the key determinant in a student's choice of books. According to a research study for The Publishers Association in 2005, 83 per cent of students who received a strong textbook recommendation from their lecturer purchased a book, compared to 30 per cent of those who received a weak recommendation (Carpenter et al.). The research showed a low propensity to buy books which are not recommended – 74 per cent said they had not bought any other new books.

Direct sales

Most print books are sold via booksellers (including Amazon) to end-users. Some booksellers, especially the specialist, sell by mail order and may produce catalogues. Internet booksellers, book clubs, and direct selling companies are the main direct sales channels. But some publishers sell a proportion, or indeed a major proportion, of their products directly to end-users.

Consumer publishers rarely solicit direct print orders because until recently most are unable to identify readers and addresses, and many of their books are priced for the retail outlets, too low for their distribution systems to supply one paperback book cost effectively by mail order. Publishers may use Amazon or other distributors to sell direct-to-consumer. However, in so doing the publisher passes the important customer data to the retailer. Readers of ebooks are usually tied to a particular retailer's ecosystem, and this discourages direct purchases from the publisher. There are companies, notably Harlequin in the area of romance, which have built a direct relationship with their consumers and have a high proportion of their ebook sales from their website. The development of a community around content also encourages direct sales.

College textbook publishers, in response to declining campus sales and the growth of internet purchasing, have attempted to encourage direct purchase by offering incentives to students. The publishers of specialist online services sell directly to defined professional markets (for example legal, accountancy, finance and business), although some of their print products pass through booksellers and library suppliers. The academic and STM publishers likewise actively solicit direct orders – or through intermediaries – of high-level books from academics, scientists and professionals. Publisher displays at conferences can also be an effective method of reaching these markets.

Academic publishers promote their journals or databases directly to researchers and librarians primarily to secure institutional subscriptions from libraries. The bundling of packages of journals now leads librarians to choose packages that offer the best value. However, journal publishers also offer subscriptions at much lower rates for personal use, which are supplied directly. Their aim is to convert personal subscriptions into full-priced institutional subscriptions. The schools market is ideal for the direct marketing of books and new media, since schools may buy multiple copies with repeat purchases direct from the publisher. Discounts are given by quantity rather than to any intermediary.

The vehicle for direct marketing may be an email, space advertisement, website information, an insert in a magazine or book, or a mailed item (a catalogue or leaflet and personalized letter) or an app. Whatever the means, the marketer encourages direct purchase (sometimes by special offers) and includes a response facility which eases ordering and payment (by freepost, telephone, or email, and using a credit card) or which facilitates, for example, a journal subscription via the library. By assessing the response rates, direct marketing allows the statistical testing of the effectiveness of different offers and creative approaches (such as the design of the email, letter or leaflet), their timing and frequency, and of the vehicle.

The mailing list is of prime importance. It should be accurate, up-to-date, and appropriate for the product. List brokers may be used, lists are rented or acquired free, and are tested initially. Lists may be gathered from firms which specialize in constructing lists in educational, academic and professional areas, from associations, journal subscribers, and conference delegates, and from authors. In time the best lists are the publisher's own, built from successive sales and recorded and coded into the publisher's own database or customer relationship management (CRM) system. In the UK lists must be held in accordance with the Data Protection Act. Sometimes they are rented from, or to, other publishers. The most likely customers are targeted regularly with the most appropriate titles, and varying amounts are spent to acquire and keep different levels of customer. The publisher's author base may be a fruitful set of contacts.

Postal mailings can still be done very cheaply and, for example, some publishers use mail houses in India. While email provides a highly cost-effective method of mailing, companies must ensure that its use stays within the law. The advice from the Information Commissioner's Office in the UK is that:

> email, text, picture and video marketing messages are all considered to be 'electronic mail' … You cannot transmit, or instigate the transmission of, unsolicited marketing material by electronic mail to an individual subscriber unless they have previously notified you, the sender, that they consent, for the time being, to receiving such communications. (ico.gov.uk, accessed 4 August 2013)

Direct marketing sells books quickly (most feedback is usually in weeks, not many months) and a response rate of 1 or 2 per cent would be thought a success, depending on the costs and type of book, though rates of up to 5, 10 or 15 per cent plus are possible. If poorly executed, much money can be lost even though the books are sold at full price or at a modest discount. Telemarketing, by a publisher's own staff or by a retained agency, is sometimes used to follow up a mailshot, for example, to reach teachers and professionals at their place of work. It may be used to follow up renewals of journals and online reference subscriptions.

Best practice is to ask individuals to opt in to receiving marketing messages rather than opt out

Analytics

The role of data analytics has grown with the explosive availability of data. If the publisher does not collect data, it cannot be analysed. Digital marketing especially lends itself to scrutiny. For example, the design of emails effects response rates or the timing of tweets to maximize re-tweets. There are many tools available to monitor social media activity in relation to a publisher and its authors and books. Direct contact with customers allows the recording of traffic and referrals, and the assessment of publicity campaigns by channel. Readers' activity on a publisher's website can be monitored to assess where they come from, what their behaviour is and how they are converted to do something, in order to collect and segment information about them. Resulting transactional data impacts back on marketing strategies. Publishers that have built strong direct contacts with large numbers of customers, say teachers in schools, use Customer Relationship Management (CRM) systems to segment their customers and to plan marketing activities. The internal relationships between marketing, sales and customer services continue to develop.

Now read this

Alison Baverstock, *How to Market Books*, 5th edition, Routledge, 2014.
Philip Kotler, Gary Armstrong, Lloyd C. Harris and Nigel Piercy, *Principles of Marketing*, 6th European Edition, Pearson, 2013.

Sources

Philip Carpenter, Adrian Bullock and Jane Potter, 'Textbooks in Teaching and Learning: The views of students and their teachers', *Brookes eJournal of Learning and Teaching*, 2:1 (October 2006).
Jenny Hartley, *The Reading Groups Book*, revised edition, Oxford University Press, 2002.
Mintel, *Book and E-book Market Research*, September 2012.
National Literacy Trust, *Children's and Young People's Reading Today: Findings from the 2011 annual survey*, 2012.
Nielsen BookScan, *Travel Publishing Year Book* (2012).
Angus Phillips, 'How Books Are Positioned in the Market', in Nicole Matthews and Nickianne Moody (eds), *Judging a Book by Its Cover: Fans, publishers, designers, and the marketing of fiction*, Ashgate, 2007.
Angus Phillips, 'Jane Austen Gets a Makeover', *Logos*, 18:2, 2007.
Angus Phillips, *Turning the Page: The evolution of the book*, Routledge, 2014.
Al Ries and Jack Trout, *Positioning: The battle for your mind*, McGraw-Hill, 2001.
Jane Rogers (ed.), *Good Fiction Guide*, Oxford University Press, 2001.
John Sutherland, 'Brave New World', *Financial Times*, 9 October 2004.
Felicity Wood, 'The Mighty Booth', *The Bookseller*, 2 August 2013.

Web resources

www.anobii.com Online reading community.
www.bookmarketingsociety.co.uk Book Marketing Society.
www.consumerbarometer.com How people research and shop for books.
www.goodreads.com Site for readers and book recommendations.
www.jellybooks.com A web app for exploring, sampling and sharing books.
www.klout.com Klout – helps marketers to identify and engage with top influencers.
www.lboro.ac.uk/microsites/infosci/lisu/ Statistics from LISU on libraries in the UK.
www.literacytrust.org The National Literacy Trust is a UK charity 'dedicated to building a literate nation'.
www.literaryfestivals.co.uk Literary festivals in the UK.
www.themanbookerprize.com Man Booker Prize for Fiction.
www.mediauk.com Media UK contacts database.
www.publisherspublicitycircle.co.uk Publishers Publicity Circle – holds monthly meetings for publicists from publishers and freelance PR agencies.
www.socialmention.com Social Mention – social media search engine.

CHAPTER 11

Sales and distribution

While it is the job of marketing to understand the needs of the market and promote books to the relevant audiences, it is sales staff who stimulate the visibility of products and their demand through the various channels to market. They realize income by sustained and regular face-to-face selling to key intermediaries. The roles within sales, distribution and marketing continue to be transformed by changes in the retailing of printed books and ebooks through intermediaries, and by the rise of direct marketing and attempts by publishers to sell to end-users. A combination of the dominance of the internet booksellers (for example Amazon), the shift of bookselling chains to central buying, frontlist sales through supermarkets and the decline of independent bookselling, has led to a change in focus of sales staff in recent years. Publishers maintain key roles selling to the main accounts, but have drastically reduced the number of field sales representatives (reps) who visit bookshops and have created new in-house roles in direct selling, website or platform development and data analytics. They also use third parties such as sales and merchandising agencies. It is also important for publishers to ensure that their books are listed online with sufficient metadata, and to deploy search engine optimization as a way of attracting purchasers.

In the area of print and ebook distribution, the larger publishers run their own operations. Small and medium-sized enterprises (SMEs) usually use third parties – larger publishers or independent distributors. Publishers typically derive most of their sales revenue from a small number of customers, and small revenue from a great number. This so-called Pareto effect suggests that 20 per cent of customers might account for 80 per cent of total sales.

SALES

In consumer publishing, a big order from a supermarket can still put a book amongst the bestsellers, and high street booksellers remain important for the visibility of books. But Amazon has taken market share for print and come to dominate in the area of ebooks. The internet provides a route to sell the 'long tail' – the books that are not regularly stocked in bookshops (see Chapter 13) – and smaller publishers have found they can compete effectively online. Customers searching online for a relevant title can come across slow-selling backlist titles as well as the current bestsellers. Since independent booksellers rely on the trade wholesalers with their own sales forces, many have lost face-to-face contact with publishers. However, they may deal with selected publishers from which they receive higher discounts than from wholesalers.

With Western markets relatively mature, publishers look to Eastern and Southern markets to boost sales of English language editions. Export sales staff will make visits to key markets and use local distributors and agents. If the market is sufficiently strong, the company may set up its own office, which may be a sales and marketing office or possibly a full local publishing company. Publishers may also have joint ventures – companies set up in partnership with domestic publishers. This would normally be where the local laws do not allow wholly owned foreign investment, or where local company expertise is necessary to penetrate the market. Alternatively the English language publisher may want to sell the rights to their books (see Chapter 12) or enter into copublication deals – where they co-operate with domestic companies on particular projects.

Rights sales are covered separately in Chapter 12

Sales forecasting and inventory control

Sales forecasting and translating them into the actual number to print of a book at the outset, especially one of expected high sales volume, is part of the risk decision for the publisher. The view of the sales department is critical. Too high an initial print run would lead to a large stock write-off if the book does not sell; printing too few and being unable to fulfil demand quickly enough on reprint would lead to lost sales and antagonize the book trade and readers. For consumer book publishers, the all-important Christmas market of short intensity is the most difficult to predict, with surprise and often quirky bestsellers popping up each year. In the UK, on super Thursdays (in late September and early October) hundreds of hardback Christmas titles are published (often three times the monthly average): 'It's a seasonal harbinger as reliable as the depressing appearance of the first high-street Christmas trees. In a three-week autumn frenzy, publishers blanket shelves virtual and real with the books that will compete in the lucrative Christmas charts' (*Independent*, 27 September 2012).

In theory, the sales department of a consumer book publisher should receive the orders from the book trade three months ahead of publication – in practice, orders often arrive after the publisher has set the print run quantity. Therefore the publisher has to forecast. The management of the sales department has conventionally based their forecasts on judgement and experience, historic data of the firm's similar books, and the conversations they have held with the book trade's senior buyers. More recently they have the aid of forecasting software, either the publisher's own or supplied by specialist firms; and historic and real-time data of actual book sales made through retailers, as supplied by Nielsen BookScan. Publishers are increasingly using analytics to work out the optimum combination of price and revenue, and may opt for a short initial run so that they can gauge the likely balance of sales between pbook and ebook. The ability of printers to deliver smaller quantities quickly has also ameliorated the publisher's risk of over-stocks, while print on demand and ebooks enable books to remain available without inventory costs.

Tom Holman writes:

Plenty of printing decisions are still based on what publishers hope they will sell rather than cold calculation – but the availability of high quality data and market intelligence means predicting demand has become a much more exact science. The improvements are due in large part to the rise of Nielsen BookScan, which has given publishers far more accurate records of how many copies of their books are selling, as well as where and when. Basing future sales on past performance isn't always reliable, but publishers credit BookScan with transforming forecasting. Combined with the publisher's own sales data, it has reduced the likelihood of rash overprints, improved the timeliness of reprints and cut back on returns. (*The Bookseller*, 9 February 2007)

The international college textbook publishers, academic and STM publishers face the challenge of managing stock levels in their warehouses throughout the world and the shipping of stock between them. For example, the UK sales office in the early new year would have forecast the adoption demand of a college textbook in the UK and northern Europe to be purchased by students in the autumn and would have the stock (printed overseas during the summer) to meet that demand. But what if, in September, at the critical UK buying period, another publishing centre overseas receives an unexpected and large direct order from an institution, likely to be repeated annually thereafter, which they cannot fulfil? The stock earmarked for the UK and Europe is immediately shipped out of the UK to the overseas centre, dangerously lowering the UK stock levels. But they may have other warehouses elsewhere with small quantities of available stock from which they can replenish the UK.

How sales data can inform publishing decisions

Richard Knight, Before his retirement Richard was Business Development Director of Nielsen BookScan

E★PERT

Publishers have had to adapt to a market that contains both physical and digital product and it is imperative that they understand the interaction between both product formats. The economics of printing books is changing radically as smaller print runs are needed due to digital penetration. Analysis of the data from physical sales is required alongside an understanding of the penetration of digital products. The use of normalized sales data is the only accurate and cost-effective way to ensure that publishers achieve the balanced market view they require.

The principal benefits to publishers from accurate weekly *physical* book sales data have been:

- The ability to size categories and genres accurately so that better ROI predictions can be made.
- Controlling inventory through better print and reprint decisions. This area is even more important in the digital era because print volumes still dominate significantly over digital copies but are reducing year on year.
- Spotting genres that have suddenly burst into life – erotic or vampire fiction for example. Early adopters into these growth spikes can benefit hugely.

- In the academic and trade non-fiction sectors, monitoring sales will allow a determination of when or if a new edition should be published. It also allows a publisher to see how a competitor's edition is performing and then plan the launch of a new title or reprint of an existing edition.
- Comparing the number of copies distributed into the market against actual sales from the market allows for an estimate of the level of 'stock-in-trade', which will then indicate the likely scale of returns.
- Analysis of average sales prices for different formats, and the percentage of the market taken at each price point will inform which format is most likely to succeed.
- Comparison of market shares – you might believe you have been successful but with sales data analysis you can prove this.

The tracking of sales of *digital* products is in its infancy but the need to verify category or genre size and the proportion of digital and physical products within the category is paramount to a successful sales campaign. In the digital product area the key benefits of sales data derive from:

- The identification of category sizes and the physical split between physical and digital products.
- How the above is changing over time: is digital product penetration static or growing or shrinking – and at what rate?
- Price point comparisons between digital and physical product.
- Analysis of discounts given to consumers, and the effect on sales of price changes.
- Digital format analysis – which file formats are dominant?

Roles in the sales department

The sales director, usually supported by a UK sales manager and an export sales manager, plans and organizes the sales effort, and negotiates the terms of trade with the main customers. At the most senior level, the negotiation of terms imposed by Amazon, Apple and others is exceptionally difficult and fraught. The sales management comments on editors' new book proposals – forecasting sales and advising on pricing. They are involved in decisions on covers, discussions around marketing campaigns, and the management of stock, especially of key titles. In consumer publishing, the sales management may use the technique of dynamic pricing for ebooks, for example lowering prices for a limited period to stimulate titles showing a decline in sales. The large publishing houses now employ specialists in pricing and analytics.

Key account managers will present all new titles six months ahead of publication to the buyers of key accounts, and discuss the plans for promotions to be run by the publisher and retailer. Co-op promotions to increase book visibility may be based around special price offers, summer reading or back to school campaigns. There are changing policies amongst the chains when it comes to the delegation of buying decisions to branch buyers, but most buy centrally and roll (or scale) out order quantities to their branches. Scale-outs will always apply to major new books and promotions but the local managers might still have the ability to increase orders. Supermarkets buy centrally from publishers and stock may then be delivered via wholesalers.

Another sales role is the manager who undertakes so-called 'special sales' to customers beyond the traditional book trade, such as to non-book wholesalers, non-book retailers, direct sales companies (such as the Book People), newspapers and magazines (for example cover mounts), and sometimes to remainder or promotion book imprints. Non-book retailers are unlikely to have the skill or time to select titles. Some publishers operate vendor managed inventory systems for them. In academic, STM and professional publishing, special sales encompass direct supply deals made with institutions and businesses, such as bulk sales of textbooks to universities. Special editions may be customized and printed for companies to give away to staff or their customers. Pharmaceutical companies purchase reprints of journal articles for distribution to medics. Furthermore, some STM, reference and directory publishers sell advertising space in their books and journals to supplement their income; and on their websites (though advertising revenue is much lower than for print).

The licensing of content (ebooks, journals and databases) to libraries (public, school, university and corporate) is exceedingly complex. The large STM publishers license their content directly. Other publishers use one or more of the aggregation companies supplying the library sectors, through which the licensing and distribution are controlled – the licensing and loan usage models are under constant evolution.

In medium to large publishers the UK market sales manager (supported by in-house staff) runs the sales force. Small publishers may not be able to afford the high cost of employing their own reps, in which case they will normally hire the services of a freelance sales force. If a publisher employs its own full-time reps, each one will cover a discrete area (a territory), and is supplied with a car, a laptop/tablet, and receives expenses and a salary. Some publishers, more often the consumer firms, pay bonuses for exceeding sales targets. The reps usually live in their territories and meet together with the in-house staff only at the sales conferences (two to four times per year), where they learn about the new books, promotional plans and priorities. The reps are sent or can access all the promotional material (advance information sheets, jackets and covers), publicity and marketing details, and feedback orders and reports on their activities, and on the response of customers.

If the publisher chooses the freelance option they will expect to pay between 10 and 15 per cent commission on their net sales. The sales force will work in exactly the same way as an in-house sales team, and will expect the same level of information and sales material. The downside of this arrangement is that the reps will be selling in many other lists and so the publisher will not necessarily be given any special treatment. Equally there are no hidden costs, and the more the team sells, the more they earn.

Sales staff keep in constant contact with intermediary buyers through email and telephone, for example by alerting them to new titles dropped into the publishing schedule or titles receiving media and social media attention. Some companies have their own telesales specialists to support and complement the field force or outsource the activity; in the area of academic publishing this activity is carried out by the reps. Telesales are also used to reach accounts that are not cost-effective to visit, not primarily booksellers, or too geographically remote. Calling can be focused on new and backlist titles and brands, taking orders from regular buyers or speculative cold calling, as well as conducting market research.

The management of the sales channels is vital. Each channel to market offers different sales prospects and margins. Some imprints, brands or individual titles are more suitable for some channels than others. Furthermore the management of the channels is affected by the publisher's distribution arrangements. Whilst physical retail has been in decline, accounts are managed with the growing number of internet retailers and distributors, and aggregators supplying products to institutional and corporate markets, some of which are specialist. In order to sell the publisher's books, internet retailers need to be supplied over six months in advance with rich and correct metadata.

Terms of sale

Publishers sell books to retailers on the following terms. The definitions are open to variation, but the important distinction is between firm orders and sale or return. The risk for publishers is lower with firm orders, while the risk for booksellers is lowered if there is the guarantee that they can return unsold stock. If a book is returned to the publisher, the bookseller usually pays for the return delivery, unless otherwise agreed.

Firm orders

On firm orders the bookseller agrees to accept the books, to pay for them (preferably on one month's credit, unless otherwise agreed) and not to return them for credit. Powerful booksellers will request a higher discount on firm sales and are likely to be more cautious on the quantity ordered. Firm orders are typically used by publishers on direct bulk sales to organizations (for example education and corporate).

Sale or return

Most booksellers will want to operate on the basis of sale or return to ensure they are not left with unsold stock. Within a specified period they can return books (provided that they are in saleable condition) for credit, or in exchange for other books. The bookseller's account is invoiced at the time of supply, and payment is due at the expiry of the agreed credit period (which could be between 30 and 90 days).

The terms of trade between publishers and their customers – discounts, credit periods and levels of returns – are subject to regular negotiation. As the large retailers have gained in strength, the consumer publishers essentially trade with them on a sale or return basis on longer credit terms. Discounts are discussed in more detail in Chapter 13, page 308.

Ebooks

The problem of returns is solved with the sale of ebooks, but there are still issues
to be sorted out around the terms of trade. The wholesale model is prevalent
with set discounts given to intermediaries, and there have been controversial
experiments with the agency model (see Chapter 2, page 38). The ebook is sold
under licence from the publisher to either the intermediary, which then licences
to the end purchaser, or directly to the consumer.

Selling in and selling through

It is important to realize that sales staff do not merely walk into the head offices
of the chains or into individual shops with a bag of new titles to sell, authorize
the return of unsold books and leave. In a rapidly changing world, affecting
publishing and retailing, and of changing consumer preferences, the retailers
must concentrate their time and effort on marketing and selling the right titles
to their customers. The role of the rep or key account manager extends to
representing the constituent parts of the publisher – the sales and marketing
departments, and the editorial thinking behind projects – to the retailers, and
helping them market and sell to their customers effectively.

Key account managers will discuss forthcoming titles with the major
booksellers, looking to push those books most suitable for each. Sometimes a
book is seen as, for example, a Waterstones title, one that could do especially well
in their shops. Promotional plans will be discussed, both those planned by the
publishers and suitable promotions being run by the bookseller. Promise of a
sizeable spend on marketing can be required to get a title taken seriously by the
major chains. While a retailer may bear the cost of a promotion themselves, more
often extra discount is required from the publisher to secure a place for a book in
a promotion, and co-op payments may be required from the publisher to secure a
prime position in a chain's Christmas campaign or similar.

A consumer publisher's senior in-house staff see the main book buyers twice
a year around nine months ahead of the main seasons – in February/March for
September to January titles, in August/September for the February to August
titles. They prioritize the lead titles which are part of major promotions, discuss
other new books and important backlist. Monthly presentations to the key
accounts follow, around five months ahead of publication. Frequency of
presentations varies among publishers.

What has changed the practice of selling in is the widespread use of sales
data. Booksellers can check on an author's track record, and will not be impressed
by wild claims by the publisher. When they are unsure about a new title, they will
want to check the author's previous sales to firm up their opinion. As Kate
Kellaway writes,

> In the past, publishers could fudge sales figures. Now, thanks to Nielsen
> BookScan, there is nowhere to hide. It is possible to look up sales data
> on any novelist faster than you can say Zadie Smith. And if a book flops
> commercially, or, to use publishing parlance, 'doesn't work', a postmortem
> can be briskly conducted. Equally, if it does 'break out' (desperado publishing

slang for success), the scale of its popularity can be precisely assessed.
(*Guardian*, 25 March 2007)

Those field reps who do visit individual accounts will keep a file on customers,
listing their interests and opening hours. By appointment, they visit mainly
booksellers – the branches of the chains and significant independents – any
wholesalers or library suppliers within their areas, and other outlets which justify
the high cost of calling. The reps prepare their own folders with clear plastic
sleeves containing neatly placed covers, and other information to show buyers.
The folder contains the covers of forthcoming books over, for instance, the
following six months, and the lead titles are usually at the front. They use the
folder as a visual aid to sell books on subscription (in advance), and the catalogue

SKILLS

Sales

Common features of all good sales staff are their energy, self-motivation and
discipline which get them out of bed very early, and help them work long hours.
They need a strong knowledge of print and digital markets, and competitor
activity. On meeting buyers of differing levels of seniority, sales staff need to be
alert and make a good first impression. Listening and watching they adjust their
selling style and procedure to a buyer's character and mood. They need to be
flexible, pitching their style within a range from soft to hard sell, and sense
when – and when not – to talk. They are part amateur psychologist, part actor.
Strong negotiation skills are required, especially when dealing with key
accounts, and they should present their firms honestly, be diplomatic and have
authority. When a buyer asks for special terms, or some other favour, a sales
manager must be able to make decisions which are best for the company but
at the same time attractive for the customer. Their marketing and customer
service skills give the publisher a competitive edge.

Field reps should have clean driving licences and be happy to drive many
miles. Being alone, they need to be well organized to keep up with the emails
and manage their own time. A good field rep knows the books and the
customers' businesses and their customer profiles, interests and systems.
Although reps are given priorities, their skill is to determine which books are
best for their area and each outlet, and what size of order is suitable. They
gain the confidence and respect of buyers by recommending books that prove
themselves. Educational and college reps (also called consultants) must have a
lively interest in education and the ability to get on well with the kind of
people in those professions and understand their attitudes, mindsets and the
conflicting pressures they work under. Overt hard selling is inappropriate.
Rather they need to be able to talk about the problems faced by teachers,
the kinds of materials used, and the ways a teacher likes to use them, and
then have to be able to suggest and promote suitable products – as well as
demonstrate online and other resources. In the higher education sector they
need to understand the purchasing systems of the institutions, as well as give
sales presentations and product demonstrations.

for covering the backlist. Tablets may be used to display covers and marketing materials and there are interactive catalogues such as the Edelweiss system – bespoke catalogues can be created for individual stores. Reps rarely carry finished copies, apart from exceptions such as children's illustrated books. A high level of connectivity allows the reps to provide current information on stock availability, order status, and sales history, and to send information, such as orders and reports, back to their publishers in the evening. Reps may tweet or blog about their favourite titles; they can also use social media to pick up on trends to pass on to buyers.

A rep's aim is to obtain advance orders (or subscriptions) on forthcoming books usually three months ahead of publication from all the main bookshops, in time to inform the print run decision. As most independents place orders electronically, and not through the reps, the reps want the orders to be sent to their publishers, not via higher discount wholesalers. During a call they will cover the new books to be published in a certain period. However, smaller and infrequently visited bookshops may be sold new books post-publication.

The meeting with the bookshop buyer takes place in an office, the stock room or on the shop floor. The first few minutes are spent discussing trade gossip and the shop. Reps provide the main contact between booksellers and publishers, and should be able to supply the most recent information on all the firm's titles and to determine what information would be useful, and what marketing and promotions the bookseller could use.

The rep usually leads off with a major, strongly promoted title. The prime aim is to put the buyer in a positive buying frame of mind. Two to three minutes are spent in presenting a lead title. Showing the cover and the AI, the rep talks about the book and author, covering such aspects as its contents, what part of the market it is aimed at, why it is good, previous books by the author, the promotion, and sometimes the competition. Although more time is devoted to the main titles, the rep generally has under a minute per title, just one or two sentences, to sell it. One approach is to have a key positioning line, which helps place the book in the mind of the buyer. The 'new Harry Potter' is overused, but similar lines can be created. If the book is of local interest or is going to receive other publicity, this is mentioned. Mention of participation in an online book club, for example, will guarantee a good subscription. Vanessa Di Grigorio, a sales rep for a number of publishers in the USA, wrote on her blog: 'my job is to pick out what books will work for certain stores, and which books deserve to be highlighted. My job is to get people excited. In a way, you could say that my job is to talk to people about books – a lot' (publishingcrawl.com, accessed 4 October 2013). Reps keep records of orders, so that they can remind buyers of orders placed on authors' previous books.

Training is usually required to sell well, both in negotiation and interpersonal skills. To avoid diluting the buyer's interest the rep, aware of his or her buying pattern and customers, concentrates on those titles likely to sell in that particular shop – retailers' customer profiles differ greatly. There is a common understanding between an experienced rep and a good buyer with regard to the titles and order quantities that can be sold in that particular shop. Weak buyers need help. A good buyer is often aware of the books before the rep calls and can estimate within a few seconds the number of sales. But a buyer may want a larger quantity than the rep had in mind or conversely may place an order which the rep

Advance orders are called subscriptions

feels is too low. Knowing that the book is selling well elsewhere or sensing that the buyer does not appreciate some aspect, the rep mentions that and suggests a higher quantity. If the rep is trusted, the buyer may increase the order. Part of the persuasion may involve the rep in allowing greater freedom on returns within the firm's overall policy. But selling too many copies which are merely returned eats away at the bookseller's and publisher's margins, and erodes the trust between rep and buyer. It is a waste of time for both the bookseller and the publisher.

While there are bookshops which expect reps to do their stock checking and re-ordering for them, booksellers' electronic stock control systems should in theory override a rep's intervention, provided that the book has been ordered in the first place. In practice reps may tactfully remind buyers of new and backlist titles missing from the shelves, reshelve misplaced titles or mention a title that is gaining media attention. When visiting the branch of a chain, the rep will check that the store is complying with the display and positioning of key titles as agreed with head office.

Backed up by attractive POS material, the rep tries to persuade the bookseller to mount special window or instore displays to increase visibility by offering incentive terms if necessary. They will receive emails from head office with news of media coverage which is relevant to titles on the list. The bookseller may ask the rep to arrange an author signing session in the shop, and will negotiate any cost attached. Reps also feedback promotional needs requested by customers or promotional ideas used by other publishers which could be emulated; and occasionally reps make editorial suggestions. They may also chase debts and support marketing on author events.

Academic sales

Academic sales forces are smaller than those of consumer book publishers. Reps visit a limited range of bookshops, such as campus stores, which stock their titles, and may call on specialist mail-order booksellers and library suppliers which supply books to home and export markets. Additionally they may visit campuses in order to identify courses and the lecturers who make the decisions to recommend textbooks. While to a limited extent they encourage academics to order personally, or through their library, monographs and reference books (and sometimes journals and online services), their main thrust is to secure textbook adoptions. Using the promotional material and occasionally bound copies, they present the most relevant texts to individual lecturers who, if interested, are followed up by email and are sent inspection or gratis copies of the physical edition, or access to a digital edition. Increasingly rep visits are being replaced by emails inviting lecturers to order inspection copies directly.

Reps may also demonstrate any supporting electronic resources, arrange for password access for the lecturer, and promote any customization possible of the company's titles. The major publishers employ specialists to conduct further technical demonstrations. The rep also undertakes market research, such as looking at reading lists to check new and old adoptions or recommendations, and discussing with lecturers trends in subjects generally and particularly in relation to the firm's and competitors' titles. Sometimes they pick up new ideas and potential authors, to be developed by editors.

There is a great disparity amongst publishers regarding the proportion of the reps' time spent visiting booksellers and campuses. Many firms rely on direct promotion and reps devote most time to academic booksellers, whereas the reps of the larger textbook publishers may emphasize college calling. Owing to the difficulty of combining bookseller and college calling cycles, they may separate the activity. The busiest time of college-related shops (which derive 70 per cent of sales from five months of the year) and pop-up shops in universities is from the start of the academic year through to Christmas, followed by a secondary peak in the New Year to serve semester course starts. Thus the rep's key period, from mid-summer onwards, is the run-up to September. Although good booksellers forge links with lecturers and solicit reading lists around May, reps alert buyers to adoptions from information gathered from campus visits and from inspection copy requests, and then inform librarians. There are online reading list services such as the one run by Blackwell (readinglists.co.uk).

Reluctant buyers are eventually triggered into building up their stock by the students. Only a small number of booksellers stock monographs and high-priced reference books. Such books are supplied by bookshops in response to orders, and in fact most of such sales have transferred to the internet. However academic reps also sell titles more dependent on retail exposure – these may be used by students as background reading or for reference. Examples are OUP's series of Very Short Introductions and their Oxford Paperback Reference titles. A crucial aim is to get bookshops to stock and display the books – otherwise sales are lost. Booksellers are encouraged to distribute promotional material and to mount special displays at back-to-college time. Another activity is setting up and attending exhibitions at academic conferences. Large firms employ full-time staff solely for conferences. Against the background of the decline in campus bookstores and the reluctance of booksellers to hold stock of academic titles, conference exhibitions provide an opportunity for academics to see the publishers' main titles.

The sales staff of the major journal publishers concentrate their efforts on negotiating big deals with the main customers: the research intensive universities, through their librarians, and library consortia throughout the world.

Schools publishing

School textbook publishers and some children's book publishers employ a core of full-time educational reps (also called consultants) supplemented with term-time reps – often parents or ex-teachers. The large publishers have separate sales forces covering primary and secondary schools, and possibly the further education sector. Additionally, they may appoint specialist advisers (ex-teachers) in the major subject areas. They provide product training for reps, give talks to teachers and promote to local advisers. A rep for a large company may cover just two counties while one in a small company may have to cover a whole region. During term time reps usually visit two to three secondary schools per day or up to five primary schools. Large primary schools warrant coverage similar to a secondary school. The number of schools visited per day is related to their proximity.

Educational publishers may hold two or three sales conferences a year, before the opening of terms, at which the commissioning editors present the new books and digital resources. The marketing/sales manager directs the priorities.

Conferences enable the reps to report on sales, and on the response from their schools. The key period and busiest time for reps is the spring term when teachers select what they will use for the next school year – their financial year usually begins on 1 April. The summer term is quieter; the winter term becomes progressively more important towards the end. In small primary schools, headteachers usually choose the materials to be used; in secondary schools and large primary schools, departmental heads have the most influence. Thus a rep will try and see them, sometimes by appointment to talk about forthcoming titles, but mainly to show them finished copies. Teachers are asked what they are using and whether they are satisfied. If it is a competitor's book and there is a sign of hesitation, this provides an opening for a rep to discuss the merits of their books.

Experienced reps know the content not only of their own books but also of their competitors too, and recount the experience of teachers in other schools. If a teacher shows sufficient interest a rep will ask for an inspection copy to be sent. Occasionally copies of key books are left behind. Although priority is given to new books, especially those introducing a comprehensive course of study for National Curriculum core subjects, the promotion of the backlist is vital. Reps promote the use of digital products and services (CD-ROM and online; and for interactive whiteboards), and their role in this area becomes one of a consultant, advising on what resources work well. In those schools which manage their own budgets, reps encourage direct orders to the publisher, offering incentive discounts on sizeable quantities if necessary.

Market research includes the regular feedback of information such as teachers' suggestions, the response of teachers to their own and competitors' books, information on competitors, buying policies, local authority guidelines affecting purchases, and gaps in the market. Sometimes reps suggest ideas for books to the commissioning editors, give advice to teachers who are considering authorship and discover new authors. The market for digital content was stimulated by the government's provision of eLearning credits over a five-year period up until 2008; in response publishers developed a range of CD-ROM and online products, including those for interactive whiteboards.

Apart from visiting schools, reps ensure that their books are included in the school library, maintain contact with inspectors and local authority advisers, and sometimes conduct seminars. They are also involved in setting up and staffing local exhibitions, and the major exhibitions linked to national subject conferences held in vacations. Generally speaking, reps who work long hours during term time benefit from the school holidays.

INTERNATIONAL SALES

There are various ways of organizing export sales staff within a publishing house. In small firms the sales director may be responsible for home sales and for export arrangements, spending perhaps one or two months abroad annually. In larger firms there is a separate export department headed by an export sales manager, who reports to the sales director. An export manager may be supported by office staff. In still larger firms, there may be an international sales director in charge of staff such as regional sales executives or area export managers, who look after all the group's lists in specific territories. They are usually responsible for all export sales within their territories and for the arrangements and relationships made with the distributors and booksellers. As an alternative the sales team can be organized by list or imprint but this is less economic as it means several people are travelling to the same part of the world.

Territories are usually roughly divided by continent: Europe, Asia, India, Middle East, Africa, Australia, Canada, South America, and the Caribbean. The USA can be handled in many different ways but trade publishers will aim to sell rights, rather than their own edition, into this lucrative market. Larger houses will have several people covering the world; smaller companies may only have one person, who inevitably has to prioritize the most appropriate markets. The major players may well have their own companies in Australia, Canada, India, or South Africa, and the sales role becomes more one of product manager.

A characteristic of staff in international sales is that they are usually expected to spend anything from three to six months abroad. For example, medium and large UK publishers may employ sales representatives who cover parts or the whole of Europe or other areas of the world. Broadly, the larger the company, the smaller the geographical area covered by each representative; but compared to the home market their territories are vast and their calls to importing book trade customers far less frequent. They are either home-based, travelling regularly, or resident overseas. Some of the major publishing groups station their nationals in small offices in countries outside the fields of operation of their overseas firms. They are mainly concerned with promoting the firm's books, liaising with and supervising arrangements made with local distributors, opening up the market

Penguin India, started in 1987, publishes a range of fiction and non-fiction books, predominantly by Indian authors. It also publishes in local languages

International sales

The ability to speak preferably two or more languages is invariably required, but is not a top priority: most customers can speak English to some extent. But linguistic ability enables you to understand and relate that much better to the market and customers. Fluency in one or more of the European languages such as French, German, Spanish and Italian, and semi-fluency in some is ideal. Standard Arabic and Chinese are sometimes particularly desirable for certain firms. Export sales staff have a commitment to publishing and exporting, and have to enjoy working with books. First and foremost sales people, they have a burning desire to ring up the till, to increase profitable turnover. Most of the personal skills required for selling to the home market are paralleled in export selling; but exporters face the complexities of understanding many different and diverse markets and need an appreciation of the political, social, economic and cultural factors pertaining to each country, as well as a sensitivity to and enthusiasm for the market. Good exporters are able to sell and adapt to different environments and situations fast; they are good at building up relationships with key customers. Sales staff must like travel, and have the self-motivation to work far away from headquarters, take high-level decisions, and cope with loneliness (they could be travelling three months of the year).

SKILLS

and, when appropriate, employing local representatives. The export-orientated ELT divisions of major publishers typically have their own export sections deploying all of the above methods. Publishers may also employ full-time local nationals in some areas to represent their interests.

Export arrangements

The staff numbers of export departments are paradoxically far smaller than the home sales side because much of the work of promoting and selling books is carried out abroad. The international publishers with world rights in an author's work have greater control to set published prices and uniform publication dates in different parts of the world. Those publishers without world rights may be in competition with other publishers in some markets. International sales staff of UK publishers who are selling into open markets, for example Europe, will be keen to publish UK trade and ebook editions ahead of the equivalent US publisher's editions. There is mixed evidence, depending on the market, as to the impact of translation deals on the sales of English language editions. For example, Dutch publishers will rush to translate a potential bestseller ahead of the arrival of the English edition in their market. In Germany it may be the success of a novel once translated which encourages sales to those wanting to read the original English language edition. By contrast sales of the English edition of *Fifty Shades of Grey* fell in Slovenia once a translation was published.

The main export arrangements are as follows but ebooks can of course be sold directly to customers right around the world.

Sister companies and branches

In countries where there are firms connected through ownership with the originating publisher, such sister firms usually have the exclusive right to distribute. For example, Oxford University Press has a number of branches around the world. Nevertheless, certain titles or whole lists may be licensed to, or distributed by, other firms. Some US-focused consumer imprints of major international publishers are distributed in the UK by independent distributors such as Turnaround. Branches or sister companies may develop publishing operations aimed at their own domestic market and for export throughout the group.

Exclusive market

A stockholding agent may have the exclusive distribution rights for the publisher's output within a certain export territory. The agent services the orders originating from customers within the territory and collects the money. Normally the agent carries out the promotion and sales representation as well. Such agents may be wholesalers, booksellers, importers or branches of other publishers. Sometimes, exclusivity is restricted to part of the publisher's output or important named customers within the territory deal directly with the publisher.

Non-exclusive markets

In countries not covered by the exclusive stockholding agents or the publisher's overseas firms, the publisher deals directly with the local book trade. However, non-exclusive distribution arrangements may be made with certain local 'preferential' stockists (such as wholesalers), who receive more favourable terms from the publisher. The local booksellers can order either directly from the publisher or from the stockist. Some stockists also promote and sales-represent the publisher's books.

Sales on commission

Freelance agents can be appointed to promote and represent the books in specified countries – usually but not always in open markets, and carry many publishers' lists. Those representing publishers in the UK are based in the UK or abroad. They receive a commission of between 10 to 15 per cent on net sales revenue from the territory.

Terms of trade

The agents, wholesalers and booksellers trading in the books receive discounts from the exporting publisher, usually off the publisher's recommended price, in the same way as in the UK. They then add their costs and profit which can result in book prices being higher than those in the originating publisher's home market. However this situation is now changing as consumers are able to compare prices around the world and choose the most favourable option. Customers' credit periods in export markets are longer (90–120 days from date of invoice) but can extend to six months or more from slow-paying parts of the world. They also have to allow for import duties and freight costs, which often fall to them to pay. Wherever possible firm sales are made, and rarely are books actually returned from export markets. Publishers will ask for a POD (proof of destruction) and then credit the customer accordingly.

There are different terms that apply to the shipping of books:

- *Free on board* (FOB) – the publisher delivers the books free to the buyer's appointed UK shipping agent. Buyers within a country may co-ordinate and nominate a UK export company that will consolidate orders.
- *Ex-warehouse* – the customer bears the cost from the publisher's (or printer's) door. This is a common basis for trading.
- *Cost, insurance and freight* (CIF) – the publisher bears all the costs up to their arrival in a port or town. In return for saving the customer cost and (if the goods are sent air freight) time, the discount and credit period may be cut back.
- *On consignment* – the customer pays only on sales made and has the right to return unsold stock. This may be used for substantial orders.

Other export sales, not directly instigated by the publisher, are made by the UK and US export wholesalers, booksellers, and library suppliers. The largest are internationally based and promote, sell and distribute books worldwide – such firms are major 'home' customers of academic and STM publishers. An alternative arrangement is to work with such companies to help them promote the books in export markets. Sales can then be correctly recorded in the publisher's accounts as export. Some end-users seeking the cheapest source of supply (especially libraries) 'buy round' the publishers' arrangements by ordering books from suppliers which ignore exclusive territorial markets. Furthermore, internet bookselling of print and ebooks has broken down national frontiers for the trade of different kinds of books in different languages.

Promotion and personal selling

Communication with the international network is vital. Retailers and intermediaries must be persuaded to concentrate on promoting and selling the firm's titles rather than those of others. Constant contact takes the form of the supply of information through mailings, email, telephone calls and overseas visits. The AIs, catalogues, sales documents, covers, and point-of-sale material cascade on to the local network who use that material to publicize the publisher's titles within their markets. Originating publishers and the distributors operate online systems through which information on titles can be accessed by trading partners worldwide. Some agents prepare their sales documentation from information supplied while others use material produced by the originating publisher. They adapt the titles' metadata as necessary. For example, the original book description may be too difficult to understand by readers for whom English is their second language. Agents may generate free media publicity, secure reviews, mail catalogues, conduct email and social media campaigns, sometimes place advertisements, attend exhibitions and operate a textbook inspection copy service.

The originating publisher may also send promotional material to booksellers, libraries, British Council offices, academics and professionals, send books for review to learned journals, send complimentary copies of textbooks to influential people and operate an inspection copy service from the UK. The promotional efforts of publisher and agent may overlap. Of equal importance is the quality and regularity of the response from agents and representatives. They provide feedback on their activities and on market conditions, and specific feedback on individual titles, such as requests for more material.

Overwhelmingly, however, export sales are generated by personal selling. The publisher's senior sales staff give presentations to agents and main customers on their visits to their offices, at book fairs, and in their own countries. Their trips may last two, three or more weeks, and encompass half a dozen countries and up to 30 to 40 customers. They primarily sell to agents' sales managers or directors concerned with imports and may brief the agent's reps at a conference. They discuss all aspects of their trading relationship and assess agents' effectiveness. The reps need to develop an excellent knowledge of their markets in terms of pricing and what genres, subjects and authors work well. This knowledge can also feed back into commissioning decisions.

Sales reps may be working directly with customers in certain markets. They try to get subscriptions for new books, do not overlook the backlist, respond to complaints and collect debts. When appropriate they supply promotional copy for inclusion in the catalogues of wholesalers or retailers, check orders in order to avoid expensive distribution mistakes, and sometimes co-ordinate booksellers' ordering. Academic reps may call on lecturers and librarians in order to secure textbook adoptions, facilitate inspection copy orders and encourage booksellers to carry out joint promotions and exhibitions. ELT reps promote and sell courses directly to private language schools, state schools and to government agencies.

While some bestselling series sell well across international markets, other titles may have variable patterns of sale. What goes well in one country may not work in another market. Book formats and covers may have to be varied to take account of international differences in taste and societal norms. International sales staff view titles with their markets in mind, and may join both editorial and covers meetings. Sales of physical books by region are given in Table 11.1 (digital sales are not yet broken down by territory).

Diane Setterfield's gothic novel, *The Thirteenth Tale* (2006), had modest initial sales in the UK despite reaching the top of the *New York Times* bestseller list

Table 11.1 UK exports of physical books 2012 (*source*: The Publishers Association)

Region	£m
Europe	436
East and South Asia	184
Middle East/North Africa	162
North America	141
Australasia	139
Sub-Saharan Africa	92
Other Americas	52

DISTRIBUTION

The remainder of this chapter is devoted to how books are distributed through the supply chain. The distribution of books and journals in digital and print formats, and new media products, is massively complex and critical to the publisher's role of getting its product into the customers' hands at the right time, and if in print, in the right quantities. The key aspects of print distribution (sometimes called logistics) are:

- customer care,
- accuracy in order fulfilment,
- speed and reliability in dispatch,
- physical protection of the product,
- economies in dispatch, and
- credit control.

Failings in these areas lead to lost sales, diminished retail display, increased cost to the publisher and loss of confidence by bookseller and reader; improvements give the publisher a competitive marketing edge.

It is acknowledged that the system in the UK for the distribution of physical books is highly efficient, helped by the relatively small size of the country. Even so book distribution is an enormous challenge and exhibits unusual characteristics.

Many other kinds of goods produced by manufacturers (often on continuous production lines) are supplied directly to wholesalers and then on to the retailers. But publishers hire printers to manufacture the books which are usually delivered to the publisher or its distributor. Printers may also distribute new books direct to retailers and wholesalers, and POD printers direct to readers. In material handling terms, book distribution presents extremes, ranging from one or more copies or other media products up to a container load. Publishers face the return of unsold books from the UK book trade (typically in the range of 10 to 20 per cent of sales), which are credited accordingly; and if the books are damaged or of low value they destroy them. KPMG in 1998 estimated that the average cost of publishers' distribution represented 13 per cent of sales, while that of a consumer goods manufacturer was 6 per cent.

Publishers carry an enormous range of new and backlist products stored for a long time. In the main, publishers supply retailers – individual shops or their centralized warehouses – directly. Despite the growth of the wholesalers, book wholesaling in the UK is concentrated mainly on consumer books. The customers for books extend beyond the retail trade – to schools and to individuals needing single copies (for review and inspection if not digital, and mail-order sales). Publishers receive massive numbers of small orders, the profits from which may not cover the distribution and credit cost. For some publishers, referring direct sales from individuals to internet retailers, which pay affiliate fees, is more cost-effective than fulfilling such orders themselves. Yet physical stores demand faster and more reliable distribution in order to compete against internet retailers and other kinds of products. UK publishers export vigorously and distribute to most countries from the UK via a myriad of arrangements and carriers.

Industry standards

The foundation stone on which all book trade electronic transactions and information systems are based was the introduction in 1967 of the 10 digit standard book number (SBN). By 1970 it had become internationally accepted. In 2007 it was extended to 13 digits to make it consistent with the European Article Numbering (EAN) system (now international) used to identify many kinds of products and from which bar codes are generated. The ISBN incorporates in the following sequence the prefix of the 'book' product identifier 978 (979 will be introduced when the current stock of numbers is exhausted); the country or region or language group (for example English speaking countries either 0 or 1, French 2, German 3); the publisher identifier (the larger the publisher's output and demand for ISBNs, the smaller the number of digits are assigned to it); and the unique identifier of each book or edition. The last digit is a check to ensure the preceding digits are correct. ISBNs are used by publishers to identify tradable products such as different print and ebook formats, audiobooks and CDs. ISBNs are obtained by publishers from the national ISBN agencies: in the UK operated commercially by Nielsen and in the USA by Bowker. The digital identifier for journals is the International Standard Serial Number (ISSN).

In 1979, TeleOrdering was launched in the UK by Whitaker. This enabled booksellers to transmit orders electronically overnight into publishers' computers. TeleOrdering was the book trade's first proprietary electronic trading system deploying an early form of electronic data interchange (EDI). EDI facilitates the exchange of data between computer systems, saving trading partners' time, errors and cost by avoiding the use and handling of paper and making it unnecessary to rekey information. By the early 1990s most main UK bookshops had installed electronic point of sale (EPOS) systems which read the bar codes on books. The collection of EPOS data from the UK general retail market by Nielsen from the late 1990s aids stock management during the rise and fall of a title's sales.

EDItEUR is the international book trade standards body that co-ordinates the development of the infrastructure standards for EDI and other e-commerce standards for book and serial transactions, bibliographic and product information, digital publishing, and rights management and trading. It is supported in its drive towards electronic ordering, invoicing, information gathering and transmission, by BIC (Book Industry Communication) in the UK and the BISG (Book Industry Study Group) in the USA. The adoption of 'standards' is critically important to the trading of physical and digital products, and there are many agencies in the UK, Europe and in America working on standards for the description and trading of different categories of products. However, for the publishing industry and the intermediaries, three main areas stand out.

Product information

First, the development of standardized product information – a classification system whereby publishers describe the bibliographical details of their products consistently – and second the technical and procedural standards whereby they electronically communicate that information and its updating to others, such as to the bibliographic providers, wholesalers and retailers (see Chapter 10, page 243).

Supply chain

The second area relates to the supply chain (print and digital) and covers bar codes; B2B ecommerce transacted through EDI (orders, acknowledgements, delivery notes, invoices, credit notes, and price and product availability); and the standardization of the authorization procedures for returns in order to reduce costs. The UK Industry Returns Initiative (IRI) has led to returns requests being sent by booksellers electronically, with credits taking place automatically when stock is returned. There is no precise data, but the IRI is believed to have made reductions in the cost of returns. Under the IRI no returns are authorized until three months after publication or once 12–15 months have elapsed since the title was supplied to the shop.

In 2007 a bookseller in Holland, BGN, introduced radio frequency identification (RFID) into its stores. Called a smart bar code, a RFID tag can be inserted into a book, enabling fast scanning of the books within a store. This raises the possibility of smart shelving, which recognizes what stock is sitting there, and for customers to go through self-service tills. However so far there has been little demand for this technology from other book retailers.

Digital publishing

As publishers license and sell their products online either via intermediaries or directly to end-users from their digital warehouses, there is a need for common standards to facilitate electronic copyright management in order to trigger payment systems. For instance, an intermediary may want to print on demand a publisher's title or to customize a product including chapters from a range of book sources, or a researcher may want to follow-up an electronic journal reference in an article from another publisher's journal server.

The classic digital identifiers – the ISBN and ISSN – are the basis for electronic rights management systems at the macro level. One problem around ebooks is that this system has not necessarily kept pace – for example, an ebook could be published on Amazon's Kindle Direct without an ISBN; also each ebook edition (say Kindle, ePub, or PDF) may be given a new ISBN making the tracking of sales data more difficult. The Association of American Publishers sponsored the concept of a micro-level identifier – the digital object identifier (DOI) which is now promoted by the DOI Foundation (doi.org). The idea behind DOI is that it is a simple or dumb number which can be attached by the publisher to an object, such as a journal abstract, author's name and address, or book chapter, or piece of text or an illustration – whatever the publisher considers could be reusable or tradable. The publisher maintains a continually updated directory, which acts as a routing system where the dumb number is associated with the publisher's internet address. The publisher's database stores the most accurate information about the DOIs such as the copyright ownership, terms and conditions of sale and prices. The journal publishers were amongst the first publishers to deploy DOIs, although the take-up in other areas has been slow.

Warehousing and distribution

There are three main types of distribution arrangement: *self-distribution* by a publisher to retailers; *fulfilment only* of the orders generated by the publisher; or *full service distribution*, which 'outsources the entire publisher-to-book-buyer transaction, including dispatch, invoicing and credit control' (booksellers.org.uk, accessed 27 October 2013). The major publishing groups run their own distribution and place the facility away from the headquarters, while the very small publishers with insufficient turnover to attract a distributor have to do it themselves from their office or garage. Amazon runs a consignment scheme called Advantage, which can be used by small publishers or authors who self-publish. Publishers set the list price of the printed book, off which Amazon receives a 55–60 per cent discount and has the right to sell it at a discount to its customers, and Amazon keeps in stock quantities as low as two copies. At the end of each month, Amazon pays the publisher for sales in the previous month.

Small and medium publishers either distribute themselves or commonly use independent distributors (such as in the UK, Central Books or Turnaround for consumer titles, Marston Book Services, NBN or Turpin for academic and STM). They may use larger publishers which offer their services to smaller publishers such as TBS (The Book Service Ltd) owned by Random House, Macmillan Distribution, and Bookpoint and Littlehampton Book Services owned by Hachette all of which are eager to increase their turnover. Alternatively, they may use wholesalers such as Bertrams and Gardners in the UK, and Ingram in the USA, which also act as distributors.

> The basic difference [between a distributor and a wholesaler] is that a distributor will handle orders from both bookshops and wholesalers on terms set by the publisher and will also hold all of the publisher's stock. This will normally incur charges for receiving, storing, dispatching and handling stock, on agreed terms and rates. In addition they will invoice and collect payment on behalf of the publisher. A wholesaler on the other hand will sell on the terms that they agree with the retailer, and will invoice and collect payment on their agreed terms with the customer and undertake the associated credit risk. (Gardners.com, accessed 15 August 2013)

Publishers may use a mixture of services, supplying direct sales themselves but using third parties for trade and export sales. Third-party distributors offer to publishers the complete service of bulk storage, invoicing, customer service and cash collection, and delivery for which they charge around 12 per cent of sales: less for larger publishers and more for smaller publishers. Such distributors have extended their reach, for example to beyond the physical and internet book trade to libraries, schools and universities, and to members of the public, in home and export markets. They increasingly offer additional services to client publishers, such as sales representation, marketing, print on demand, ebook distribution and negotiation with aggregators, hosting a white label website (a plain copy of the publisher's site), and platforms. Global ebook distribution has become increasingly complex and difficult to manage. Publishers may operate their own digital warehouse (Digital Asset Distribution, DAD) or outsource it to a distributor or specialist company, such as Gardners, Ingram (CoreSource), or ePubDirect etc. Some distributors also offer to publishers Digital Asset Management (DAM) which includes a complete audit trail to ensure the publisher knows where its content is at all times.

The supply chain for books

Books can be supplied directly from the publisher or through a distributor or wholesaler (see the figure below for the physical supply chain). Smaller bookshops source the majority of their stock from the wholesalers, which offer a next-day service. The trend is towards fewer and larger distributors. Size gives to the distributor the turnover to invest in expensive electronic book handling and warehouse systems, the ability to bulk up order values, greater leverage in debt collection, and the securing of lower rates with carriers. With the development of faster and more reliable transportation systems, including air freight, there is a movement away from overseas stockholding agents to direct supply from the UK, giving a greater opportunity to price books more competitively in many markets. The independent third-party distributors occasionally go bust, which can be a disaster for the publisher if unable to retrieve its cash and books from the receiver.

Short-run printing and print on demand are embedded in book distribution. They reduce the need for the publisher to hold speculative inventory and enable

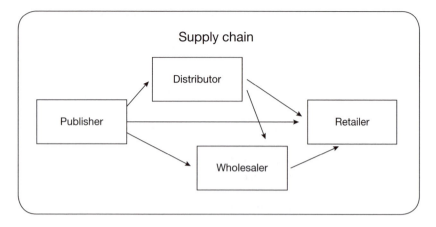

slow moving backlist titles to remain in print. Indeed for some specialist or academic titles, journal back issues, or ebook originals, the need is removed to hold any stock at all. The publisher may export and import via printing in the local sales market. A book is produced in response to an order, or an agreed minimum order is kept in stock, and the publisher's POD supplier dispatches it direct. Third-party distributors serving publishers may have their own POD facilities or have alliances with such printers.

Some publishers have built their own platforms for the delivery of online content; others use third parties. High levels of investment are required to develop online services and, for example, it is estimated that Elsevier spent £200 m on the establishment of their platform ScienceDirect. For ebooks, publishers may distribute through a third party, or opt for direct supply. In practice most consumer sales in the UK go through Amazon. Libraries prefer ebooks on a common platform and there are companies such as OverDrive (trade) or ebrary (academic) that will supply content from a variety of publishers.

There have been developments to develop direct sales of digital textbooks, and for example CourseSmart makes content available digitally to HE students, faculty and institutions. Instructors can obtain inspection copies and rather than buy the books there is a rental model for students (access expires after 360 days).

The distribution of physical books

The 'trade side' of distribution is concerned with processing received orders, raising invoices, credit control and documentation. Once orders are received, the invoice is raised, and the documentation, labelling and physical distribution begin. There are many standardized codes which tell a trade customer a book is unavailable for various reasons. The Standard Address Number (SAN) and Global Location Number (GLN) are identifiers of a physical location of a bookseller and are an essential part of EDI and other ecommerce transactions. New books or reprints not yet in stock are recorded on a 'dues listing' and dispatched when available unless otherwise instructed. Export orders need additional documentation to comply with the receiving country's import regulations and taxes; there can also be censorship of titles in China or in countries in the Middle East. On orders to mainland Europe some publishers invoice in euros or local

> ScienceDirect from Elsevier offers articles and chapters from more than 2,500 journals and nearly 20,000 books

currencies and offer banking arrangements. Pro-forma invoices may be sent to new or unsafe customers – with a non-existent or poor credit history – before the books are dispatched. Most publishers supply books to UK booksellers carriage free, whereas booksellers in Europe will pay their own carriage.

The customer services department handles return requests and resolves queries from booksellers regarding problems of distribution and of accounts; or from end-users who may make comments on social media. The textbook inspection copy service and mail-order or subscription sales are usually handled by separate departments. Adverse comments made by readers or users on social media, internet retailers and book recommendation sites may need a fast response.

The warehouse includes the bulk store of books and journals (and of any raw paper reserves), into which deliveries are made from printers, and a 'picking' area where titles and back-up stock are positioned for easy location (new books and fast-selling titles in prime sites). The invoices may include the location of titles in the order in which they are 'picked'. The collated orders move to the packaging and dispatch area. Dispatch involves knowing the most economic, speedy and reliable method (road carrier, shipping, air freight, post) and negotiating bulk deals with carriers. If the publisher bears the cost, the incentive is to lower costs to increase profitability; when the customer pays (for example on FOB export orders) the incentive is to assist them to save money, a marketing service. In order to treat mainland Europe as an extension of the home market and to compete against US publishers, some UK publishers are using pan-European delivery networks operated by the same carriers as used in the UK. In so doing, the publisher controls the level of service door-to-door, avoids dealing with dozens of carriers and attains economies. For the internet retailer Amazon, they may choose to supply an order from their own warehouse or from third-party wholesalers.

While the computer monitors stock levels, there are staff who physically check the stock and check the returns (the barcodes aid the task), liaising with the sales office where appropriate. The application of computers to order-processing, distribution and dispatch provides key information for management, such as reports on dues, sales by title, by area, by representative (and comparative monthly reports), type of customer, discount structure, return levels, stock and re-order levels, method of dispatch, carriage charge analysis and debtors.

Looking into the future, we may see publishers abandoning their own warehousing and distribution, preferring to concentrate on core competences in editorial, sales and marketing. Investments in digital platforms and services will bring a greater reward.

Now read this

Chapter 13, The sales channels for books in the UK.

Sources

Publishers Association, *PA Statistics Yearbook*, 2012.

Web resources

www.bic.org.uk Book Industry Communication, UK.
www.bisg.org Book Industry Study Group, USA.
www.booksellers.org.uk The Booksellers Association (UK and Ireland).
www.doi.org International DOI Foundation.
www.editeur.org International standards body for the book and serials
        industry.
www.publishingcrawl.com Blog from authors and industry professionals.

CHAPTER 12

Rights sales

The author–publisher contract sets out the scope of the publisher to license various kinds of rights to other firms: the licensing business model. These rights allow the licencees to exploit the book across different dimensions – by media, territory and language. Rights sales can be important to a publisher since the income attracts little by way of direct costs and is often simply extra profit. To be compared directly to sales income, the revenue from rights sales should be multiplied by a factor of six to eight. In consumer book publishing, where the contract is frequently drawn up by the author's agent, there may be a more limited grant of rights to the publisher – for example, agents may choose to retain film and TV rights, serial rights and translation rights to handle themselves.

Industry data rarely separates out rights income but a biennial survey from the Publishers Association in 2013 (to be annual in future) put a value on the rights sales for the larger publishers and the major literary agents in the UK. The total income in 2012 was £178 m, with 28 per cent from co-editions. Foreign language co-editions accounted for 88 per cent of the co-edition sales; the remainder were English language co-editions. For foreign language co-editions, 53 per cent of sales were in Western Europe. For the English language co-editions, 80 per cent of sales were to USA and Canada, and 20 per cent in the UK, including book clubs. Other income included translations (£29 m), permissions (£29 m) and English language reprints (£29 m). Under the sale of other rights, the area of electronic rights totalled £31 m, mainly in the sectors of academic and reference publishing; however, figures for this area are not wholly representative as many publishers do not classify electronic arrangements (for example with aggregators) as rights deals.

RIGHTS WORK

The selling of rights may be done by editors and sales staff. However, medium to large publishers normally employ specialists to sell rights actively. A small department may consist of a rights manager and assistant; a larger one has staff specializing in particular rights such as translation, particular areas of the list or regions of the world. A publisher may choose to use subagents abroad (for example in mainland Europe, the USA, China and Japan), who receive a commission of, say, 10 to 15 per cent on rights sales made.

In the pre-digital age, there was a clear distinction between a sales department which sold printed copies to intermediaries (for distribution) and a rights department which licensed rights to other firms (mainly publishers). However, ebooks and other digital resources are often sold via intermediaries and those arrangements are now usually undertaken by the sales department. Former distinctions and demarcations between rights and sales are breaking down, as are the ways publishers organize the activities.

Publishers face a perennial question as to whether they would make more or less money by licensing a book to a local publisher (for instance in the USA) or distributing the book into that territory themselves. For example, a motivated local publisher operating under a rights deal may sell more copies but may pay a royalty or (if importing printed copies) pay a lower price per copy to the originating publisher; or the originating publisher under a distribution arrangement may sell fewer copies but receive a higher price per copy. A further complication arises with ebooks. In the former, print-only world, printed editions of English language consumer books would be published at different times in different territories (in this case countries) by different publishers. With ebooks, even though territorial rights can still be maintained under contract with internet retailers (at least in theory), consumers would not understand their inability to buy an ebook in their country when it is evidently published elsewhere. A lack of availability also fuels piracy. Ebook publication is expected to occur at the same time throughout the world. Thus a UK consumer book publisher holding world English language rights might have been unable to sell print rights to a US publisher, but it might publish itself the ebook in the USA. UK agents face the same difficulty. They may have withheld US rights from the UK publisher, but have been unable to find a US publisher. This has prompted some UK agents to publish ebooks in the USA under their own arrangements in the hope that they might make an eventual sale to a US publisher.

The large publishers maintain separate contracts departments which put into the contractual detail the outcome of the agreements reached with authors, agented authors and with publishers from whom they have bought rights; some may also handle contracts with licensees, although in many companies these contracts are handled by rights sales staff. There are also contract specialists who offer their services to publishers and agents. Rights staff may also check and monitor the contracts made between the publisher and authors, and offer their expertise on copyright and media law.

Separate permissions staff may carry out necessary reactive work, which involves responding to requests for copyright permission to reproduce limited amounts of material (such as extracts of text, tables, technical illustrations) from the firm's books in other publications or media. Usually granted is a non-exclusive licence to reproduce the material for a particular use, with due acknowledgement, for a specified edition, quantity and language throughout the world, though the territories may be limited. The applicant is charged a fee, usually equally shared by the originating publisher and author. The Copyright Licensing Agency (CLA) in the UK facilitates the collection of fees from educational and other organizations wishing to copy extracts for class sets, coursepacks and other uses. Such 'collective' – or 'secondary' – licensing schemes are used by publishers when it is not possible or practical for them to license users directly. The money collected is shared between the publisher and the author. There are similar schemes throughout the world, such as the Copyright Clearance Centre (CCC) in the USA, that have reciprocal arrangements with each other.

Many books have no significant rights sales income, but some (such as in consumer publishing, especially in adult and children's highly illustrated colour books) earn much or depend on rights deals for viability. Where agents are involved, many rights may be reserved and not available to the publisher, limiting what then can be sold. For example, a publisher buying volume (essentially print and ebook) rights for a specified territory will not be able to sell translation rights unless these are specifically added to their licence for the agreed territory. By contrast, the non-consumer publishers will aim to acquire all rights, throughout the world, from their non-agented authors. As the major publishers consolidate their position worldwide, they gain the capability of publishing books themselves in foreign languages through their subsidiary companies, rather than licensing

Copyright Licensing Agency

Kevin Fitzgerald CMG, Chief Executive of the Copyright Licensing Agency

E★PERT

The Copyright Licensing Agency Ltd (CLA) was set up by UK authors and publishers to manage collective licensing on their behalf for the copying of extracts from publications. CLA was established in 1982 by the Authors Licensing and Collecting Society (ALCS) and the Publishers Licensing Society (PLS) to license the limited photocopying of books, journals and magazines. Today CLA also licences printed music, and digital copying and storage. Visual creators are also represented through an agency agreement with the Design and Artist Copyright Society (DACS).

CLA licenses organizations from the business, education and government sectors and permits limited copying under blanket licences, in most cases in return for one single annual fee. Through reciprocal agreements with sister organizations in other countries, the licences also include rights to copy from titles published in all major overseas territories. CLA is currently collecting some £75 m per year in licence fees. This money is allocated to individual copyright owners on the basis of the titles copied in the relevant period.

This core licensing activity connects creativity with industry by ensuring that copyright owners receive a fair reward when their works are copied as well as providing easy, legal access to a wide range of publications – such as trade and consumer magazines, journals, books, law reports and press cuttings – for businesses, schools, colleges, government and public bodies.

In 2012 CLA signed up to self-regulation through the British Copyright Council. The first Independent Code Review on the effectiveness of this regulation was due in spring 2014. By supporting copyright owners through collective licensing, CLA plays a major part in maintaining the value of their work, thereby sustaining creativity and the creative industries in the UK which provide some 7 per cent of the UK GDP and generate millions of jobs.

translation rights to others. The major educational and academic publishers have the ability to sell their products digitally and directly to end-users without the use of intermediaries.

Rights work involves close contact with the editorial, production, promotion and sales departments, and also the royalty and accounts departments. Selling to customers, who are mainly editors or directors of other firms, has to be carried out in a regular and personal way, and good negotiation skills are required to negotiate deals and contracts. Travel includes attending the major rights fairs of Frankfurt and London, Bologna (for children's books), and BookExpo America. Staff who sell many books of international appeal, such as highly illustrated colour non-fiction, travel widely and frequently, making sales trips to countries in addition to their attendance at relevant fairs. There is a great deal of paperwork – correspondence, maintaining customer mailing lists, and record keeping – and after fairs and sales visits considerable follow-up is required. Rights managers have to keep track of trends around which countries are likely to be fruitful sources of business – for example, China has assumed much greater importance in recent years as the economy and the publishing sector there have experienced fast growth. In Europe, there are variations between countries in terms of the number of books bought per head of population, and in recent years markets such as Greece, Spain and Italy have been badly affected by the economic recession. Those countries with a tradition of cheap paperback publishing are likely to have higher sales per capita.

As in other areas, rights selling is aided by technology. For example, there are specialist rights databases such as Bradbury Phillips, and rights components of larger systems such as Biblio3 and Klopotek, which enable rights staff to keep track of their submissions and sales and can automate many procedures such as chasing customers for decisions and payments. The international book fairs are creating virtual market-places for the trade of rights. As content is chunked into ever smaller units, whether chapters or pictures, there are software solutions for tracking their sale, ownership of the rights and royalties payable. Selling by rights staff may be done by telephone or email, using a variety of tools, such as specialist rights websites, email alerts for new titles, advance information sheets, sample pages and catalogues; databases can be transported and material shown to customers on laptops, tablets or even smartphones. However, for high-quality illustrated books customers still want to see physical materials. For publishers selling translation rights of fiction, for example into English, sample chapters may need to be available to overcome language barriers.

The rights department may get involved with a title before the author has signed the contract. An editor may ask the rights manager to assess the title's rights sales potential, particularly if that affects the author's advance, or the viability of the book depends on rights sales. This can be particularly important for highly illustrated books with significant origination costs, where co-edition sales may be required. Sample covers and page spreads may be shown at the Frankfurt Book Fair to gauge the likely interest in a proposal. Around the delivery of the manuscript, the titles are assessed and a strategy is drawn up regarding the choice of possible customers, and how and when they will be approached. There are many kinds of rights and the deals struck are both intricate and varied. The main subsidiary rights are described on the following pages. Sometimes, the author's approval is needed before deals are concluded, and it is any case a courtesy to keep them informed.

The Frankfurt Book Fair is held in October each year. In 2013 there were over 7,000 exhibitors and 26,000 visitors

Book fairs

Lynette Owen, Copyright and Rights Consultant

EXPERT

Book fairs are key events in the publishing world calendar, providing a meeting place for publishers, agents, distributors and retailers to pursue their business on a face-to-face basis; authors may also attend for book launches and cultural events. Some book fairs admit the public, who can attend literary events and in some cases purchase books at a discount.

Rights trading is a major feature of many book fairs. Although this business is conducted year-round by letter, telephone and email, book fairs provide a focus for new titles on offer. The key fairs for rights business are: Frankfurt, held in October and covering all types of publication and featuring exhibitors from all over the world; Bologna, from 2008 held in late March and covering children's books and some educational publications; and London, now held in mid-April.

BookExpo America, held annually in early June and based in New York until 2015, is primarily an event for US publishers to showcase their new publications to the US book trade, but it also provides an opportunity for British and other publishers to meet US publishers on home territory.

Other fairs in Western Europe have varying roles: Salon du Livre (in Paris in March) and Göteborg (late September) are largely cultural events, whilst Liber (held immediately before Frankfurt and alternating between Madrid and Barcelona) is primarily a forum for Latin American publishers to meet Spanish publishers.

In central and Eastern Europe there are now many fairs, although most are 'selling fairs' for local publishers to sell books to the visiting public. The Warsaw Fair, held every year in May, provides a rights forum, whilst the Moscow International Book Fair (early September) provides an opportunity to meet many Russian publishers who do not always attend Western book fairs. The rather oddly named Non-Fiction Fair is held in Moscow in late November/ early December and is rather more upmarket, with book launches and discussion panels. Fairs have also been established in Prague, Budapest and the Baltic states, where the book fair rotates between Estonia, Latvia and Lithuania. In the Balkans there are fairs in Belgrade, Bucharest and most recently in Thessaloniki.

In the Middle East the Cairo Book Fair was long the major event as a sales fair, but in recent years Abu Dhabi and Sharjah have established themselves as rights market places; each offers a subsidy scheme for rights deals, with Abu Dhabi funding the cost of rights purchase and Sharjah the costs for translation. Further afield there are book fairs in Calcutta and Delhi (sales rather than rights events), Seoul (June), Tokyo (July) and Beijing (late August/early September). Beijing is a major rights fair and Tokyo is seeking to build up this aspect of its business. In Latin America, Guadalajara (December) is being promoted as a rights event.

Literary agents and publishing rights staff start work on book fairs early and appointments are planned and confirmed many weeks before the event itself. Many literary agents arrive in Frankfurt before the fair commences and hold appointments in their hotels; many overseas publishers arrive ahead of the London Book Fair and visit publishers and agents in their offices. Random callers at book fair stands may be accommodated, but prebooked appointments are now the order of the day.

Rights sellers attend book fairs armed with information and material on existing and forthcoming projects and work under considerable pressure; usually no more than half an hour is available for each appointment. Traditionally, sellers remain based on their own stand or in an agents' centre, whilst buyers move around the fair from meeting to meeting. The physical conditions at some fairs can leave much to be desired! A rights appointment will usually start with a discussion of any outstanding business, followed by a presentation of new projects; the rights seller will aim to select titles appropriate to the customer and may be switching languages from appointment to appointment. Projects may be offered on the basis of an exclusive option (more common for academic and professional titles, where the potential buyer will need time to obtain specialist reviews), multiple submission to more than one potential buyer, or a full-scale auction where would-be buyers will have to compete with each other on the basis of terms set by the seller.

Although rights trading is conducted all year round and has been much facilitated by email, book fairs remain extremely important as much rights business depends on personal relationships, knowledge of the taste of the potential buyer (particularly important in trade publishing) , face-to-face discussions and occasional serendipitous discoveries. Deals may be finalized for projects submitted before the fair, and new deals started which may be finalized weeks or months later. Business is often extended beyond a full working day at the fair with breakfast meetings, receptions and dinner after the fair; publishers are social animals and many a deal has come about as a result of a chance encounter in less formal circumstances than a fair appointment.

The period after a book fair is usually extremely busy, and traditionally the onus is on the rights seller to follow up with each customer promptly after the fair, confirming what has been agreed, drawing up contracts for any deals finalized at the fair and providing any information or sample material promised to the potential buyer. For educational, academic and professional titles, decisions tend to be taken some weeks or months after the fair itself – for trade titles, decisions may be made more quickly.

In the age of the internet, the future value of book fairs has sometimes been questioned, but most publishers would agree that they remain hugely important events and that 'virtual' events would not be an adequate substitute for regular personal contact and the buzz of a well-run book fair.

SUBSIDIARY RIGHTS

Reprint rights

With the emergence of consumer book publishers that publish both hardbacks and paperbacks, the selling of English language reprint paperback rights by originating hardback publishers to separate paperback publishers is now rare. But a small or medium-sized publisher, while capable of selling a trade paperback itself, may not be able to sell a mass-market paperback edition demanding different distribution channels. Thus it could access that market by licensing that edition to a larger publisher. The *No. 1 Ladies' Detective Agency* by Alexander McCall Smith was first published in 1998 by Polygon, a small Scottish publisher, before appearing as an Abacus paperback in 2003. Similarly a mainstream publisher might buy the print rights to a self-published work, as Simon & Schuster in the USA did in 2012 with *Wool* by Hugh Howey.

The key features of such deals are as follows. The seller defines the rights granted: the exclusive right to publish a particular kind of edition in specified territories is stated; and the duration of the licence is set out (for example eight years). The buyer prints its own edition and pays royalties on copies sold to the originating publisher. These royalties are shared between the author and the originating publisher. A rising royalty scale – the royalty rate increases when sales reach a certain figure – and the size of the advance (representing a proportion of future royalties) are negotiated. The advance payable is usually split, with part payable on signature of the contract and the balance on publication; it is shared with the author in a proportion agreed in the rights section of the author–publisher contract.

An offset fee is payable in order to reproduce the original setting of a book

The buyer will pay the originating publisher an offset fee, not shared with the author, for the right to reproduce the text prior to printing, and sometimes a fee for use of the digital files of the book. The timing of reprint publication is set so as not to undermine the originator's other sales.

North American rights

The USA is by far the largest and richest English language market. Agents, on behalf of authors and book packagers, may retain US rights or North American rights (the USA plus Canada). But if held by the publisher and the book is not to be sold via the publisher's North American firm or through a distribution arrangement, the rights may be licensed. Sometimes US publishers request Spanish language rights for their territory.

Selling to US editors is carried out at a distance or personally when they visit the UK en route to the Frankfurt or Bologna Book Fairs, or at such fairs. The London Book Fair has grown in importance over recent years. Sometimes, the rights manager attends the annual US book fair, BookExpo, or visits New York to see a number of publishers. UK-based scouts of US publishers may be used; and UK editors are also in contact with US publishers. The submission method may be simultaneous – the chosen editors from several different US houses receive the material at the same time – or occasionally full-scale auctions are held. Editors may be given the proposal, manuscript, or proofs. Depending on the stage reached, the rights manager uses the author's previous sales figures, the jacket and blurb, pre-publication quotes, the UK subscription order, reviews and details of other rights sales to stimulate interest.

There are essentially two types of deal. In the first, a reprint deal, the US publisher manufactures its own edition, pays royalties and an advance which are shared by the UK publisher and author – for trade titles, usually the larger share goes to the author, for example 75 to 80 per cent. In effect the UK publisher acts as the author's agent. For academic titles, the share may be 50/50 or 60/40 in the author's favour. Additionally the US publisher may pay for the use of a digital file of the book, or perhaps of the illustrations only. Alternatively, they may pay an offset fee at a rate per page. This type of royalty exclusive deal tends to be used on most fiction and on some illustrated books of considerable US interest. It may also be used if the US publisher needs to make (agreed) changes to the text, for example adding American references or perhaps Americanizing the terminology and spelling.

In the second type of deal, the UK publisher co-prints the US edition together with their own UK edition, substituting the US publisher's imprint and ISBN. This is an English language co-edition. The bound copies are sold at a small marked-up price; and the author's royalty of say 10 per cent of the UK publisher's net receipts is usually included in the price paid. This type of deal can apply to any illustrated consumer book, and could also be used for academic books published by UK firms without a strong US presence. However, the \$–£ exchange rate will affect the viability of co-edition sales to the US market. Proprietary co-editions can be made with retailers, for instance, a UK children's book publisher may customize a book for Walmart or Costco. The co-edition business model (sometimes called co-publishing) can be applied to any market channel which can be defined.

A non-exclusive licence allows a publisher to enter into agreements with other third parties

Whichever applies, the US publisher is granted an exclusive licence, sometimes for the full term of copyright, but usually for a shorter period with provision to renew. The US publication date is stated, the UK publisher is obliged to supply the material by a set date, and the US publisher has to publish by a certain date. Contractual limitations are essential to forestall premature release of an ensuing US paperback or remainder, which could jeopardize export sales of a UK paperback. The price paid or the royalty rates, and advance, are negotiated as well as the exact territories. The US publisher, which is granted exclusivity in the USA and its territories (US publishers also commonly request Canada), is

Rights

Rights staff preferably know French or German, and if concerned with co-editions especially, Italian and Spanish as well. But negotiations are mostly in English. However senior the role, the work can involve much administration.

The essential prerequisite for selling is knowledge of the books and customers. Editorial insight into the firm's new titles alongside lateral thinking aid the assessment of rights prospects and their worth, the drawing out of salient points and the realization of sales revenue. With highly saleable titles, skilled judgement is needed on the kind of approach and its timing to selected customers.

The perception of customers' needs entails an understanding of the way they run different kinds of businesses – for example their product range, markets, business models and financial structure – in different cultural, political and economic contexts. It is also important to recognize personal interests and tastes – especially in fiction and children's publishing – and national reading trends. Dealing with small numbers of senior people regularly and personally demands the development of good and close relations. Sales skills encompass the enthusiastic promotion of titles in writing, on the telephone and in person, even when there is scant information available on a new title. Where customers are in competition or when time is short in co-printing, they have to be pressured and manoeuvred to clinch deals quickly.

Negotiation skills allied to experience, numeracy and fast thinking help a rights person to tell if a customer is offering too low an advance or too little in a co-printing deal. The full implications and catches in customer contracts must be spotted and adverse clauses removed or modified. Where physical or digital elements are supplied, a knowledge of production processes and terminology is required. As so much of the job involves remembering and recording which books are on offer and who is looking at what, a meticulous, methodical mind which registers fine detail is essential. The consequences of selling the same book twice in the same territory are horrendous, although this is unlikely given the use by many publishers of rights managements systems.

Long working days precede and follow the major fairs, such as Frankfurt, at which customers are seen in back-to-back, half-hourly appointments during the day, and informally into the nights, over a week. The job calls for immense stamina and a strong voice box.

excluded from the UK publisher's territories (for example usually the UK, the Commonwealth countries and mainland Europe, although the latter markets can prove a bone of contention), and has the non-exclusive right to distribute their edition in other countries. The US publisher may be granted other rights within their agreed market, such as book club or serial right, and pays a proportionate share of revenue from such sales to the UK publisher. This is in turn shared with the author in the proportion agreed in the subsidiary rights section of the author–publisher contract. With some co-edition deals the US publisher may be territorially limited to North America, and the subsidiary rights granted may be fewer.

Translation rights

With the globalization of publishing, sales of translation rights have continued to grow. Translation sales lead the way into emerging markets such as Eastern Europe, the Baltic countries, South America and Asia, and help fend off piracy. Acquiring translation rights gives the licensee the right to publish a work in a particular language. In the case of adult consumer books, translation rights (for some or all foreign languages) are often retained by agents. But if they are held by the publisher, the titles are promoted abroad by email and telephone, and personally at major book fairs or through sales visits. For trade titles, appropriate publishers within a language market area are selected and sent material simultaneously. Academic titles take some time to be reviewed and are often offered to only one publisher at a time on an exclusive option basis. Foreign language editions may increase export sales of the English language edition owing to the book's increased exposure, but there may also be an argument that the translation rights for adult titles should be withheld, for example in European markets with a high ability to read English such as the Benelux countries and Scandinavia, to encourage the sales of the English language edition (by contrast, children's books would best be read in the local language). Continental European publishers will want to race their translations of consumer titles through to capitalize on the original publication and to avoid loss of sales from purchasers of the English edition. They also have to contend with the English language ebook, which may be highly competitive on price.

For many titles, the translation deal will be on the basis of a licence where the foreign publisher translates and produces the book, and pays royalties and an advance to the original publisher. There may also be a charge for the digital files of any illustrations to facilitate production of the translated edition. The advance is usually lower than for English rights, and some publishers work on an advance equivalent to half of the royalty likely to be earned on the first print run. Occasionally a lump sum is requested to reproduce a set quantity. This can be a good arrangement for those territories where print runs are small, book prices are low and the customer may not be able to provide accurate or regular data on the number of copies sold. The purchasing publisher is granted an exclusive language licence for a particular edition, and other rights for a set period, and may be granted rights for that language throughout the world. Practice varies as to whether the deal includes ebook rights in the local language, and for countries where there are concerns about piracy, the rights are often refused. Sometimes, on a consumer book, a Spanish, Portuguese or French publisher is excluded from Latin America, Brazil or Quebec, respectively, since rights can be sold separately in different territories for the same language. The author receives say a 50 per cent share of the royalties if academic, or up to 80 or 90 per cent if popular trade. There are some novelists whose sales in translation greatly exceed their English language sales – for example the US novelist Jonathan Carroll. The rewards to

Window display in
Moscow of cookery
books by Gordon
Ramsay

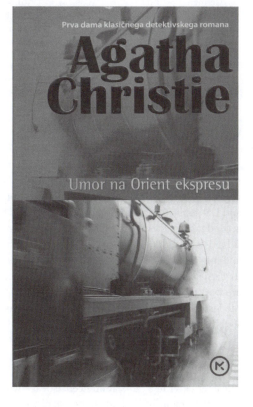

The Slovenian edition
of Agatha Christie's
*Murder on the Orient
Express* (Mladinska
Knjiga). Her books
have been translated
into over 45
languages and have
sold over 2 billion
copies worldwide

academic authors from translation are usually in terms of prestige and the dissemination of their work, rather than financial, but for textbooks the cumulative effect of lots of small deals over a number of years is an aid to both longevity and profitability.

Table 12.1 Top 10 translated languages (*source*: www.unesco.org/xtrans, accessed 5 September 2013)

Original language	Number of translations
English	1,263,024
French	223,575
German	205,969
Russian	103,041
Italian	68,939
Spanish	54,109
Swedish	39,853
Japanese	29,038
Danish	21,149
Latin	19,652

Table 12.2 Top 10 target languages (*source*: www.unesco.org/xtrans, accessed 5 September 2013)

Target language	Number of translations
German	301,884
French	239,982
Spanish	228,495
English	228,495
Japanese	130,639
Dutch	111,267
Russian	100,785
Portuguese	78,838
Polish	76,697
Swedish	71,206

UNESCO has a historical database of translations which can be consulted online (see Tables 12.1 and 12.2). A search on the Index Translationum reveals the most popular original languages, with English heading the table. This clearly gives UK and US publishers an advantage when it comes to selling translation rights. The second table shows the top target languages, into which translations are made. What is often commented on is the imbalance in the number of translations from and into English. The website Three Percent showcases translated literature and its name derives from the low proportion of books published in the USA which are works in translation. Between 2000 and 2008 the UK and Ireland saw a modest rise in the number of translations published – from 1,721 to 2,207 titles (publishers.org.uk).

Foreign language co-editions

The alternative to a translation licence deal – which is used for many highly illustrated colour books and children's picture books – is for the foreign language publishers to supply the digital files of their translations to fit around the four-colour illustrations. This type of licence is called a foreign language co-edition. Several language editions are then printed together by the original publisher or packager in order to gain economies of scale. The printing press usually has five cylinders carrying the printing plates. Four cylinders carry the plates which print the four-colour illustrations (made up of yellow, magenta, cyan and black), and the fifth cylinder carries the plate of the text printed in black outside the areas of the illustrations. The press operator changes the fifth plate for each language edition printing. The ordered quantities, carrying each publisher's imprint, are usually supplied royalty inclusive. Digital colour presses allow production of shorter runs.

English and foreign language co-edition deals are central to the work of rights staff of highly illustrated adult and children's publishers and packagers. For example, the publication of a children's picture book may depend upon co-editions to make it viable, and accordingly the content may need to be sensitive to cultural differences. Rights staff usually initiate deals well in advance of publication with English language publishers and book clubs (although the latter are now far less significant channels to market) using the book's contents, and mock-ups of the jacket and blads of selected double-page spreads. The co-printing of foreign language editions may follow because their publishers may translate from the finished text and layout. The English and foreign language co-printing of children's books of few words can coincide. Negotiations with customers on the price paid per copy, the timing of the deals and their combined printing can be critical for a book's viability.

A blad is a sample printed section

Co-editions may be combined with TV tie-ins, own-brand titles and sponsorship deals. The complexity of these deals, involving close contact with the production department, makes it very difficult for authors' agents to enter this form of rights selling. Peter Usborne, founder of the children's publisher Usborne, comments about co-editions:

> You have to invest in each of the books you produce – you have to create something that is more expensive than your partner can afford to create so that they will buy it from you rather than making it themselves. (*The Bookseller*, 19 October 2007)

Digital rights

The licensing of electronic rights became important for publishers in some areas, such as reference and academic publishing, as a staging point whilst they set up their own digital platforms. If smaller companies do not have the resources and skills to establish digital services, they will look to sell to third parties. Even for bigger players, the sale of electronic rights on a non-exclusive basis may provide useful external income. Customers could be media companies, such as those producing games (especially for children/YA), rather than other publishers, and the possibilities of the internet and mobile technology continue to be explored. In China and Japan, for example, hand-held dedicated readers are produced for reference works such as dictionaries. The *Oxford English Dictionary*, or smaller lexical works, are licensed by OUP to numerous platforms and devices, including the Kindle. There is growing interest in travel content and language phrasebooks being available on mobile phones.

Journal and reference articles and whole books may be licensed to aggregators, such as EBSCO and ProQuest, which offer content from a variety of publishers to academic or public libraries and other institutions. Academic publishers offer site licences for their own electronic services to institutions such as universities – the licences outline the conditions under which the service is to be used. In the USA, libraries have formed consortia to negotiate the terms for access to online databases. In the UK Jisc arranges licences for databases and ebooks on behalf of UK higher and further education (jisc-collections.ac.uk). Access will be passworded and there may be limits on the number of concurrent users for an ebook. Universities have also negotiated off campus access, using authentication systems such as Shibboleth or Athens. Responsibility for this type of arrangement may vary – in some companies it is handled by sales staff, in others by rights staff.

E★PERT

Licensing electronic rights – a starter for 10

David Attwooll, Director of Attwooll Associates Ltd, a publishing consultancy and licensing agency specializing in electronic media

Finding the right partners in the area of electronic rights usually requires active hunting, and there are technical issues around delivering content. Electronic rights deals can be very time consuming and, as with all rights, can be done in-house or outsourced to a specialist agency. Alongside the distribution of ebooks through e-vendors in a range of markets (now the norm for many publishers), content can also be licensed to a wide range of other e-customers. Here are some pointers:

1. Electronic markets are more various than book markets, and can be segmented in similar ways. But they can also be sorted by ebusiness type, including:
    - library 'aggregators' of data,
    - ebook companies,
    - apps for mobile phones and tablets,
    - internet service providers (ISPs) and portals,
    - hardware manufacturers,
    - elearning vendors,
    - company websites, and
    - mobile phone companies.
2. Understanding your e-customer's business model facilitates successful licensing deals – for example, do they charge subscriptions, sell individual ebooks, or rely on advertising revenue?
3. What do you actually own? What rights do you have to sell or license? Conducting an audit of your intellectual property assets (including image rights) is a critical first step.

4. Information-based content works well on screen and in searchable databases, especially non-fiction and learning materials not organized in continuous prose. Any metadata enabling users to find immediately what is relevant to them is extremely valuable: the structure and formal tagging of content (including images) are key elements.

5. Electronic file formats are becoming more generic. Using a flexible data structure such as XML facilitates many deals. Many e-customers (especially ebook companies) will also take adapted PDFs. For ebooks, ePub has become the standard format.

6. There are some industry norms for electronic licensing deals. First, licensing deals are non-exclusive. The definitions of e-rights granted will not usually be territorial or by retail sales channel (as for print rights), but by specific product, platform and market. Definitions should prevent data being reused in other products (possibly in small chunks) by the same e-companies. Regarding payment terms, for licences to aggregators of larger data products, minimum annual guarantees and a royalty based on usage are often achievable. By contrast, ebook agreements are distribution deals, so revenues are retrospective, and should be seen as net of an agreed discount (rather than a royalty).

7. Online users expect up-to-date content, and publishers may be required to provide updates. This is both an organizational problem and a commercial opportunity to add greater value.

8. Licence periods should be short and some control over the start date should be specified (since launches are often delayed).

9. Security of data is essential and should be covered in the contract. Similarly, it does not make sense to license unabridged, valuable data to a paying customer who is then giving it away free on the web. Smaller subsets are usually sufficient here.

10. Acknowledgements and feedback: in addition to full publisher and copyright credits it is often possible to negotiate links to the publisher's website. Analysis of actual usage can be specified in the agreement and is extremely useful in improving editorial content.

The ebook is now usually regarded as a form of distribution rather than as part of the sale of electronic rights. Publishers selling electronic rights, for example in reference content, datasets or images, will protect themselves by granting short-term, non-exclusive or narrow exclusive licences, in particular languages, limited to specific formats or platforms, with performance guarantees and advances. Licensing on a non-exclusive basis means that new companies, technologies and business models can be tried out. Strict controls on the use of the publisher's brand may be written into the contract to minimize any damage to its reputation. In the days of the dotcom boom, sizeable money up front could be on offer for the right content but those sums are now far harder to negotiate. The publisher may prefer fixed annual fees to royalty deals based on untested business models. Alternatively they may enter into joint ventures in which costs and income are shared in agreed proportions, for example to develop apps or APIs (application programming interface) with developers. Publishers seeking to sell electronic rights need to ensure that they hold their content in a suitable form such as XML. Such files can be returned from the typesetter or planned from the outset. Extra value will come from higher levels of structure and metadata in the content for sale.

Serial and extract rights

First serial rights are more valuable since the extracts appear before the book's publication

Selling serial rights is granting the right to a newspaper or magazine to publish extracts from a book. Serial rights can be valuable in the case of celebrity or political memoirs, with the first serial the more important because it will appear before the book's publication, and can offer a national newspaper or magazine a scoop of some kind. These rights are often but not always retained by authors' agents. Sometimes first serial rights can be sold to two different publications; for example David Blunkett's memoirs, *The Blunkett Tapes* (2006), were serialized in both the *Guardian* and *Daily Mail*. The second and subsequent serial rights appear after the book's publication and may be sold to a succession of regional or evening newspapers, or magazines, at rates equal to or above that paid for original articles of comparable length, or for zero on the basis that the coverage will stimulate sales of the books. Ideas for extracts, which may come from the editor, are marked on the manuscript or proof and sent to chosen feature editors of newspapers and magazines some months ahead of the book's publication. The author's share of first serial rights (often as much as 90 per cent) may be offset against the advance, so as well as providing valuable publicity for the book, the sale of such serial rights could be valuable financially. In some consumer book publishers, the marketing department sells serial rights instead of the rights department. The sums payable for serial rights declined significantly with the onset of the financial crisis across the world economy, alongside the long-term decline of print newspapers, which are now tending to invest more in developing additional online content.

Film, TV, merchandising, audio and games

Film rights to *The Horse Whisperer* (1995) were sold for $3 m before the author Nicholas Evans had even finished the novel

Publishers, other than the major trade houses, are often unfamiliar with selling rights to film and TV production companies and use specialist agents – the larger agenting firms have developed an expertise in this area. Usually production companies will acquire, for a fee, an option in a novel, which gives them the right to come back within a fixed period and purchase the full rights to take a film into production. Lynette Owen comments on the chances of a work making it on to the screen:

> between 5 per cent and 10 per cent of options are exercised and of those perhaps one in ten finally proceeds to production; television options have a higher success rate than film options. Since options should be paid for rather than granted free of charge, the income is nevertheless welcome. (Owen, 6th edition, page 281)

Preferred partner arrangements with production companies enable publishers to sublicense film and TV rights (rights for merchandising and games may often be included in those arrangements) and in turn acquire the rights to publish books of upcoming programmes and films. The Harry Potter films became an incredibly successful franchise, earning around $8 bn in box office revenues. As new media and formats arise, partners may work together to exploit cross-media opportunities spanning the publishing, film, merchandising and games industries.

Audiobook rights can be licensed exclusively in two forms: abridged and unabridged. Some of the main trade publishers operate audio divisions which either produce their own audio books or license titles from agents or other trade publishers without their own audiobook lists. There are also independent and specialist audiobook publishers. Unabridged audiobooks used to be produced largely by specialist publishers supplying public libraries, which may also publish large print books – another right available for licensing. In recent years there has been a trend towards unabridged editions as the main offer. Books can also be licensed for reading or dramatization on radio. The use of high-profile narrators and the availability of different formats – from CDs to digital downloads on to devices such as iPods and mobile phones – have stimulated sales of audiobooks (see page 87). They are especially suitable for the US market, given the long distances involved in travel by car there.

On the insistence of J. K. Rowling, the audiobooks of Harry Potter, read by Stephen Fry, are wholly unabridged

Other rights

Examples of other rights include condensation, promotional reprint rights (low-cost editions for a mass market), large print, rights for the visually impaired, including Braille and Moon (tactile reading systems) and text-to-speech (generally granted for free), and English language paperback licensing rights to export territories. Material may also be licensed for use in customized textbooks for college courses or in coursepacks (although in the UK the latter arrangements are normally made via the CLA).

Many trade author–publisher contracts still refer to the grant of book club rights to the publisher by the author. However, in the UK, the book club sector (which sold books to customers at a discount by mail order) has declined severely in the face of competition from discounting by retailers and direct sellers, both terrestrial and online, and for many people the term book club is now more often associated with reading groups. Formerly a major force in the book trade, Book Club Associates was first sold by Bertelsmann in 2008 and was then bought by a home entertainment company, the Webb Group, in 2011, but it now operates more like an online retailer, purchasing copies of the original publisher's own stock at high discount rather then preordering copies with a book club imprint; authors then receive their contractual royalty percentage based on the sum received. The same applies to the few remaining children's book clubs. In such cases arrangements would usually be handled by sales rather than by rights staff. The Folio Society specializes in offering special editions of titles in handsome decorated bindings – in some cases they may be prepared to buy book blocks, or may obtain a reprint licence to manufacture themselves, in which case arrangements would be handled by rights staff.

Now read this

Lynette Owen, *Selling Rights*, 7th edition, Routledge, 2014.

Sources

International Literary Market Place, Bowker For book publishing contacts on a global scale.
Literary Market Place, Bowker Annual guide to the US publishing business, available online or in print.
Lynette Owen (ed.), *Clark's Publishing Agreements: A book of precedents*, 9th edition, Bloomsbury Professional, 2013.
Publishers Association, *PA Statistics Yearbook*, 2012.

Web resources

www.audiopub.org US Audio Publishers Association.
www.cla.co.uk Copyright Licensing Agency.
www.copyright.com Copyright Clearance Center (CCC).
www.lunch.publishersmarketplace.com Publishers Marketplace (USA).
www.rochester.edu/College/translation/threepercent/ Three Percent is aimed at those interested in discovering contemporary international literature.

CHAPTER 13

The sales channels for books in the UK

Publishers operate through a variety of sales channels, and the choice of channel will depend on the sector in which they operate. The sales success of consumer books, for example, may depend on retail exposure and as we saw in Chapter 10, page 224, an important purchase prompt is being visible in the shops. High street booksellers remain vital to the visibility of books but the decline in physical retail, and the rise of internet sales, challenges publishers to make their books discoverable to those consumers who do not regularly visit a physical, or 'bricks and mortar', store. Also, as with many other products, consumers may use the high street store to discover a title and then purchase it online.

Table 13.1 shows the source of purchase for physical books in the UK. Over time the trend has been for the share of supermarkets and the internet to grow, and for chain bookshops, independents, bargain bookshops and book clubs to suffer a decline. By comparison in 2005 the market share of internet retailers was 8 per cent, and of supermarkets 8 per cent. With the growth in ebook sales, the proportion taken by the internet of all books sold is higher still. There is naturally a mixed purchasing pattern across channels and in 2013 83 per cent of book buyers had purchased online, and 76 per cent had used a bricks-and-mortar store (Mintel).

Table 13.1 Market share by volume in the UK book trade (*source*: www.booksellers. org.uk, accessed 5 October 2013)

	Market share (%)		
	2010	2011	2012
Internet	25	30	38
Chain bookshops	30	27	28
Supermarkets	14	12	14
Other shops	11	11	7
Bargain bookshops	8	10	6
Book club/direct seller	6	6	5
Independent bookshops	5	4	3

The UK book trade has seen a great many changes over the last 30 years. These include the collapse of the Net Book Agreement in 1995 (the official end came in 1997), which led to price discounting, and the development of large chains on the high street. Smaller shops have closed and medium-sized businesses have been swallowed up by their larger rivals – for example, Waterstones acquired Ottakar's in 2006. The late twentieth century saw the arrival of the superstore concept from the USA – large, welcoming shops with a wide range of stock (typically 50,000 to 80,000 titles) and coffee shops. The first Borders superstore opened in Oxford Street in 1998; and Waterstones in Piccadilly in 1999.

E★PERT

Independent bookselling for the twenty-first century

Patrick Neale, Co-owner of the Jaffé & Neale bookshop and café, Chipping Norton, Oxfordshire

With one bookshop closing every week for the last ten years, there is little need to list the challenges facing high street bookshops. Second only to pubs, bookshops have become the victim of supermarket pricing strategies and the dominance of stay at home shopping and entertainment. We are only just beginning to face the onslaught of the ebook revolution which could make bookshops seem even less relevant.

And there is the irony. Research has shown that, although people may like to read their books on a tablet, nearly two-thirds of customers want to discover them in a bookshop. This has opened the whole debate about how bookshops can make money from 'showrooming' books that are subsequently bought online or for an e-reader. Twenty-first century bookselling is linked to the ability of high street retailers to adapt and respond to the massive changes that people have made to the way they shop. These are a few of the ways they can face these difficult days:

First, bookshops need to embrace new technology and not allow themselves to be perceived as only for the technologically incompetent. This could be through offering ebooks and e-readers to their customers or by using social media to reach the widest possible customer group. Be this Twitter, Facebook, or blogs, shops need to demonstrate that they are part of the future and not a museum piece.

Second, independent booksellers need to connect with the interest groups and movements that are suspicious of globalization. So whether it is becoming part of the 'Shop Local' or the Transition Movement, or participating in the outrage at the tax arrangements of multinationals, bookshops need to join in the clamour to save communities and keep the humanity in people's lives.

US bookshops have developed a clear message for their customers explaining that buying a few books a year more from them makes them viable allowing customers to gain pride in their community and keeping more than one channel of book purchase available. This has been best demonstrated by the Indiebound campaign (indiebound.org). This call to arms was followed in the UK in 2012 by the 'Books are My Bag' campaign, where publishers, recognizing the value high street bookshops bring, helped to fund a national campaign to remind consumers that real bookshops are the best place to buy real books.

Finally, and most importantly, bookshops need to demonstrate their value to customers. They may not be the cheapest and they may not have the most efficient distribution network in the world, but they can provide services and style that no one else can offer. The ways that this can be done are too numerous to list, but to name a few: staging literary events and festivals, providing personal shopping services, discovering the best possible read (not those that have been the most hyped), and creating an atmosphere of friendly and intelligent service supported by great coffee and cake.

It is essential to overcome the lazy assumption that bookshops are old fashioned. They can be lively meeting places where the customer feels valued and can have their cultural batteries recharged. The real challenge for bookshops is that most of what they offer and provide does not require a purchase and so they have to make sure that their cultural capital provides revenue that will keep them in business for the next century. There are many bookshops flourishing in what looks like impossible conditions. They are doing so because they have found a large enough group of customers who understand the value of what they provide and are willing to pay for it. It is essential for the independent to differentiate their offer from that of other book suppliers and make sure that their customers enjoy the service provided.

Both Borders and Waterstones were badly affected by the growth in sales through the internet and supermarkets. In 2007 came the news that Borders had sold their UK operation to the serial entrepreneur Luke Johnson and his private equity firm, and the chain closed for business in 2009 (the US company closed in 2011 with the loss of over 500 stores). Waterstones was forced to close some of its bookshops in both 2011 and 2013. The supermarkets have become so significant to consumer publishers that in 2007 HarperCollins launched a new mass market list called Avon. Called 'channel publishing', the list was to target supermarket sales of three popular genres – chick lit, romance, and crime/thrillers. Supermarkets can call the shots, as they do in other product areas, demanding large discounts as well as payments to remain preferred suppliers. Publishers have responded not only by changing what they publish but also by forming larger groups, which can offer a constant supply of likely bestsellers.

The independent bookshops have had a torrid time faced with price discounting not only in the high street chains but also online and by the supermarkets. A bookseller may find it cheaper to buy a book from Tesco or Amazon than directly from the publisher. In 2014 the number of independents had fallen below 1,000 shops – compared to over 1,400 in 2007, and more than 1,800 in 1997. The ones that survive have sought to make a niche for themselves by offering excellent service (effectively hand-selling to customers), prompt ordering, and stressing their place in the community. Just as consumers are being encouraged to buy from local suppliers in other product areas, the independents are emphasizing their value in an increasingly homogenized high street. Other book outlets of significance to particular kinds of publishers include airport terminal shops, especially at Heathrow and Gatwick, which sell enormous quantities of paperback fiction, travel and business books (flight delays are a boon for book sales).

ONLINE

In the UK online bookselling means Amazon. With an international brand, heavy discounting on a large range of titles, 24/7 access, and features such as giftwrapping, the internet bookseller has built up a powerful presence in the UK market. Members of the Amazon Prime service have free one-day delivery on physical titles, and can borrow ebooks for free, with a choice of hundreds of thousands of titles. The selection of books dwarfs what can be found in any terrestrial bookshop, opening up a window for smaller publishers, which may be struggling to get their titles into the chains, and for backlist titles. For specialist and academic titles the main supply route is now through Amazon; the same is true for many self-published authors of both pbooks and ebooks.

The concept of the 'long tail' was coined by Chris Anderson in relation to books and music. Usually books that are not selling in sufficient numbers are returned to the publisher. Yet the internet provides a means of marketing and selling these titles. If we add up this long tail of slow-selling books, Anderson suggested that it could add up to a greater source of revenue than the bestsellers prominent in bookshops. Although the theory has attracted some criticism, for example that the web seems to amplify the blockbuster hits, the idea does strike a chord with publishers, which have seen internet bookselling open up a new channel for backlist books which had disappeared from terrestrial retail display. The book return rates are much lower, and the internet provides a good route for the fulfilment of low-value single book orders.

The original model was for Amazon to source books from the wholesalers, avoiding the need for a large investment in warehousing. By 2013 the company ran eight of its own distribution centres (more were promised) – five in England, two in Scotland, and one in Wales – enabling it to provide fast supply of bestselling lines. Many titles are still supplied from wholesalers and dispatched in Amazon-branded boxes. Working practices at Amazon's distribution centres came under some criticism in 2013. The jobs can be physically demanding – pickers can walk between seven and 15 miles a day, and hand-held computers both navigate them around the aisles and allow management to measure their productivity. 'Managers could also send text messages to these devices to tell workers to speed up ... "People were constantly warned about talking to one another by the management, who were keen to eliminate any form of time-wasting," one former worker added' (*Financial Times*, 8 February 2013). That same year saw Amazon also come under fire for the amount of tax it paid, with its UK subsidiary paying only £2.4 m on sales of £4.3 bn in 2012 (bbc.co.uk, 16 May 2013).

For some, online purchasing will never match the experience of browsing in their local or high street bookshop, but especially for those without ready access to a bookshop, the internet provides a convenient and cost-effective method of obtaining books. There is the added convenience of ebooks for either study or leisure reading – when you have finished a thriller late at night you can simply download the next title in the series straight away. Even the most ardent buyers of books on the high street use Amazon as well, with 66 per cent of Waterstones' customers also buying from Amazon, and 61 per cent of customers of independent shops (2013 figures from Mintel). The positive attitudes of consumers to the online retailing of books can be seen in Table 13.2. In the area of ebooks Amazon had a totally dominant position in 2013, with 79 per cent of people who accessed or downloaded ebooks using the Kindle platform – 9 per cent used Apple's iBookstore (Ofcom).

Table 13.2 Attitudes of book buyers in the UK (2013) to online book retailers (*source*: Mintel)

	Proportion in agreement with statement (%)
Online book retailers offer the cheapest prices for books	49
It's difficult for high street bookshops to compete with online book retailers	47
It's more convenient to shop from online book retailers than go to bookshops	46
Online book retailers have the best range of titles (available in both physical and electronic format)	35
Online book retailers have the best promotional offers	33
Online book retailers encourage me to look for more titles from my favourite author	32
Online book retailers are becoming too dominant in the book market	23
Online book retailers have too much control over the book industry	16

Amazon has so far held off competition from new or existing players in the book market. Play.com started to find a place in the market selling from its offshore base in Jersey, but changes to the tax arrangements on products which attracted VAT (it was selling DVDs and similar goods tax free) forced it to become a marketplace for third party sellers. It is now owned by the Japanese company Rakuten (which also purchased the ebook retailer Kobo). The supermarkets have their internet operations but have not yet created a compelling offer in the area of ebooks. Based in Gloucester, the Book Depository aimed to service the long tail. Rather than hold stock, it met customer orders from the optimal source – publisher, wholesaler or distributor – and offered free delivery to many parts of the world. Its independent status came to an end when it was purchased by Amazon in 2011. A former director of the Book Depository teamed up with the wholesaler Bertrams in 2012 to launch the online retailer Wordery. The US retailer Barnes & Noble brought its Nook device to the UK in 2012 backed up by its own website. Innovations around a hybrid model of 'clicks and bricks' have also been developed by some shops (for example Waterstones), with a facility to reserve books online and pick them up from a store. Direct sales of consumer books (both pbook and ebook) from the websites of publishers remain minimal.

Online content

In sectors such as professional and journals publishing, the model for publishing has shifted from the delivery of books and printed journals to the supply of content online. Educational publishers produce DVDs, website add-ons and online subscription services for schools. Many publishers will sell through third parties and use rights sales to take advantage of online markets, but some have built their own platforms to sell directly to their markets. Companies such as ProQuest and EBSCO offer sales channels for publishers, providing ejournals, ebooks and databases to libraries, companies and other institutions.

Digital downloads of audiobooks are available from a variety of websites including iTunes and Audible (Amazon). Silksoundbooks is a collaboration of actors and performers who came together and decided to record their favourite classic literature for you to enjoy. Headed by [the actor] Bill Nighy, many of the artists involved believe so much in the project, that they have waived performance fees in favour of taking shares in the company. (silksoundbooks.com, accessed 7 October 2013)

Some technical book publishers are also selling digital voice audio.

THE CHAINS AND SUPERMARKETS

There is no doubt that bookselling has become much more professional in the last 30 years, and there are high street shops which offer a good range of stock amongst pleasant surroundings, with added value from coffee bars, attractive areas for children, and a range of events taking place. Some shops have aimed to become destination stores – welcoming and lively in their approach.

The chain booksellers differ in their character, and have aimed to develop distinctive brands. The general retailer WHSmith has broad product categories of Stationery, 'News and Impulse', and Books. It operates two core businesses: Travel, with 643 stores at airports, railway stations and motorway service stations; and High Street, with 621 stores on virtually all of the high streets in the UK. The book selection differs between these businesses. In the area of e-readers and ebooks, it began a partnership with Kobo in 2011 and by 2013 there were 250 Kobo Shops in-store. The retailer attracts all demographics but parents of children aged 5 to 15 are an important part of the customer base. In its Travel shops, the 'typical

The original Dillons shop was founded in 1936 by Una Dillon (1903–93). The chain was sold to HMV in 1998 and put under the Waterstones brand in 1999

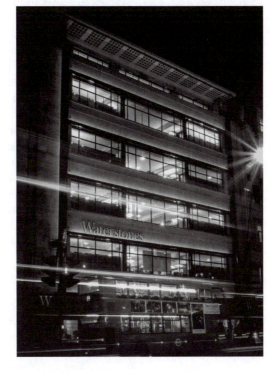

The exterior of Waterstones in Piccadilly, London. Europe's largest bookshop, it has over 8 miles of shelving and up to 200,000 titles in stock

customer has less time to browse than the High Street customer and is more interested in reading materials for a journey as well as purchasing food, drink and confectionery' (whsmithplc.co.uk, accessed 5 October 2013).

Waterstones, owned by the Russian oligarch Alexander Mamut since 2011, had around 270 shops in 2013. An average-sized Waterstones store has a range of around 30,000 individual books, with 200,000 titles in the largest store. During the 1980s Waterstones competed fiercely with the Dillons chain of shops, opening well-designed branded stores, typically carrying a much larger range of stock than traditional bookshops. The two chains were brought together by their parent company HMV, which acquired Dillons in 1995 and Waterstones in 1998. They were called 'upmarket' booksellers, exemplified by their wide range of hardback and trade paperback titles and the depth of backlist titles stocked. However the size of these stores became dwarfed in the late 1990s by the opening by Waterstones and Borders of flagship superstores carrying upwards of 150,000 titles. The demographic for Waterstones is skewed towards men, and its customers are also 'affluent, being significantly more likely than average to be from the AB socio-economic group and have a gross household income of over £50,000' (Mintel). To some astonishment from the book trade, in 2012 the retailer announced a co-operation with Amazon in the area of ebooks: 'After previously describing Amazon as "a ruthless, money-making devil", Waterstones' managing director, James Daunt, announced in May that he was teaming up with the US internet store and would sell and promote its Kindle tablets and e-readers in the UK's premier book chain' (bbc.co.uk, 24 October 2012).

> Waterstones dropped the apostrophe from its name in 2012 in order to provide 'a more versatile and practical spelling'

The academic-orientated Blackwell chain dominates the ownership of campus-related bookstores (Waterstones closed some of its campus stores in 2013). Blackwell has over 40 outlets in the UK including its flagship store in Oxford, which boasts the world's largest room with books on display for sale. Another important academic chain, with 20 campus shops in 2013, is John Smith's. One issue for academic shops is how to attract footfall outside the two peak sales periods of the autumn and the new year. Some campus shops now stock stationery, music and gift items; and in 2013 Blackwell announced a new digital strategy of providing resources sourced from a variety of publishers.

There are smaller chains such as Foyles, which has six shops in London and one in Bristol. It is famous for its large shop in Charing Cross Road, where a range of events are held: 'it's not just Booker winners and learned thinkers who present their work in the Gallery; we now offer regular concerts with stars from Ian Bostridge and Sarah Chang to Jamie Cullum and Kit Downes' (foyles.co.uk, accessed 5 October 2013). James Daunt has his own small chain of six upmarket shops in London, which avoid discounting: 'The shelves of Daunt Books interweave travel guides with a world of literature; the shop's cloth bags are de rigueur for London literary locavores' (*New York Times*, 26 September 2013).

How the chains operate

The largest chain dedicated to books, Waterstones, operates centralized buying, that is book buyers at head office select titles presented to them by the publishers' sales or key account managers. This usually prevents the publishers' sales representatives from selling titles directly into their branches. In 2009 the chain opened its own distribution hub at Burton upon Trent, to receive books from publishers before distribution around its stores. As required, for example to source books from smaller publishers, the company also uses the wholesalers. WHSmith is its own wholesaler – it operates centralized buying from publishers and owns its own warehouse at Swindon, which receives stock from the publishers and then distributes the books to its branches. The chains have central marketing departments which organize, often in collaboration with publishers' sales and marketing staff, consumer advertising, in-store promotion, and author signings in the branches.

Supermarkets and other non-book retailers

Other kinds of big retail chains, such as the supermarkets, buy centrally and receive their stock either directly from publishers or via wholesalers. The supermarkets often offer massive discounts on bestsellers, usually up to 50 per cent of the recommended price. In 2007 *Harry Potter and the Deathly Hallows* was sold by Asda at £5.00 compared to the recommended retail price of £17.99. In general the supermarkets make larger margins on books than they do on the purchasing of food. Although the supermarkets' share of the overall book market is relatively limited, their share of sales can reach 50 per cent for top bestsellers, which explains why they can ask for discounts as high as 65 per cent or more. Specialist merchandisers, for example Oakwood Distribution (owned by Tesco), stock the shelves in supermarkets and monitor stock levels. Beyond the range stocked in-store there are many more titles available as pbooks and ebooks through the online stores of Tesco, Asda (owned by Walmart) and Sainsbury's – in 2013 Tesco unveiled its own low-priced Android tablet, the Hudl; and in 2014 its ebook platform blinkbox. Tesco is the leader amongst the supermarkets in the

sale of books, followed by Asda and Sainsbury's: 'Tesco achieves its position through a strong peak in buying among the C2 socio-economic group which represents its core shopper, while Asda is particularly successful at targeting the DE socio-economic group. Both of these are segments of the market which the major high street book chains like Waterstones often struggle to reach' (Mintel). The more upmarket profile of Sainsbury's may explain why it is not as successful, as its customers may be purchasing at bookshops.

Books are available in many other kinds of retail outlets, which the publishers reach through wholesalers. For example, the merchandising wholesalers serve newsagents, convenience general stores, ferry port outlets and garages. They will check and replenish stock of mass-market paperbacks, and remove slow-selling titles for destruction. Books are sold through garden, DIY and leisure centres, and specialist shops such as computer stores and toy shops.

BARGAIN BOOKSHOPS

Of declining importance are the bargain bookshops, which occupy high street positions, sometimes on short leases granted by stressed landlords. Publishers have a long history of ridding themselves, albeit quietly, of their mistakes in printing too many copies. When a title's sales are insufficient to cover the cost of storage, it may be pulped or remaindered through bargain outlets. Some publishers never remainder in the home market so as not to damage their brand and sales of full-price stock. The greater usage of short-run printing has reduced the need to remainder.

The promotional book publishers provide the bargain chains with a ready supply of newly created low-priced books. Such publishers and the remainder dealers are well represented at the London and Frankfurt Book Fairs, and have their own London fairs, organized by Ciana, in January and September. A bargain chain may also sell new titles at deep discounts alongside remaindered titles, and may sell other goods such as stationery and artist's materials.

WHOLESALERS AND INTERMEDIARIES

Trade wholesalers

Many of the independent bookshops stock from 12,000 to 20,000 titles. Most purchase their stock from the two large trade wholesalers, which offer next-day delivery. Gardners, owned by the Little Group and based in Eastbourne, stocks over 400,000 titles at any one time and supplies many of the large trade retailers. Waterstones buys all its books from small publishers through the wholesaler. Bertram Books, owned by Connect Group (formerly called Smiths News), is based near Norwich; it has over 200,000 titles in stock. Wholesalers can also act as distributors for small publishers, and they have installed POD facilities and digital warehouses for ebooks as additional services.

From the late 1980s, the trade wholesalers revolutionized the speed and efficiency of book distribution through their supply to the independent bookshops, which were faced with a myriad of publishers' invoicing systems, and publishers' warehouses which could be slow and inefficient. The wholesalers' growth was grounded in their focus on customer service to booksellers. They offered the convenience of dealing with just a few invoicing systems, rather than those of dozens of publishers; of online bibliographic information systems (including marketing and purchasing advice); of online ordering; and of consolidated orders with fast and reliable delivery. The wholesalers became the booksellers' stockroom. If the trade wholesalers had restricted their ambitions to the independent booksellers they too would have faced eventual decline. But they extended their reach into serving the retail chains and supermarkets, entered the school library supply market (long restricted to specialist suppliers) and began to export. At the end of the 1990s, they received a fillip from the emerging internet booksellers, such as Amazon UK, which initially drew their stock from the wholesalers.

Book market information

The retail outlets summarized above account for most of the UK retail sales of books. The publishers sell their new titles directly to the retailers (or via wholesalers). But the data of actual sales made by the retailers to their customers is of critical importance to the retailers, wholesalers and publishers. The installation by retailers of electronic point of sale (EPOS) systems, reading the bar-codes on covers when sales are made, enables the retailers to monitor the rate of sale of titles and to control their inventory (by reordering the titles which sell or by returning unsold titles to the publisher). The effect of EPOS installations was that booksellers placed smaller orders more frequently (provided that a title was stocked in the first place) and expected faster deliveries.

For pbooks Nielsen BookScan collects the sales data by title from almost all of the different kinds of book retailers from across the country and from internet booksellers, and produces various bestseller charts which are published in *The Bookseller* weekly and in other media. Bestseller lists for ebooks became available in 2013 using data from publishers.

Data is also sold to interested parties. Thus, for example, publishers cannot only monitor the sales performance of their own titles – their rise and fall – but also that of competitors. Publishers armed with that information are in a far better position to respond to the needs for quick reprints or not. However, the data cannot help publishers' sometime over-optimism or misjudgement of printing too many copies of a new title at the outset, or that of booksellers' stocking too many copies in the knowledge that they can return unsold stock.

Returns

The return of unsold print books to publishers from retailers and wholesalers is an expensive and wasteful characteristic of the book business, which was estimated by KPMG in 1998 to cost the industry £100 m. Around 14 per cent of books (by sales value) are returned to the publisher, and book wastage still accounts for 20 per cent of production in trade publishing. This has rightly raised ecological concerns – is it right to have such a culture of wasteful distribution within the book industry?

This is alongside the issue of book miles – books may be printed the other side of the world, say in India, before entering the warehouse, say in Oxford: 'As each order is processed, books that have already travelled nearly 8,000 miles to get to Oxford now set off on their travels again' (Bullock and Walsh, page 9). In the area of environmental impact, many publishers are trying to achieve carbon neutral targets; and the larger companies have shown an interest in corporate social responsibility (CSR), given their sourcing of work from companies around the world, often in developing nations. For example, Pearson is a founding signatory to the UK Global Compact, which 'has successfully engaged many thousands of global companies in considering their responsibilities towards labour standards, human rights, environmental management and in tackling corruption' (pearson.com, accessed 25 September 2013).

Library suppliers

The public, academic and corporate libraries are supplied by booksellers and library suppliers. The UK public library market has been difficult and long gone are the days when library sales supported hardback runs of new titles. There has been continued consolidation amongst the main library suppliers. Following the collapse of the Net Book Agreement, the public libraries sought higher discounts – above 30 per cent – through collective regional purchasing consortia, while still demanding a large amount of bibliographic selection support and book processing from the suppliers such as Askews, Holt Jackson and Peters (which specializes in children's books). The entry of the trade wholesaler Bertrams into the public library market, through the purchase of Cypher, caused consternation amongst the library suppliers and publishers, who have conventionally segmented this channel through different discounts and terms. In 2007 Gardners purchased Askews, followed by Holt Jackson in 2008, in a further consolidation of the wholesaler and library supply market. Blackwell's, Dawson and Coutts (owned by the giant US wholesaler Ingram) served academic markets, but consolidation again occurred with the acquisition of Dawsons by Bertrams in 2011 and the withdrawal of Blackwell's from library supply in 2013 (with its contracts sold to Dawsons). The library suppliers export, especially academic and STM titles, sometimes under tendered contracts, to national and regional government libraries, and university and corporate research libraries. Ebooks are sold or rented through the ebook platforms run by the library suppliers, for example dawsonera from Bertrams.

Discounts

Under the wholesale model, publishers sell their books to retailers and intermediaries at different discounts off their recommended retail prices (RRP). They aim to keep their discounts secret and by law must not collude with rival companies. The main factors affecting discount levels are:

- the type of book – hardback , paperback, ebook; consumer or non-consumer,
- the role and value the intermediary plays in the supply chain,
- the balance of power between the buyer and seller,

- historical precedent, and
- the size of order on a particular book or group of books.

For some publishers, the best discount is zero. The intermediaries are cut out of the supply chain entirely or are dealt with on low, or 'short', discounts. For example, the learned journal publishers may grant a discount to the subscription agents of 0 to 5 per cent. The highly specialist publishers producing very high-priced information products sold directly to professional markets may grant a discount of 10 to 20 per cent on an order received from a bookseller. The school textbook publishers may grant a discount of 17 to 20 per cent to a school supplier such as a bookseller, specialist school contractor or local authority purchasing organization. In such examples, the publishers generate the demand themselves and can supply end-users directly – the intermediaries provide a convenient service to the end-users. If schools are supplied direct, a discount of 10 to 15 per cent may be offered as an incentive, based on the size of the order or as part of a special offer (for example, if orders are received by a certain date).

The standard discount to booksellers for academic books is 30 to 35 per cent; college textbook publishers offer discounts of up to 40 per cent. The publishers argue that they have achieved the adoptions through their own promotion. The terrestrial booksellers argue that they are physically stocking the titles for student purchase and displaying other titles that they might buy. Textbook discounts have risen to some extent from the pressure exerted by the chains, especially Waterstones and Amazon. However, the retailers' leverage on the textbook publishers for increased discounts is far less than on the consumer publishers. The major publishers are resistant and are building their direct supply capabilities.

In consumer books, the discounts are more varied and are the highest in the world. In 2012 they averaged around 62 per cent for print titles across fiction, non-fiction and children's (Publishers Association). For ebooks they could reach 65 per cent and Amazon could ask for the publisher to bear the cost of the VAT payable. A small publisher might give a discount of 40 per cent to Waterstones and 55 per cent to a wholesaler, but the question then arises as to how widely their titles will be stocked. To get shelf space a larger publisher will offer higher discounts and will pay for its titles to be prominently displayed front of store. These co-op charges can amount to many thousands of pounds, and can be asked for by other retailers such as the supermarkets. The terrestrial retailers argue that their expensive display space generates the sales for the publishers; smaller publishers become frustrated by their inability to access the system. In order to survive, they have found new routes to market through Amazon or direct sales.

OTHER SALES CHANNELS

Direct sales

A proportion of children's publishers' sales and a very high proportion of educational publishers' sales do not pass through retailers. Furthermore, some publishers, especially those issuing specialist academic and professional titles, or highly niche trade titles, may sell them directly to end-users by conventional means or through the internet, and there are other sales channels available, such as sales at special events or fairs.

Book clubs

The Folio Society was founded in 1947 by Charles Ede, with the dream of publishing beautiful books that would be affordable to everyone

Sales to book clubs are handled by publishers under rights deals. Book clubs conventionally occupied a major segment of mail-order sales to consumers. Founded in 1966, Book Club Associates (BCA) was a major player in book publishing when there were fixed prices and few alternatives to the high street shops. It found it difficult to retain members in the face of new retail competition offering deep discounts. For example, Amazon emails information about new or discounted titles to customers with the relevant profile. Previously owned by Bertelsmann, BCA is now part of the Webb Group. Another book club is the Folio Society, founded in 1947, which specializes in handsome illustrated hardbacks in a range of bindings.

Direct selling companies

Some companies sell books (and other products) directly to customers in the workplace, their local sports centre, or at home. They employ 'agents' who receive a percentage on sales, and allow customers time to examine the books before they purchase. The companies order very large quantities of selected titles from publishers on a non-return basis, and sell them at a discount off the publisher's price of between 50 to 75 per cent, usually six months after publication. The pre-eminent company is The Book People, which had revenues of over £90 m in 2012. Through the internet or the telephone, or through its distributor network in a range of workplaces, customers buy at deep discounts off the recommended price.

Scholastic ran 13,000 book fairs in schools across the UK and the Republic of Ireland in 2013, reaching over four million children

Children's books

Children's books sell well when displayed face out alongside other kinds of products, whether in the multi-product WHSmith chain, or amongst groceries or toys, where parents are likely to have their children in tow. They are available in

supermarkets, toyshops, and internet retailers. Like the educational textbook publishers, children's publishers also supply their books directly to schools when their books are used to support the National Curriculum.

The school is an important outlet for children's books, providing a setting where children's books leap through the adult sales barrier and important word-of-mouth recommendations amongst children themselves take place. School book fairs have grown enormously and involve the supplier (Scholastic is the largest seller) providing the school with upwards of 200 titles displayed face out on special mobile bookcases. The school benefits from a sales commission or free books.

Used books

Worthy of note in any discussion of the sales channels for books is the burgeoning second-hand or used book market. Oxfam has over 100 specialist bookshops, alongside its sale of books in its other retail outlets and online. The internet has revolutionized the search and sale of second-hand books: Amazon sells second-hand copies through its Marketplace scheme; and AbeBooks (acquired by Amazon in 2008) lists millions of new, used, rare and out-of-print books from thousands of booksellers. As Theodore Dalrymple comments:

> if there is a particular book that you want urgently, the internet is a wonder: you type in the title, you pay by credit card, the book arrives the next day. There is no need any longer to resort to the bookfinder, that strange professional searcher after needles in haystacks, who guards his sources more jealously than any journalist and, I suspect, would not reveal them under torture. (*Daily Telegraph*, 3 December 2012)

Publishers are concerned about the impact of second-hand print sales on the sales of new books, and authors of course receive no royalties on sales past the initial purchase. In 2013 Amazon secured a patent which would enable it to sell ebooks second hand. How likely this is as a development is difficult to determine at the time of writing but if it goes ahead, 'secondhand ebooks would be very likely to cannibalise sales of new ebooks, and probably to a greater extent than piracy because it will be legal, easy and entirely without emotional repercussion' (*Forbes*, 8 February 2013). Textbook publishers have to issue new editions on a regular basis to counteract the attractions for students of buying second hand. There is also concern about the sale of used books described as being like new. These could be unwanted review copies or returns that have found their way into the second-hand market. There are other channels for used books, including initiatives such as BookCrossing, which encourages readers to leave books in a public place to be picked up by others. Started in 2001 BookCrossing asks readers to tag a book before releasing it 'into the wild', enabling the book's progress to be tracked (bookcrossing.com).

Sources

Chris Anderson, 'The Long Tail', *Wired*, 12:10, October 2004.

Adrian Bullock and Meredith Walsh, *The Green Design and Print Production Handbook*, Ilex, 2013.

Philip Kogan, 'Independent in a Sea of Conglomerates', *Logos*, 18:2, 2007.

Robert McCrum, 'Fear the Revolution', *The Observer*, 1 July 2007.

Laura Miller, *Reluctant Capitalists: Bookselling and the culture of consumption*, University of Chicago Press, 2006.

Mintel, *Books and E-Books*, September 2013.

Sarah O'Connor, 'Amazon Unpacked', *Financial Times*, 8 February 2013.

Ofcom, *Online Copyright Infringement Tracker: March to May 2013*, prepared by Kantar Media, 2013.

Publishers Association, *PA Statistics Yearbook*, 2012.

John Sutherland, 'Brave New World', *Financial Times*, 9 October 2004.

John B. Thompson, *Merchants of Culture*, Polity, 2012.

Web resources

www.booksellers.org.uk The Booksellers Association represents over 4,000 retail outlets.

www.booktokens.co.uk Book tokens were first introduced into the UK in 1932; their story is told here.

www.readitswapit.co.uk Readers swap books online.

CHAPTER 14

Getting into publishing

Publishing is a popular career choice and there is strong competition to enter the industry. Digital developments – from ebooks to apps and interactive fiction – have been prominent in the media, highlighting the exciting opportunities for new entrants unafraid of new technologies or fast-paced change. Companies have broadened out their view of what comprises a good candidate, to include digital literacy, an entrepreneurial mind-set, and an appreciation of changes across other media and throughout society. There is also a greater variety of job roles to consider, as these merge across functional boundaries (for example production editor), take on a digital focus (for example digital product manager), or venture into multimedia (for example media research and commissioning).

Although many junior jobs that are advertised state that previous publishing experience is necessary, entry to publishing is paradoxically mainly at the bottom. You should therefore snatch any kind of work in any area of publishing, whatever the size of firm. Publishers usually recruit only to fill vacancies which, at the entry level, often occur at no more than a month's notice. Working on a placement, a short-term contract, or covering for a permanent employee's maternity leave, can be a good opportunity. Once in, you will be learning, gaining personal impressions of various jobs by talking to people, and, what is more, be in a position to hear about future jobs. From that bridgehead, it is usually easier to obtain a second job than the first, by moving sideways or upwards within or outside the firm. The Publishing Training Centre originally developed the National Occupational Standards for Publishing for the main job categories, which are now available from Creative Skillset. They list job competences against which candidates may be assessed.

Do not fear that your first job will necessarily determine your subsequent career. It is best to complete at least a year in the first job, but two to three job changes in the first five years are not uncommon. At the outset, it is preferable to think first of the kinds of books you would be interested in publishing and hence the type of publishing company (sometimes it can be problematic to move across publishing sectors); and second of the kind of work for which you feel you might have a particular aptitude.

To increase your chances, good office skills and computer literacy (knowledge of Microsoft Office) are necessary for all jobs. Experience of administrative work and proofreading skills are desirable. Strong writing and analytical skills will be sought, which may have been exercised in a piece of research at university. The ability to use publishing software such as Adobe InDesign and experience of ePub file conversion are highly useful alongside familiarity with social media and online communities. An understanding of HTML is increasingly important (set up your own website on WordPress); and explore Google Analytics. If you are a bookseller and want to move into publishing, two to three years of bookselling is ample. For any newcomer to the industry, work experience at a publisher will help your CV stand out, and a temporary job with a publisher during the summer may lead to the elusive first full-time appointment. The ability to drive is also useful.

FIRST STEPS

Market research

You must carry out research on publishing in general and on your target publishers in particular, and especially you should research the books these firms publish. Read the trade press available in print or online – for example *The Bookseller* (UK), *Publishers Weekly* (US), Publishing Perspectives (international), BookBrunch (UK), Publishers Lunch (US); Book2Book (UK), Digital Book World (US); read book reviews and sign up for Goodreads; and visit libraries and bookshops to look at publishers' books and to seek advice from librarians and booksellers. You can also follow publishers on Twitter and visit their Facebook pages. For specialist areas visit the appropriate library or bookshop. When visiting bookshops, during their quiet periods try to talk to the manager who deals directly with the central office or publishers' reps. When you have narrowed down the field or have secured an interview, you must visit the publisher's website and catalogue before any further approach is made.

> The London Book Fair held in April provides a great opportunity to view the output of publishers

Networking

Networking is a key publishing skill and once developed will stand you in good stead even when you are settled in the industry, when you may be searching out new prospects for your business. Contacts in publishing provide insight into particular firms, offering you advice, spreading knowledge of your abilities, and alerting you to impending vacancies. Sometimes these contacts are influential enough to secure you a preliminary discussion or interview, though rarely a job itself. Therefore, first tap your family and personal connections; if you draw a blank there, take the initiative. You can network by joining the Society of Young Publishers (SYP) in a variety of locations including London, Oxford and Scotland. It holds frequent meetings and an annual conference, at which senior publishers speak, and publishes the journal *InPrint*. Membership is not restricted to people employed in publishing. Women in Publishing (WiP) holds regular meetings in London. Membership is open to women of any age in publishing, unwaged and students. You may be able to attend meetings of the Independent Publishers Guild (IPG) in London and around the country (small and medium-sized publishers), or go to events of organizations such as the Oxford Publishing Society

(OPuS), BookMachine, or the Publishers Publicity Circle (PPC). Publishing groups and professional connections on LinkedIn provide contact opportunities, especially in non-consumer publishing.

In 2014 LinkedIn had over 300 m members

QUALIFICATIONS

Most entry into publishing requires an undergraduate degree, and common subjects are English, History and Modern Languages. People with degrees in science and other specialities, such as law or medicine, are at a premium for publishers in those areas; and publishers developing digital products and services would love to recruit graduates from mathematics and computer science. A teaching background or experience in English language teaching is particularly useful for educational and ELT publishing, and African studies or experience of working for Voluntary Service Overseas for international educational publishers. Some legal background is useful for rights and contracts positions. Language degrees are desirable for rights and export sales departments of all kinds of publishers. The level of degree is less important. Those with doctorates seeking their first junior job may face the difficulty that they are that much older than competing younger applicants. Some of the major publishers offer graduate recruitment schemes. For example, under the long-running Macmillan scheme, a small number of graduates are selected each year and are given an accelerated, diverse and international experience to shape them for management positions.

Pre-entry qualification

Traditionally the only departments in which formal vocationally orientated qualifications were highly desirable were graphic design and production. For marketing posts publishers have come to recognize the benefits of qualifications from the Chartered Institute of Marketing (CIM). The pre-entry publishing courses, which used to concentrate on copy-editing and production skills, now also cover the business and marketing aspects of publishing. At undergraduate level, students can choose to study publishing on its own or along with other disciplines. There has been a large increase in the range of courses available at undergraduate and graduate levels, with student places around several hundred per year. Their links with publishers, various work experience schemes for students, and the rise of their former students into management positions have undermined the traditionalist view that pre-entry vocational training is a waste of time. Attaining a BA or MA in Publishing does not guarantee a job in publishing but it substantially increases the chances – the established courses score impressive success rates. Some publishers, recognizing the quality of graduates from the main programmes, advertise job openings directly on their websites.

Work experience

There are some websites that advertise work experience, and some of the larger publishers have established mechanisms for recruiting students keen to gain, mostly unpaid, placements. You can write to the HR departments or if you have

any contacts inside a publisher, use them to find out who it would be best to contact. Work experience is an excellent preparation for a career in publishing. By working in different departments you can gain first-hand experience of the different functions, find out about your aptitudes, and build a network of contacts: employers may treat it as an extended interview. Whilst there continues to be a large amount of unpaid work experience offered, there is a trend towards paid assignments (see the information at bookcareers.com).

Other experience which increases a job applicant's attractiveness includes editing your school or college magazine, marketing and website work, and short-term work in a bookshop.

FINDING VACANCIES

Recruitment agencies

There are a variety of agencies that recruit for publishers. Examples are Atwood Tate, Judy Fisher, Inspired Selection, PFJ Media Recruitment, and Redwood. Some specialize in more senior positions and will help headhunt staff from rival companies. The agencies regularly advertise junior positions on their own and other websites. Some of the agencies encourage job hunters to register with them, offer free advice, and they will forward the details of likely candidates when a vacancy occurs. It is unlikely they will take someone on their books without a publishing degree and six months of work experience within the industry.

Publishers also use agencies to recruit for temporary positions. There is always a demand from publishers for temporary staff to fill jobs vacated by people on holiday or ill. In London this is a good way of getting the feel of different publishers and can lead to a permanent job.

Advertisements and search

Advertisements for publishing jobs appear in *The Bookseller* and the national press (mainly the *Guardian* on a Monday). Some companies use more generic recruitment websites, such as Monster, and publishers outside London may advertise locally. The high cost of advertising has prompted many publishers to advertise jobs on free websites, such as those of the IPG, SYP, and the Oxford International Centre for Publishing Studies; and on their own career web pages, as well as on Facebook and Twitter. Many jobs, especially in trade publishing, are not advertised at all, and publishers prefer to use word-of-mouth recommendations, especially referrals from their own employees. You need to use a variety of search engines to find internships, and try different keywords, such as 'publishing work experience' or 'publishing opportunities': look through all result pages. Career-based websites, such as Prospects (UK) can be useful.

YOUR APPLICATION

Preparing your CV and covering letter

To secure an interview you must attract the publisher's attention by submitting a compelling and immaculately tailored CV and covering letter, without spelling mistakes, inconsistent punctuation or ungrammatical sentences. Many of those applying for their first publishing job, as well as those applying for subsequent positions, fail on these points at this initial hurdle.

A typical CV (or résumé) will have the following headings:

- personal details,
- personal statement – a short description of your attributes and personal qualities,
- education,
- relevant previous employment and work experience, paid and unpaid – other employment can be moved later on in the CV,
- skills and qualifications (include evidence of digital and commercial aptitude),
- personal interests, and
- references.

The CV is an organized summary of the key facts (not opinions) about yourself. Use bold to highlight headings (avoid underlining) and choose a readable and professional typeface; avoid boxes and photographs. Bullet points may be a useful way of emphasizing essential points about a job or your degree – projects undertaken, achievements and skills developed. While emphasizing your assets, the CV must be truthful. Each element, backed with evidence, should prove to the publisher that you have the qualities and skills for the job: omit those that do not.

It should not be longer than two A4 pages. For those with little work experience, the chronological CV laid out in a form style is usually the best approach. The information is listed in chronological order under headings.

Under personal details give your full name, contact address with home and mobile telephone numbers, email, date of birth, and nationality. The education section lists college and school details, with dates, courses taken, grades achieved, special projects, scholarships, prizes. Highlight any occupational training courses which show relevant skills.

If you have relevant employment and work experience, you will want to put the details near to the top of the CV, usually in reverse chronological order – the most recent first. Provide employers' names, your job titles with duties and responsibilities, promotions, special awards and accomplishments (for example ideas that reduced costs, increased profitability, streamlined administration) – a few key points for each job. Relevant work outside publishing should be emphasized, for example office, library or bookshop work, preparing a firm's literature or magazine, market research, mailing list management, public and customer relations, teaching and work overseas.

Whatever the CV format, the skills emphasized may be those pertaining particularly to specific jobs, for example design or proofreading, and those which are more generic, such as computer literacy, website development, driving, languages, numeracy, administration, communication (for example, presentations, telesales and email). At management levels, applicants often start their CVs with a personal statement highlighting their achievements, skill and experience. This is followed by sections on their career history and key skills.

Activities and interests may be incorporated under the above headings or listed separately. If you are about to leave full-time education, your skills and keen interests (for example, photography, sport) assume great importance because with little work experience they mark you out. You should list your leadership or administrative positions and achievements. Older candidates who have missed out on entry level jobs need to build a portfolio of projects.

The CV usually ends with the names and telephone numbers of your two or three referees who can convey your character, stability and competence to perform the job. Brief them beforehand. One should act as a character reference. You can state, if necessary, that they should not be contacted without prior consultation. It is increasingly common to say that references are available on request.

Use factual, concise, simple language – without abbreviations or jargon – and active verbs. Have someone who is literate or familiar with recruitment check and edit your CV. It is vital to avoid basic spelling and grammatical errors: for example, check your use of apostrophes and avoid mixing up their and there (do not rely on spell checkers). Use good quality white paper (avoid colour printing and coloured paper). Set good margins with adequate spaces top and bottom. Leave one line space between sections. Try not to break a section at the bottom of the first page (a heading should be followed by at least two lines of text, or carried over).

Covering letter

The covering letter accompanies the CV. Its purpose is to show the publisher the benefits of employing you, to whet the publisher's appetite to learn more about you – to read your CV and to call you to interview. The letter should be no longer than one page of A4, say three to five short paragraphs, printed on white A4 paper (the same as the CV). If you are applying for your first job in publishing you will not have space, nor would it be desirable, to expound at length on your love of books and reading.

The letter should be headed with your name and contact details and addressed to the head of the department to which you are applying, to the HR department, or, if replying to an advertisement, to the person stated. It is vital to spell correctly the names of the manager and publisher. Start with a brief and simple statement of your reasons for writing – for example that you are applying for position X, advertised in journal Y, on Z date, or are seeking work, or mention a mutual contact referral – and that you enclose your CV.

Orientate the letter to the job, firm, your suitability and enthusiasm:

- State briefly your current position, for example about to leave college with expected qualifications.
- Show your research of the publisher by referring to recent or future books or promotions.
- Stress your motives and suitability: your relevant experience, skills and enthusiasm. Link your attributes to those specified in the advertisement, and you may want to use similar phrasing. Convey your enthusiasm by anchoring it to some credential, or a relevant fact.
- Give positive reasons for making the career step and for your keen interest in the job.
- Sign off using 'Yours sincerely' and sign your name above your printed name.

Use relatively short paragraphs rather than a few long ones; use plain English, concise and precise language, and the active voice. Avoid clichés and unappealing abruptness. To judge tone, try reading the letter aloud the next day, or ask someone else, such as a tutor or senior colleague, to read and proofread it. Ask them what overall impression you have conveyed in the letter – employers welcome the right level of enthusiasm. Remember you are trying to persuade a stranger to interview you.

Application form

Some publishers supply application forms. Make copies of the form if not supplied electronically. Follow the instructions and read it right through twice before starting. Take particular care with your full answers to the major open-ended questions or 'other information'. Use the photocopies for drafting and layout. If necessary, attach an extra sheet. You may be allowed to attach your CV and a covering letter.

What to do now

If you have been shortlisted, the publisher will contact you to arrange the interview. You may receive a rejection – like the majority – or worse, hear nothing.

Difficult as it is, do not let depression and frustration colour future applications. No application is wasted: elements can be reused and modified. Some publishers hold strong but rejected applicants on file.

Direct approach to publishers

Since many publishing jobs are not advertised, writing speculatively to publishers can work; but be prepared to write a large number of applications. Many publishers have high staff turnover at junior levels or need to cover maternity leave and these continually create new opportunities. Because so many humanities graduates apply to the London consumer book publishers and their editorial departments, you increase your chances if you apply to other sectors and departments. There are many opportunities in sales, marketing and production, as well as in the out-of-London educational, academic and journal publishers.

Some publishers do not reply to speculative approaches, others hold impressive candidates on file, to be approached later if a job arises. Some will call you for a preliminary discussion which may lead to an interview, or are prepared to offer advice, possibly recommending you for interview in another house. If you hear nothing or receive a letter of rejection, yet are still very keen on that publisher, telephone the manager and persuade him or her to make time for a short chat. People whose commitment to publishing is so strong and who persist usually get in.

INTERVIEW

Preparation

First impressions count at interview, including your appearance, body language and tone of voice

If you are called to interview, acknowledge quickly. If you decide not to go, say so, and give others the opportunity. Prepare thoroughly beforehand. First, research the publisher, its books or promotions. Why do you find them interesting? This greatly improves your chances. Second, think of answers to probable questions. As a publisher, what would you be looking for? Publishers are transitioning from print to digital. They always looked for a mix of creativity and commerce, now in addition it is digital capability and adaptability. What are your particular strengths? From your research, you should be able to deal with questions that relate to your interest in the job and test your knowledge of the publisher. Also you should be prepared to discuss what you think are the most important skills needed. You may be asked what you feel would be the most mundane or frustrating parts of the job and how you would cope with them.

The thinking you put into your CV and letter is apposite to questions such as:

- Why do you want to go into publishing? (Don't say 'I love reading and books'.)
- How is your previous experience applicable?
- Why do you think you are suitable?
- What are your major strengths?
- What makes you think you will be good at this job?

- What are your interests or hobbies?
- How do you assess current developments in the industry?
- What books do you read? – asked especially by consumer book publishers. Cite books which correspond to their interests and be prepared to analyse briefly why you think they work.

Be prepared for questions which probe facts, explore your feelings, judgement and motivation. You may well be asked to explain why you left a job. Do not blame the previous employer or specific individuals. Acceptable reasons include: 'I left for a better opportunity' or 'for more challenging work', or 'to broaden my experience'. Redundancy, even if no fault of your own and a common affliction of many in publishing, can be related to the circumstances of the particular firm. Beware of quoting shortcomings that may be applicable to the new job.

You will need to show that you have thought of medium-term career goals, while stressing your preparedness to commit yourself to the job for an effective time-span. Many new entrants apply, for example, to the marketing and sales departments, with the ambition of becoming editors. You may confess that legitimate target to a manager of another department but you must show strong commitment to the job applied for, otherwise you will be rejected.

Book publishing is an ideas business from start to finish. 'What ideas do you have?' may be asked of any applicant in any department. Do not sit dumbfounded. There may be no 'correct' answer – the question is more of a test of initiative and of common sense. Come up with your own questions to ask the interviewer. The best ones relate to clarifying features of the job and showing your knowledge of and keen interest in the publisher. Questions relating to the job include its main aspects, what factors promoted its creation, limits of authority, responsibility and independence, whom you would be working with most closely, terms and conditions, and future prospects. Those relating to the publisher (such as on new developments) could arise from your research. However, you should ask only a few questions – you are the one being interviewed. You could ask questions to which in part you can guess the answer and which will elicit a positive response. Be careful not to ask questions that are out of your depth, or cheeky, or ask the publisher to give you unreasonable special treatment.

You may want to take samples of printed material on which you have worked – for example a college magazine, book, promotional material, or a project from your degree. By recounting quickly the brief, the decisions and initiatives taken, the problems overcome, the people involved, you can reveal your analytical, creative, decision-making and organizational abilities, teamworking skills, your ideas and effectiveness in dealing with people, and your success.

Your face-to-face interview

You will need to judge the correct standard of dress for the interview. The style and atmosphere of publishers differ markedly, and some departments, such as accounts, may be more formal than others. On the whole it is best to appear businesslike and well dressed and groomed. You must not be late so allow plenty of time, and make sure you know the precise location of the interview. If you are unavoidably delayed, telephone and apologize. On arrival announce yourself to the receptionist and if time allows examine the publisher's material available in the reception. Some interviews include tasks and tests.

While some interviewers will greet you at the door, your first test may be to enter the room confidently (an important skill for most jobs). You should greet the interviewer and shake their hand positively. First impressions count, so do not forget to smile, and make sure you come across as confident and relaxed. Throughout the interview try to mention those assets which reveal your suitability and enthusiasm, anchor your skills in hard evidence, and ground accomplishments by giving examples. Reveal your research of the publisher, but do not over-praise or lecture.

Maintain eye contact with the interviewer and listen to the questions. Do not mumble yes/no answers. Answer questions fully, but judge the length and depth of your reply by watching the interviewer's verbal and non-verbal cues, and interest level. Be prepared for the interviewer's follow-up questions. When stating views make sure your reasoning is sensible and fairly firm, not vague, arrogant or inflexible. The danger of talking too much, apart from boring the interviewer, is to go beyond the question and introduce irrelevant facts or opinions, either of which could inadvertently reveal weaknesses. Indeed an interviewer may keep quiet and let you hang yourself. Interviewers tend to form negative impressions more readily, and on less information, than they form favourable impressions; their judgements are apt to be coloured by one or two striking attributes of candidates; and they tend to reject on negatives rather than select on positives.

A quality that most interviewers want to see, which can illuminate all others, is enthusiasm. It means having a positive outlook that shines through whatever subject is being discussed. Do not give the impression that you are not really interested in the job. The more nervous you become, the faster you may talk. Strive for measured animation. Undue modesty will conceal you, while boasting is damaging. If you have been dishonest in your CV or overstated the case you will be unable to substantiate your claims. Depending on the job, you may want to take along a portfolio of your design work or journalism. You will need to judge in the interview how much importance to give the portfolio, depending on the level of interest shown by the interviewer. Finally, the most intangible and important part of the whole exercise is whether the interviewer likes you and thinks you will fit in because most publishers are relatively small businesses (or profit centres within a large corporation) and publishing is a personal business. Some managers set great store on their quality of life expressed by the work they do and the people they have around them.

Having asked your own questions, by the end of the interview you should have a clear idea of what the job entails, what will happen next, who will make the next move, and the timescale. Publishers typically use either one or two interview stages. If called to a second interview, be armed with ideas that might help the publisher – but do think them through.

YOU'RE IN!

When the publisher is pretty sure it wants you, your references may be checked – but not always. If you are the chosen candidate reply quickly if you decide either to decline or accept the offer. There is usually little or no room for negotiation on salary in junior jobs. A question you may be asked at interview or subsequently is 'What salary are you expecting?' It is preferable to pass the responsibility back to the publisher to make the first offer by asking, for instance 'What are you planning on paying the best candidate?' Publishers rarely state salaries in advertisements and there is great variation in salary ranges between different publishers.

Publishers differ markedly in style of management and atmosphere, and have their own culture around dress code, level of formality, and hierarchy. The first months at work are a crucial period for quickly assimilating the politics of the organization and learning how to work within it, how to get things done, how to win and retain the regard of new colleagues. Tactics such as throwing your heart into the new job and being seen to arrive early and leave late – putting in extra hours when projects require – will establish an enduring reputation.

Career paths

It was mentioned earlier that the first jobs within the first few years may not necessarily determine a career path. Many new entrants have little idea of the work of the departments they join and may find they develop an aptitude and liking for the work. It is possible to move across to other departments and areas of publishing, but over time it becomes progressively more difficult: there are usually candidates who have acquired specialist knowledge of that particular area of publishing.

In small firms with few staff and less departmentalism it may be easier to move around the firm and learn different jobs, sometimes simultaneously. But such knowledge may not be considered by a larger firm to be specialist enough. In contrast, junior staff in large firms while often finding it more difficult to cross the more pronounced departmental boundaries, may gain in-depth expertise afforded by the greater resources of the publisher. People move from small to large firms, which usually pay much higher salaries at the top, and vice-versa: for example, middle-ranking staff of large firms may attain more senior jobs in smaller firms. The promotion of staff with little management experience to departmental management positions is common.

Unlike huge industrial concerns and the civil service, not even the largest publisher has a big enough staff pyramid to be able to fill staff vacancies from within at the time they occur. Publishers are not rash enough to advertise career pathways which cannot be fulfilled but in some large firms there are visible grade progressions within departments. Although some staff progress upwards in publishers, a few rapidly, it has become rare to spend a whole lifetime with one firm. Rather most people move from one publisher to another, sideways or hopefully in an upward direction. The possibility of getting stuck in any job at any level is ever present.

In moving around companies, most people tend to stay with the type of work in which they have acquired expertise. If moving between functions is far from easy, moving across the major types of publishing is even more difficult. Generally speaking people stay within consumer, educational or academic publishing (unless, that is, they have more transportable administrative and IT experience).

Many employers use social media for recruitment, including LinkedIn, Facebook and Twitter

Many have expertise that is applied to the publishing of books and associated products for certain markets and their contacts inside and outside publishing are orientated accordingly.

Some people in their early 30s may want to change direction, for instance, to move from academic to consumer book publishing, or vice-versa. But they are up against people already in that area so their chances of getting a job at the same level of seniority and salary are much more remote. As you increase your expertise of an area, the more valuable that expertise becomes and it can be difficult to throw it aside and turn to something else. That said, people do move between departments and types of publishing at all stages of their careers, up to and including managing directors. Traditionally they have been in a minority but there are indications that this may be changing.

Corporate reorganizations and takeovers inevitably affect careers. Employees unfortunately cannot choose their new owners. After a takeover, staff from the acquiring company may enhance their position in the larger organization, whereas the former management of the bought company is realigned. The managers may stay, leave or be downgraded. The more junior staff may leave as the new owners rationalize the departments, for example, by cutting out competing editorial units, merging production and design and rights departments, amalgamating the sales forces, centralizing HR, accounting and distribution services, and relocating offices (even across the Atlantic). Many staff who leave with their redundancy payments reappear in other publishers, start their own businesses in specialist services or consultancy, or go freelance.

Freelance work, for example in editorial, design or web design and marketing offers the freedom of working at home without the rigours and costs of commuting to work. Creative Skillset estimates that 48 per cent of UK publishers use freelancers, and that they represent 22 per cent of the workforce. The growth in self-publishing increases the demand from authors for freelance editorial, production and other services. Outside the general hubbub of a publishing house, and with fewer interruptions, freelancers may be able to work faster and plan their day to their own rhythm. But forced to maintain a flow of work and pressured to meet deadlines, the freelancer's day often extends far into the night, to weekends and public holidays. It can be difficult to turn work down given the uncertainties of a freelance existence. The best way to obtain work is through personal recommendation, professional contacts, or by personal approach. Industry bodies such as the SfEP (Society for Editors and Proofreaders) and the Society of Indexers maintain registers of freelancers. The National Union of Journalists recommends hourly rates for editorial work such as proofreading.

Many people in their 30s reach a plateau below management level and fear that their rapidly approaching fortieth birthday is their last chance to make a change. With increasing age the possibilities of movement diminish. However, many senior jobs are filled by people roughly between the ages of 37 to 45. After that, unless an individual is particularly well known or brilliant or specialized, changing companies becomes progressively more difficult. By the age of 50, with the same provisos, it becomes very difficult indeed – there may be no alternative but to stay put until retirement. Another factor constraining intercompany movement is the housing market and the accessibility of a range of firms. House prices in the south-east region are higher and increase at a faster rate than in the

> **Over a fifth of the UK publishing workforce are freelance**

rest of the country; they rise particularly steeply towards the centre of London. A company away from the centre may offer to pay relocation expenses, but you should consider the possible career step after that. If you move home too far out, you may be taking a one-way rather than a return ticket.

Staff of commercial publishers are very attractive to the many public, private and voluntary sector organizations with their own publishing operations. Moreover, the contacts made and skills learnt in publishing can be applied to other commercial enterprises, not necessarily concerned with publishing. In commercial and not-for-profit publishing, staff have been traditionally recruited from within the industry; and publishing staff tend to be retained unless they leave voluntarily or are forced out. It has been a relatively closed world. However, with the growth of digital publishing and the highly commercial outlook of most publishers, the industry now also looks outside for fresh talent. Managers may come from other industries, as well as staff with IT and logistics backgrounds, and consumer publishers may look for experience of other media industries, such as games, or for brand management expertise from retailing. Publishing businesses have changed dramatically over the last decades and continue to do so at dizzying pace.

Post-entry training

Most people in publishing learn on the job by observing the successes and mistakes made by themselves, colleagues, and other publishers and applying that experience to each new project: knowledge is passed on or reinvented. Few publishers give sufficient emphasis to training of their junior staff in their early 20s, or for that matter of senior staff who, while having specialist knowledge of their field, may often lack a broad overview of the business and general management knowledge; let alone an MBA. Publishers may then complain that they face shortages of talent when recruiting for senior posts. If you are fortunate enough to work in a firm that trains, take all the opportunities offered. But if not, the initiative is yours to seek out relevant meetings such as those of the SYP and WiP, and to make the time to attend courses. There are numerous courses offered part-time by the main teaching institutions and by professional organizations such as ALPSP (Association of Learned and Professional Society Publishers), the Publishing Training Centre and the SfEP.

Salaries

Within book publishing there is a great variation in salaries and no trade-wide statistics are available. There are salary surveys undertaken by bookcareers.com and the IPG. Traditionally, the many junior jobs in publishing, particularly in editorial, have low starting salaries, in part a consequence of large numbers chasing few jobs. Estimates of the typical starting salary in publishing in 2013 were around £18,000 to £20,000. Some people argue that the incidence of low pay and the high proportion of female employment at junior levels are not unconnected.

Those who move jobs on a regular basis may find they have increased their salaries above the levels of those who are content to stay for a long time in the same company. The law of supply and demand affects salaries across different types of publishing. For example, publishers wanting staff with a humanities background have a large choice and tend to pay lower salaries than legal and medical publishers, which may find it more difficult to recruit staff with the relevant academic qualifications or experience. Moreover, some people like to work in areas which they see as having intrinsic interest and accept lower salaries than if they worked in other fields of publishing. This has applied particularly to those in the literary and prestigious end of publishing.

On the marketing and sales side, salaries have been approaching those of general commerce; but at the top end, the salaries of most directors of publishing companies do not equate with those earned by the heads of large fast-moving consumer goods industries. At the very top, chief executives earn salaries many times those of the lowest paid staff, in some cases more than 15 times.

Diversity in publishing

There is a high proportion of women in pre-entry courses and in publishing, particularly London consumer book publishing, to the extent that some publishers wonder how to attract more men into the profession. About 70 per cent of the workforce is female. In senior management there is a higher proportion of men than in the publishing workforce as a whole, but the position of women has improved at board level. There are a number of prominent women in senior positions across the industry.

An industry study (*Ethnic Diversity in Publishing*, 2006) found that 92.3 per cent of employees within the publishing industry are from a white background, while 7.7 per cent are from a black and minority ethnic (BME) background. Although this matches the proportions within the UK as a whole, it does not reflect the ethnic make-up of London (71.2 per cent white/28.8 per cent BME), where most of the respondents were based. There is clearly an opportunity for publishers looking to broaden the readership for their books. Helen Fraser, then Managing Director of Penguin, said: 'A workforce that mirrors the population, especially urban populations where the majority of books are sold, will be able to tap into the whole market' (Kean, page 11). Equality in Publishing (Equip) promotes equality across publishing, bookselling and agenting.

Now read this

Alison Baverstock, Susannah Bowen and Steve Carey, *How to Get a Job in Publishing*, A & C Black, 2008.

Sources

BML (Book Marketing Limited), *Ethnic Diversity in Publishing*, September 2006.
Creative Skillset, *Publishing Labour Market Intelligence Digest*, 2011.
Danuta Kean (ed.), *In Full Colour*, Supplement to *The Bookseller*, 12 March 2004.

Web resources

www.publishingeducation.org Association for Publishing Education.
www.alpsp.org Association of Learned and Professional Society Publishers.
www.bookcareers.com Independent careers advice service.
www.bookmachine.org Book Machine.
www.bookmarketingsociety.co.uk Book Marketing Society.
www.booktradecharity.wordpress.com The Book Trade Benevolent Society offers practical, emotional and financial support to anyone who works or has worked in the book trade, as well as their dependants.
www.bytethebook.com Byte the Book.
www.careersatrandom.co.uk Random House Group's careers website.
http://creativeaccess.org.uk/ Charity founded in 2012 to help tackle the under-representation of ethnic minorities in the media.
www.creativeskillset.org Creative Skillset.
www.equalityinpublishing.org.uk Equality in Publishing.
www.indexers.org.uk The Society of Indexers.
www.ipg.uk.com Independent Publishers Guild.
www.opusnet.co.uk OPuS (Oxford Publishing Society).
http://publishing.brookes.ac.uk/ Oxford International Centre for Publishing Studies.
www.prospects.ac.uk Official graduate careers website.
www.publishers.org.uk Publishers Association – there are pages on training and publishing courses, and helpful career profiles.
www.publisherspublicitycircle.co.uk Publishers Publicity Circle.
www.publishingtalk.eu Publishing Talk.
www.sfep.org.uk Society for Editors and Proofreaders.
www.thesyp.org.uk Society of Young Publishers.
www.train4publishing.co.uk/careers Publishing Training Centre's pages on careers.
www.wipub.org.uk Women in Publishing.
www.writersandartists.co.uk Writers' & Artists' Yearbook.

Glossary of publishing terms and abbreviations

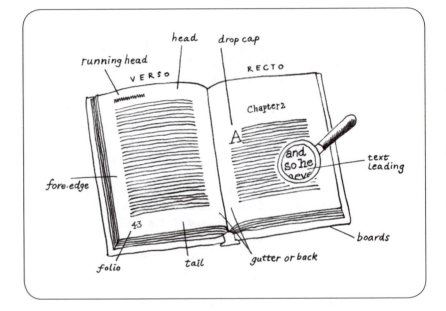

AAP Association of American Publishers

add-on extra value added into a product, for example a DVD in the back of a printed book

advance sum paid in advance to the author in anticipation of the author earning royalties from sales of their work. Advances may be paid on signature of contract, delivery of the typescript, and on publication

advance copy printed copy available ahead of publication. Advance copies are sent to the author and used in marketing

Aga saga Novel set amongst the Aga-owning English middle class

agent a literary agent may act on behalf of an author and negotiate the contract for a book with the publisher

aggregator an aggregator will license the rights to distribute content online from a variety of publishers

airport edition   export paperback edition of a book sold at airport shops ahead of the main paperback edition

AI sheet   advance Information sheet containing essential bibliographic and marketing information

APC   an article processing, or publishing, charge

app   application for mobile devices such as smartphones and tablet computers

BA   Booksellers Association of the United Kingdom and Ireland

backlist   a publisher's established titles; *compare* frontlist

BIC   Book Industry Communication

big deal   a large bundle of journals sold by a publisher as one package

blad   sample printed section

blurb   the selling copy that appears on the back cover or front jacket flap of the book

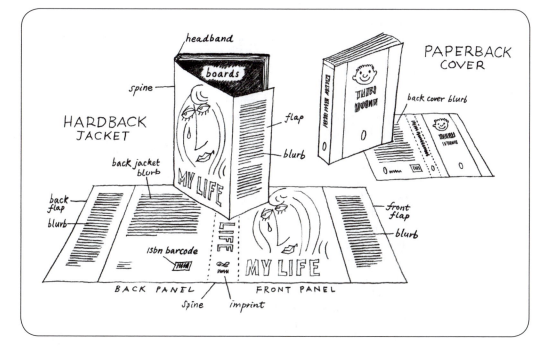

book club   traditionally a mail order bookseller; now also a reading group

born digital   products originated in digital form

BRIC   shorthand for the fast-growing economies of Brazil, Russia, India and China

bulk   a paper's thickness

bundling   journals are often packaged up into bundles of titles for sale to institutions such as university libraries; also a printed book and ebook may be bundled together

cascade journal   part of a hierarchy of titles; articles submitted to the top of the cascade may be rejected but still published by a lower-ranked journal within the cascade

chick lit   genre of fiction principally aimed at single women in their 20s or early 30s

CIP   Cataloguing in Publication

CIVETS   shorthand for the second wave of fast-growing economies of Colombia, Indonesia, Vietnam, Egypt, Turkey and South Africa

CLA   Copyright Licensing Agency

CMS   content management system

co-edition   An additional part of the print run sold to a third party. There are both English and foreign language co-editions

commissioning   creating a new project and signing up an author; or acquiring the rights to publish a work from the author, their agent or another publisher

contract   legal agreement between the author and publisher, outlining the rights acquired by the publisher, financial terms, and the responsibilities of both author and publisher

co-publication   joint publishing agreement between two or more companies

copy-editing   editing the author's manuscript with regard to style and consistency to eliminate errors and improve the text for the reader

copyright   the protection which gives authors and other creative artists legal ownership of their work – it establishes their work as their personal, exclusive property. © is the copyright symbol

coursepack   a collection of chapters and articles, photocopied or accessed electronically, for teaching use in higher education

cover-mount   special edition of a book attached to the front of a magazine, or bundled with a newspaper

CRM   customer relationship management

crossover title   a children's book with an adult market

CSR   corporate social responsibility

CTP   computer to plate

CUP   Cambridge University Press

DAD   digital asset distribution

DAM   digital asset management

depreciation   reducing the value of stock in the company's accounts

digital rights management (DRM)   the technical means by which the access to digital content is controlled

discount   publishers give retailers a discount off the recommended price to encourage them to list or stock their titles

DK   Dorling Kindersley

DNB   *Dictionary of National Biography*

DOI   digital object identifier

dummy   A mock-up of the final printed book, mainly used for selling illustrated books to retailers or overseas customers

ebook   electronic book; a vanilla ebook echoes – or is a straight transfer from – print; an enhanced ebook has added value such as audio and video

ECM   enterprise content management

EDItEUR   international standards organization for the book trade

EFL   English as a foreign language

ELT   English language teaching

embargo   restriction placed by a publisher on a book to prevent it either being sold or covered in the media prior to its official publication date

EMEA   Europe, the Middle East and Africa

enhanced ebook   ebook with additional features such as audio and video

EPC   Educational Publishers Council of the Publishers Association

frontlist   a publisher's new titles; *compare* backlist

GLN   global location number

goodwill   assets that contribute to a publisher's competitive advantage, including its brand and employees

house style   the set style imposed during the editing of a text – elements include spelling, grammar, capitalization and hyphenation

HSS   humanities and social sciences

HTML   HyperText Markup Language

imprint   a list of books within a publisher's overall publishing programme. Each imprint will have its own flavour and direction

institutional repository   a digital collection of research papers by members of an institution such as a university

intellectual property (IP)   a publisher's IP includes its copyrights, licences and trade marks

IPR   intellectual property rights

IRI   industry returns initiative (UK)

ISBN   international standard book number

ISSN   international standard serial number

Jisc   formerly termed the Joint Information Systems Committee, Jisc is funded by the post-16 and higher education councils of the UK

JPEG   joint photographic experts group

licence   a licence gives a publisher the sole, exclusive right to publish an author's work and sell it as widely as possible. The publisher also licenses a book to other publishers, for example for translation. A *non-exclusive* licence enables the publisher to sell content – for example for digital use – to a number of companies

licensed publishing   an exclusive licence granted to a publisher to exploit in book form a product or character

list-building   taking a strategic view of commissioning in order to create a new publishing list or expand the present publishing programme

litho   offset lithography. This form of printing is still common for long print runs

LMS   learning management system

long tail   first proposed by Chris Anderson in 2004 in *Wired* magazine, the idea that there is greater total value in the long tail of less popular products (available over the internet) than in the more widely available hits

manuscript (ms)   the author's version of the work; *also* typescript. It was originally handwritten

MARC   machine readable cataloguing

marketing mix   product, price, place and promotion

mass market paperback   'A format' paperback – 178 x 110 mm; *compare* trade paperback

mega journal   fast-growing open access title, covering a broad subject area

metadata   data about data. This enables content to be categorized and found more easily in online searches

MOOC   massive open online course

moral rights   additional to copyright, these statutory rights granted to the author are the right to paternity, the right of integrity, the right to prevent false attribution, and the right to privacy

NBA   Net Book Agreement (UK)

NBI sheet   new book information sheet – also known as AI

NSR   net sales revenue

OA   open access

OEBF   open ebook format

OED   *Oxford English Dictionary*

OER   open educational resources

ONIX   online information exchange

online marketing   use of the internet for marketing. Activities include the use of social media, search engine optimization, email marketing and website promotion

on-screen editing   copy-editing on screen rather than on a paper print-out

ontology   the structure of a set of data

OUP   Oxford University Press

overheads   the ongoing costs of running a business, for example office costs and salaries

PA   Publishers Association (UK)

packager   separate from a publisher, a packager supplies an edited and designed book for the publisher to market and sell

patron-driven acquisition   free access is given to content, for example a set of ebooks, and payment is then triggered by usage past a certain threshold

pay per view   pay as you go model for content, for example purchasing a single article from a journal or a chapter from a book

pbook   printed book

PDA   personal digital assistant; also patron-driven acquisition

PDF   portable document format

peer review   the evaluation by reviewers of an academic author's work

PLS   private language schools

POD   print on demand. Digital printing enables the economic printing of short runs. True print on demand is the ability to print single copies to order

POS   point of sale

positioning   placing the product in the mind of the consumer

post-print   journal article as revised after peer review; *compare* pre-print

PR   public relations

pre-print   commonly accepted as the version of an article submitted to a journal, before peer review; *compare* post-print

print run   the number of copies printed of a pbook

production values   the quality of the paper, design, printing, binding and cover of a book

proofreading   reading proofs of a book in order to spot mistakes missed at the copy-editing stage as well as any errors introduced in the design and production stages. Proofs can be read against the original copy or by eye (with no reference to the original version)

proposal A document outlining the content and market potential of a proposed title

PS PostScript

puff endorsement used on the book's cover, ahead of the book being reviewed

REF Research Excellence Framework, UK

remainder publisher's surplus stock sold off cheaply

returns unsold books sent back to the publisher by the retailer

RFID radio frequency identification

royalty the share of the income from a book paid by the publisher to the author; royalty rates will vary according to format and the source of the income (for example from subsidiary rights)

SAN standard address number

schema the structure of an XML document

serial rights the right to sell selections from a work to a newspaper or magazine. *First* serial rights cover extracts before the book's publication; *second* serial rights are for extracts published on or after publication

smart content content with an added layer of semantic meaning

STM scientific, technical and medical. STEM adds in engineering

subsidiary rights Rights a publisher can acquire in addition to the volume rights of publishing their own edition as an ebook and pbook – examples of subsidiary rights are translation rights and serial rights

TIFF tagged image file format

trade paperback 'B format' paperback – 198 x 129 mm; *compare* mass-market paperback

trade publishing publishing of books that are sold through the book trade; also known as consumer publishing

Unicode an encoding system which gives a unique identity to each character, 'no matter what the platform, no matter what the program, no matter what the language'. (unicode.com, accessed 1 October 2007)

USP unique sales proposition – what makes a book stand out from the competition

VAT value added tax

version of record published version of a journal article with the final formatting

viral marketing spreading a marketing message using social networks

VLE virtual learning environment

wasting disposing of unsold stock

Web 2.0 the new generation of the web in which users upload as well as download

widget mini web plug-in with sample content that can be emailed or copied on to the user's social networking pages

wiki Collaborative website. The name derives from the Hawaiian word *wikiwiki* – quick

WIPO World Intellectual Property Organization

WOM word of mouth

XML Extensible Markup Language

Bibliography

The relevant sources and suggestions for further reading are given at the end of each chapter. This list pulls together key texts and resources.

Journals and periodicals
The Author
The Bookseller
Learned Publishing
Logos
Publishers Weekly
Publishing News
Publishing Research Quarterly
Scholarly Publishing

News services
BookBrunch
Book Trade.info
Paid Content
Publishing Perspectives

Industry databases and information resources relevant to publishing
Book Facts Online
GPI Country Reports
Mintel
Nielsen BookData
Nielsen BookScan
Outsell

Industry data is also available from the websites of the industry associations:
www.booksellers.org Booksellers Association
www.publishers.org.uk Publishers Association
www.stm-assoc.org/ International Association of Scientific, Technical & Medical
    Publishers

Books

Chris Anderson, *Free: The future of a radical price*, Random House, 2009.

Chris Anderson, *The Long Tail: How endless choice is creating unlimited demand*, Random House, 2006.

Diana Athill, *Stet*, Granta, 2000.

Tricia Austin and Richard Doust, *New Media Design*, Laurence King, 2007.

Phil Baines, *Penguin by Design: A cover story 1935–2005*, Allen Lane, 2005.

Phil Baines and Andrew Haslam, *Type and Typography*, Laurence King, 2005.

David Bann, *Book Production Control*, 2nd edition, Class Publishing, 2012.

David Bann, *The All New Print Production Handbook*, RotoVision, 2006.

Alan Bartram, *Making Books: Design in British publishing since 1945*, British Library, 1999.

Alison Baverstock, *How to Market Books*, 5th edition, Routledge, 2014.

Alison Baverstock, Susannah Bowen and Steve Carey, *How to Get a Job in Publishing*, A & C Black, 2008.

Eric de Bellaigue, *British Book Publishing as a Business*, British Library Publishing, 2004.

Michael Bhaskar, *The Content Machine: Towards a theory of publishing from the printing press to the digital network*, Anthem Press, 2013.

Sven Birkerts, *The Gutenberg Elegies: The fate of reading in an electronic age*, Faber, 2006.

Carole Blake, *From Pitch to Publication*, Pan, 1999.

Clive Bloom, *Bestsellers: Popular fiction since 1900*, Palgrave Macmillan, 2002.

Sue Bradley (ed.), *The British Book Trade: An oral history*, British Library, 2008.

Manfred H. Breede, *The Brave New World of Publishing: The symbiotic relationship between printing and book publishing*, Chandos, 2008.

Robert Bringhurst, *The Elements of Typographic Style*, version 3.1, Hartley & Marks, 2005.

Adrian Bullock, *Book Production*, Routledge, 2012.

Adrian Bullock and Meredith Walsh, *The Green Design and Print Production Handbook*, Ilex, 2013.

Judith Butcher, Caroline Drake and Maureen Leach, *Copy-editing: The Cambridge handbook for editors, copy-editors and proofreaders*, 4th edition, 2006.

Jen Campbell, *Weird Things Customers Say in Bookshops*, Constable, 2012.

Robert Campbell, Ed Pentz and Ian Borthwick (eds), *Academic and Professional Publishing*, Chandos, 2012.

The Chicago Manual of Style, 16th edition, University of Chicago Press, 2010.

Clayton M. Christensen, *The Innovator's Dilemma: When new technologies cause great firms to fail*, Harvard Business School Press, 1997.

Joseph Connolly, *Eighty Years of Book Cover Design*, Faber & Faber, 2009.

Bill Cope and Angus Phillips (eds), *The Future of the Book in the Digital Age*, Chandos, 2006.

Bill Cope and Angus Phillips (eds), *The Future of the Academic Journal*, 2nd edition, Chandos, 2014.

Robert Darnton, *The Case for Books*, Perseus, 2009.

Gill Davies, *Book Commissioning and Acquisition*, 2nd edition, Routledge, 2004.

Gill Davies and Richard Balkwill, *The Professionals' Guide to Publishing: A practical introduction to working in the publishing industry*, Kogan Page, 2011.

Christopher Davis, *Eyewitness: The rise and fall of Dorling Kindersley*, 2009.

Dictionary of Printing and Publishing, 3rd edition, A & C Black, 2006.

Ned Drew and Paul Sternberger, *By its Cover: Modern American book cover design*, Princeton Architectural Press, 2005.

Susan Elderkin and Ella Berthoud, *The Novel Cure: An A to Z of literary remedies*, Canongate, 2013.

Simon Eliot and Jonathan Rose, *A Companion to the History of the Book*, Blackwell, 2007.

Jason Epstein, *Book Business: Publishing past, present, and future*, Norton, 2002.

John Feather, *A History of British Publishing*, 2nd edition, Routledge, 2005.

David Finkelstein and Alastair McCleery (eds), *The Book History Reader*, 2nd edition, 2006.

Simon Garfield, *Just my Type*, Profile, 2010.

Albert N. Greco, Jim Milliot, Robert Wharton, *The Book Publishing Industry*, 3rd edition, Routledge, 2013.

Susan Gunelius, *Harry Potter: The story of a global business phenomenon*, Palgrave Macmillan, 2008.

Richard Guthrie, *Publishing: Principles and practice*, SAGE, 2011.

Frania Hall, *The Business of Digital Publishing: An introduction to the digital book and journal industries*, Routledge, 2013.

Jenny Hartley, *The Reading Groups Book*, revised edition, Oxford University Press, 2002.

Barbara Horn, *Editorial Project Management*, Horn Editorial Books, 2006.

Barbara Horn, *Copy-editing*, Horn Editorial Books and Publishing Training Centre, 2008.

Independent Publishers Guild, *The Insiders' Guide to Independent Publishing*, Independent Publishers Guild, 2010.

Walter Isaacson, *Steve Jobs*, Little, Brown, 2011.

Jeff Jarvis, *What Would Google Do?*, HarperCollins, 2009.

Ros Jay, *The White Ladder Diaries*, White Ladder Press, 2004.

Chris Jennings, *eBook Typography for Flowable eBooks*, PagetoScreen ebook, 2012.

Hugh Jones and Christopher Benson, *Publishing Law*, 4th edition, Routledge, 2011.

Andrew Keen, *The Cult of the Amateur*, Nicholas Brealey, 2007.

Arthur M. Klebanoff, *The Agent*, Texere, 2002.

Miha Kovač, *Here comes the Book: Never mind the web*, Chandos, 2008.

Marshall Lee, *Bookmaking: Editing, design, production*, 3rd edition, Norton, 2004.

Lawrence Lessig, *Free Culture*, Penguin, 2004.

Jeremy Lewis, *Penguin Special: The life and times of Allen Lane*, Viking, 2005.

Noah Lukeman, *The First Five Pages: A writer's guide to staying out of the rejection pile*, Oxford University Press, 2010.

Hugh McGuire and Brian O'Leary (eds), *Book: A futurist's manifesto*, O'Reilly Media, 2012.

Ruari McLean, *The Thames and Hudson Manual of Typography*, Thames and Hudson, 1980.

Tom Maschler, *Publisher*, Picador, 2005.

Nicole Matthews and Nickianne Moody (eds), *Judging a Book by Its Cover: Fans, publishers, designers, and the marketing of fiction*, Ashgate, 2007.

Daniel Menaker, *My Mistake*, Houghton Mifflin Harcourt, 2013.

Jason Merkosi, *Burning the Page*, Sourcebooks, 2013.

Laura Miller, *Reluctant Capitalists: Bookselling and the culture of consumption*, University of Chicago Press, 2006.

Michael Mitchell and Susan Wightman, *Book Typography: A designer's manual*, Libanus Press, 2005.

Sally Morris, Ed Barnas, Douglas La Frenier and Margaret Reich, *The Handbook of Journal Publishing*, CUP, 2013.

Simone Murray, *The Adaptation Industry: The cultural economy of contemporary literary adaptation*, Routledge, 2011.

Ian Norrie, *Mumby's Publishing and Bookselling in the Twentieth Century*, 6th edition, Bell & Hyman, 1982.

Lynette Owen (ed.), *Clark's Publishing Agreements: A book of precedents*, 9th edition, Bloomsbury Professional, 2013.

Lynette Owen, *Selling Rights*, 7th edition, Routledge, 2014.

Angus Phillips, *Turning the Page: The evolution of the book*, Routledge, 2014.

Alan Powers, *Front Cover: Great book jackets and cover design*, Mitchell Beazley, 2001.

Paul Richardson and Graham Taylor, *A Guide to the UK Publishing Industry*, 3rd edition, Publishers Association, 2014.

R. M. Ritter, *New Hart's Rules: The handbook of style for writers and editors*, Oxford University Press, 2005.

R. M. Ritter, *The Oxford Style Manual*, 2003.

R.M. Ritter, Angus Stevenson and Lesley Brown, *New Oxford Dictionary for Writers and Editors*, 2005.

Lucienne Roberts and Julia Thrift, *The Designer and the Grid*, RotoVision, 2002.

André Schiffrin, *The Business of Books: How international conglomerates took over publishing and changed the way we read*, Verso Books, 2001.

Mike Shatzkin, *The Shatzkin Files*, Kobo Editions, 2011.

Kelvin Smith, *The Publishing Business: From p-books to e-books*, AVA, 2012.

Erik Spiekermann and E. M. Ginger, *Stop Stealing Sheep and Find Out How Type Works*, 2nd edition, Adobe Press, 2003.

Claire Squires, *Marketing Literature: The making of contemporary writing in Britain*, Palgrave Macmillan, 2007.

David Stam and Andrew Scott, *Inside Magazine Publishing*, Routledge, 2014.

Iain Stevenson, *Book Makers: British publishing in the twentieth century*, British Library, 2010.

Rachel Stock, *The Insider's Guide to Getting Your Book Published*, White Ladder Press, 2005.

Simon Stokes, *Digital Copyright: Law and practice*, Hart Publishing, 2013.

Brad Stone, *The Everything Store: Jeff Bezos and the age of Amazon*, Little, Brown, 2013.

Michael F. Suarez and H. R. Woudhuysen (eds), *The Oxford Companion to the Book*, 2010.

Mira T. Sundara Rajan, *Moral Rights*, OUP, 2011.

Don Tapscott, *Grown Up Digital: How the net generation is changing your world*, McGraw-Hill, 2008.

John B. Thompson, *Books in the Digital Age*, Polity Press, 2005.

John B. Thompson, *Merchants of Culture*, Polity Press, 2010.

Michael Upshall, *Content Licensing: Buying and selling digital resources*, Chandos, 2009.

Margaret Willes, *Reading Matters: Five centuries of discovering books*, Yale University Press, 2008.

Maryann Wolf, *Proust and the Squid: The story and science of the reading brain*, Icon Books, 2008.

Thomas Woll, *Publishing for Profit*, 4th edition, Chicago Review Press, 2010.

World Intellectual Property Organization, *Managing Intellectual Property in the Book Publishing Industry*, WIPO, 2008.

Sherman Young, *The Book is Dead: Long live the book*, UNSW Press, 2007.

Gabriel Zaid, *So Many Books: Reading and publishing in an age of abundance*, Sort of Books, 2004.

Index

Bold page numbers refer to tables.